CW00343898

INTERNATIONAL ORGANIZATIONS
AND GLOBAL CIVIL SOCIETY

INTERNATIONAL ORGANIZATIONS AND GLOBAL CIVIL SOCIETY

Histories of the Union of International Associations

Edited by Daniel Laqua, Wouter Van Acker and
Christophe Verbruggen

BLOOMSBURY ACADEMIC
LONDON • NEW YORK • OXFORD • NEW DELHI • SYDNEY

BLOOMSBURY ACADEMIC
Bloomsbury Publishing Plc
50 Bedford Square, London, WC1B 3DP, UK
1385 Broadway, New York, NY 10018, USA

BLOOMSBURY, BLOOMSBURY ACADEMIC and the Diana logo are trademarks
of Bloomsbury Publishing Plc

First published in Great Britain 2019

A catalogue record for this book is available from the British Library.

A catalog record for this book is available from the Library of Congress.

ISBN: HB: 978-1-3500-5563-6
ePDF: 978-1-3500-5561-2
eBook: 978-1-3500-5562-9

Typeset by Deanta Global Publishing Services, Chennai, India

To find out more about our authors and books visit www.bloomsbury.com
and sign up for our newsletters.

CONTENTS

Part II
THE UIA IN A WORLD OF INTERNATIONAL ORGANIZATIONS

Part III
EXPLORING THE UIA'S PUBLICATIONS AND DATA

LIST OF FIGURES

LIST OF TABLES

LIST OF CONTRIBUTORS

Nancy Carfrae is a senior staff member in the Secretariat of the Union of International Associations in Brussels, Belgium.

Thomas Davies is Senior Lecturer in International Politics at City, University of London, UK.

Martin Grandjean is Junior Lecturer in Contemporary History at the Université de Lausanne and the École Polytechnique Fédérale de Lausanne, Switzerland.

Sarah Hellawell is Lecturer in Modern History at the University of Sunderland, UK.

Daniel Laqua is Associate Professor of Modern European History at Northumbria University in Newcastle upon Tyne, UK.

Matthias Middell is Professor of Cultural History at Leipzig University, Germany.

Katja Naumann is a Senior Researcher at the Leibniz Institute for the History and Culture of Eastern Europe, Leipzig, Germany.

Philip Post is a PhD candidate in History at Leiden University, the Netherlands.

Nico Randeraad is Associate Professor of History at Maastricht University, the Netherlands.

W. Boyd Rayward is Professor Emeritus in the History of Library and Information Sciences at the University of Illinois, Urbana-Champaign, USA, and at the University of New South Wales, Australia.

Bob Reinalda is a Fellow and Senior Researcher in International Relations at Radboud University in Nijmegen, the Netherlands.

Pierre-Yves Saunier is Professor of History at the Université Laval in Quebec City, Canada.

Wouter Van Acker is Associate Professor of Architectural Theory and History at the Université Libre in Brussels, Belgium.

Marco H. D. van Leeuwen is Professor of Historical Sociology at Utrecht University, the Netherlands.

Christophe Verbruggen is Associate Professor of Social and Cultural History at Ghent University and Director of the Ghent Centre for Digital Humanities, Belgium.

ACKNOWLEDGEMENTS

We thank the contributors for their enthusiasm and their willingness to produce chapters that were specifically tailored to this project. The book is the result of a sustained dialogue and we are glad that the authors responded so positively to our suggestions. In order to ensure the coherence of our volume, we arranged two meetings – one at the Mundaneum in Mons (2016) and another at the Université Libre in Brussels (2017). Our discussions proved highly stimulating and allowed us to make significant progress on the path to publication. We are grateful to the Mundaneum's chief archivist, Stéphanie Manfroid, both for hosting the first of these events and for providing access to the collections of her institution. Financial support for our initial meeting was provided by the international research network 'The Transnational Dynamics of Social Reform', led by Nico Randeraad and funded by the Netherlands Organization for Scientific Research (NWO) and the research project TIC Collaborative, funded by the Belgian Federal Science Policy Office (BELSPO).

From the very beginning, Bloomsbury has been exemplary in its support and its editors have effectively guided us through the publication process. The anonymous peer reviewers have been thoughtful and constructive in their remarks, which have helped to shape this project.

The Union of International Associations has shown a remarkable openness to this undertaking. We are highly appreciative of its support – especially as we stressed from the outset that, rather than producing a celebratory volume, we were aiming for a scholarly book that gives due attention to various problems and shortcomings. Representatives of the organization – including Jacques de Mévius, Nancy Carfrae and Leslie Selvais – have contributed to our discussions and provided valuable access to a range of sources.

LIST OF ABBREVIATIONS

CIAM	Congrès International d'Architecture Moderne (International Congress of Modern Architecture)
CISA	Congrès International des Sciences Administratifs (International Congresses of Administrative Sciences)
CISH	Comité International des Sciences Historiques (International Committee of Historical Sciences)
COW	Correlates of War
CSW	Commission on the Status of Women
DKZ	Deutsche Kongress-Zentrale (German Central Office for Congresses)
ECOSOC	Economic and Social Council of the United Nations
IAV	Internationaal Archief voor de Vrouwenbeweging (International Archive for the Women's Movement)
ICIC	International Committee on Intellectual Cooperation
ICW	International Council of Women
IFHTP	International Federation for Housing and Town Planning
IGO	Intergovernmental organization
INGO	International non-governmental organization
IIB	Institut Internationale de Bibliography (International Institute of Bibliography)
IIP	International Institute for Peace
ILO	International Labour Organization
IO	International organization
IPB	International Peace Bureau
IPR	Institute of Pacific Relations
IR	International relations
ISS	Institut des Sciences Sociales (Institute of Social Sciences)
IULA	International Union of Local Authorities
NGO	Non-governmental organization
OCDF	Office Central de Documentation Féminine (Central Office of Female Documentation)
OIB	Office International de Bibliographie (International Office of Bibliography)
PIU	Public international union
SCHM	Scientific and Cultural History of Mankind
SESP	Société des Études Sociales et Politiques (Society for Social and Political Studies)
UIA	Union of International Associations
UIV	Union Internationale des Villes (International Union of Cities)
UNESCO	United Nations Educational, Scientific and Cultural Organization

UNICEF	United Nations International Children's Emergency Fund
UNRRA	United Nations Relief and Rehabilitation Administration
UNU	United Nations University
UPEACE	University for Peace
WILPF	Women's International League for Peace and Freedom

INTRODUCTION: RECONSTRUCTING THE IDENTITIES OF AN INTERNATIONAL NON-GOVERNMENTAL INTELLIGENCE AGENCY

Daniel Laqua, Wouter Van Acker and Christophe Verbruggen

In January 1919, delegates to the Paris Peace Conference gathered to discuss the construction of a new international order in the wake of the First World War. The event raised substantial expectations, as reflected in a plethora of petitions and resolutions addressed to the 'peacemakers' in the French capital.[1] One such submission came from the Union of International Associations (UIA), whose *Charter of Intellectual and Moral Interests* stated that the 'great international associations' had been furthering the cause of international cooperation for half a century. Now was the time to acknowledge their work by including a 'Charter of Intelligence' alongside a 'Labour Charter' and an 'Economic Charter' within 'a kind of Global Constitution of the League of Nations'.[2] The document encapsulated many of the UIA's core tenets: a belief in the role played by international associations in the making of global order; the impetus to bundle the efforts of such bodies; and a conviction that any future 'world constitution' would need to pay attention to intellectual matters.

Many organizations can choose between multiple founding years, and the UIA is no different. It was formally established in 1910 as a result of the World Congress of International Associations in Brussels. Already four years prior to this event, however, a meeting had decided to start gathering information on the growing number of international organizations, partly with a view to facilitating cooperation between them.[3] In the first instance, this body was intended to unite the documentary services of international organizations that were based in Belgium. The Central Office of International Institutions was the product of these discussions. Operative from 1907 onwards, it soon reached well beyond its home country, seeking to cover 'international life' in its manifold guises. An early outcome was the first edition of its *Annuaire de la Vie Internationale*, which sought to document 'international life' across more than 1,300 pages.[4]

The UIA eventually absorbed the Central Office. From 1910 until the 1930s, it combined the documentary quest of its forerunner with a second strand of action: the project of bringing together international organizations in a variety of shared ventures. This impetus manifested itself in six 'world congresses of international associations' between 1910 and 1927. It also became evident in the opening of the Palais Mondial (1920), based within the larger, government-owned Palais du Cinquantenaire in Brussels. This 'world palace' hosted not only the headquarters of the UIA but also its International Museum and several organizations associated with its Belgian co-founders Henri La Fontaine and Paul Otlet. Otlet in particular considered the palace to be but a building brick for a greater venture: until his death in 1944, he energetically promoted his vision of a *Cité Mondiale*, a world capital city. After the Second World War, a reborn UIA reduced its scope, focusing on the core business of providing information services within a world of international non-governmental organizations (INGOs). To this day, the UIA's *Yearbook of International Organizations* constitutes an unparalleled and regularly updated data resource.

Why should we revisit the UIA's history now – a century after diplomats in Paris laid the basis for the League of Nations, whose features differed manifestly from the UIA's vision of a world organization? As we argue, the UIA's case addresses issues of ongoing relevance. We live in an age of substantial debate about global governance and the role of civil society therein. It is therefore hardly surprising that scholars have traced earlier schemes, designs and arguments relating to 'the global' as a site of intellectual enquiry or sphere of action.[5] Moreover, a growing body of literature sheds light on the historical development and role of international organizations, both governmental and non-governmental ones.[6] This general drive is illustrated by recent assessments of the League of Nations and its specialized bodies as well as attempts to trace the history of the United Nations (UN).[7] The UIA offers rich material on these phenomena as it had a dual identity: it served as an information hub on international organizations while constituting an INGO in its own right.

The UIA exemplifies the wider phenomenon of internationalism – a term that describes the attempt to foster links across nations through congresses, conferences and organizations. Several historians have considered internationalism, both as an idea and as a practice, across a longer time span.[8] The UIA can be seen as a proponent of 'cultural internationalism' – a phenomenon that, according to Akira Iriye, was based on the conviction that 'a more peaceful world order could develop … through the efforts of individuals and organizations across national boundaries to promote better understanding and to cooperate in collaborative enterprises'.[9] Taken together, the chapters in this book show how cultural internationalism was articulated and practised. They consider the role of 'intellectual cooperation' which, in the interwar years, was a byword for cultural and academic exchange. The contributions by Sarah Hellawell, Daniel Laqua and Christophe Verbruggen partly place the UIA within this framework, while Matthias Middell and Katja Naumann explore an alternative case of academic cooperation.

Strikingly, many scholars who discuss international organizations – whether governmental or non-governmental ones – rely on UIA data and its underlying typologies, without necessarily noting how the UIA's internationalist agenda has shaped this material. The present volume critically interrogates the construction and use of its datasets, most notably in Pierre-Yves Saunier's chapter. Following on from this, Bob Reinalda, Martin Grandjean and Marco Van Leeuwen test the potential of these data collections to trace particular patterns and developments. Our focus on the material produced by the UIA draws attention to one major aspect of the book: the authors do examine not only the UIA's role within the history of international relations (IR) in general but also its relevance for the *disciplinary* history of IR. Thomas Davies's chapter makes an explicit contribution to this field, considering the UIA's publications within the wider context of IR theory and its development.

The emphasis on data and information explains why, somewhat tongue-in-check, the title of the introduction refers to an 'international non-governmental intelligence agency'. At first sight, the term may seem surprising: our research presents no evidence for cooperation with secret services or security forces – notwithstanding the UIA's presence in a city that also hosts the NATO headquarters. But on closer inspection, the label makes sense. Christophe Verbruggen's chapter explains how the UIA's work served the interests of the Belgian government, at least until the early 1920s. Several contributors to this volume draw attention to Madeleine Herren's arguments about support for international congresses and associations as an alternative form of foreign policy.[10] Herren's work is also relevant in another respect: she has shown how, during the occupation of Belgium in the Second World War, officials from National Socialist Germany sought to harvest the UIA's material for their own purposes.[11] Verbruggen's chapter discusses this episode within the context of the UIA's quest for 'patronage'.

An Organization and Its History

The UIA's long history makes it a prism through which we can study the field of international organizations and its changing dynamics. As an organization that sought recognition at the international level, it had to respond to external developments: the impact of war and conflict; the diversification of the wider field of international associations; the shifting political map, both in terms of post-war border re-drawings and in terms of decolonization; and the emergence of intergovernmental organizations – first the League of Nations and then the UN – as potential patrons, partners or rivals.

We can distinguish between four major phases in the UIA's development. The *first period* covers the years from the 1890s to the organization's formal establishment in 1910. Co-founders Otlet and La Fontaine initially collaborated in sociological and bibliographical ventures. In 1895, they set up the International Institute of Bibliography (IIB), partly with a view to promoting the Universal Decimal Classification, which they had developed on the basis of the Melvil Dewey's classification scheme. Both the IIB and the International Office of Bibliography – a related institution funded by the Belgian government – conducted documentation work, including the ambitious undertaking of a universal card catalogue. Boyd Rayward's chapter in this volume covers this period and considers key impulses, including the collaboration with Catholic politician Cyrille Van Overbergh. Importantly, the sociological, bibliographical strand was complemented by La

Fontaine's prominent role in the international peace movement, which saw him serve as president of the International Peace Bureau (1907–43) and resulted in the award of Nobel Peace Prize in 1913.

The *second period* lasted from 1910 to the 1940s, constituting the UIA's 'Otlet-La Fontaine years'. In this era, the organization was engaged in a variety of ventures. In particular until the outbreak of the First World War, it undertook extensive documentation efforts. It was in this second period that the UIA maintained its International Museum, held sessions of its International University and campaigned for a *Cité Mondiale*. Although the organization sought to project vigour to its potential backers, initial cooperation with the Belgian government and the League of Nations soon gave way to disappointment, as highlighted by Christophe Verbruggen. However, as Wouter Van Acker and Sarah Hellawell show, the UIA continued to forge links with other organizations well into the 1920s.

After the Second World War, the UIA entered its *third phase*. As discussed by Nico Randeraad and Philip Post, it faced the challenge of 'carving out a role' in a world whose parameters had changed, both through Cold War power dynamics and the creation of the UN system. Randeraad and Post trace the UIA's quest for cooperation with, and recognition by, the UN. Its focus now rested squarely on the provision of information services, contrasting with the wider-ranging aspirations that had characterized the first two phases. Interactions between the UN, activists and academics are also tackled elsewhere in this volume, including in the chapters by Sarah Hellawell, Daniel Laqua, Matthias Middell and Katja Naumann. Moreover, the contributions by Thomas Davies and Bob Reinalda note that UIA publications provided a forum for those who sought to appraise the role of INGOs within the international system in this period.

Since the 1990s, the organization experiences its *fourth phase* – not so much because of any change in its conceptual underpinnings but through the influence of digitization and globalization. The UIA was an early adopter of computing technology for data processing, and the digital age provided new possibilities for the organization. A CD-ROM version of the *Yearbook* appeared between 1994 and 2008. The UIA's online presence grew from 1999 onwards, with the *Encyclopedia of World Problems and Human Potential* as well *Yearbook* data becoming available online. Moreover, ongoing talk about globalization has drawn particular attention to the world of INGOs, and the UIA is in a good position to contribute to such debates. Nancy Carfrae's epilogue outlines the work currently undertaken by the organization.

It was in the first two phases that the UIA seemed at its most vibrant, driven by the energy of its founders and optimism about the ability to shape the international order. Most historical accounts on the UIA have focused on the endeavours of its founders Paul Otlet and Henri La Fontaine. In contrast to the many monographs on Otlet available today, there is no single academic volume devoted to the UIA itself.[12] A long essay written in 1970 by former UIA secretary-general Georges Patrick Speeckaert continues to be the most detailed survey of the organization's development up to that point.[13] Nearly forty-five years since its original publication, Boyd Rayward's pioneering Otlet biography remains an important source for studying the UIA's early years as it contextualizes the work of the Belgian bibliographer and offers a detailed picture of the UIA's picture until his death in 1944.

More recently, some researchers have foregrounded the UIA in their work on internationalism and transnational cooperation.[14] Unlike these studies, this book ventures well beyond the lifetime of the UIA's founders. Of course, the first two periods of UIA history still receive substantial attention in our volume – and this is inevitable, as the UIA's field of action was much broader at that time. However, many contributors actively trace its history well into the more recent past, either by considering legacies of its work or by using the material compiled by the UIA over the years.

The UIA and Global Civil Society

The concept of 'global civil society' has attracted significant scholarly interest since the 1990s.[15] The term itself did not figure in the UIA's early discourse, which largely revolved around words such as 'world society', 'world citizenship', 'mondialism' and 'cosmopolitism'. Yet while the expression 'global civil society' is of relatively recent origin, the phenomenon that it describes has a history on which the UIA's activities can shed fresh light. One major function of the concept is heuristic: to grasp and to understand 'a vast interconnected and multi-layered non-governmental space that comprises many hundreds of thousands of self-directing institutions and ways of life that generate global effects'.[16] Data-gathering efforts such as the UIA's *Yearbook* or the *Civil Society Index* of CIVICUS have delivered important empirical material on civil society organizations, providing us with sense of their growth, variety, contours and complexity – something that would otherwise remain elusive.

The concept of 'global civil society' highlights possibilities for expanding transnational publics and spaces of representation – transcending the state system and existing social, economic and political configurations. The UIA sought to represent global civil society in two ways: it documented the work of international non-governmental actors; yet, in its early years, it also aspired to being a mouthpiece for them. The very premise of the UIA's activism was to unite and to thicken the social tissue of private international associations, and thus to help build a conglomerate of societies whose members could interact across great distances and political boundaries. As several contributions to this volume show, the UIA's universal ambitions and its status as a civil society organization made for complex relationships with the state authorities and intergovernmental organizations from which it sought backing.

In its early phase, the UIA still believed in the possibility of integrating and centralizing an open-ended group of associations. By contrast, in the second half of the twentieth century, a reconfigured UIA concentrated on its project of documenting the existence and work of INGOs. Mapping the world of networked communities, as the UIA has consistently been doing, might seem only to prove the very existence of new players, but it is also indicative of the 'hybridity, reflexivity, mobility, and performativity' of these interlinked communities, which demands a new format for politics of this networked world.[17] Such pursuits evidently carry and reinforce particular assumptions. Lina Dencik has argued that notions of global civil society present 'an inherently globalised liberal narrative' about the media's role.[18] The UIA's publications – from the *Annuaire de la Vie Internationale* to the *Encyclopedia of World Problems and Human Potential* (launched in 1972) – certainly advanced narratives about the role of international organizations and also, implicitly, about the value of such publishing ventures.

The UIA's universalism was subject to inherent contradictions from the start. For instance, gender bias clearly shaped practices within internationalist milieus as well as access to international institutions. Yet the literature in History and IR also shows how women activists combatted marginalization at the national level through transnational cooperation and engagement with international organizations.[19] In this volume, Sarah Hellawell draws attention to intersections and parallels between the women's movement and the UIA. At the same time, she highlights inconsistencies, gendered assumptions and exclusionary practices in the Union's work and internationalism more generally.

The concept of 'global civil society' evidently raises wider questions about the UIA's relation to global inequalities. From its foundation, its centre of gravity was in Europe, and its early ventures hardly challenged colonial practices or notions of a civilizational hierarchy. Indeed, as indicated in Boyd Rayward's chapter, the UIA's creation fed into the agenda of Belgian expansionism, of which actions in the Congo were another manifestation. The organization's adherence to imperial paradigms becomes evident if one considers an episode that is referenced in Daniel Laqua's chapter: the UIA's encounter with Pan-Africanism and one of its key figures, the African American thinker and activist W. E. B. Du Bois. Pan-Africanism was a globally oriented and diverse movement. As Hakim Adi has pointed out, it encompassed 'a variety of ideas, activities, organizations and movements that, sometimes in concert, resisted the exploitation and oppression of all those of African heritage'.[20] Interactions with this movement revealed the boundaries of the world view espoused by the UIA in the 1920s.

Following Otlet's invitation, parts of the Pan-African Congress of 1921 took place at the Palais Mondial.[21] As one of many events held on UIA premises, the event reflected the Union's quest to become a centre for different international ventures. Otlet also hoped that this collaboration would result in developing a section for the International Museum.[22] Delegates gathered in Brussels for three days, following on from initial debates in London and preceding their concluding session in Paris. Muzong W. Kodi has analysed the background to the Brussels meeting and the controversy it attracted in Belgium: Belgian observers conflated Du Bois's Pan-Africanism with the black nationalism of Marcus Garvey. They interpreted popular unrest in the Belgian Congo – linked to Simon Kimbangu's messianic movement – as evidence of the headway made by Garveyism.[23] The press also cast suspicions on the co-organizer of the Brussels congress, Paul Panda Farnana, whose Union Congolaise promoted Congolese interests in Belgium.[24]

At the London segment of the congress, delegates had stressed that race should not be a factor in measuring claims to 'civilization'. Their declaration demanded local self-government and access to educational opportunities while denouncing Africa's exploitation for economic gain. Although the document offered criticisms of colonial practices in several countries, it did not condemn colonialism categorically. Nonetheless, within the Belgian context, these remarks were deemed too radical.[25] At Brussels, Otlet therefore drafted an alternative statement which the congress president – the West African politician and member of the French Chamber of Deputies, Blaise Diagne – 'declared adopted in the face of a clear majority in opposition'.[26]

In Paris, delegates returned to their earlier declaration and, as such, the Brussels deliberations remained a brief interlude. Yet the episode is instructive for what it reveals about the UIA. It highlighted the limited terms in which the organization conceived global action, namely through institutional relationships. Otlet's draft called for an 'international association … [of] all those willing to assist, in all countries, in the education, progress, and protection of the coloured race' and suggested that this association 'should co-operate with the institutions classed together in the International Centre at the Palais Mondial in Brussels'.[27] Meanwhile, with regard to Pan-Africanism, the 1921 discussions indicated the movement's potential for working with international organizations: while dealings with the UIA were limited, delegates did stress their desire to cooperate with the League of Nations.[28]

After the Second World War, the UIA's focus on data gathering and data provision meant that direct collaboration with political movements became even less likely. At the same time, its very role as a documentation centre allows us to trace the cultural or geographical biases of organizations that are often seen as embodiments of global civil society.[29] In this volume, Bob Reinalda, Martin Grandjean and Marco van Leeuwen show how UIA data can highlight shifts in the global balance of the world of international organizations. Their figures remind us that imbalances were not peculiar to the UIA – a point that also emerges from Matthias Middell and Katja Naumann's discussion of historians' engagement with global questions.

Using and Representing Data

From the outset, the UIA and sister organizations such as the IIB did more than merely collect large amounts of information. They used a standardized method of indexation and tried to reduce data complexity through innovative visual methods. In this context, one needs to distinguish between visual language (including the use of infographics), data visualization and data analytics. As illustrated in Figure I.1, the UIA traced changes in the world of international organizations through basic descriptive statistics, including tables, line and graphs.

Early on, the UIA embraced relational thinking as captured by the 'network' metaphor – a term that gained currency in the early twentieth century.[30] In this

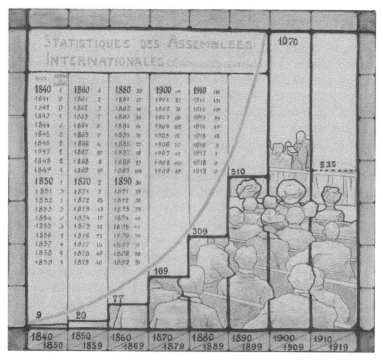

Figure I.1 Infographics depicting the rise of international events (congresses and conventions), 1840–1920 (undated). *Source:* Scan no. 009082, AFF, Mundaneum.

period, a visual vocabulary to communicate social characteristics emerged, elements of which are still being used today.[31] Paul Otlet himself developed a visual language that deployed metaphors and symbols, as illustrated by his depiction of a Universal Network of Documentation as a series of concentric circles. Figure I.2 offers examples from a UIA brochure published in the run-up to its second congress.

The development of graphic methods depended fundamentally on advances in technology and data collection.[32] After the Second World War, the step was made from the use of visual language to direct data-driven visualization. The UIA and its collaborators played a pioneering role in this respect (Figure I.3). UIA secretary Anthony Judge embraced data visualization in an age of rapidly growing computing power. His exploration of computer-aided visualizations went beyond the use of metaphors and artistic depictions of knowledge. Judge himself contributed to the development of network theory as applied to the study of international associations.[33] From the late 1960s onwards, he reflected critically on the use of mathematical graph theory for the analysis of networks. Graph theory is the base of formal network analysis and computer-aided network visualizations made possible by the emergence of user-friendly computer programmes. At this point, it became possible to do more than just summarize and visualize network data, and network characteristics or structures could be calculated more easily.

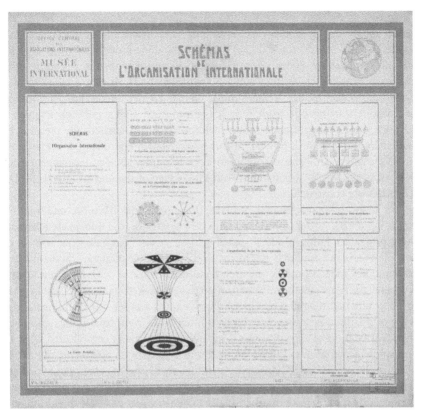

Figure I.2 Overview of different visualizations depicting international organizational life (undated, c. 1912). Concentric circles in the bottom left corner. *Source:* Scan no. 00009029, AFF, Mundaneum.

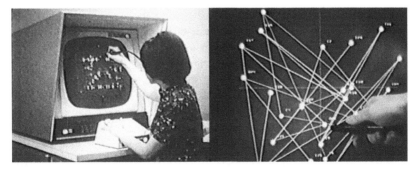

Figure I.3 UIA staff member and image of computer-aided, data-driven experiments that started in 1971. *Source:* UIA, 'Visualization – Alternative Representations of Information Gallery of Network Visualizations'. Available online: https://uia.org/visualizations-gallery (accessed 30 April 2018).

Today, in the face of digitization, new digital tools and an abundance of online data, new possibilities are emerging. The increasing availability of both structured and unstructured digital data and the dissemination of relatively user-friendly applications make it possible to tackle complex phenomena more easily. However, scholars sometimes apply network methods, distant reading tools or visualization techniques without fully realizing their theoretical implications or without starting out from research questions.[34] Using network analysis to advance the understanding of data – without creating aesthetically pleasing but artificial complexity – is crucial. In this book, Martin Grandjean and Marco van Leeuwen use an innovative combination of infographics, data visualization and data analytics, while displaying critical knowledge of the way in which the UIA datasets were constructed.

For many scholars, (spatial) visualization techniques have become a way of exploring data in order to come up with new questions and unexpected findings. Such projects might include a spatial and/or visual component as well as the use of web-based research platforms and (open) linked data.[35] Semantic web technologies indeed provide the architecture for working with large amounts of data and semi-automatic information retrieval. Linked data was – to a certain extent – already imagined by Otlet.[36] But we must temper our ambitions and be wary of misinterpretations. Linked data often lacks contextual information, and the identification of organizations – let alone persons – is complicated by name and language variations. There is a future and a need for an open reference service based on an 'open science' participatory model, consisting of collaboration between scholars who can provide contextual information on (the history of) international organizations, as well as international actors who can add self-definitions and information regarding their work. There is ample opportunity for the UIA to build on its early work and to engage in such ventures.

This Book

This volume is the first major scholarly study to combine an investigation into the UIA's early years with an analysis of its more recent past. To this end, we have brought together experts from a variety of fields, including History, Political Science and IR, Architecture, Digital Humanities as well as Library and Information Studies. The publication thus offers an inter- and multidisciplinary picture of an organization whose own work covers very different spheres.

The book is divided into three parts. *Part I* examines key stages in the UIA's development. Boyd Rayward's chapter explores the contexts in which the organization emerged, covering seemingly conflicting strands that nonetheless led to its creation. His appraisal of Cyrille Van Overbergh's impact acknowledges an often overlooked contribution. Christophe Verbruggen shows how the UIA sought to attract support from a variety of sources. Following on from this, Daniel Laqua examines the UIA's work in the aftermath of the First World War, analysing its 'International University' scheme within the wider context of intellectual reconstruction. Finally, Nico Randeraad and Philip Post show how the UIA redefined its purpose in the aftermath of the Second World War. Their contribution is important as this reorientation shapes the organization's work to this day.

The UIA was based on the premise that international organizations constituted key factors in international life. *Part II* therefore focuses on such entities. Sarah Hellawell discusses the interactions between the UIA, international women's organizations and intergovernmental organizations. Wouter Van Acker raises the question of how organizations sought to build their legitimacy. He examines how the UIA and the Union Internationale des Villes built one another's legitimacy through collaboration. Matthias Middell and Katja Naumann offer a stark contrast to Van Acker's discussion: they discuss the international collaborative patterns established by historians. While some historical congresses featured in UIA publications and while UIA leaders developed their own historical narratives about the progress of internationalism, there was little direct interaction. Moreover, as the authors show, the slow emergence of the International Committee of Historical Sciences (CISH) also seemed to question the narrative promoted by the UIA. Their final part, however, notes that CISH eventually engaged with global questions. As such, their chapter offers an interesting counterpart to the UIA's own work.

Part III provides an in-depth investigation of the material produced by the UIA. As Thomas Davies demonstrates, the work of its founders can be read as part of the wider history of early IR theorizing. Yet Davies also shows how the UIA's periodicals in the period after the Second World War contrasted with the dominant Realist paradigm. Pierre-Yves Saunier then examines the contexts in which UIA publications were being produced and used. His piece forms the context for the two remaining contributions in this section, which draw on the UIA's data and publications. Bob Reinalda does so with a focus on the secretariats of international organizations. Meanwhile, Martin Grandjean and Marco van Leeuwen use the material to identify and visualize particular patterns in the development of international congresses and organizations.

On the whole, the book notes not only the ambitions but also the limitations and problems associated with the UIA and its protagonists. As the UIA secretariat expressed an interest in our findings, we invited its staff to contribute an epilogue. Nancy Carfrae's contribution adds two further dimensions to our study: first, it shows us how the organization perceives its own history and underlying principles; second, it brings the volume up to date, summarizing the organization's current activities.

Somewhat fittingly for its subject matter, this book documents the work of an international organization, and it does so on the basis of transnational cooperation. While the scope of our publication certainly pales in comparison to the UIA's massive publishing ventures, we hope that this book contributes not only to the historical understanding of the UIA itself but also to the analysis of phenomena which, in the eyes of its founders, were key features of 'international life'.

Notes

1 See, for example, Margaret MacMillan, *Paris 1919: Six Months That Changed the World* (New York: Random House, 2001), 53–62.

2 *La Charte des Intérêts intellectuels et moraux: Memorandum adressé à MM. les Délégués de la Conférence de la Paix, à Paris par l'Union des Associations Internationales* (Bruxelles-Paris, février 1919) in 'Union des Associations Internationales II', box HLF 218, Henri La Fontaine papers, Mundaneum, Mons.

3 Meetings of Fédération Documentaire des Institutions Internationales, séance préparatoire du 5 juillet 1906, box 229, Hoover Institution, Stanford University.

4 *Annuaire de la Vie Internationale: Unions, associations, instituts, commissions, bureaux, offices, conférences, congrès, expositions, publications, 1908–1909* (Brussels: Office Central des Institutions Internationales, 1909). The only other edition appeared four years later: *Annuaire de la Vie Internationale, 1910–1911* (Brussels: Office International des Associations Internationales, 1913).

5 Sebastian Conrad and Dominic Sachsenmaier, eds, *Competing Visions of World Order: Global Moments and Movements, 1880s–1930s* (Basingstoke: Palgrave, 2007); Mark Mazower, *Governing the World: The History of an Idea* (London: Penguin, 2012); Duncan Bell, *Reordering the World: Essays on Liberalism and Empire* (Princeton, NJ: Princeton University Press, 2016); Or Rosenboim, *The Emergence of Globalism: Visions of World Order in Britain and the United States, 1939–1950* (Princeton, NJ: Princeton University Press, 2017).

6 Akira Iriye, *Global Community: The Role of International Organizations in the Making of the Modern World* (Berkeley, CA: University of California Press, 2004); Thomas Davies, *NGOs: A New History of Transnational Civil Society* (London: Hurst, 2013); Bob Reinalda, *Handbook of International Organization* (Abingdon: Routledge, 2013); Daniel Gorman, *International Cooperation in the Early Twentieth Century* (London: Bloomsbury, 2018).

7 For recent work on the League, see, for example, Patricia Clavin, *Securing the World Economy: The Reinvention of the League of Nations, 1920–1946* (Oxford: Oxford University Press, 2013); Susan Pedersen, *The Guardians: The League of Nations and the Crisis of Empire* (New York: Oxford University Press, 2015). For work on the UN, see, for instance, Paul Kennedy, *The Parliament of Man: The Past, Present, and Future of the United Nations* (New York: Vintage, 2006); Amy Sayward, *The United Nations in International History* (London: Bloomsbury, 2017).

8 Glenda Sluga, *Internationalism in the Age of Nationalism* (Philadelphia: University of Pennsylvania Press, 2013); Patricia Clavin and Glenda Sluga, eds, *Internationalisms: A Twentieth Century History* (Cambridge: Cambridge University Press, 2016); Jessica Reinisch, 'Agents of Internationalism', *Contemporary European History* 25, no. 2 (2016): 195–212.

9 Akira Iriye, *Cultural Internationalism and World Order* (Baltimore, MY: Johns Hopkins University Press, 1997), 27.

10 Madeleine Herren, *Hintertüren zur Macht: Internationalismus und modernisierungsorientierte Außenpolitik in Belgien, der Schweiz und den USA 1865–1914* (Munich: Oldenbourg, 2000).

11 Madeleine Herren, '"Outwardly … an Innocuous Conference Authority": National Socialism and the Logistics of International Information Management', *German History* 20, no. 1 (2002): 67–92.

12 W. Boyd Rayward, *The Universe of Information: The Work of Paul Otlet for Documentation and International Organisation* (Moscow: VINITI, 1975);

Françoise Levie, *L'Homme qui voulait classer le monde: Paul Otlet et le Mundaneum* (Brussels: Les Impressions Nouvelles, 2006); Jacques Gillen, Stéphanie Manfroid, and Raphaële Cornille, eds, *Paul Otlet. Fondateur du Mundaneum (1868–1944): Architecte du savoir, Artisan de paix* (Liège: Les Impressions Nouvelles, 2010); Alex Wright, *Cataloging the World: Paul Otlet and the Birth of the Information Age* (New York: Oxford University Press, 2014). The literature on Henri La Fontaine is more limited – essentially two edited volumes: Jacques Gillen, ed., *Henri La Fontaine, Prix Nobel de la Paix en 1913: un belge épris de justice* (Brussels: Éditions Racine, 2012); *Henri La Fontaine: un prix Nobel de paix: tracé(s) d'une vie* (Mons: Mundaneum, 2002).

13 Georges Patrick Speeckaert, 'A Glance at Sixty Years of Activity (1910–1970) of the Union of International Associations', in *Union of International Associations, 1910–1970: Past, Present, Future* (Brussels: UIA, 1970), 19–52.

14 Anne Rasmussen, 'L'Internationale scientifique 1890–1914' (PhD diss., Ecole des Hautes Etudes en Sciences Sociales de Paris, 1995); Herren, *Hintertüren zur Macht*; Daniel Laqua, *The Age of Internationalism and Belgium, 1880–1930: Peace, Progress and Prestige* (Manchester: Manchester University Press, 2013).

15 Helmut Anheier, Marlies Glasius and Mary Kaldor, 'Introducing Global Civil Society', in *Global Civil Society 2001*, ed. idem (Oxford: Oxford University Press, 2001), 3–22; Mary Kaldor, *Global Civil Society: An Answer to War* (Cambridge: Polity, 2003); Randall Germain and Michael Kenny, *The Idea of Global Civil Society: Politics and Ethics in a Globalizing Era* (London: Routledge, 2005); Gideon Baker and David Chandler, *Global Civil Society: Contested Futures* (London: Routledge, 2005); Don Eberly, *The Rise of Global Civil Society: Building Communities and Nations from the Bottom Up* (New York: Encounter Books, 2008); Mary Kaldor, Henrietta Moore, Sabine Selchow and Tamsin Murray-Leach, *Global Civil Society 2012: Ten Years of Critical Reflection* (Basingstoke: Palgrave, 2012).

16 John Keane, *Global Civil Society?* (Cambridge: Cambridge University Press, 2005), 20.

17 Jodi Dean, Jon Anderson and Geert Lovink, *Reformatting Politics: Information Technology and Global Civil Society* (New York: London, 2006), xx.

18 Lina Dencik, *Media and Global Civil Society* (Basingstoke: Palgrave, 2012), 3.

19 Karen Garner, *Women and Gender in International History: Theory and Practice* (London: Bloomsbury, 2018), 99–148; Leila Rupp, *Worlds of Women: The Making of an International Women's Movement* (Princeton, NJ: Princeton University Press, 1997); Deborah Stienstra, *Women's Movements and International Organizations* (Basingstoke: Palgrave, 1994). For an example of recent interest in feminism's global dimensions, see Francisca de Haan, Margaret Allen, June Purvis and Krassimira Daskalova, eds, *Women's Activism: Global Perspectives from the 1890s to the Present* (London: Routledge, 2013).

20 Hakim Adi, *Pan-Africanism: A History* (London: Bloomsbury, 2018).

21 Otlet to W. E. B. Du Bois, 17 December 1920, in W. E. B. Du Bois Papers, Series 1A. General Correspondence [hereafter: Du Bois Papers], in Special Collections and University Archives, University of Massachusetts Amherst Libraries, available online via http://credo.library.umass.edu.

22 Otlet to Paul Panda Farnana, 20 April 1921, ibid.

23 Muzong W. Kodi, 'The 1921 Pan-African Congress at Brussels: A Background to Belgian Pressures', *Transafrican Journal of History* 13, no. 1 (1984): 48–73.

24 Françoise Levie, author of the Otlet biography *L'Homme qui voulait classer le monde* (and director of the 2002 film with the same title) has also made a film on Paul Panda Farnana: *Panda Farnana, un Congolais qui dérange* (2011).

25 W. E. B. Du Bois, 'The Pan-African Movement', in *W. E. B. Du Bois Speaks: Speeches and Addresses 1920–1963*, ed. Philip Foner (London: Pathfinder, 1970), 199–203.

26 Du Bois, 'The Pan-African Movement', I 201.

27 The 'Otlet Declaration' is cited in J. Ayodele Langley, *Pan-Africanism and Nationalism in West Africa, 1900–1945: A Study in Ideology and Social Classes* (Oxford: Clarendon Press, 1973), 81.

28 'Manifesto to the League of Nations', *The Crisis* 23, no. 1 (1921): 18.

29 On issues related to this, see Katja Naumann and Klaas Dykmann, 'Changes from the "Margins": Non-European Actors, Ideas and Strategies in International Organizations', *Comparativ* 23, no. 4–5 (2013): 9–20.

30 The sociologist Georg Simmel is often cited as a founding father of social network analysis because he started thinking in terms of actors and (concentric) circles: Mario Diani, 'Simmel to Rokkan and Beyond: Towards a Network Theory of (New) Social Movements', *European Journal of Social Theory* 3, no. 4 (2000): 387–406.

31 Linton Freeman, 'Graphic Techniques for Exploring Social Network Data', in *Models and Methods in Social Network Analysis*, ed. Peter Carrington, John Scott and Stanley Wasserman (Cambridge: Cambridge University Press, 2005), 248–69.

32 For an overview, see, for example, Michael Friendly, 'A Brief History of Data Visualization', in *Handbook of Data Visualization*, ed. Chun-houh Chen et al. (Berlin: Springer, 2008), 15–56.

33 See, for example, Anthony Judge, 'Visualization of the International Organization', *International Associations* 22, no. 5 (1970): 265–81; idem, 'International Organization Networks: A Complementary Perspective', in *International Organizations: A Conceptual Approach*, ed. A. J. R. Groom and Paul Taylor (London: Frances Pinter, 1977), 381–413.

34 See Christophe Verbruggen, Thomas D'haeninck and Hans Blomme. 'Mobility and Movements in Intellectual History: A Social Network Approach', in *The Power of Networks: Prospects of Historical Network Research*, ed. Florian Kerschbaumer et al. (Abingdon: Routledge, forthcoming 2019).

35 See, for instance, TIC Collaborative, a Virtual Research Environment for the study of nineteenth/early-twentieth century international organizations and (scientific) congresses. Available online: http://www.tic.ugent.be (accessed 30 April 2018).

36 For a good discussion and overview, see Wright, *Cataloging the World*, 162–73. See also Charles van den Heuvel, 'Web 2.0 and the Semantic Web in Research from a Historical Perspective: The Designs of Paul Otlet (1868–1944) for Telecommunication and Machine Readable Documentation to Organize Research and Society', *Knowledge Organization* 36, no. 4 (2009): 214–26.

Part I

THE DEVELOPMENT OF THE UIA

Chapter 1

CREATING THE UIA: HENRI LA FONTAINE, CYRILLE VAN OVERBERGH AND PAUL OTLET

W. Boyd Rayward

This chapter explores the events and relationships that led to the foundation of the Central Office of International Institutions in 1907 and the Union of International Associations (UIA) in 1910. It investigates the tangle of potentially conflicting political orientations, personal ties and institutional affiliations of the triumvirs involved in the creation of these organizations: Henri La Fontaine (1854–1943), Cyrille Van Overbergh (1866–1959) and Paul Otlet (1868–1944). Paradoxically, they considered the Central Office and Union to express national expansionary interests – Belgium as a centre for internationalism – but also to reflect, and perhaps help regulate, an emergent form of what they called 'international life'. They regarded the latter as a globalizing trend that had been abundantly documented in the two massive *Annuaires de la Vie Internationale* of the Central Office. Their collaboration involved the mutual accommodation of different personal circumstances arising from their educational backgrounds and the various organizations of which they were members.

Henri La Fontaine, the oldest of the three, was scion of a wealthy Brussels family and a law graduate of the Free University of Brussels. He interned with two distinguished lawyers, Jules Bara and Auguste Orts, both of whom were active in the Belgian parliament as radically anticlerical liberals.[1] He became secretary to the jurist Edmond Picard who, for forty years, was one of the leading philanthropists, cultural animators and controversialists in the artistic and literary life of *belle époque* Brussels. Admitted to the Brussels Bar, La Fontaine appeared with Picard on several cases before the Court of Appeals.

As a young man, La Fontaine joined one of the oldest and most prominent Belgian lodges, Les Amis Philanthropes of which he became twice Worshipful Grand Master in a career-long dedication to freemasonry. The lodge was politically liberal and anticlerical. It had also been an important influence – not long after the formation of the Belgian state – in the creation of the Free University of Brussels. La Fontaine became an active member of the Belgian Workers' Party when it was founded by a number of his socialist colleagues in 1885. He was also among a small group of radically progressive intellectuals who launched the Université Nouvelle in 1894 to offer a revolutionary challenge to what they believed had become the Free University's reactionary approach to the social and human sciences.[2] And, like his former *maître* Picard, La Fontaine entered the Senate as a socialist, following the first elections under an extended franchise in 1894. La Fontaine was passionately pacifist and internationalist in his sympathies. In 1889 he helped to set up the Belgian section of the English-based International Arbitration and Peace Association, which had developed such sections across Europe. Throughout his long career, he was a leading figure at the Universal Peace Congresses and in the Interparliamentary Union. He became president of the International Peace Bureau in 1907 and held this office until his death in 1943. In 1913 he was awarded the Nobel Peace Prize.

Cyrille Van Overbergh's background could not have been more different.[3] Born in Kortrijk in West Flanders, he attended the Catholic University of Louvain. He too graduated in law but his internship was with François Schollaert, a Louvain-based lawyer who had recently been elected to the Belgian Chamber of Representatives for the Catholic Party. Even before graduation, Van Overbergh had become active in the Flemish urban guild movement led by Schollaert's brother-in-law, Joris Helleputte.[4] When Helleputte – deeply religious, anti-liberal and anti-socialist – founded the Belgian Democratic League in 1891 'for the church and the people', the young Van Overbergh was described as having become his right hand.[5] At Louvain, Van Overbergh had also became deeply involved with the efforts of Désiré Mercier, later cardinal and head of the Catholic Church in Belgium, to create a neo-Thomist Higher Institute of Philosophy.[6]

Van Overbergh's subsequent professional career was that of a high-ranking bureaucrat in government agencies under the political control of the Catholic Party. When Schollaert was appointed Minister of the Interior and Higher Education in 1895, Van Overbergh became his principal private secretary. He subsequently served in a range of senior administrative posts associated with Schollaert's ministerial responsibilities, covering areas such as higher education, arts and sciences.

Paul Otlet was the youngest of the three men. He grew up in a milieu of luxury and privilege.[7] His father, Edouard, was a financier and industrialist who created and lost a large fortune setting up companies to build tram and railways – at least thirty-five of them according to Paul – throughout Europe and many other parts of the world.[8] Between 1874 and 1900, Edouard Otlet represented the Catholic Party in the Senate. Paul Otlet was educated at an elitist Jesuit school in Brussels, the Collège Saint-Michel, before entering the Catholic University of Louvain. He followed his studies at Louvain with a period of independent study at the Sorbonne in Paris, where he cast off his Catholicism, capitulated to agnosticism and embraced positivism and evolutionism.[9] He subsequently transferred to the Free University of Brussels, where he took a law degree. In 1891, he became an intern of Edmond Picard, for whom La Fontaine had acted as secretary some years earlier. Picard was an Otlet family friend who for many years represented Edouard Otlet's complicated legal affairs.

In order to understand how these different personalities and orientations shaped the processes that ultimately produced the Central Office and the Union of International Associations, the chapter initially examines the context of Brussels positivism and contemporary attitudes to the social sciences. It then discusses the Belgian Catholic milieu of politics and higher education and its alternative approach to social theorizing. It suggests that the UIA's founders integrated their different intellectual interests, organizational structures for the international management of information and a commitment to pacifism into the wider vision of a new, knowledge-based world polity. They believed that their Central Office and UIA would give this vision an identity and administrative reality.

Bibliographic Collaborations, the Brussels Positivist Milieu and the Creation of the International Office and Institute of Bibliography

The origins of what was to become the administrative and physical hub of the Central Office of International Associations lie in the expanding and diversifying bibliographical collaboration between Otlet and La Fontaine. This began in Brussels in 1892 in the positivist, anticlerical and short-lived Société des Études Sociales et Politiques (SESP) and continued in the Institut des Sciences Sociales (ISS) in 1894.[10] Working with several colleagues under Edmond Picard's guidance, Otlet had embarked in 1891 on the publication of a periodical bibliography for law. The work was based on principles that Picard had enunciated, linking bibliography to the positivism that characterized the period's approach to science.[11] Otlet himself had explored these ideas, attempting to understand the impact a bibliography of the kind he had embarked upon might have on the organization and conduct of the social sciences.[12]

In March 1892, he had suggested combining his bibliographical work with La Fontaine's bibliographical activities for the SESP. Essentially positivist in outlook, the SESP declared itself to be 'exclusively devoted to scientific research', with its mission being to 'observe the facts, to let them speak, to set itself above passions and prejudices'.[13] Central to its work were its journal, the *Revue Sociale et Politique*, its library and especially its bibliographical service for which La Fontaine assumed primary responsibility.

The International Office of Sociological Bibliography, which the two men created within the SESP, became increasingly independent of the society as the latter fell on hard times. According to one observer, it was eventually absorbed by the ISS, although the principles underlying the two organizations could not have been more different.[14] Ernest Solvay, a prominent Belgian industrialist and philanthropist, set up the ISS in 1894 essentially to investigate his own sociological and economic theories.[15] La Fontaine and Otlet played a prominent role in the initial organization of the Institute.[16] La Fontaine was given financial responsibility for managing the substantial funds that Solvay provided for it. Otlet undertook unsuccessful negotiations for the SESP's *Revue Sociale et Polique* to become a joint publication with the ISS. Their Office of Sociological Bibliography became the Institute's administrative centre, with La Fontaine in effect acting for its first year as the Institute's combined secretary-treasurer. The Office undertook to cover all secretarial needs of the ISS and 'to catalogue such documents, to create such statistics, to carry out such physical research as indicated by the Institute'.[17] In addition, it agreed to put its bibliographical collections and other resources at the disposition of the ISS. For these services, the Institute agreed to pay the Office an annual sum for three years, further funding to be negotiable after that.

Having been asked by Solvay how best to extend and formalize the work of the ISS, Otlet and La Fontaine drafted a series of proposals regarding the bibliographical support which, they argued, the Institute would eventually need for the research of its members and collaborators.[18] The complex of tasks that they now projected for an independent, self-sustaining International Office of Sociological Bibliography went far beyond anything that the ISS might have been expected to support. In fact, Otlet suggested raising capital to support the International Office by incorporating it as a cooperative society in which there would be different levels of investment.[19]

Otlet and La Fontaine's bibliographical experience had begun with the compilation and publication of relatively straightforward periodic bibliographies for the social sciences. But these undertakings had suggested to them that the SESP's positivist commitment to identifying and synthesizing facts – ideas to which they themselves subscribed – required something much more developed in terms of both system and comprehensiveness. Bibliography was seen to have powerful internationalist implications.[20] What was needed now was a bibliographical office that could ensure the creation of a universal listing of materials related to all of the disciplines, would support a 'Universal and International Library' and an international bibliographical institute that, not limited to law or sociology, would coordinate worldwide the activities of learned societies and other organizations with an interest in bibliographic matters.[21] Such an organizational infrastructure would enable the identification, collation and integration for the rapid and precise deployment of 'facts' that were fragmented, widely dispersed, 'unprocessed' and thus unready for use.

But a critical tool was missing. For the systemization and coordination of its work, the International Office of Sociological Bibliography had to develop a classification system that could allow the coordination and integration of bibliographical activities wherever they were taking place. Otlet's discovery early in 1895 of the latest edition of the Decimal Classification, first published in 1876 by the American librarian Melvil Dewey, came as a revelation to the two men. It seemed as if it could easily solve the classification problem that had hitherto appeared to be intractable of enabling international cooperation and synthesis of scattered bibliographic work. Its possibilities seemed almost inexhaustible. It covered the entire universe of knowledge and, with its seemingly simple, potentially infinite decimal divisions and subdivisions into tens, appeared to enable that coverage in a practical, straightforward way.[22]

With the Office of Sociological Bibliography reasonably well established and their plans for its extension underway, La Fontaine and Otlet embarked on organizing an international conference on bibliography for September 1895. This led to official recognition and the provision of a legal basis for what was now simply called the International Office of Bibliography (OIB).[23] They secured the agreement of Edouard Descamps to preside at the conference. As a member of the Belgian Senate, eminent jurist and professor of law at the University of Louvain Descamps gave the meeting weight and visibility and helped to secure government patronage for the conference. And indeed, it is the publication of Descamps's closing address that gives us an account of the conference's immediate background, objectives and outcomes.[24]

The conference recommended that a Universal Bibliographical Repertory be undertaken, that its entries be classified by the Decimal Classification and that this should be translated immediately into French, German and Italian. To secure the necessary participation and support of governments in setting up the OIB to manage the Universal Repertory and related services, it was resolved that the Belgian government should be asked to create an international bibliographic union of governments. The conference also resolved that an International Institute of Bibliography (IIB) be created as 'a vital and permanent centre' where individuals, institutions and associations could assemble to work together for the progress of the science of bibliography.

Two weeks later, the legal basis for the OIB to become an agency of the Belgian government was established by Royal Decree under the signature of the Minister for the Interior and Public Instruction, François Schollaert. The OIB was to have as its object the creation and publication of a Universal Bibliographical Repertory, and 'to study all the questions related to bibliographical work'.[25] The decree also indicated that the government would make available an appropriate locale for the Office and would provide a subsidy towards the costs of its work.

Official support for the OIB and IIB came not from leading members of liberal, socialist, rationalist, francophone organizations. Instead, it came from Catholic centres of political power and from the intellectual and philosophical commitments of members of the Catholic University of Louvain, from Catholic politicians originating for the most part in the Flemish community – though conducting their public life in French as was the custom at the time. Especially important in this was the connection between Edouard Descamps, François Schollaert and the latter's protégé, Cyrille Van Overbergh.

The Louvain Connection: Catholicism, Descamps, Schollaert, Van Overbergh and Mercier

Edouard Descamps's support for the OIB–IIB continued beyond the conference of 1895. He was gazetted president of the OIB by the Royal Decree that established the office, and he continued actively in this role until 1907. Apart from his distinction as professor at the University of Louvain, he had also been elected as senator for the district of Louvain in 1892, a position he held for more than forty years. He was a fervent apologist for Léopold II's interests as sovereign of the Congo Free State.[26] As an international jurist, he was active in the Interparliamentary Union, where his study on international arbitration set out an influential position that varied considerably from that advanced by La Fontaine in the Universal Peace Congresses.[27]

Profoundly religious, he was oriented towards the ultramontane tradition of the Catholic Church.[28] He wrote a number of works on the reconciliation of Christianity with law and the sciences. These publications brought him within the sphere of the neo-Thomist Higher Institute of Philosophy, set up tentatively in 1889 in the Catholic University of Louvain by Désiré Mercier. The Institute's aim was not only to investigate and accept the findings and methods of modern science, but also to demonstrate that positivism had moral, psychological and spiritual limitations that the faithful could transcend through a reformulation of the philosophy of Saint Thomas Aquinas.[29] Descamps's religious position was sympathetic to Mercier's anti-positivist but science-based approach to religious eschatology.

To express his sense of obligation and gratitude for more than ten years of support by Descamps, Otlet addressed him directly in 1907 at the opening ceremony of the Collective Library of Learned Societies. This had been formed by the deposit of the library collections of twenty-five Brussels-based organizations in a facility provided by the government. It was to be administered by, and to become an integral part of the collections and services of, the OIB–IIB.[30] Descamps had just resigned as OIB president to head the Belgian government's newly created Ministry of the Sciences and Arts.

> Minister, Dear President, behold the steps covered since the year 1895, when we convoked at the Hotel Ravenstein the first International Conference of Bibliography. You will remember those modest beginnings. We had 40,000 cards [*sic* – the number was 400,000][31] but we were without a library, without government-supported international relations, without a locale, without collaborators, without a budget. Today we have all of this.[32]

The links between Descamps and Schollaert were close and Louvain-based. Schollaert had been a student in the Louvain's Faculty of Law of which Descamps was such a prominent member. Schollaert had been elected to the Chamber of Representatives for the administrative arrondissement of Louvain in 1888. He had authorized the official recognition of the OIB not long after having been appointed Minister for the Interior and Public Instruction in 1895. Descamps joined him in the government as Minister for Sciences and the Arts not long before Schollaert became Belgian prime minister in 1908. Schollaert was to add Descamps's portfolio to his own responsibilities upon the latter's resignation in 1910. But there is also another important connection involving Schollaert. Upon his designation as minister in 1895, he appointed Cyrille Van Overbergh as his Chief of Staff.

Van Overbergh emerges as a major figure in the penultimate developments leading to the creation of the Central Office and the UIA. In 1924, *L'Indépendance*

Belge described La Fontaine and Otlet as the 'Siamese twins' of the Palais Mondial, as the complex of institutions created by the two men was called after the First World War. But from 1895 until the war, observed Glycas, 'they were helped by a third person who acted in the wings rather than on the stage: M. Cyrille Van Overbergh. [He] it was who from the start attracted the favour of M. Schollaert to the Office. It is he who ten years later knew how to attract the sympathetic interest of King Leopold II.'[33]

As mentioned above, Van Overbergh had been deeply influenced by the anti-socialist Catholic worker's organizational activities of Schollaert's brother-in-law, Joris Heleputte. Helleputte himself had been elected to the parliament at the same time as Schollaert and when the latter became head of the government in 1908, Helleputte entered his cabinet and over the subsequent years occupied a number of portfolios.[34] Thus, at the outset of his career, Van Overbergh had the closest connections in parliament to these two intimately related, influential members of the governing Catholic Party. He quickly transitioned from chief of Schollaert's staff in 1895 to Director General of Higher Education in the Ministry of the Interior and Public Instruction in 1899 and Director General for Arts and Sciences in 1910.

In the period from 1895 to 1910, despite all sorts of bureaucratic difficulties, Otlet and La Fontaine had *entrée* to and support of two closely related ministers and their departments: the Ministry of Interior and Public Instruction (Schollaert) and of the Arts and Sciences (Descamps). In Van Overbergh, they had the attention of one of the most senior bureaucrats in these ministries – someone who was supportive of their work and aware of its potential to underpin a larger national and international role for Belgium.

Otlet and Louvain

Otlet is the figure that connects the Office and Institute of Bibliography to the Louvain-based milieu of support discussed above. From his days as a student at the University of Louvain, Otlet had maintained a small circle of close friends who were to become important in the development of Désiré Mercier's Higher Institute of Philosophy. They were among the first collaborators whom Otlet attracted to the work of the OIB. When the *Revue Néo-Scolastique* began publication in 1894 with Mercier as editor-in-chief, Otlet's colleague, Maurice De Wulf, was designated the *Revue*'s managing editor. The Royal Decree of 1895 had gazetted De Wulf – whom Mercier had appointed professor of philosophy in his Higher Institute – a member of the OIB's 'management committee', along with Descamps as its president. Following the OIB's establishment, De Wulf immediately aligned the *Revue Néo-Scolastique* with its work and developed tables of the Decimal Classification for the field of philosophy. From July 1895, the *Revue* included a classified bibliography of philosophical works, 'Sommaire idéologique des ouvrages de philosophie' – a title echoing Otlet and La Fontaine's earlier periodical bibliographies for law and sociology. Its entries were intended for eventual inclusion in the OIB's Universal

Bibliographical Repertory.[35] The series continued as a supplement to the *Revue Néo-Scolastique* until the outbreak of the First World War. Working with De Wulf was Armand Thiéry, a brilliant albeit eccentric scholar who had been Otlet's closest school friend at the Collège Saint-Michel.[36] Now beginning his academic career, Thiéry sought Otlet's advice on the use of the Decimal Classification for an encyclopaedic dictionary of philosophy he was contemplating compiling. He noted that Mercier was 'charmed to find you among us once more and hopes that this will be often and more and more'.[37]

Van Overbergh, also an intimate friend of Otlet's,[38] was one of the small number of religious young men on whom Cardinal Mercier was eventually to rely as founding academic staff for the Higher Institute of Philosophy. Mercier declared that Van Overbergh, Thiéry and Simon Deploige in particular 'formed a cohort of young Catholics the like of which he had rarely encountered'.[39] In new arrangements for the Institute in 1893 – implemented in 1895, 'before an audience of hundreds of students' – Van Overbergh began to present a formidable programme of lectures on contemporary socialism. He offered these lectures annually until the academic year 1911–12 in what constituted an evolving study and critique of socialism and its Marxist connections.[40]

In 1899, Van Overbergh created the Belgian Society of Sociology. It was a curious enterprise very much dominated by its president. It met regularly in Brussels in his offices as Director General of Higher Education – not, as one might expect, in Louvain. On the face of it, its objectives resembled those of the earlier SESP: 'to undertake the study of social facts without *a priori* conception, without class or political biases; to be objective'. But as Van Overbergh was to indicate forty years later, the approach was by no means positivist. 'We wanted to show', he said, 'that Catholics could undertake sociology, that they aren't restrained by their religion.' Its concern was with the procedures of 'true sociology', the examination by the members of the society, who represented various disciplines, of the sociological implications of these branches of knowledge. He dismissed the kind of work undertaken within the Sociological Institute of Solvay, which had grown out of the ISS, as not sociological but a form of economics. From 1900 until 1906, reports of discussions within the society were published in the form of a supplement, *Le Mouvement Sociologique*, edited by Van Overbergh, to the *Revue Néo-Scolastique* of the Higher Institute of Philosophy.[41]

The Belgian Society of Sociology's work took a distinct turn in 1904 when the Society began to discuss how to carry out a systematic sociological study of the 'primitive peoples' whose conversion to Christianity was being undertaken by missionaries in colonial territories. This discussion led to a 'Sociological Study of the Peoples of Inferior Civilization' and eventually to the creation of the International Bureau of Ethnology (with Van Overbergh as president), which emerged from the Mons International Congress of World Economic Expansion of 1905.[42] The methodology proposed was to distribute detailed questionnaires widely to officials in the field, missionaries, scholarly experts and any others who might have useful knowledge. The results were then to be collated onto separate detachable sheets organized by a rigid scheme of subject headings that allowed the comparative study according to the same criteria of all of the aspects of the life and belief of the indigenous populations being studied.[43] As the study got underway, it became clear that its results – not only in terms of volume but also with its documentary methodology of detachable pages – could not be continued as a supplement to the *Revue Néo-Scolastique*. In 1907 Van Overbergh undertook to edit a new journal not only of discussion but one in which increasingly the results of the ethnographic studies of Congolese tribes could appear in the new format, *Le Mouvement Sociologique International*. This was published jointly by the Belgian Society of Sociology and Otlet and La Fontaine's IIB.[44]

The Imperialist Agenda: International Congress of World Economic Expansion, 1905

Van Overbergh was responsible for organizing the 1905 Mons Congress of World Economic Expansion and acted as its secretary-general. Reminiscing forty years after the event to Pierre de Bie, he commented that as a 'friend of Leopold II', he had suggested to the King in 1905 that 'a general congress of all international learned societies having their offices in Belgium' would be an appropriate addition to the 75th anniversary celebrations of national independence.[45] The major thrust of the Mons Congress, however, was to bring together representatives of various foreign governments, learned societies, Belgian government administrations and various Belgian civil, religious and military bodies to explore issues of colonial administration and development, especially the preparation of personnel for service in posts in overseas colonial agencies.[46] While its discussions canvassed a variety of national interests, given the overwhelming number of Belgian participants, the emphasis was on the Congo Free State.

At a congress reception, Leopold II expressed sentiments not directly about the expansion of Belgian economic and other interests in the Congo, but about a broader general international role for Belgium. Van Overbergh enthusiastically reported these remarks: 'Little Belgium can become more and more the capital of a notable intellectual, artistic, civilizing and economic movement, can become a modest but useful member of the great family of nations performing its small part in the service of Humanity.'[47]

Otlet acted as one of the secretaries and rapporteurs for section 5 of the congress: 'Civilizing Expansion into New Regions', which was particularly concerned with the ethnographic study of indigenous peoples, the recruitment, induction and living conditions of colonial personnel, and with services such as colonial museums, libraries, and information services. Descamps presided over the section and, as congress secretary-general, Van Overbergh participated in its discussions.[48] There was considerable interest in the questionnaire-based ethnographic project of the Belgian Society of Sociology and the congress recommended the setting up of what became the International Bureau of Ethnology with Van Overbergh at its head.

Otlet submitted a lengthy report on the vital importance of gathering, organizing and disseminating various kinds of information in support of successful colonial expansionary, civilizing and economic initiatives. The International Office and Institute of Bibliography in Brussels, he argued, provided a model of what was needed organizationally in terms of objectives and methodologies, and could function as a kind of centre for these new functions.[49] Unsurprisingly, the congress adopted several resolutions in favour of the idea and in support of the OIB's work.[50]

Van Overbergh and Otlet had increasingly started to work together in the run-up to the Mons Congress. Otlet had suggested that they 'examine the possibility of grouping existing international institutions on a federative basis'. He had pencilled a note on the draft of his long letter about this: 'Point of departure of many ideas to be recast.' In the context of Belgium's anniversary year, he noted Leopold II's speeches on the prospect of creating 'a greater Belgium'. Otlet suggested that the work of the Mons Congress would 'be truly complete if an organism grouping international institutions could crown its work'. A great number of these organizations already existed in Belgium. Moreover, geographically 'at a crossroads of ideas as well as territories' and always sensitive to 'great world movements', Belgium should be the country 'to coordinate elements of progress in all domains' and to facilitate all that leads towards 'the universal life to which the Humanity of tomorrow is summoned'. In analysing what one might call the 'aggrandizing' work of the new body he was proposing, Otlet laid out the range of issues that would eventually be addressed by the World Congress of International Associations five years later.[51]

While both Otlet and Van Overbergh were ready to pursue this idea following the Mons Congress, a difficulty had arisen in the form of a potentially conflicting initiative in Monaco.

International Pacifism and International Organizations

As an agency of the Belgian government, the OIB had begun to gather information for a directory of Belgian scholarly and professional organizations in 1904.[52] At about this time, it also started to compile another directory, dedicated to *international* agencies that had established their headquarters in Belgium.[53] This was part of a much larger survey of international associations in general. Van Overbergh, in offering a rationale for this survey, pointed out that the Belgian Society of Sociology had carried out 'two enquiries on the basis of a systematic questionnaire. ... One dealt with pure sociology ... the other was concerned with people of an inferior civilization.'[54] He now suggested 'applying the method ... to social structures', such as 'international association in its modern sense, one of the most characteristic expressions of the solidarity of peoples'.[55] In commenting on this study, De Bie described it as 'a sort of comparative analysis of 18 international associations with various objectives. They are described according to a schema involving their definition, history, their classification by genre and species, their creation, their life, their evolution and their method of dissolution.' It took up more than 300 pages when published in the *Mouvement Sociologique international*. De Bie, not having understood its status as a preliminary 'report' or a work in progress, went on to say misleadingly: 'apparently there was no follow-up to this preposterous (*abracabrant*) attempt'.[56]

At much the same time, however, a similar initiative had been introduced by the International Institute for Peace (IIP), which Prince Albert I of Monaco had created in 1903. The IIP was an outcome of the Universal Peace Congress held in the principality the year before. The Monaco-based body aimed to ensure the publication of documentary works related to matters of international peace, arbitration, armaments, the statistics of war and related topics. The task of organizing the IIP was given to the French pacifist Gaston Moch.[57] Moch was well known to Otlet and La Fontaine, both because of his role in the French peace movement and because he was among a small group of French pacifists who had purchased the prominent Brussels daily newspaper, *L'Indépendance Belge*, in 1896.[58] The IIP's first publication, in fact, was La Fontaine's *Bibliographie de la Paix* in 1904.[59]

In 1905 the IIP began to sponsor the publication of an *Annuaire de la Vie Internationale*, compiled by another of La Fontaine's colleagues in the peace movement, the Austrian journalist Alfred Fried. Through the relatively simple listings in his *Annuaire*, Fried sought to suggest that an international civilization was appearing and that 'international relations are more advanced than is generally admitted'.[60] Fried had suggested to Moch that the Institute should also set up a 'Bureau for International Life' to encourage the development of the 'processes of internationalization which are appearing in all the domains of human activity'. Moch had taken the idea to the Prince of Monaco, who agreed to a small but insufficient subsidy to support it. Fried, Moch reported to Otlet, had then suggested that as 'the Congress of World Expansion was assembling in Mons, ... the King of the Belgians would certainly associate himself with the Prince in founding the Bureau'. Otlet informed Moch that he and La Fontaine had already begun to collect data for an international directory of associations, suggesting 'a practical arrangement, an agreement for collaboration ... , to make the *Annuaire* a publication of the Institute for Peace, the Institute of Bibliography and the Bureau of International Relations'.[61] Following negotiations with Fried, in which La Fontaine played a major role, the Austrian agreed to cooperate. The directories that Otlet and La Fontaine were planning were considered to form a second series of Fried's *Annuaires*. Fried was listed as a co-editor; the IIP agreed to transfer its support to the Belgian venture; and Fried was paid.[62]

While Van Overbergh and Otlet were working on their inventory of international organizations, they were also holding discussions with representatives of various Brussels-based international organizations to explore cooperation in the field of documentation – matters that Van Overbergh stressed were of a limited nature and intended to represent an eminently practical form of cooperation. La Fontaine seems not to have been involved in these meetings. In their communications, Van Overbergh and Otlet – as, respectively, president and secretary of a 'provisional committee' – noted that these initiatives were intended to follow up on the discussions held at Mons in 1905. The list of organizations initially to be approached was drawn from those headquartered in Brussels with which the OIB–IIB was already associated.[63] The preliminary idea was to create an office for international organizations on the model of the Cooperative Library of Learned Societies that was then in the process of being set up as part of International Office and Institute of Bibliography.[64]

In mid-1907, twenty of these associations formally agreed to the creation of a Central Office of International Institutions. The objectives proposed for it, however, had now both widened and been generalized from the earlier focus on documentation and bibliography.

> The programme of the office has been defined as: to establish a centre to facilitate the action and undertakings of institutions which have international objectives; to study questions of organization, coordination of effort, standardization of methods, in what is common to or similar for these diverse institutions; to create cooperation between the institutions, especially for information, documentation and the extension of relations; to contribute thus to the organization of a pacific internationalism.[65]

At its meeting in January 1908, the General Assembly of the new body took several important decisions about the Office's future work: to complete the survey of international organizations by encouraging all who had not done so to return the survey questionnaire that had been circulated; to publish the *Annuaire de la Vie Internationale*; and to organize a world congress of international associations in Brussels. It also agreed that there should be a close connection between the 'positive work of the international associations' and the 'pacific propaganda' of the peace societies associated with the International Peace Bureau (IPB). This last resolution reflected the important position that La Fontaine had ascended to the year before as president of the IPB and made explicit an international pacifist link between the two bodies. Up to this point, the negotiations concerning the Central Office had been left to Otlet with his Louvainiste and governmental associations, though the collaboration between him and La Fontaine remained as close as ever in the ongoing developmental work of the OIB–IIB. But now, the Central Office's turn to the world of international pacifism provided a basis for La Fontaine taking up his role as the third triumvir in its creation and management and for the international pacifist movement itself to become one of the Office's and subsequently the UIA's principal axes of action.[66]

From the Annuaire to the World Congress of International Associations

The Central Office immediately embarked upon a major initiative: to complete the collection, analysis and publication of the data from the survey of international associations that had been set up by Van Overbergh with Otlet and La Fontaine's help. The first volume of the monumental *Annuaire de la Vie Internationale* – published jointly by the Central Office, the IIB and the IIP – appeared in 1909.[67] Otlet and La Fontaine's analyses of the survey data gave powerful support to the idea that international associations and organizations now embraced every area of human activity and thought, were ever increasing in numbers and now played a constitutive, expanding role in international life.[68] Moreover, the survey provided a basis for identifying possible participants and themes for a Word Congress of International Associations in 1910, the organization of which the General Assembly of the Central Office had authorized in 1908.

Opening in the Palais des Academies in Brussels on 9 May 1910, the World Congress of International Association was described as an event of 'rare importance and ... exceptional interest'.[69] It was one of the many professional and scholarly meetings at the Brussels world's fair that year. But in a way, it was also their summation – amounting to the 'congress of congresses' that Otlet and Van Overbergh had speculated about in 1905. It created the Union of International Associations, lifting what had been confined to international associations located in Brussels to a fully international level. It formally endorsed the work of what was now called the Central Office of International *Associations* (rather than 'Institutions') as the headquarters organization for the Union.

It can be argued that the Central Office was little more than a re-badging and extension of the collections and services of the OIB–IIB, but with a major addition. A last component of the new structure arose out of an exhibition of documents and artefacts of various kinds illustrating the work of the international associations.[70] The congress recommended that it form the basis of an International Museum to be managed by the Central Office.[71]

Envoi: An Antinomy Resolved

The UIA's foundation has generally been considered to be the partial outcome of the continuous, rapid and quite extraordinary development of the OIB and IIB in the fifteen years that preceded it. The OIB and IIB had merged organizationally into a complex structure comprising bibliographical, iconographic, museological, archival, publishing and library-related functions, the housing of which, modestly supported by the government, had gradually spread across a number of disparate locations in central Brussels. Ever growing in numbers of participants, pre-war international conferences of the IIB were held in 1897, 1900, 1908 and 1910. Together, the Office and Institute of Bibliography had developed such an institutional heft and reach during this period that they could clearly function as the institutional centre or core for the expansion of activities represented by the International Office and UIA.[72]

In a linear conception of the UIA as emerging directly from the OIB, the connections to Catholic politics and institutions and to Belgian state expansionist initiatives, essentially through Cyrille Van Overbergh, tend to disappear. Played out in this narrative, however, is the resolution of complex personal differences of attitudes, beliefs and group memberships between the three founders that in a sense reflect broader polarities and divisions in Belgian society at that time.

On one side of a kind of antinomy was the freethinking, anticlerical, masonic, internationalist, pacifist, socialist and methodologically positivist approach to the social sciences of Henri La Fontaine. He and his colleagues in the international peace movement were animated by a liberal vision of a future peaceful world society developing its global influence by harnessing knowledge and creating new knowledge-based institutions. All of the organizations he was associated with – even the Belgian Alpine Club, of which he was a devoted member and office-holder – were dominated by a left-leaning political and social francophone elite.

On the other side of this antinomy was Cyrille Van Overbergh, devoutly Catholic, anti-socialist, anti-positivist, seeking a method in the social sciences in harmony with the ultimate objectives of the Catholic Church. For him and his colleagues, their belief in the ultramontane traditions of the church led to a commitment to a vision of the ever-widening influence of the church's institutions and values both within Belgium and abroad.

The resolution was provided in part by Paul Otlet, who did not espouse any particular political or religious allegiance – neither socialist nor Catholic. Like La Fontaine, he had been educated at the freethinking, liberally oriented Free University. Unlike La Fontaine, however, he did not join the movement to break away from that university to create the Université Nouvelle with its iconoclastic approach to the study and popularization of the social sciences, though he later lectured at it. Like La Fontaine, his commitment to 'facts' suggested a positivist approach to sociology, but he never abandoned a belief in the limits of knowledge, in the idea of something pervasive, profound and beyond – the Great Unknown – with all the religious overtones inherent in such a notion.[73] Like Van Overbergh, he had also studied at the Catholic University of Louvain, to which he retained a number of personal connections. Unlike La Fontaine, with his long career in the Belgian Senate, he had no aspirations to political office. Nor did he express any interest in the kind of high-level administrative career enjoyed by Van Overbergh, who also eventually entered the Senate.

La Fontaine and Otlet had become colleagues and friends in the early 1890s. Their collaboration and friendship lasted from their first meetings to the end of their lives in the mid-1940s. Van Overbergh was also a friend and colleague of Otlet's, even if the connection was not so intimate or to last so long as that with La Fontaine. Otlet acted as a kind of *trait d'union*, a hyphen, between La Fontaine and Van Overbergh and their distinctive world views and the memberships in which these views manifested themselves. He functioned as a kind of 'boundary object' or, to adapt the sociological theory put forward initially by Starr, Griesmer and Bowker, a 'boundary person' on whom could be projected different and sometimes conflicting interests and values but who could assimilate them in such a way as to allow the cooperation and mutual assistance of diverse individuals and groups.[74]

Moreover, the intellectual domain that Otlet represented, and to which La Fontaine had initially and independently been drawn, is a kind of meta-discipline unlikely to engender the methodological or theoretical conflicts that often shake traditional scientific disciplines or the partisanship characteristic of deeply felt political and social organizational memberships. This is bibliography or documentation, what we might now call 'knowledge organization', and the intellectual and technological problems it poses, and has always posed, of how most quickly and effectively to make information available to whoever needs it, regardless of the form in which it is recorded or represented.

Van Overbergh's interest and activities in the UIA largely ceased with the return of peace at the end of the First World War, during the course of which, however, he was largely responsible for keeping the Central Office alive and active. Otlet and La Fontaine, by contrast, were committed to a post-war vision of an emerging, peaceful, information-rich world polity in which the Office and UIA – and the myriad of organizations whose work would be coordinated and synergized by them – would play a major supportive role. They dedicated themselves to trying to realize this vision throughout the rest of their lives.

Notes

1   Robert Abs,'Fontaine (Henri-Marie La)', in *Biographie Nationale publiée par l'Académie Royale de Belgique*, tome 38, 1973), cols 214–22; Jacques Gillen, ed., *Henri La Fontaine, Prix Nobel de la Paix en 1913: un belge épris de justice* (Brussels: Éditions Racine, 2012); *Henri La Fontaine: un prix Nobel de paix: tracé(s) d'une vie* (Mons: Mundaneum, 2002).
2   On the Université Nouvelle, see, for example, Wim van Rooy, 'L'Agitation étudiante et la fondation de l'Université Nouvelle en 1894', *Revue Belge d'Histoire Contemporaine* 7, no. 1 (1976): 197–241; Edmond Picard, *Une Nouvelle Université à Bruxelles* (Brussels: Imprimerie Veuve Monnom, 1894); *L'Institut des Hautes Etudes à l'Université Nouvelle de Bruxelles* (Paris: Librairie de l'Art Social, 1897); Wouter Van Acker, 'Sociology in Brussels, Organicism and the Idea of a World Society in the Period before the First World War', in *Information Beyond Borders: International and Cultural Exchange in the Belle Époque*, ed. W. Boyd Rayward (Aldershot: Ashgate, 2014), 150–1.
3   Emmanuel Gerard, 'Cyrille Van Overbergh', in *Nationaal Biografisch Woorenboek*, vol .13 (Brussels: Koninklijke Vlaamse Academie, 1990), cols 607–19; Christian Wenin, 'Chronique Generale: Cyrille Van Overbergh', *Revue Philosophique de Louvain* 57, no. 54 (1951): 291.
4   Jan De Maeyer and Leen Van Molle, eds, *Joris Helleputte 1852–1925,* vol. 1 (Leuven: Leuven University Press, 1998), 258.
5   Jan de Maeyer, 'La Ligue démocratique et ses antécédents', in *Histoire du mouvement ouvrier chrétien en Belgique*, ed. Emmanuel Gérard and Paul Wynants, vol. 2 (Leuven: Leuven University Press, 1994), 38.
6   Louis De Raeymaeker, 'Les Origines de l'Institut supérieur de Philosophie de Louvain', *Revue Philosophique de Louvain* 49, no. 3 (1951): 505–633.
7   W. Boyd Rayward, *The Universe of Information: The Work of Paul Otlet for Documentation and International Organisation* (Moscow: VINITI, 1975); Françoise Levie, *L'Homme qui voulait classer le monde* (Brussels: Les Impressions Nouvelles, 2006); *Cent ans de l'Office International de Bibliographie, 1895–1995: les prémisses du Mundaneum* (Mons: Mundaneum, 1995).
8   Michel Dumoulin, 'Otlet (Edouard-Barthelemi-Lucien –Joseph)', in *Biographie nationale publiée par l'Académie Royale de Belgique*, vol. 41, cols 600–12. For Paul's assesement, see Levie, *L'Homme qui voulait classer le monde,*16.
9   His diaries of the period reveal his religious struggles. See Rayward, *The Universe of Information*, 19.

10 Van Acker, 'Sociology in Brussels', 144–7.
11 Edmond Picard, 'Préface', in *Bibliographie générale et raisonnée du droit belge: relevé de toutes les publications juridiques parues depuis 1814 réunies ...* (Brussels: F. Larcier, 1882), i, vi, viii and ix.
12 Paul Otlet, 'Un Peu de Bibliographie', in *Le Palais: Organe des Conférences du Jeune Barreau de Bruxelles* (Brussels: Alfred Vromont, 1891): 254–71 [translated as 'Something about Bibliography', in *International Organisation and Dissemination of Knowledge. Selected Essays of Paul Otlet*, ed. W. Boyd Rayward (Amsterdam: Elsevier, 1990), 11–24].
13 'Statuts de la Société de la Société d'études sociales & Politiques', *Revue Sociale et politique* 1 (1890): 15. See especially Auguste Couvreur, 'La Société d'Etudes Sociales et Politiques: son origine –son but', *Revue Sociale et politique* 1 (1890): 1–9. On La Fontaine and Otlet's involvement, see Kaat Wils and Anne Rasmussen, 'Sociology in a Transnational Perspective: Brussels, 1890–1925', *Revue Belge de Philologie et d'Histoire* 90, no. 4 (2012): 1278–9.
14 Dick May, 'L'Institut Solvay et le "comptabilisme"', *Revue Politique et Parlementaire* 8, no. 22 (1896): 385–97.
15 On the Institut des Sciences Sociales, see Jean-Francois Crombois, *L'Univers de la Sociologie en Belgique de 1900 à 1940* (Brussels: Editions de l'Université de Bruxelles, 1994); Wils and Rasmussen, 'Sociology in a Transnational Perspective', 1283–8; Van Acker, 'Sociology in Brussels', 147–50.
16 For their roles in the early meetings in 1894–95, see the procès-verbaux copies, available in Mundaneum: Box HLF 121 Institut des Sciences Sociales.
17 [Agreement headed] 'Institut des Sciences Sociales, Bruxelles 12 Avril 1894 entre 1. L'Institut des Sciences Sociales ... . 2. L'Office international de Bibliographie ...', Mundaneum Box HLF 121, Institut des Science Sociales 1894–1895.
18 'Institut des Sciences Sociales, Rapport présenté à M Ernest Solvay'; letter from Paul Otlet, 18 November 1894 to Messieurs, 'A la suite du désir exprimé par M Solvay ... priant d'en prendre connaissance avant la réunion de demain', Mundaneum Box HLF Box 121.
19 'Office International de Bibliographie, Société Coopérative Statuts', undated typed draft with MS corrections by La Fontaine; also separate brief manuscript notes by Otlet, especially 'Liste des obligataires' and 'Liste des sociétaires', Mundaneum Box HLF 121.
20 Edmond Picard, 'Préface', i, vi, viii, ix; Otlet, 'Something about Bibliography', 254–71.
21 'Institut des Sciences Sociales, Rapport présenté à M Ernest Solvay'.
22 Rayward, *The Universe of Information*, 85–111.
23 Paul Otlet and Henri La Fontaine, 'Création d'un Répertoire Bibliographique Universel: note préliminaire', *IIB Bulletin*, no. 1 (1895–96): 15–38. [Translated as 'Creation of a Universal Bibliographic Repertory: Preliminary Note' in *International Organisation and Dissemination of Knowledge*, 25–50]; see also Rayward, *The Universe of Information*, 37–57.
24 'Discours [de clôture] de M. le Chev. Ed. Decamps, 'Conférence Bibliographique International rapport général I', *IIB Bulletin*, no. 1 (1895): 4–9.
25 'Création à Bruxelles d'un Office International de Bibliographie: Rapport au Roi', *IIB Bulletin*, no. 2–3 (1895): 58–61.
26 J. M. Jadot and P. Coppens, 'Le Baron Edouard Descamps, écrivain antiesclavagiste et Ministre d'Etat de l'E.I.C. [sic]', *Bulletin de l'Institut Royal Colonial Belge* 25, no. 2

(1954): 497–541; Daniel Laqua, *The Age of Internationalism and Belgium, 1880–1930: Peace, Progress and Prestige* (Manchester: Manchester University Press, 2013), 60.

27 Sandi Cooper, *Patriotic Pacifism: Waging War on War in Europe, 1815–1914* (New York: Oxford University Press, 1991), 94–5.

28 Romain Yakemtchouk, 'Descamps (Edouard-Francois-Eugene), Baron', *Biographie Nationale publiée par l'Académie Royale de Belgique*, vol. 4, cols 198–247.

29 De Raeymaeker, 'Les Origines de l'Institut supérieur'.

30 'Bibliothèque collective des associations et institutions scientifiques et corporatives: Programme … règlement … local de la Bibliothèque collective', *IIB Bulletin*, no. 11 (1906): 20–6.

31 'Discours [de clôture] de M. le Chev. Ed. Descamps', 5.

32 'Discours de M. Paul Otlet: Bibliothèque collective des Sociétés Savantes, Bruxelles, décembre 16, 1907', *IIB Bulletin*, no. 12 (1907): 290.

33 Glycas, 'Nos Enquêtes: le Palais Mondial VI: les hommes'. M. Cyrille Van Overbergh, M. Henri La Fontaine, M. Paul Otlet, *L'Indépendance Belge*, 20 June 1924.

34 Roger Ernotte, 'Helleputte (Georges-Augustinus)', *Biographie Nationale publiée par l'Académie Royale de Belgique*, vol. 35, cols 373–9.

35 Maurice De Wulf, 'Introduction', *Revue Néo-Scolastique* 2 (1895): 3–6.

36 Rayward, *The Universe of Information*, 12.

37 Armand Thiéry to Paul Otlet, 28 November 1896, Mundaneum Box PPPO 0681.

38 They were corresponding with the intimacy of friends as early as 1889 (see Van Overbergh to Otlet, Louvain, 12 October 1889, Mundaneum Box PPPO 0677). Subsequently their personal correspondence was always couched in the friendliest terms.

39 De Raeymaeker, 'Les Origines de l'Institut supérieur', 561.

40 Versions of these lectures were published in the *Revue Néo-Scolastique*. See for example Cyrille Van Overbergh, 'Le Socialisme scientifique d'après le Manifeste communiste', *Revue Néo-Scolastique* 3(1896): 272–315. In his later years, Van Overbergh's lifelong studies of Marxism resulted in the publication of several major works.

41 The information in this paragraph is from Pierre de Bie, 'Les Débuts de la sociologie en Belgique III: les Sociétés belges de sociologie et le centre universitaire', *Recherches sociologiques* 17, no. 2 (1986): 193–230.

42 *Documents préliminaires et compte rendu des séances. Congrès International d'Expansion Economique Mondiale tenu à Mons du 24–28 septembre 1905 sous le haut patronage de sa Majesté le Roi Léopold II et du gouvernement Belge* (Brussels: J. Goemaer, Imp. du Roi, 1905), 183–6.

43 'Enquête ethnographique internationale', *Le Mouvement Sociologique* (Supplément à la *Revue Néo-Scolastique*) 6, no. 4 (1905): 173–212.

44 *Le Mouvement sociologique international; notice sur un nouveau type de revue documentaire publié par la Société belge de sociologie en conformite avec les desiderata de l'organisation systématique de la documentation universelle*, IIB Publication 83 (Brussels: Institut International de Bibliographie, 1907).

45 De Bie, 'Les Débuts de la sociologie en Belgique III', 216.

46 'Liste des délégués des gouvernements étrangers', 'Liste des délégués officiels du gouvernement belge', 'Liste des membres', *Documents préliminaires et compte rendu des séances*, xli–xlvi, xlvii–li, lii–cxlvii. See also Laqua, *The Age of Internationalism and Belgium*, 34–5.

47 Cyrille Van Overbergh, *La Réforme de l'Enseignement d'après le Premier Congrès International d'Expansion Mondiale, Mons, 1905*, vol. 1 (Brussels: Oscar Schepens, 1906), xxiv. For the wider context, see Madeleine Herren, 'Governmental Internationalism and the Beginning of a New World Order in the Aftermath of the First World War', in *The Mechanics of Internationalism: Culture, Society, and Politics from the 1840s to the First World War*, ed. Martin Geyer and Johannes Paulmann (Oxford: Oxford University Press, 2001), 129–33.

48 *Documents préliminaires et compte rendu des séances*, xxvi.

49 Paul Otlet, 'L'Organisation rationnelle de l'information et de documentation en matière économique: examen des moyens d'assurer aux services de renseignements des musées coloniaux et commerciaux, ainsi qu'aux offices de renseignements industriels et commerciaux indépendants, une plus complète utilité au point de vue de l'expansion mondiale', *Congrès International d'Expansion Economique Mondiale tenu à Mons les 24–28 septembre, 1905, Rapports: Section V, Expansion Civilisatrice vers les Pays Neufs* (Brussels: Hayez, 1905).

50 *Documents préliminaires et compte rendu des séances*, 204.

51 The quotations in this paragraph are from Otlet's letter to Overbergh, 10 September 1905, Mundaneum Box PPPO 242 1, 'Fondation de l'UIA'.

52 *Annuaire des sociétés scientifiques, artistiques et littéraires de Belgique. 1904–1905*, IIB Publication no. 66 (Brussels: IIB, 1905).

53 *Institutions Internationales ayant leur siège en Belgique*, IIB publication 87 (Brussels: IIB, 1907).

54 This survey was to continue and to result in multiple volumes of ethnographic studies.

55 Cyrille Van Overbergh, 'L'Association Internationale: enquête sur les structures sociales', *Le Mouvement Sociologue International*, enquête no 3 (Brussels: IIB, 1907), 3–4.

56 De Bie, 'Les Débuts de la sociologie en Belgique', 220.

57 Nadine Lubelski-Bernard, 'Les Mouvements et les idéologies pacifistes en Belgique: 1830–1914' (PhD diss., Université libre de Bruxelles, Brussels, 1977), 95–6.

58 Lubelski-Bernard, 'Les Mouvements et les idéologies pacifistes en Belgique: 1830–1914', 101–3.

59 Henri La Fontaine, *Bibliographie de la Paix et de l'Arbitrage international* (Monaco: Institut International de la Paix, 1904).

60 Alfred Fried, ed., *Annuaire de la Vie Internationale* (Monaco: Institut International de la Paix, 1905), vii. Fried's *Annuaires* were issued in 1905, 1906 and 1907.

61 Gaston Moch to Paul Otlet 30 November 1905; Otlet to Moch 13 December 1905. Mundaneum Box PPPO 242 PO 1 Fondation de l'UIA.

62 Daniel Laqua, 'Alfred H. Fried and the Challenges for "Scientific Pacifism" in the Belle Époque', in *Information Beyond Borders*, ed. Rayward, 186. See also 'Institut international de la paix, Monaco'. Available online: https://uia.org/s/or/en/1100020742 (accessed 31 July 2018).

63 'Note Confidentielle: Les Congrès internationaux suivants sont en rapport avec l'Institut International de Bibliographie pour la Bibliographie', in folder 'Procès-verbaux (origines) de l'Office Central des Institutions Intles (sic)', Mundaneum Box PPPO 241 1, 'Fondation de l'UIA'.

64 [Paul Otlet], *Rapport lu à la Réunion des Représentants des Institutions Internationales le 4 juin 1907*, Institutions internationales ayant leur siège en Belgique; IIB Publication 87 (Brussels: IIB, 1907).

65 'Office Central des Institutions Internationales', *Office Central des Institutions Internationales Bulletin* no. 1 (March 1908): 5.

66 'Office Central des Institutions Internationales', 7–9.

67 *Annuaire de la Vie Internationale, 1908–1909* (Brussels: Office Central des Institutions Internationales, 1909); *Annuaire de la Vie Internationale, 1910–1911* (Brussels: Office International des Associations Internationales, 1912).

68 Paul Otlet, 'L'Organisation Internationale et les Associations Internationales', *Annuaire de la Vie Internationale, 1908–1909*, 29–166.

69 'Le Congrès des Associations Internationales', *L'Indépendance Belge*, 10 May 1910.

70 'Exposition-Musée des Associations Internationales à Bruxelles: Préface … Catalogue', *Congrès Mondial des Associations Internationales, première session, 1910. Actes: Documents préliminaires, Rapports, Procès-verbaux, Code*, Office Centrale des Associations Internationales Publication 2a (Bruxelles: Office Centrale des Associations, 1913), 244.

71 Paul Otlet, 'L'Organisation international et les musées', in *Actes: Documents préliminaires, Rapports, Procès-verbaux, Code, Congrès Mondial des Associations Internationales, première session, 1910*, vol. 2, procès des verbaux des séances (Brussels: Office Centrale des Associations Internationales, 1912), 1207–11.

72 Louis Masure, *Rapport sur la situation et les travaux pour l'année 1912* (Brussels: IIB, 1912), 123; *Union of International Association: A World Centre* (Brussels: UIA, 1914).

73 See the sections 'L'Inconnu, le mystère, le secret' and 'L'Equation du monde' in Paul Otlet, *Monde: Essai d'Universalisme* (Brussels: D. Van Keerberghen et Fils, 1935), 393–401.

74 Susan Leigh Star and James Griesmer, 'Institutional Ecology, "Translations" and Boundary Objects: Amateurs and Professionals in Berkeley's Museum of Vertebrate Zoology', *Social Studies of Science*, 19 no. 3 (1989): 387–420; Geoffrey Bowker and Susan Leigh Star, *Sorting Things Out: Classification and its Consequences* (Cambridge, MA: MIT Press, 1999).

Chapter 2

THE UIA AND THE PATRONAGE OF INTERNATIONALISM: FROM THE *BELLE ÉPOQUE* TO THE SECOND WORLD WAR

Christophe Verbruggen

'Follow the money' is not only a phrase in popular culture: it can also be an approach to studying the organizational dynamics of non-profit organizations and their quest for financial resources. This chapter scrutinizes the patronage of internationalism and processes of negotiation between the UIA and its patrons. The idea of 'patronage' has the advantage over concepts such as philanthropy, charity or *mécénat* in that its potential definition is much broader. It denotes all resources that constitute the object of exchange between patrons and their clients, but it can also describe the process of exchange itself. It is both the act of giving and the personally or politically motivated intention to support someone else's work.[1]

There are several broad categories of patronage, each with its own subcategories: individual and collective patronage; governmental support; and, to a certain extent, the market. Intergovernmental organizations such as the League of Nations constitute another potential source of patronage. In the world of non-governmental organizations, membership or subscription to support the operation of an organization cannot always be distinguished from a genuine purchase of a good or service. As commercial aspects are tackled in Pierre-Yves Saunier's chapter, the focus here will be on the other categories.

While the chapter is concerned with patronage in its different guises, the discussion adds to our understanding of philanthropy, which has multiple meanings in itself. What most definitions of philanthropy have in common is that they view it as a third sector between the state and the market and as a process that cannot be separated from changing power exertion and mechanisms of social distinction. As Thomas Adam has put it, philanthropic culture involves 'the decision to give for a chosen cause in a specific way to engineer society according to the philanthropist's wishes'.[2]

Philanthropy played an important role in the history of pacifism and internationalism. Early on, businessmen directly or indirectly supported pacifist endeavours. Even more important was self-funding by which wealthy activists used their inherited family capital to stage events or publish periodicals.[3] In the early twentieth century, the scale and the coordination of philanthropic efforts became amplified. Moreover, the twentieth century was an era in which American philanthropy was intertwined with American cultural diplomacy.[4] Founded in 1910, the Carnegie Endowment for International Peace played a pioneering role in terms of its international scope. As the Endowment was the first important body to subsidize the UIA, the relationship between these two organizations highlights the growing American influence on European internationalism. To this day, Andrew Carnegie and his 'gospel of wealth' serve as an important example for wealthy capitalists who see it as their duty to apply their successful way of conducting business to solve global social problems.[5]

The relative importance of philanthropy can only be measured by assessing it alongside other forms of support. This is where the concept of patronage enters the picture. The distinction between patronage and philanthropy is often made by reserving the former to the individual support given to an artist or a person in need of help.[6] Even more than philanthropy (which is also a process) patronage implies a continuous dialectical and often asymmetrical interaction. Bearing these points in mind, the chapter considers the different kinds of material backing, encouragement and financial aid that the UIA received from other actors, as well as the motives and frameworks for this support.

Seeking and Finding Carnegie Funding

Katarina Rietzler has shown convincingly how the Carnegie Endowment for International Peace successfully 'plugged' into the various currents of the European peace movement.[7] Its intervention was a game-changer. News about the Endowment's creation spread like wildfire among European pacifists, who stumbled over one another in their quest for support.[8] In early 1911, Henri La Fontaine approached the Carnegie Endowment to gain funding for both the International Peace Bureau (IPB) – the body that federated national peace societies – and for the UIA.

By this stage, La Fontaine was a prominent figure within the international peace movement, having become IPB president in 1907.[9] As shown by Boyd Rayward's contribution to this volume, La Fontaine was active in a range of fields, including sociological associations, the *Université Nouvelle* and the Belgian Workers' Party. His involvement in international pacifism thus formed part of a broader reformist endeavour and extended to the Union of International Associations.[10] In 1911, La Fontaine prepared a memorandum to attract subsidies for the UIA, casting the Union as, above all, a pacifist organization. The document proposed that the UIA's Central Office be provided with a budget that it would distribute – on behalf of the Carnegie Endowment – among 'national groups of internationalism'.[11]

These suggestions bore the potential for misunderstandings, as a similar request was made by – and approved for – the IPB. The confusion only increased because at the time, rumours circulated that the Peace Bureau would move from Berne to Brussels. La Fontaine admitted that such a move would not be a good idea because without support from national governments, organizations such as the IPB and UIA could not survive.[12] The Swiss government was the first to subsidize the Peace Bureau, followed by a few Scandinavian countries. The Bureau would almost certainly have lost this support in case of its relocation. Another reason to remain in Berne was the fact that, at the time, there was no general law in Belgium providing international organizations with a civil legal personality.[13] Yet it is clear that the discussion about the role and potential move of the IPB troubled the relations between La Fontaine and Nicholas Murray Butler, president of the Carnegie Endowment for International Peace.[14] For the American benefactors, the experience of distributing money through the IPB in Europe was not worth repeating. Soon, plans were made for the establishment of a European section of the Carnegie Endowment, to be placed under the auspices of the foundation's trustees.

Notwithstanding the difficulties that existed from the start, from 1912 onwards the UIA received an annual subsidy of $ 15,000 from the Carnegie Endowment. The trustees' formal decision almost literally echoed the UIA's mission statement: they wished to support the Union in fostering a spirit of internationalism, to aid individual associations and improve their efficiency, to establish relations with branches in each country and, last but not least, 'to develop international documentation and to give such documents a permanent and systematic character'.[15] However, the UIA had expected more, and before the decision was approved, its leaders approached the Endowment again with detailed budgets and publication plans. They claimed that their future was in the hands of American benefactors. Belgian and other European millionaires, they argued, were only interested in private art collections, personal luxury and, 'if they were generous', works of charity. For La Fontaine it was clear: 'It is only in the US that the idea like that which is the base of our work can be comprehended. The American people is cosmopolitan; its mission is to pacify the world, I would willingly say, to civilize it.'[16] And who better than the UIA to realize this 'civilizing effort'?

The attempt to generate goodwill and obtain a larger budget ultimately failed. According to Butler, it was inconceivable and, indeed, undesirable that the Carnegie Endowment would remain the UIA's sole patron. He and the other trustees would do everything possible to convince the many 'generous minded men around the world' about the importance of the Union's work – but the organization would really have to find other financiers.[17] Seen from this perspective, Carnegie funds were conceived as seed capital for increasing support among both private individuals and European national governments. La Fontaine took the gauntlet, expressing the hope that many would follow the good example given by Carnegie: 'perhaps even Governments themselves will comprehend that is in their interest to aid in drawing man together'.[18]

The UIA's report identified three groups that could be addressed. First, it might be possible to develop the commercial potential of UIA publications. Yet, as La Fontaine pointed out, the documentary nature of these publications made it difficult to convince a Belgian financier or publisher to invest in these publishing projects. A second solution was that other international organizations would pay for the UIA's services and expertise – but unfortunately most organizations hardly had enough resources for their own operations. Only the then Brussels-based Interparliamentary Union, which also promoted international arbitration, was persuaded to do so.[19] Governments were the third and final group that could be addressed. However, the results of the UIA were not yet of such a nature as to convince national governments to provide state support as they did for other international organizations, including the IPB. Moreover, in partial contradiction to earlier comments, La Fontaine's report insisted on the UIA's independence. His conclusion was clear: the Union *had* to rely on philanthropists.[20]

Almost simultaneously, La Fontaine wrote a personal and emotional letter to Butler about the choice between 'life and death'. The situation had become intolerable for the UIA founders, who no longer had a social life as they did everything by themselves.[21] La Fontaine agreed with IPB vice-president Bertha von Suttner, who supposedly said that even in the United States, there was only one benefactor who really cared about their endeavours: Andrew Carnegie. La Fontaine suggested that, as a captain of industry, Carnegie should know better than anybody else that no venture could succeed without adequate resources.[22] He continued to alternate between sending formal and personal letters to Butler, but without making much impression. On the contrary, in April 1913, the UIA was granted the same amount of money but with a clear warning: the trustees thoroughly appreciated its work, but felt uncomfortable about being the sole benefactor. They had to be able to withdraw at any time. What they did not communicate was the general decision to phase out subsidies for the different European pacifist organizations that depended on them.[23]

The Limits of Private Belgian and American Patronage

The trustees were rightly suspicious about La Fontaine's claims. The Belgian peace leader was wrong in suggesting that there were no European philanthropists with an interest in science and intellectual cooperation. Indeed, La Fontaine did not have to look very far. One of the most active European patrons of scientific internationalism, physiology, sociology and research-based business administration moved within the same Brussels-based cultural circles that La Fontaine frequented: the chemist and entrepreneur Ernest Solvay. During his lifetime, Solvay spent millions on philanthropic work.[24] Other well-known contemporaries of Solvay and acquaintances of La Fontaine and Otlet who became patrons of science and internationalism included Solvay's brother Alfred and the industrialist Raoul Warocqué who, like La Fontaine, was a freethinker and freemason.

There were differences between these potential Belgian patrons and the way in which Carnegie operated. In line with his enlightened paternalistic vision of labour relations, Solvay was personally involved in all the institutions he funded, aiming to organize the world in a more just and, above all, rational way.[25] The transnational scope of Belgian sociology was facilitated by his sponsorship.[26] Most of his initiatives were located in each other's vicinity in the Cité Scientique, situated in the Parc Léopold in Brussels. It is remarkable that Solvay never provided any significant direct funding to the UIA. After all, Otlet and La Fontaine had been actively involved in the sociological ventures funded by Solvay, and their organicist interpretations of internationalism resembled one another.[27] Moreover, Solvay's name appears on lists with expressions of sympathy for UIA-related projects, and in 1907 he became the president of Otlet and La Fontaine's International Institute of Bibliography (IIB). He also expressed an interest in helping to fund a World Palace for International Associations on the Mont des Arts.[28] But such promises did not translate into concrete funding. Solvay had his own priorities, which did not match those of the Union.

Still, we might argue that Solvay was one of the UIA's patrons, as he provided moral and intellectual encouragement. Indeed, the Union was also not only interested in financial support, but also in moral and diplomatic patronage. For instance, UIA leaders expected the Carnegie Endowment to play a mediating role in its attempt to gain a foothold in the United States.[29] When Andrew Carnegie visited the UIA's Brussels headquarters in 1913, it attracted the attention of ambassadors and ministers, highlighting the diplomatic resonance of philanthropic endeavours.

The outbreak of the First World War changed the overall framework for such cooperation. From December 1914, all payments from the Endowment were suspended. The UIA's documentary activities to some extent continued, as the Belgians managed to keep matters financially afloat with loans from Van Overbergh and Otlet, who remained in Brussels for parts of the war years.[30] Meanwhile, La Fontaine headed to the United States, travelling the country to give lectures on pacifism, the war situation in Belgium and much more. Thanks to La Fontaine, some American money reached occupied Brussels, but a more important observation is that First World War did not change the trustees' attitude towards the European funding requests.

In 1920, a delegation from the Carnegie Endowment visited the UIA and the remaining amount of the subsidy amount for the tax year 1915 was paid, albeit without a commitment to future support. From January 1921 onwards, correspondence became more intensive and directed to both the Carnegie Endowment's European Center and the trustees.[31] After years of lobbying in which increasing disillusionment and bitterness became apparent – for instance when Butler passed through Brussels without paying the UIA a visit – the final negative verdict came in 1922. The fact that La Fontaine was a member of the consultative board of the European Centre did little to change this. All funds would only be used to support philanthropic work that was directly managed by the Carnegie Endowment.[32] In the following decades, several new attempts were made to convince the Carnegie Endowment and the Rockefeller Foundation, but the answer remained the same.[33]

The UIA and Belgian Politico-Intellectual Diplomacy

As both Madeleine Herren and Daniel Laqua have shown, the Belgian state supported the involvement in international congresses and associations as an alternative to traditional forms of foreign policy.[34] Until his death in 1909, King

Leopold II financially and morally backed various Belgian-based international organizations, in particular those in line with his expansionist ideology.[35] In 1910, this 'Leopoldist' doctrine was also the starting point for a confidential working document in which the Union outlined its expectations from the Belgian government: moral, diplomatic and financial support coordinated by the Ministry of Foreign Affairs (instead of the Ministry of Arts and Sciences).[36]

At first sight, the Union did not gain much official funding before the war.[37] Yet there was indirect support since another one of La Fontaine and Otlet's ventures – namely the IIB – received 50,000 francs each year. Moreover, the Union's conferences of 1910 and 1913 were organized with the 'patronage' of the Belgian government. In addition, the government approved Otlet's proposal to use a section of its Palais du Cinquantenaire in Brussels. The UIA would not have to pay rent and only be responsible for maintenance and heating costs.

In the immediate aftermath of the First World War, discussions about official support for the UIA were partly shaped by the wartime aid that Belgium had received thanks to American efforts. In 1914, Herbert Hoover had launched the Committee for Relief in Belgium, an unprecedented global philanthropic enterprise.[38] Its local partner – responsible for food distribution in occupied Belgium – was the Comité National de Secours et d'Alimentation, which was headed by Solvay and Emile Francqui, a fellow businessman and patron of science. After the war, it became clear that a substantial part of the hundreds of millions of dollars donated by governments, associations and private individuals had not been spent. The plan was to invest these funds in the universities and scientific institutions as a means of rebuilding the country. Belgian universities received 20 million francs in total (3.8 million US dollars). A similar sum was divided between the Mining School, the Colonial School, the newly established University Foundation and a national research fund. Hoover also promoted the creation of an exchange programme between American and Belgian scholars.[39]

Otlet and La Fontaine campaigned to gain a share of the funds. In early 1920, Edward Anseele – the socialist Minister for Public Works – informed Otlet that he would propose using some of the available capital to construct a new Palais Mondial at the Parc of Woluwe on the outskirts of Brussels. This 'world palace' was to host the UIA headquarters and related institutions headed by La Fontaine and Otlet.[40] Solvay also supported the idea of granting the UIA some of those funds. However, the plan was opposed by Catholic prime minister Léon Delacroix – who had been involved in the relief fund during the War – and probably also by Émile Francqui.[41] Instead, extra money went into Belgo-American scholarly exchange programmes.[42]

Nonetheless, the UIA remained suited to the government's post-war ambitions, as the country's official policy continued to focus on attracting international organizations to Belgium. A few years later, however, the initial enthusiasm had evaporated. The turbulent relationship with the Belgian government and its patronage of the UIA in the interwar years therefore merits further discussion. Its development can only be understood in connection with wider changes in Belgian foreign policy, in particular the attitude towards the League of Nations. Party-political differences were an additional factor.

During the war, the UIA's work had seemed to gain greater appreciation within official circles. Via La Fontaine, the Union was asked to continue its documentation efforts and its campaign for the establishment of a post-war League of Nations.[43] Moreover, in 1919, the Belgian parliament approved several measures in support of the UIA, partly with a view to strengthening the candidacy of Brussels as host city for the League of Nations. In anticipation of a new Palais Mondial, extra space was made available in the Palais du Cinquantenaire and an additional annual subsidy was approved alongside a one-off investment of 100,000 francs for the UIA's *Quinzaine Internationale* ('international fortnight') of 1920. Last but not least, parliament passed a law to give international organizations such as the UIA legal personality.[44] The aim of the *Quinzaine* was to bring an international 'elite' of experts to the Palais Mondial, which hosted all UIA-related activities.

Financial support from the Belgian government alone was not enough to help the UIA realize its wide-ranging ambitions. An internal note from in 1920 reveals the Union's strategy: other governments (beyond Belgium's one), philanthropists and in particular the League of Nations would be asked to provide financial and moral support for the Union as a whole and for particular initiatives.[45] Individual states were free to 'protect' the Union, while the League was supposed to become 'le très haut protecteur'.[46] The UIA's leaders expected that their technical expertise would be recognized and that they could continue their publications under the League's auspices and with its financial support. They also anticipated League funding and patronage for their International University, which is being discussed in Daniel Laqua's contribution to this volume.[47]

The Belgian delegates at the League, including La Fontaine himself, did everything to promote the UIA's interests. A first result came in 1920 when a subsidy of 1,500 pounds – the equivalent of a year's budget – was granted for the publication of the *Code des Voeux Internationaux*, which ultimately appeared in 1923, compiling resolutions from various international organizations.[48] The League's formal decision to grant the UIA this sum explicitly stated that it was not a subsidy for the International University: it was a one-off contribution and by no means 'a precedent to be cited by other international institutions'.[49] To the League Assembly, the arrangement was presented as a quick win: in default of the technical work done by the UIA, it would have been the League's responsibility to publish such information.

A few months later, League secretary-general Eric Drummond repeated how important the UIA's efforts in the spreading of documentation and information had been. His words were and continue to be used by the Union to emphasize the League's moral patronage: according to Drummond, the UIA's efforts were a 'vast enterprise of international intellectual organization, characterized by the breadth of its conception and design'.[50] But at the same time, the League's International Bureaux Section – headed by the Japanese diplomat and intellectual Inazō Nitobe – slowly but surely took over many of the UIA's documentary activities, in particular by launching its *Répertoire des Organisations Internationales/Handbook of International Organisations*.[51]

After the decision to locate the League's headquarters in Switzerland, the Belgian diplomatic efforts shifted to what would later become the International

Committee on Intellectual Cooperation (ICIC).[52] At the instigation of La Fontaine and Otlet, the Belgian delegation at the Paris Peace Conference had pushed for the stimulation of intellectual cooperation as an important task for the future League of Nations. The line of reasoning behind the Belgian proposition to the League of Nations Assembly in 1920 was that manual work and intellectual work deserved equal attention.[53] In August 1921, the UIA convened a conference on intellectual work in Brussels. The event not only resulted in the draft statutes of the International Confederation of Intellectual Workers: it was also another step towards the growing attention for cultural affairs within the League of Nations.[54] Based on a proposal by French statesman Léon Bourgeois, the Council of the League finally decided in 1922 to establish the ICIC. The keyword of Bourgeois's proposition was 'exchange', in particular the exchange of knowledge.[55] It is therefore not surprising that the UIA and the IIB viewed themselves as the 'foundation stones' of this exchange.[56]

Initially chaired by the philosopher Henri Bergson, the ICIC comprised eminent scientists and intellectuals who were appointed on the basis of their reputation. To their own surprise, neither Otlet nor La Fontaine was selected as members of the committee. Yet they could live with the selection of their friend and socialist politician Jules Destrée.[57] Later on, they therefore experienced it as a real betrayal when Destrée withdrew his support for the Palais Mondial and the UIA.[58] It seemed as if Destrée regarded himself as a representative of the international 'intellectuality' and not an advocate of Belgian matters, including the UIA's work.[59] In other instances, however, he was not afraid to defend Belgian interests. Destrée was not the only ally who abandoned them. Press coverage was increasingly sceptical about an enterprise that what cast as utopian and expensive.

Patronage and the Palais Mondial

In early 1924, increasing tensions culminated in an open conflict with the Belgian government. Otlet framed this conflict as 'L'Affaire du Palais Mondial'. The immediate cause for the controversy was the expulsion from parts of its premises in the Palais du Cinquantenaire to make space for a commercial exhibition of (mainly British) rubber manufacturers. The conflict, however, went much further, and there was a direct link between the international political arena and a rapidly deteriorating relationship with the Belgian government.

The first stage of the 'Affaire du Palais Mondial' coincided with the League's declining interest in the UIA, which ultimately manifested itself in the establishment of an intellectual coordination centre in Paris, the International Institute of Intellectual Cooperation. In July 1924 the French government offered to set up such a body in Paris, proposing to endow it with a budget of an annual amount of 2 million French francs. When this generous offer was accepted, Albert Einstein and other eminent ICIC members expressed their concern that the international committee had begun to promote a French agenda.[60] As Daniel Laqua has argued, efforts for intellectual cooperation 'were hampered by the power-politics of governments',[61] and such power-political aspects also manifested themselves in the Belgian attitudes to the UIA in this period. According to Otlet, the negative sentiment towards the Palais Mondial grew after Belgium's involvement in the Ruhr occupation of 1923, which the Union Belge pour la Société des Nations (associated with La Fontaine and Otlet) had criticized.[62] Moreover, given the strength of Franco-Belgian ties in this period, the Belgian government showed little inclination to compete with the French proposal to host an International Institute of Intellectual Cooperation. Accordingly, when Otlet proposed to bring together all the Brussels scientific institutions including the university, the UIA and the American-funded new institutions into a 'Centre-Cité International', official reactions were lukewarm, to say the least.

Only in May 1926 did the Minister of Science and Arts present some encouraging news. As long as no alternative solution was found, all organizations, documentation and collections were allowed to stay where they were. It was no coincidence that this letter came from the then minister Camille Huysmans, a socialist and internationalist intellectual who had been secretary of the Second International. Apart from having a background in internationalism, Huysmans also frequented the same Brussels-based cultural and masonic circles as La Fontaine. For the UIA and its International Museum, this fresh commitment was the start of a creative period with innovative visualizations and a renewal of its exhibitions. Nonetheless, the consecutive coalition governments showed little interest in doing more than maintain the status quo.

In 1934, the relations between the UIA and the Belgian government reached a new boiling point.[63] This time, the conflict was more serious, and the UIA was requested to vacate the Palais du Cinquantenaire and thus abandon its Palais Mondial. The organization was given only a few months to complete this operation. The reactions were – understandably – furious. The conflict was again framed as the 'Affaire du Palais Mondial'. Now that the UIA's leaders had apparently lost the support of the Belgian government altogether, it was time to test alternative action repertoires. Next to petitions, press releases, personal letters, awareness lecture series, they also organized a highly mediatized sit-down strike or 'open-air office' the day after the news became public, as depicted in Figure 2.1.[64]

Otlet and La Fontaine also attempted to revive alternative kinds of patronage. During the first episode of the 'Affair' in 1924, they had set up a group called 'Les Amis du Palais Mondial'. Members did voluntary (documentary) work and were the first to be mobilized when needed, for instance for the 'open-air office' performance.[65] After the closure in 1934, they adopted the tried and tested idea of channelling individual philanthropy into an endowment, named the 'Comité Belge de Patronage et d'Entraide du Palais Mondial – Dotatio Mundaneum'.[66] A leaflet was printed and distributed, but the press did not pick it up. The *Dotatio* quickly faded away. La Fontaine's carefully maintained press file shows how the mood was reversed compared to the palmy days right after the war. Not so much the UIA – of which most newspapers did see the point – but certainly the Palais Mondial and the universal aspirations of the International Museum hit a wall of incomprehension.[67] It is also striking that when using quotations from

Figure 2.1 Sit-down strike by Paul Otlet and his collaborators after the expulsion from the Palais Mondial in 1934. *Source:* Mundaneum, Mons.

'personalities' in their propaganda, La Fontaine and Otlet increasingly had to return to statements from the past. Although the collections and documents were no longer accessible, the work of the IIB and the UIA continued in Otlet's private home.

In the end, only one option remained: to file a lawsuit against the Minister of Public Works, who was responsible for allocating public buildings. The official in question was the socialist politician Hendrik De Man, another old acquaintance of La Fontaine. The intention was to put the Belgian government under pressure – but the response was rather laconic. The decision was in the hands of the judge and the fact that a court case might drag on for years was not a matter of concern.[68] Moreover, the Royal Museum of Art and History – which was to receive the space vacated by the Palais Mondial – was not interested in a compromise. The eminent Egyptologist Jean Capart, with whom Otlet had cooperated well in the past, acted as the Royal Museum's representative yet also cast himself as a representative of the state. He emphasized that, in contrast to the UIA and its International Museum, his own museum was not a private entity.[69] The space should be used for the archaeological (Egyptological) collection and nothing else – certainly not for a private museum and documentation centre.

In his statement, Capart mocked Otlet's universal aspirations. In this respect, the transcript of a telephone conversation between Otlet and Hendrik De Man's head of cabinet, Robert Lemoine, is enlightening. The conversation revealed great scepticism about a project that was perceived as unrealistic and even esoteric. There could, for instance, be no question of state support for an exhibition where outdated and unscientific propaganda for theosophy could be seen.[70] The court case was heard in October 1936, but it was never concluded or officially settled. In 1939 – after years of years of immobilism – an informal settlement was reached. The UIA and the IIB were given an unused wing of the Palais du Cinquantenaire.[71] The intellectual and symbolic capital of the UIA seemed to have been revalued again.

The Totalitarian Quest for Documentation

Until the publication of an article by Madeleine Herren, there was much uncertainty about the history of the UIA during the Second World War.[72] A number of errors – for example claims that the archives of the UIA were destroyed by the Germans – are still being repeated in some of the literature.[73] In fact, the records were integrated into the files of the German Central Office for Congresses (Deutsche Kongress-Zentrale, DKZ), which after the war were transferred to the Hoover Institution at Stanford University. The DKZ was founded in 1934 and became part of the Reich Ministry of Public Enlightenment and Propaganda. It regulated every international event that took place in Germany as well as the participation of German citizens in congresses and conferences abroad.

Already before 1939, the DKZ had cooperated with the UIA. After the start of the war, DKZ director Karl F. Schweig quickly saw the opportunity to transform his national body into an international institution. One way of doing so was to use the UIA's expertise and documentation.[74] Shortly after the German invasion, the Germans occupied the Palais du Cinquantenaire for 'military reasons'. The collections of the UIA and its affiliated organizations were moved to the Institute of Anatomy in the Parc Léopold where, at least initially, the Union was allowed to continue its activities.

Now over seventy-two years old, Otlet saw his life's work threatened more than ever. By that point, La Fontaine was no longer active and Otlet was alone in his quest for patronage. Shortly before the outbreak of the war, he had tried to convince the US president Franklin D. Roosevelt to accept a transfer of his entire collections to America. There was no answer and from December 1940, Otlet started negotiations with the Third Reich. He attempted to convince the Germans to invest in a new Palais Mondial and even ordered some sketches in a style that integrated fascist architectural features.[75] However, in almost all his correspondence with the occupiers, he continued to emphasize the possibility of applying the principle of extraterritoriality for the (future) Palais Mondial, meaning that the latter would be exempt from German law and jurisdiction. He even tried to convince King Leopold III of Belgium, who remained in Brussels during the war, of this idea.[76]

Otlet repeatedly stressed the UIA's private character, implying a reliance on private donations and contributions. A contribution from the DKZ did not exclude further financial support from the German-controlled Belgian government, but Otlet was more interested in subsidies coming from private organisms.[77] The Palais Mondial held no appeal for the German authorities, but the UIA's material on international organizations did. DKZ director Schweig intended to retain the research centre in Brussels, albeit under German (military) control, with German funding and in close cooperation with German intelligence agencies.[78] According to a Brussels-based SS Untersturmführer, Otlet could not be trusted, notwithstanding his recent cooperative attitude. According to the SS, Otlet was known for his socialist sympathies and anti-German sentiments as well as being a freemason (which he was not).[79] A new, seemingly more trustworthy administrator was appointed and Otlet was slowly but surely pushed aside. It is striking, however, that Otlet's legal argumentation about the UIA's status, including diplomatic privileges and extraterritoriality, was adopted by the internationalized DKZ in Berlin.

For a few months, the UIA continued its documentary work in Brussels – yet it proved impossible to escape National Socialism's centralizing agenda. Eventually, the rest of the documentation that the Germans considered important was transported to Berlin. With the war developments heightening German mistrust towards all matters international, the DKZ's internationalization soon ended. In 1943, all the files came into the hand of the intelligence agencies.[80] As Madeleine Herren has argued, the German authorities opposed the idea that the DKZ 'should be built up from a mere documentation agency into an independent organization'.[81] Ultimately, this vision and conception on documentation was similar to the UIA's vision and organizational structure. Initially, the National Socialist authorities thought it would be sufficient to control and instrumentalize these (information) networks, but as the war progressed the DKZ was marginalized as well.

At first sight, it seems that, in the autumn of his life, a disillusioned and desperate Otlet went quite far in his attempt to work with the Germans. But it is also possible to contextualize his actions in terms of a decades-long quest for patronage. From 1922 onwards, the UIA experienced a period of decline as the Belgian government, the League of Nations and philanthropists all retreated from backing Otlet's ventures. Otlet sought support from multiple sources but also reiterated his earlier beliefs. For instance, in his correspondence with the German occupier, he stressed more than ever the non-governmental, private character of the UIA and his other endeavours.

Epilogue: A Lifetime of Patronage

Of all forms of patronage for non-profit organizations, only one remained a constant factor throughout and beyond the lifetime of Otlet and La Fontaine: the patronage provided by the UIA founders themselves. Their total inherited wealth was not of such a nature to give the Union financial independence, let alone that an endowment could be created with which the UIA could realize its wide-ranging objectives. However, during their lives, both protagonists spent their family money (included their wives' inheritance). La Fontaine also used the money he had gained when receiving the Nobel Peace Prize in 1913. Both UIA leaders were regularly responsible for arranging transitional financing and loans – but even more important was the time that they spent on their projects. For several decades they did not pay themselves a wage and, as a senator, La Fontaine also provided symbolic capital.

Their final will and testament are enlightening. Paul Otlet changed his testament dozens of times.[82] In one of his first 'testaments spirituels' in 1917 he already made clear that it was impossible to divide his personal papers, library and documentation. Like all his endeavours, they were indivisible. He suggested in several changes that it was his will to establish a proper endowment. The central aim of the projected 'Otlet-Van Nederhasselt' Endowment was to continue his work through the UIA.[83] In 1938 (in line with the telegram he sent to Roosevelt one year later), he considered a radical turn. He investigated the idea of donating his fortune to an American institution, deeming Europe no longer the right place for his work. Several other changes followed, which further refined the goals of the foundation, and he also changed its name: the 'Otletaneum' would guarantee the unity of his thinking and his personal papers. The UIA was not explicitly mentioned anymore. Meanwhile, his wife's fortune would remain in the family.

La Fontaine's last will was more concise. When he died in 1943, he left his fortune and library in equal shares to the UIA and the IPB.[84] The money – the equivalent of at least one year's budget – was enough to relaunch the UIA's activities after the war, but certainly not enough to create a fund that would guarantee enough interest and income to give the UIA a carefree financial future. However, La Fontaine's money and Otlet's intellectual capital certainly provided the seed funding for the UIA's entry into a new era in world history.

Notes

1 Helmut K. Anheier and Regina List, *A Dictionary of Civil Society, Philanthropy and the Non-Profit Sector* (London: Routledge, 2005), 196.

2 Thomas Adam, 'Philanthropy and the Shaping of Social Distinctions in Nineteenth-Century U.S., Canadian, and German Cities', in *Philanthropy, Patronage and Civil Society: Experiences from Germany, Great Britain, and North America*, ed. idem (Bloomington, IN: Indiana University Press, 2004), 17. See also Thomas Adam, 'Philanthropy', in *The Palgrave Dictionary of Transnational History*, ed. Pierre-Yves Saunier and Akira Iriye (Basingstoke: Palgrave, 2009), 832–4.

3 Rudolf Broda is good example of the many activists who used family capital to fund pacifist and related activities. See Christophe Verbruggen and Julie Carlier, 'Laboratories of Social Thought: The Transnational Advocacy Network of the Institut International Pour La Diffusion des Expériences Sociales and its Documents du Progrès', in *Information Beyond Borders: International Cultural and Intellectual Exchange in the Belle Époque*, ed. W. Boyd Rayward (Farnham: Ashgate, 2014), 123–42.

4 Inderjeet Parmar, *Foundations of the American Century: The Ford, Carnegie and Rockefeller Foundations in the Rise of American Power* (New York: Columbia University Press, 2012); Katharina Rietzler, 'Of Highways, Turntables and Mirror Gazes: Metaphors of Americanisation in the History of American Philanthropy', *Diplomacy and Statecraft* 24, no. 1 (2013): 117–33.

5 Matthew Bishop and Michael Green, *Philanthro-Capitalism: How Giving Can Save the World* (New York: Bloomsbury, 2009).

6 Francesca Sawaya, *The Difficult Art of Giving: Patronage, Philanthropy, and the American Literary Market* (Philadelphia, PA: University of Pennsylvania Press, 2014).

7 Katharina Rietzler, 'From Peace Advocacy to International Relations Research: The Transformation of Transatlantic Philanthropic Networks, 1900–1930', in *Shaping the Transnational Sphere: Experts, Networks and Issues from the 1840s to the 1930s*, ed. Davide Rodogno, Bernhard Struck and Jakob Vogel (New York: Berghahn, 2015), 173–94.

8 Daniel Laqua, 'Alfred H. Fried and the Challenges for "Scientific Pacifism" in the Belle Époque', in *Information Beyond Borders*, ed. Rayward, 181–99.

9 On the structure and workings of the IPB, see, for example, Sandi Cooper, *Patriotic Pacifism: Waging War on War in Europe, 1815–1914* (New York: Oxford University Press, 1991), 80–2.

10 Daniel Laqua, Wouter Van Acker and Christophe Verbruggen, 'Henri La Fontaine et la belle époque', *Henri La Fontaine, Prix Nobel de la paix en 1913: un belge épris de justice*, ed. Jacques Gillen (Brussels: Racine, 2013), 21–32.

11 Note Henri La Fontaine, 30 April 1911, in Series III: Division of Intercourse and Education, Subseries B, vol. 178, Carnegie Endowment for International Peace Records, Butler Library, Rare Books and Manuscripts Library, Columbia University, New York City (hereafter CEIP, Columbia).

12 Note Henri La Fontaine, 30 April 1911.

13 International law was not prepared for the rapid growth of non-state actors. Only from the beginning of the twentieth century did some countries start to give legal personality to what later became known as 'INGOs'. One of the advantages of receiving legal personality was the ability for formal relations with intergovernmental organizations, but also the fact that they could receive and invest subsidies more easily.

14 For a detailed discussion of the troubled relations between the IPB and the Carnegie Endowment, see Rietzler, 'From Peace Advocacy to International Relations Research', 179 and passim.

15 Division of Education and Intercourse to La Fontaine, 15 December 1911, CEIP, Columbia.

16 La Fontaine to Butler, 29 November 1911, CEIP, Columbia.

17 Butler to La Fontaine, 12 December 1911, CEIP, Columbia.

18 La Fontaine to Butler, 16 December 1911, CEIP, Columbia.

19 UIA, *Resources financières de l'UIA avant 1940 après les documents de HLF*, unpublished manuscript, 26 October 1948, UIA Archives, Brussels. The Interparliamentary Union effectively transferred its operational headquarter from Bern to Brussels in 1911.

20 *Rapport sur l'Office Central des associations internationales présenté à la Carnegie Endowment for international peace*, 21 October 1912, CEIP, Columbia.

21 See also Laqua 'Alfred H. Fried and the Challenges for "Scientific Pacifism"', 191. From 1913 to 1915, La Fontaine also received a small personal travel grant from the Carnegie Endowment to support his international activities.

22 La Fontaine to Buttler, 21 November 1912, CEIP, Columbia.

23 Rietzler, 'From Peace Advocacy to International Relations Research', 182–3.

24 Andrée Despy-Meyer and Valerie Montens, 'Le Mécénat de Ernest et Alfred Solvay', in *Ernest Solvay et son temps*, ed. Andrée Despy-Meyer and Didier Devriese (Brussels: Université libre de Bruxelles, 1997), 221–45.

25 Kenneth Bertrams, Nicolas Coupain and Ernst Homburg, *Solvay: History of a Multinational Family Firm* (Cambridge: Cambridge University Press, 2013), 138–9.

26 Kaat Wils Kaat and Rasmussen, 'Sociology in a Transnational Perspective: Brussels, 1890-1925', *Revue belge de philologie et d'histoire* 90, no. 4 (2012): 1273–96.

27 Wouter Van Acker, 'Sociology in Brussels, Organicism and the Idea of a World Society in the Period before the First World War', in *Information Beyond Borders*, ed. Rayward, 143–68.

28 Wouter Van Acker, 'Universalism as Utopia: A Historical Study of the Schemes and Schemas of Paul Otlet (1868–1944)' (PhD diss., Ghent University, 2011), 571–2; W. Boyd Rayward, *The Universe of Information: The Work of Paul Otlet for Documentation and International Organisation* (Moscow: VINITI, 1975), 151–2.

29 Memo N. Butler to Mr Haskell, 13 April 1912, CEIP, Columbia.

30 Minutes of the meetings of the administrative committee of the Union between 1915 and 1919, *exact box?*, boxes 315–19, 'Union des Associations Internationales 1910–1937', records of the Deutsche Kongress-Zentrale 1870-1943, Hoover Institution Archives, Stanford University (hereafter: Hoover Institution Archives, DKZ).

31 For instance: Demande de subvention en faveur de l'Union des Associations Internationale, unpublished manuscript (1921), UIA Archives.

32 Division of Intercourse and Education to La Fontaine and Otlet, 9 November 1922, CEIP, Columbia.

33 Earle B. Babcock to Paul Otlet, 7 May 1934, UIA Archives.

34 Madeleine Herren, *Hintertüren zur Macht: Internationalismus und modernisierungsorientierte Außenpolitik in Belgien, der Schweiz und den USA 1865–1914* (Munich: Oldenbourg, 2000); Daniel Laqua, *The Age of Internationalism and Belgium, 1880-1930: Peace, Progress and Prestige* (Manchester: Manchester University Press, 2013).

35 Jan Vandersmissen, 'The King's Most Eloquent Campaigner … : Emile de Laveleye, Leopold II and the Creation of the Congo Free State', *Belgisch Tijdschrift voor Nieuwste Geschiedenis / Revue Belge d'Histoire contemporaine* 41, nos. 1-2 (2011): 7–57.

36 UIA, *Note confidentielle sur la participation de la Belgique au mouvement international et sur les moyens de maintenir et de développer la situation*, 17 March 1910, UIA Archives.

37 UIA, Ressources financières de L'UIA avant 1940 après les documents de HLF, unpublished manuscript, 26 Oktober 1948, UIA Archives.

38 George Nash, 'The "Great Humanitarian": Herbert Hoover, the Relief of Belgium, and the Reconstruction of Europe after World War I', *The Tocqueville Review/La Revue Tocqueville* 38, no. 2 (2017): 55–70.

39 Kenneth Bertrams, 'De l'action humanitaire à la recherche scientifique: La Commission for Relief in Belgium et la création du Fonds National de la Recherche Scientifique en Belgique, 1914–1930', in *L'Argent de l'influence: les fondations américaines et leurs réseaux européens*, ed. Ludovic Tournès (Paris: Editions Autrement, 2010), 45–63.

40 Van Acker, 'Universalism as Utopia', 604–11.

41 Paul Otlet, *Memorandum sur les rapports du Gouvernement belge avec l'UAI et le Palais mondial* (Brussels: UIA, 1923), 3.

42 Kenneth Bertrams, 'The Domestic Uses of Belgian–American "Mutual Understanding": The Commission for Relief in Belgium Educational Foundation, 1920-1940', *Journal of Transatlantic Studies* 13, no. 4 (2015): 326–43.

43 Minutes of the meetings of the administrative committee of the Union between 1915 and 1919.

44 One year later, on 2 July 1920, the UIA was registered as an international association with scientific aims. Paul Otlet, *Memorandum sur les rapports du Gouvernement belge avec l'UAI et le Palais mondial* (Brussels: UIA, 1923), 7.

45 'Notes sur les resources de l'UAI et les prévisions d'avenir', 26 May 1920, box PP PO, 239, Mundaneum.

46 *Organisation future de l'état juridico-financier de l'Union,* box PP PO, 239, Mundaneum. Elaborated in: Paul Otlet, *Centre intellectuel mondial au service de la Société des Nations* (Brussels: UIA, 1919).

47 La Fontaine and Otlet to Eric Drummond, 18 August 1920, Archives UIA.

48 Rayward, *The Universe of Information,* 223–6.

49 Procès-verbal of the Eight Session of the Council, 30 July–5 August 1920, quoted extensively in: Abraham Henry Goodman, *The League and Cultural Cooperation* (University of British Columbia, 1946).

50 *Memorandum communicated on 5th September 1921,* quoted in 'The United Nations and the Yearbook of International Organizations'. Available online: https://uia.org/ ecosocres (accessed 24 April 2018).

51 Georges Patrick Speeckaert, 'A Glance at Sixty Years of Activity (1910–1970) of the Union of International Associations', in *Union of International Associations, 1910– 1970: Past, Present, Future* (Brussels: UIA, 1970), 29–31; Rayward, *The Universe of Information,* 223–8.

52 On this body, see Daniel Laqua, 'Transnational Intellectual Cooperation, the League of Nations and the Problem of Order', *Journal of Global History* 6, no. 2 (2011): 223–47; Jean-Jacques Renoliet, *L'Unesco oubliée: la Société des nations et la coopération intellectuelle, 1919–1946* (Paris: Publications de la Sorbonne, 1999).

53 Assemblée de la Société des nations 1920, *Le Travail intellectuel, proposition de la délégation belge* (unpublished manuscript), box 201, Henri La Fontaine papers [hereafter: HLF], Mundaneum, Mons.

54 For CITI, see Christophe Verbruggen, 'Intellectual Workers and Their Search for a Place within the ILO during the Interwar Period', in *Essays on the International Labour Organization and Its Impact on the World During the Twentieth Century,* ed. Jasmien Van Daele et al. (Bern: Peter Lang, 2010), 271–92.

55 *L'Organisation du Travail Intellectuel. Rapport présenté par M. Léon Bourgeois, adopté par le Conseil le 2 septembre 1921 ,* box 201, HLF.

56 'L'Activité éducative et l'Organisation du Travail Intellectuel accomplies par l'Union des Associations Internationales. Communiqué au Conseil', 5 September 1921, box 201, HLF.

57 Demeulenaere, 'Rôle et attitude des délégués belges à la Commission Internationale de Coopération Intellectuelle', in Dumoulin, *Penser l'Europe à l'aube des années trente,* 9–33.

58 Otlet to La Fontaine, 26 July 1922, UIA Archives.

59 *L'Affaire du Palais Mondial: documents* (Brussels: UIA, 1923), 57.

60 These concerns are discussed in Renoliet, *L'Unesco oubliée,* 49–53.

61 Laqua, 'Transnational Intellectual Cooperation', 246.

62 *L'Affaire du Palais Mondial,* 4.

63 Paul Otlet, *L'Union des Associations Internationales et le gouvernement belge* (Brussels: UIA, 1934).

64 'L'Affaire du Palais Mondial', *Periodicum Mundaneum,* no. 2 (1934), UIA Archives.

65 *L'Affaire du Palais mondial. Organisation de la Défense et du Développement du Mundaneum par la Ligue 'Les Amis du Palais Mondial de Belgique',* Periodicum Mundaneum, 1934, UIA Archives.

66 Dotatio Mundeaneum, 23 April 1934, box PP PO 239, UIA Archives.

67 *Union des Association Internationale, Dossier du procès (1934-…),* UIA Archives.

68   Réponse de M. Le Ministre Bovesse à M. H. La Fontaine, Sénat de Belgique, séance du 13 février 1936, UIA Archives.

69   Françoise Levie, *L'Homme qui voulait classer le monde: Paul Otlet et le Mundaneum* (Brussels: Les Impressions Nouvelles, 2006), 264–5.

70   Entrevue de M. Otlet avec M. Lemoine. Le Ier Avril 1936, 2 April 1936, UIA Archives.

71   Levie, *L'Homme qui voulait classer le monde*, 291.

72   Madeleine Herren, '"Outwardly … an Innocuous Conference Authority": National Socialism and the Logistics of International Information Management', *German History* 20, no. 1 (2002): 67. See also Benjamin Martin, *The Nazi-Fascist New Order for European Culture* (Cambridge, MA: Harvard University Press, 2016) and Madeleine Herren, 'Fascist Internationalism', in *Internationalisms: A Twentieth Century History*, ed. Glenda Sluga and Patricia Clavin (Cambridge: Campbridge University Press, 2016), 191–212.

73   Alex Wright, *Cataloging the World, Paul Otlet and the Birth of the Information Age* (New York: Oxford University Press, 2014), 240.

74   Herren, 'Outwardly … ', 85–7.

75   Paul Otlet, 'Memoire au Reich,' box 988, PP PO, Mundaneum.

76   Baron Papeians de Morchoven to Otlet, 29 January, box 317, Hoover Institution Archives.

77   UIA, 'Pour une participation belge à l'UAI', unpublished typoscript, 27 November 1941, box 317, Hoover Institution Archives, DKZ.

78   C. L. Van Loock and K. Schweig, 'Entwurf – Die Reorganisationen der Union des Associations Internationales unter Deutschen Führung', 28 January 1941, box 317, Hoover Institution Archives, DKZ.

79   SS Unterstumführer (Brussels) to the Head of the Secret Police Belgium and France, 27 February 1941, Hoover Institution Archives, DKZ. In July 1942 the SS found 'hate propaganda against the Führer' and anti-German pamphlets. Idem to director DKZ, 22 July 1941, box 317, Hoover Institution Archives, DKZ.

80   Herren, 'Outwardly … ', 85–90.

81   Ibid., 91.

82   Paul Otlet, 'Dispositions testamentaires', box PP PO 35, Mundaneum.

83   'Avec le but de continuer l'objet même des études et travaux de Paul Otlet dans l'esprit de ceux-ci et en connection avec le Mundaneum (les Instituts du Palais Mondial organisé par l'Union des Associations internationals)', 27 December 1936, box PP PO 35, Mundaneum.

84   The total share of his inheritance that went to the UIA was about 595,000 francs. I would like to thank Stephanie Manfroid for giving me a copy of his testament. See also UIA, Ressources financières de L'UIA avant 1940 après les documents de HLF, unpublished manuscript, 26 October 1948, UIA Archives.

Chapter 3

EDUCATING INTERNATIONALISTS: THE CONTEXT, ROLE AND LEGACIES OF THE UIA'S 'INTERNATIONAL UNIVERSITY'

Daniel Laqua

In September 1920, the Union of International Associations hosted the inaugural session of its *Université Internationale* at the Palais Mondial in Brussels. While this 'International University' was not a degree-awarding institution but rather a two-week lecture cycle, its programme was certainly impressive: forty-seven speakers from ten countries, including prominent figures from academia, politics and culture, gave altogether 143 lectures.[1] Further sessions followed in 1921, 1922 and 1927. The organizers conceived these events as the basis for a more permanent institution, which was to supplement the work of existing universities by providing 'an initiation into international and comparative aspects of all great questions'.[2] Intended to educate a new generation of leaders, the initiative chimed with the UIA's agenda for organizing international life: the university venture sought to 'unite universities and international associations in a movement of both higher education and higher universal culture'.

Eventually, the International University joined the ranks of several grandiose but unsuccessful schemes that had been conceived by UIA founders Paul Otlet and Henri La Fontaine. In the same period, the pair also sought to transform their institutions into an intellectual branch of the League of Nations and championed plans for a world capital city (*cité mondiale*). Like those endeavours, the International University did not reach the heights that its creators had anticipated: it never went beyond being a summer school and, notwithstanding a final attempt in 1927, its momentum had largely passed by 1923. Yet the scheme was nonetheless significant, as it represented an influential strand of internationalist thinking: many activists considered educational ventures as ways of building international cooperation.

As Joëlle Droux and Rita Hofstetter have argued, 'the field of education' offers 'a relevant platform for an analysis of transnational dynamics'.[3] Accordingly, a growing literature examines the channels through which pedagogical expertise was disseminated across national borders.[4] The UIA's undertaking relates to a particular area of educational research and practice, namely 'international education' – a field that is 'wide enough to embrace both education for international understanding ... and education for world citizenship'.[5] This chapter first analyses the ideas that underpinned the International University and traces their partial implementation. Its final section addresses legacies and echoes of this project. As a whole, the chapter contributes to our understanding of internationalism, yet it also sheds light on the history of education by helping to historicize international education.[6]

Education and Internationalism

Well before the First World War, peace campaigners aimed some of their activities at children and schools, as part of their quest to foster pacific attitudes.[7] Such efforts constituted early examples of peace education – that is, pedagogical approaches aimed at 'empowering people with the skills, attitudes and knowledge to create a world where conflicts are solved non-violently and [to] build a sustainable environment'.[8] The pursuit of these objectives extended to higher education. For instance, two proposals for an international university were submitted to the Universal Peace Congresses of 1905, a major pacifist gathering in Lucerne.[9] Congress delegates subsequently called for 'an International University, endowed by the different States, in which the most eminent personages of each should be called on to teach all that can assist human progress'. Moreover, they encouraged national peace societies 'to continue their inquiry as to the organisation of an international system of instruction and education'.[10] Subsequent Universal Peace Congresses did not result in a new institution, yet delegates reaffirmed their commitment to academic exchange.[11] Such examples highlight a conceptual link between peace education and international education: the conviction that international exchanges would foster goodwill and understanding.

American philanthropy was a second influence for such educational schemes. In 1910, Edwin Ginn established the International School of Peace in Boston, partly funded by profits he had made as a textbook publisher. The body was meant to 'educate all nations about the waste and destructiveness of war, and to promote international justice and the brotherhood of man'.[12] Although the International School eventually became the World Peace Foundation – a think tank rather than a site of instruction – it demonstrated the resonance of educational ideas within American internationalist settings. Significantly, Ginn's initiative also impacted on the shape Andrew Carnegie gave to his Endowment for International Peace.[13]

A third development occurred within universities, linked to the emergence of international student organizations that promoted cultural exchange and international cooperation. In 1898, Italian students launched the association *Corda Fratres* to foster internationalism among their peers. In 1907, their efforts were complemented by the US-based Cosmopolitan Clubs, whose members proclaimed humanity to be 'above all nations'.[14] The Cosmopolitan Clubs maintained links to the peace movement. For instance, shortly before the outbreak of the Great War, some of its members participated in a British summer school led by the renowned pacifist author Norman Angell.[15]

The UIA's founders had direct connections to each of these three pre-war strands. Henri La Fontaine was a major presence at the Universal Peace Congresses and in 1907 became president of the body that coordinated them, the International Peace Bureau. Moreover, during the Great War, Ginn's World Peace Foundation published La Fontaine's proposal for a future world organization.[16] Further interactions between the UIA and American philanthropy are discussed in Christophe Verbruggen's contribution to this volume. The UIA founders were also aware of efforts among students, covering the Cosmopolitan Club movement in their periodical.[17]

Yet links to activists and philanthropists were not the only factors that accounted for La Fontaine and Otlet's interest in international higher education. After all, the Belgians' bibliographical work constituted a transnational research venture in its own right. As early as 1894, La Fontaine had mentioned the idea of an international university, primarily in terms of providing access to scholarly literature from around the world.[18] The same year, he also became involved in the *Université Nouvelle* in Brussels – a radical educational venture that, despite having no degree-awarding powers, attracted an international cast of students and scholars.[19]

These intersections with internationalist and academic milieus help to explain the genesis of the UIA's project. By 1912, the *Annuaire de la Vie Internationale* suggested that specialists at the UIA's 'Centre International' might become the 'professorial body of a veritable international university'. It also portrayed a future 'world school' as an organic extension of traditional universities.[20] In 1913, the second World Congress of International Associations agreed on general principles for an international university.[21]

The Interwar Moment for International Education

The outbreak of the First World War prevented the immediate implementation of any such scheme. The wartime ruptures within the academic world are well known: in the present volume, Matthias Middell and Katja Naumann have noted their impact on historians, and similar observations apply to other disciplines. Tomás Irish has cautioned against viewing the divisions as complete, noting that 'ties between scholars in different countries were often much more durable than has been credited'.[22] Nor did formal academic exchanges come to a halt. However, their meaning changed, as 'the war inaugurated a move to redefine international exchange in accordance with wartime geopolitical configurations'.[23] This ambiguity was evident in Paul Otlet's wartime writings: his 500-page study of 'international problems' not only extensively discussed ruptures in the academic world, but also sought to demonstrate the ongoing momentum for international education.[24]

Academic cooperation faced significant challenges well beyond the war years. When the International University was launched in 1920, the exclusion of Germans mirrored the situation in other international academic institutions before the Locarno era.[25] This stance was far from uncontroversial. A UIA note from May 1921 reported 'two opposing attitudes': whereas some 'expressed regret not to have seen Germany immediately admitted to the International University', others suggested that the Germans would 'never become part of it'.[26] The document suggested that the time had not yet come for 'a rapprochement between yesterday's enemies, as pacification is far from being complete in the political sphere'. The International University, they argued, had to proceed in multiple steps, starting with those who were currently integrated into international structures.

Precisely because of such persistent antagonisms, the promotion of international education acquired great significance. As Akira Iriye has pointed out, school exchanges and textbook reform were prominent features of cultural internationalism in the interwar years.[27] The League of Nations ultimately developed activities in this field during the 1920s.[28] Prior to League action, however, private efforts were under way. For instance, reform pedagogues such as Beatrice Ensor and Elisabeth Rotten promoted international education through the New Education Fellowship.[29] Meanwhile, in New York, the academic Stephen Duggan established the International Institute of Education to facilitate academic exchanges and disseminate information about different study opportunities.[30] Duggan's institute cooperated with key figures in American internationalism, including Nicholas Murray Butler, the chair of the Carnegie Endowment for International Peace. According to Katharina Rietzler, the Carnegie Endowment underwent a 'transition from funding peace advocacy to the production and dissemination of knowledge on international relations' in this period.[31] As a result, 'the American leaders devoted more and more energy to projects with an academic or scientific bent'. This reorientation included not only links with Duggan's institute but also support for an 'international summer academy for the teaching of international law' at The Hague.[32]

Of course, nationalism continued to matter in university settings – yet the efforts to facilitate transnational contacts were plentiful and diverse. Students were actively engaged in this process. The 1920s and 1930s saw a revival in student mobility and a plethora of travel schemes. Moreover, with regard to Britain, Georgina Brewis has highlighted students' involvement in various transnational activities, including humanitarian relief efforts.[33] Cooperation in this period was facilitated by the creation of a host of new international student organizations. Clearly, then, the UIA's International University formed part of a much wider pattern.

Concept and Design of the International University

The International University tied in with key aspects of the UIA's post-war agenda, notably the promotion of an intellectual branch for the League of Nations. As a UIA document on the 'international organization of intellectual labour' stated, 'Humanity has to create for itself a vast collective brain.' In this respect, the International University was to serve as an intellectual 'Centre of Centres'.[34] This ambition was also apparent to external observers. For instance, when *The New York Times* reported on the International University in 1921, it described it as 'organizing [the] world's intellectual work'.[35]

At one level, the proposed institution was meant to perform traditional university functions, for instance, by operating as a 'research centre on comparative education'.[36] Yet it was also supposed to offer 'complementary education for an elite of students' and 'serve as a pedagogical centre at the service of democracy'.[37] Otlet and La Fontaine envisaged a system whereby students would participate in an international tour of distinguished universities, with a core course at the Palais Mondial. Each student who, within two years of graduation in their home country, had been to universities of at least three different countries would receive the title 'international student'. Recognition as a 'world student' was reserved for those who, within three years after graduation, had spent study time at ten universities in five countries, situated in at least two continents.

The proposed curriculum reflected two prominent strands in the thought of Otlet and La Fontaine: encyclopaedism – as exemplified by their bibliographical work – and internationalism. These dimensions manifested themselves in the plan to dedicate one university section to the 'synthesis and encyclopaedia of the sciences' and another one to the League of Nations.[38] The idea of a 'universal encyclopaedia as synthesis of ideas and knowledge' was reiterated as late as 1927.[39] Yet even in a venture with such universal ambitions, nationhood figured prominently – confirming Glenda Sluga's observations on the way in which internationalism was conceptualized in national terms.[40] From the outset, 'comparative national studies' featured alongside 'international studies' within the proposed curriculum.[41] A later document suggested that students would cover four areas: 'national problems'; 'international problems' (focusing on international organizations); 'universal problems' (providing 'the foundations of a universal spirit') and, finally, the 'sociological study of Belgium', involving visits to various Belgian institutions.[42]

The institution's intended audience reached beyond university students: it was also meant to serve as the 'educational centre for international associations' and to help develop 'the doctrine of the League of Nations'.[43] Between 1920 and 1927, the Brussels-based sessions sought to put some of these ideas into practice. On all four occasions, the International University formed part of the UIA's *Quinzaine Internationale* – an 'international fortnight' comprising congresses and meetings. The organizers enlisted participants of the *Quinzaine* events as lecturers for the university sessions and invited affiliated organizations to establish 'chairs'. In 1920, they listed thirteen such collaborations. For example, the Union Internationale des Villes – whose work is discussed in Wouter Van Acker's chapter – supplied the British town planner Patrick Abercrombie and the French economist Edgard Milhaud.[44]

The UIA anticipated formal links with the League of Nations as part of its university venture. Prior to the first *Quinzaine Internationale*, Inazō Nitobe – the League's under-secretary-general – visited the Palais Mondial, and League secretary-general Eric Dummond subsequently offered encouraging words.[45] Moreover, Nitobe contributed a lecture on 'What the League of Nations has done and is doing' to the International University session of 1920. Yet despite further correspondence, neither the League Secretariat nor the Council deemed the scheme ready for being placed under the League's auspices.[46] This stance evidently disappointed the UIA's leaders, who had hoped for such patronage.

Although the International University remained a predominantly European phenomenon, the UIA cast its venture in universalist terms. The actual implementation reflected these global ambitions only to a limited degree. For instance, the programme for the 1921 session listed three Japanese academics, but two of these talks were cancelled.[47] The same year, the lecture cycle also featured an Indian speaker, B. P. Wadia – an influential figure in international theosophy – who a few weeks earlier had attended the Paris-based world congress of the Theosophical Society.[48] The UIA's leaders were also aware of another Indian thinker: Rabindranath Tagore worked towards the aim of an international university by founding Visva-Bharati in 1921.[49] Yet, in contrast to Tagore's scheme, the UIA's venture was largely based on Western institutional and educational ideas. As one scholar has argued, it 'did not take into account the knowledge traditions' of people in non-Western territories that were under colonial rule.[50]

In considering the role of education, the UIA's founders hardly challenged the civilizational assumptions that underpinned global power-political structures. For instance, in 1919, Otlet discussed the efforts of the African American scholar and activist W. E. B. Du Bois, who organized a Pan-African Congress to coincide with the Paris Peace Conference. Otlet cited the event as evidence of a new era of 'globality' (*mondialité*) and suggested that Pan-Africanism offered opportunities for educational exchanges between the United States and Africa. However, Otlet's sympathetic portrayal was couched in the language of a 'civilizing mission'. Moreover, with regard to Belgian practices in the Congo, his article claimed that any 'errors, abuses' had ended following 'the energetic action of Belgium's parliament'.[51] Despite Otlet's ambivalent stance, his subsequent correspondence with Du Bois resulted in the UIA hosting parts of the Pan-African Congress of 1921. The event took place during the *Quinzaine Internationale*. As such, it coincided with the International University – and, accordingly, Du Bois was invited to contribute 'two or three' lectures to the latter.[52] In the end, one such lecture featured on the programme, addressing 'the situation of black people throughout the world'.[53] Furthermore, delegates to the Pan-African Congress were made aware of the university session: in a congress report, the African American author Jessie Fauset noted that 'a fine, fresh-faced youth from the International University gave us a welcome from the students of all nations'.[54]

As noted in the Introduction to the present volume, the Brussels segment of the Pan-African Congress proved controversial. Parts of the Belgian press accused it of revolutionary tendencies, whereas Pan-Africanists were disappointed that the deliberations in Brussels had muted any criticism of colonial practices.[55] Moreover, there were underlying conceptual and strategic differences about the nature of international work. From the beginning, Otlet and his fellow organizer, the Congolese activist Paul Panda Farnana, had envisaged the congress as a 'scientific' event.[56] By contrast, Du Bois placed the emphasis 'on the spiritual and inspirational side': only once a spirit of unity had been achieved would it be possible to address 'the matter of funds for scientific research'.[57] These differing priorities indicate why a venture such as the International University held limited attraction to activists – and, as such, they highlight wider difficulties in fostering links with international movements.

Scholars and Students

Cooperation with protagonists of interwar internationalism played an important role in the UIA's work – yet any university venture depended on the backing of researchers and educators. The organization seems to have had some success in this respect: by 1922, 347 professors from 23 countries had pledged their support.[58] Speakers at its sessions included some high-ranking academics, for instance Jules Payot, rector of the University of Aix-Marseille. The cast of contributors extended to experts such as Edouard Claparède and Adolphe Ferrière, who headed the Rousseau Institute – a body for educational research which later became the International Bureau of Education and nowadays is a UNESCO institute.[59] Moreover, the UIA claimed that several universities had affiliated to the International University – seemingly in line with its aims for a 'federation of universities'.[60] By 1921, it cited support from institutions in Bucharest, Lisbon, Leiden, Copenhagen, Madrid, Beijing, Poznan, Prague, Sofia, Tokyo, Warsaw, Vilnius and Zurich.[61] Impressive as this may sound, such 'affiliations' meant little. At best, they were a general expression of sympathy; at worst, an example of the UIA leaders' tendency to overstate the extent of their backing.

In the same period, the UIA also built links with a specific academic constituency: Russian exile scholars. In 1921, sixteen Russian speakers featured at the International University – from the Orientalist Vladimir Fedorovich Minorsky to anti-Bolshevik politicians such as Mark Slonim and Peter Struve.[62] Their involvement had been facilitated by contacts between the UIA and the Russian Academic Group in Paris. After the October Revolution, Russian Academic Groups had been established in several European cities, helping to sustain a 'Russia abroad'.[63] The UIA combined its 1921 lecture programme with a meeting at which it offered special services to its Russian guests: access to the collections of the Palais Mondial and the proposed creation of a repository for exile publications. A subsequent account optimistically reported that the bibliographer Nikolai Rubakin had 'agreed in principle' to transfer his Russian Library – a collection he had built after leaving Tsarist Russia in 1907 – from Baugy-sur-Clarens, Switzerland, to the Palais Mondial.[64] Despite Rubakin's long-standing links to Otlet, the collection ultimately moved to Lausanne instead.[65] Yet such discussions illustrate how the UIA sought to integrate the International University with its other activities, including the documentation work of its founders and the development of an International Museum at the Palais Mondial.

The International University evidently attracted interest from different scholars, associations and institutions. What about another core constituency, namely university students? In line with the UIA's general modus operandi, its engagement with university students was channelled through an international organization, the International Confederation of Students (*Confédération Internationale des Étudiants*, CIE). Having been founded in 1919, the CIE brought together representatives of national unions of students.[66] During the early 1920s, the UIA hosted the confederation's secretariat at its Palais Mondial, forming part of a wider strategy of attracting international associations to these premises. Reflecting their anticipated partnership, the UIA listed the CIE's leaders and national affiliates in the initial programme of the International University.[67]

Relations with the student leaders proved more ambiguous than the UIA had anticipated. During the UIA's 'international fortnight' of September 1920, the CIE's executive council met at the Palais Mondial and Otlet personally welcomed the delegates. He 'emphasized with great enthusiasm the importance of the International University's tasks' and stressed the need for the 'effective support and cooperation of all intellectual associations'.[68] Yet several CIE council members raised organizational and conceptual objections.[69] Moreover, Otlet's claims about support from national governments met with scepticism, as they seemed largely unsubstantiated. In the end, the CIE did not offer unequivocal backing. While it affiliated to the International University 'in principle', it postponed its formal adhesion to a later stage.[70] The debate in Brussels reflected wider tensions within the CIE. French and Belgian activists played a prominent role during its formative years – the Belgian Marc Van Laer managed the confederation's office at the Palais Mondial. However, other student leaders – in particular from the Netherlands and Scandinavia – feared that the CIE might become too much of a francophone or quasi-Allied venture.

Despite reservations within the CIE, the programme for the International University of 1922 noted that the confederation would organize social activities for its students.[71] Moreover, a report from the CIE's council meeting of January 1923 mentioned that the confederation could continue to base its offices 'without cost at the Palais Mondial, as hitherto'.[72] Later that year, the CIE expressed its support for the International University in two letters to the League of Nations.[73] There is, however, little evidence of an ongoing relationship beyond the early 1920s, and the CIE's operations soon moved outside Belgium.

Relations with the CIE raise the wider question of student participation. Strikingly, the preserved records offer little information on this subject. A document from 1922 is a rare exception. At the closing event of that year's International University, Ludmila Genttnerová from Czechoslovakia praised the 'hospitality and friendliness' that she had received, hoping that social bonds would result in a return visit to Prague.[74] Genttnerová's comments indicate that the Maison des Étudiantes in Brussels had hosted her alongside delegates from Italy. However, as this building – which usually catered for female students from the Free University of Brussels – housed a mere twenty-five residents, we cannot draw any conclusions about the wider number of students involved.[75]

The lack of student voices in the archival record is not entirely unexpected. The organizers focused on assembling a programme rather than a student body. This limitation is illustrated by a letter after the 1922 session. The Italian astronomer Giovanni Boccardi complained that a shortage of students had led the organizers 'to open the door to everyone'. Boccardi's concern was less with the student audience than with the calibre of speakers. He wanted professors who 'deserve this label' and suggested that 'misguided idealism' might have led the organizers to think that 'everyone should have the right to expose their ideas'.[76] In this regard, his assessment was harsh – many speakers did have strong credentials. However, Boccardi's comments highlight an intrinsic contradiction. The UIA frequently raised expectations by speaking of an 'elite' of students.[77] Yet this elitism, and an underlying desire for prestige, stood at odds with a more inclusive impulse: the hope to reach a broad audience for the cause of internationalism.

Successes and Setbacks

Notwithstanding their shortcomings, the 1920, 1921 and 1922 International University sessions attracted many distinguished contributors. Individuals such as Ferdinand Buisson – the French educator, politician and president of the Ligue des Droits de l'Homme – certainly were far from marginal.[78] With sixty-nine speakers, the 1921 programme was even more extensive.[79] Boyd Rayward has described the International University and *Quinzaine Internationale* of 1922 as 'rather small' by comparison,[80] yet with over seventy-two professors from sixteen countries giving hundred lessons, the programme still reached a considerable scale.[81]

In its quest for support, the UIA seized opportunities as they presented themselves. For instance, when an American trade delegation from the Southern Commercial Congress travelled to Europe in 1922, Otlet arranged a meeting with its director-general Clarence Owens. Having described the encounter as 'the most delightful experience of my present visit to Europe', Owens agreed to support 'the plan to build a great International University in Brussels', believing that the venture would 'inspire the peoples of the earth to promote the ideals of peace'.[82] Owens was subsequently designated as the university's 'Vice-President for the Western Hemisphere' while the Southern Commercial Congress became its 'corresponding body'.[83] Neither of these roles had practical consequences. Indeed, a report that the Americans presented to the US Congress revealed various misconceptions: it erroneously referred to the 'International University at the Palais de Ville where students from various European universities are taking postgraduate research work and lectures on cultural subjects'.[84] Nonetheless, the example illustrates how flattery could draw in potential supporters.

At the time of the American visit, there was still some optimism about the International University's prospects. Prior to the 1922 session, *Le Figaro* claimed that the project was backed by 'all the country's personalities, the government and the King himself'.[85] The French newspaper linked the initiative to a wider agenda, namely 'Belgium's evident desire … to attract anything international that it can have'.[86] In the *Journal du Droit International*, Barthélemy Raynaud – Professor of Law at the University of Aix-Marseille – seemed to anticipate steady progress: he suggested that 'the flexibility of its organization, [and] the breadth of its founders' vision' would assure the 'most beautiful future' for the university.[87] His prediction turned out to be wrong. No further sessions took place from 1923 to 1926, and the fourth International University, held in 1927, formed a somewhat sad epilogue. Boyd Rayward has noted its 'much reduced' nature and the 'insignificance' of that year's *Quinzaine Internationale*.[88] This development reflected the UIA's general fate in the later 1920s. Its decline was partly linked to worsening relations with the Belgian government, which Christophe Verbruggen has covered in this volume.

Yet the collapse of the International University was not solely due to the rift with the Belgian state. Another key factor was related to a League of Nations enquiry into different 'international university' proposals. The League's engagement with this subject was channelled through its International Committee on Intellectual Cooperation (ICIC). In 1922, the ICIC's creation had seemingly met the UIA's demand for an 'intellectual League of Nations' – but without providing a role for the two Belgians.[89] Indeed, the ICIC investigation of university schemes was not triggered by the UIA, but by a separate initiative from the Spanish government. Moreover, within the ICIC, the Indian political economist D. N. Bannerjea had produced another proposal, supporting 'an international system of education which may be at once truly national and genuinely international without being cosmopolitan or unduly propagandistic'.[90]

The Polish art historian and ICIC secretary Oskar Halecki was charged with producing a report on the matter. Being fearful of potential rivals, the UIA responded critically. Otlet asserted his organization's 'anterior rights', regarding it as 'truly inconceivable' if the League of Nations created a new university 'instead of helping an institution such as ours'.[91] Halecki subsequently described the question of an International University as 'one of the most litigious and most contested ones in the area of intellectual cooperation'.[92] The UIA's stance was only one factor – government responses to the enquiry revealed starkly contrasting viewpoints, raised by concerns that such a body might duplicate or challenge the work of national institutions.[93]

Otlet need not have worried about the League launching a rival scheme: the ICIC report dismissed plans for an International University altogether.[94] To some extent, Halecki's rejection seems surprising. After all, he had featured on the programme of International University sessions in Brussels, although his 1921 lecture on the 'accomplishments and future of the League of Nations' was cancelled.[95] Halecki did not deem a permanent institution feasible, partly because of the fragility of existing international structures and partly because existing universities were keen to avoid competition. Based on his report, the ICIC concluded in July 1924 that the imminent implementation of any 'international university' scheme was unrealistic.[96] Accordingly, later proposals submitted to the League met with a negative response.[97] Instead, the Leagues' engagement with university matters focused on more limited concerns such as the promotion of academic exchanges.

Meanwhile, outside of formal League structures, Geneva became the site of several international educational ventures during the 1920s. From 1924 onwards, Alfred and Lucie Zimmern organized the Geneva School of International Studies – also known as 'Zimmern School' – each July and August. In mid-August, this was followed by the Geneva Institute of International Relations, a two-week lecture cycle run by Britain's League of Nations Union and the US's League of Nations Association. Finally, in August–September, the International Federation of League of Nations Societies hosted its International Summer School.[98] Daniel Gorman has described these ventures as exemplifying the 'emergence of international society' in the 1920s.[99]

These were not the only Geneva-based ventures. From 1924 to 1940, the Students' International Union (SIU) opened its gates in the Swiss city. This institution was funded by American philanthropists and run by an American couple, Alexander and Maude Miner Hadden, while the Oxford classicist and ICIC member Gilbert Murray served as its president. The institution aimed not only 'to establish a student centre as a headquarters for international student groups and an institute of international relations' but also to 'promote mutual understanding and service among youth of different nationalities'.[100] The SIU staged events throughout the year, including an annual summer course that was initially led by the Spanish diplomat and academic Salvador de Madariaga. Furthermore, in 1927, William Rappard and Paul Mantoux established another, highly influential and more durable institution – the Graduate Institute of International Studies which, to this day, offers postgraduate education (now known as the Graduate Institute of International and Development Studies).

There were several parallels between these initiatives and the UIA's International University sessions. One key difference was that, from the outset, the Geneva-based schemes were more limited in scope and thus less likely to provoke objections. Moreover, compared to the Brussels activities, they drew on personal and physical proximity to the League. Madariaga served as the director of the Disarmament Section from 1922 to 1928 while Alfred Zimmern became the deputy director of the League's International Institute of Intellectual Cooperation in 1926. And prior to founding their Graduate School, Rappard and Mantoux had, respectively, headed the League's Mandates and Political Section. Such links allowed organizers to recruit leading officials for guest lectures.

By comparison, cooperation between the UIA and the League remained limited. Nor could the UIA draw on a mass membership – unlike, for instance, the League of Nations Union as co-organizer of the Geneva Institute of International Affairs.[101] The attempt to attract support elsewhere, namely in academia, was hampered by the fact that neither Otlet nor La Fontaine primarily operated in university settings. At times, they did appeal to other constituencies, as illustrated by Otlet's address to the World Federation of Education Associations in 1925.[102] By and large, however, the realization of the UIA's scheme seemed to become an ever-more distant prospect during the 1920s.

Legacies and Echoes

Patricia Clavin has stressed the importance of a long-term perspective when assessing the impact and influence of internationalist endeavours.[103] This point is relevant with regard to the UIA's initiative because, while its plan was never fully implemented, it did not sink without trace either. After the Second World War, various schemes for an international university directly referenced Otlet and La Fontaine's work.

Alexandre Marc was one activist who built on the UIA's educational undertakings. Born to Russian-Jewish parents in 1904, Marc had moved to France in his youth. After completing his studies, he became an influential figure in the 'nonconformist' movement of the 1930s, championing Third Way economics, pacifism and European cooperation through the periodicals *Esprit* and *L'Ordre Nouveau*.[104] Having spent the occupation years in Swiss exile, Marc returned to France in 1945 and soon became a leading voice for a united Europe. Marc served as secretary-general of the Union of European Federalists, contributed to the major 'Congress of Europe' at The Hague (1948) and later led the European Federalist Movement.[105] Moreover, Marc viewed education as a vehicle for international cooperation. In 1948, he set up the World Federalist University in Royaumont, north of Paris, building on the Inter-University Union of Federalists, which he had co-founded in Paris in 1946.

Marc directly referenced Otlet and La Fontaine's project in his submission to UNESCO's *International Social Science Bulletin* in 1952.[106] To him, the UIA's efforts constituted 'a first attempt to set up an International University' and 'valuable experiments deserving of attentive study'. The work of the 1920s seemed to offer insights even within the context of a new global order: 'The scheme, the syllabus and the actual work of the Brussels International University still have so close a bearing on some of the problems with which we have to grapple as a result of World War II that they provide food for thought and serve as useful pointers.'[107] Marc was not oblivious to the obstacles that such a venture might encounter. He noted that an international body should not act 'as a rival to existing universities' and credited the Brussels activists with having been conscious of this.[108]

Although his own Royaumont venture proved short-lived, Marc himself was a key player in internationalist ventures, extending to a movement that attracted some attention in the immediate aftermath of the Second World War: world federalism. The latter was compatible with Marc's Europeanism as many world federalists conceived regional federations as elements of global organization.[109] He supported the Chicago-based proposal for a world constitution of 1948 – one of the key expressions of federalist ideas. Mark Mazower has described the latter as a 'staggeringly implausible document'.[110] Yet, as Mazower's monograph on the history of global governance shows, world federalists were but one of many post-1945 ventures in which American internationalists played a prominent role.

It is therefore hardly surprising that the most extensive engagement with the UIA's scheme featured in an American publication: Michael Zweig's 1967 book on *The Idea of a World University*. Both Zweig's preface and his chapter on the 'History of the Idea of World Education' started with the UIA's efforts.[111] Elsewhere, he described the scheme as 'the first proposal for an international university to emerge after World War I'.[112] Throughout his study, he quoted extensively from UIA documents, even reprinting the International University's statutes.[113] In analysing later schemes, Zweig frequently compared them to the pioneering efforts from Brussels. For instance, he described the abortive proposal for a School of International Contacts – developed within the context of early UNESCO debates – as being 'identical in structure with Otlet's unsuccessful Brussels International University'.[114]

Zweig's study partly resulted from his personal involvement in internationalist circles. In 1960, he had participated in Americans Committed to World Responsibility, a student group at the University of Michigan. Its members influenced the creation of the Peace Corps under the John F. Kennedy administration while promoting wider ideas about international education. Elise Boulding – the American academic whose work Sarah Hellawell discusses in the present volume – later recalled 'watching the students who formed Americans Committed to World Responsibility travel across Europe gaining support for the idea of a world university'. To Boulding, the work of this group demonstrated 'how creative new institutions can be shaped by the imagination and the willingness to act of youth'.[115]

Zweig himself was not involved in subsequent work towards a world university. Instead, his activism shifted to Students for a Democratic Society, which emerged as the leading voice of student radicalism in the United States. Zweig's study appeared partly thanks to the American academic Harold Taylor, who edited the manuscript, wrote a foreword and added further material. Taylor was an influential figure in educational debates. From 1945 to 1959, he had served as president of Sarah Lawrence College, the prestigious liberal arts institution in New York State. Having left this post, he dedicated much of his subsequent career to promoting international education.[116] In his foreword to Zweig's study, Taylor suggested that a world university might help to address the ongoing Cold War tensions. As he saw it, 'the world's educational system' was 'in danger of becoming less, rather than more, internationalized as the political divisions and antagonisms multiply and coalesce into institutional forms'.[117]

To address these challenges, Taylor lent support to practical efforts at the international level. For example, when a Japanese grant helped to create the United Nations University (UNU) in 1973, Taylor led an American committee to support the new body.[118] In 1974, he further discussed UNU in a magazine for American educators, praising the idea of a 'university for the world'. According to Taylor, it was necessary to 'mobilize the intelligence of the human race to solve the world's problems on a global scale, using the powers of the imagination and intellectual to invent new solutions'.[119] Tellingly, Elise Boulding drew a direct connection between UNU and earlier efforts in the United States, claiming that the group Americans Committed to World Responsibility 'had laid the groundwork for the present United Nations University'.[120]

Based in Tokyo and partly sponsored by UNESCO, UNU bears echoes of earlier internationalist endeavours. As its charter puts it, the university was set up to study topics such as

> coexistence between peoples having different cultures, languages and social systems; peaceful relations between States and the maintenance of peace and security; human rights; economic and social change and development; the

environment and the proper use of resources; basic scientific research and the application of the results of science and technology in the interests of development; and universal human values related to the improvement of the quality of life.[121]

At the time of UNU's creation, Taylor mentioned a 'central danger', namely 'that the new institution may remain isolated within the UN system and the bureaucracies of the world academic community'.[122] Acting primarily as a research institution and think tank, UNU has sought to avoid isolation. It maintains a network of eleven UNU research and training institutes (based in ten different countries) as well as collaborating with forty institutions within the UN system.[123] By contrast, its role as an education provider has been limited: UNU only gained degree-awarding powers in 2010 and in 2016, its postgraduate cohort comprised 240 Master's students and 18 PhD candidates.[124]

Regardless of its limitations, the creation of UNU showed that a quasi-university could have a place within the UN system. In 1980, it was joined by the University for Peace (UPEACE), a Treaty Organization established by the UN General Assembly. The aims of the Costa Rica-based institution resonate with long-standing ideas of cultural internationalism. Its charter speaks of the 'clear determination to provide humanity with an international institution of higher education for peace and ... the aim of promoting among all human beings the spirit of understanding, tolerance and peaceful coexistence'.[125] At present, UPEACE runs Master's programmes on issues such as peacebuilding, development and human rights while maintaining joint degree programmes with institutions in Colombia, Ethiopia, Monaco, the Philippines, South Korea and the United States.[126] That said, recent reports still indicate a relatively small number of students.[127]

Conclusion

At first sight, the UIA's International University appears to be a product of its time, exemplifying the optimism with which many internationalists sought to build a new international order after the Great War. However, as this chapter has shown, matters are more complex. On the one hand, the sessions of the 1920s addressed long-standing concerns for education among pacifists and philanthropists. On the other hand, initiatives after 1945 showed that the idea still enjoyed resonance: even within a new geo-political configuration, the interwar project remained a point of reference.

This is not to say that the climate after the Second World War became more conducive to implementing such ideas on a large scale. Tellingly, a 1967 review of Zweig's book on *The Idea of a World University* viewed many of the arguments surrounding such an institution as idealistic and suggested that 'its prospects for the future appear to be no better than its record in the past'.[128] The subsequent creation of UNU and UPEACE does not in itself disprove this point, as these ventures remained limited in scale.

Moreover, there have been criticisms of 'world university' schemes in terms of their premises, for instance the idea 'that greater understanding of other cultures leads to peace, and that the university is an appropriate institutional model for the inclusion and study of the knowledge of all societies without the domination of the norms of any one culture over the others'.[129] From one angle, one might therefore conclude that the challenges encountered by the International University reflected problems with its very design. Yet it is also clear that there were external obstacles. For instance, inability to gain League of Nations support only partly reflected issues with the Brussels organizers, as it was also linked to the League's limited scope for action in the educational realm. Notwithstanding such challenges, the International University's contributors, partners and afterlives highlight the inspiration that such a venture could offer. As such, it demonstrates the importance of educational endeavours for the history of internationalism.

Notes

1   For these numbers, see 'Quelques dates dans l'existance d'une institution sexagénaire', *International Associations* 22, nos. 8–9 (1970): 431; *Université Internationale: Ière session 5–20 septembre 1920: programme des cours et conferences* (Brussels: UIA, 1920).

2   UIA, *L'Université Internationale: Notice et Programme* (Brussels: Palais Mondial, 1920), 3.

3   Joëlle Droux and Rita Hofstetter, 'Constructing Worlds of Education: A Historical Perspective', *Prospects* 45, no. 1 (2015): 6.

4   Eckhardt Fuchs, 'Educational Sciences, Morality and Politics: International Educational Congresses in the Early Twentieth Century', *Paedagogica Historica* 40, nos. 5–6 (2004): 757–84; Damiano Matasci, 'International Congresses of Education and the Circulation of Pedagogical Ideas in Western Europe (1876–1910)', in *Shaping the Transnational Sphere: Experts, Networks, and Issues (1850–1930)*, ed. Davide Rodogno, Bernhard Struck and Jacob Vogel (New York: Berghahn 2015), 218–38.

5   Robert Sylvester, 'Historical Resources for Research in International Education (1851–1950)', in *The SAGE Handbook for Research in International Education*, 2nd edn, ed. Mary Hayden, Jack Levy and Jeff Thompson (London: SAGE, 2015), 13.

6   Theodore Vestal, *International Education: Its History and Value for Today* (Westport, CT: Praeger, 1994); Robert Sylvester, 'Mapping International Education: A Historical Survey 1893–1944', *Journal of Research in International Education* 1, no. 1 (2002): 90–125; Ian Hill, 'Evolution of Education for International Mindedness', *Journal of Research in International Education* 11, no. 3 (2012): 245–61; Joëlle Droux and Rita Hofstetter, eds, *Border-Crossing in Education: Historical Perspectives on Transnational Connections and Circulations* (London: Routledge, 2016).

7   Sandi Cooper, *Patriotic Pacifism: Waging War on War in Europe, 1815–1914* (New York: Oxford University Press, 1991), 78–80.

8   Ian Harris and Mary Lee Morrison, *Peace Education*, 3rd edn (Jefferson, NC: McFarland, 2013), 11.

9   Bureau international de la Paix, *Bulletin officiel du XIVe Congrès Universel de la Paix, tenu à Lucerne du 19 au 23 septembre 1905* (Bern: Büchner, 1905), 23.

10   Bureau international de la Paix, *Bulletin officiel du XIVe Congrès Universel de la Paix*, 131–2.

11   Bureau international de la Paix, *Bulletin officiel du XVe Congrès Universel de la Paix, tenu à Milan du 15 au 22 septembre 1906* (Bern: Büchner, 1906), 155. One 'international university' proposal features in the annexe (195–7).

12   Robert Rotberg, *A Leadership for Peace: How Edwin Ginn Tried to Change the World* (Stanford, CA: Stanford University Press, 2007), 112.

13   Rotberg, *A Leadership for Peace*, 107–17.

14   Regarding the Cosmopolititan Clubs, and funding by Edwin Ginn and Andrew Carnegie for them, see ibid. 101.

15   David Patterson, *The Search for a Negotiated Peace: Women's Activism and Citizen Diplomacy in World War I* (New York: Routledge, 2008), 2–3.

16   Henri La Fontaine, *The Greatest Solution – Magnissima Charta: Essay on Evolutionary and Constructive Pacifism* (Boston, MA: World Peace Foundation, 1916).

17   Louis Lochner, 'Les Clubs Cosmopolites', *La Vie Internationale* 1, no. 3 (1912): 371–5.

18   W. Boyd Rayward, *The Universe of Information: The Work of Paul Otlet for Documentation and International Organisation* (Moscow: VINITI, 1975), 34.

19   Kaat Wils and Anne Rasmussen, 'Sociology in a Transnational Perspective: Brussels, 1890–1925', *Revue Belge de Philologie et d'Histoire* 90, no. 4 (2012): 1280–3.

20   'Les Études et l'Enseignement International', in *Annuaire de la Vie Internationale 1910–1911* (Brussels: Office Central des Associations Internationales, 1911), 127.

21   Henri La Fontaine and Paul Otlet, 'La Deuxième Session du Congrès Mondial', *La Vie Internationale* 3, no. 14 (1912): 511.

22   Tomás Irish, *The University at War, 1914–25: Britain, France and the United States* (Basingstoke: Palgrave, 2015), 2.

23   Irish, *The University at War, 1914–25*.

24   Paul Otlet, *Les Problèmes internationaux et la guerre* (Geneva and Paris: Librairie Kundig and Rousseau & Cie, 1916), 252–335. The concept of an 'international university' features on pages 296–7.

25   For post-war tensions between universalism and nationalism in one major body, the International Council of Scientific Unions, see Geert Somsen, 'Universalism in Action: Ideals and Practices of International Scientific Cooperation', in *European Encounters: Intellectual Exchange and the Rethinking of Europe, 1914–1945*, ed. Carlos Reijnen and Marleen Rensen (Amsterdam: Rodopi, 2014), 123–37.

26   'Université Internationale: éclaircissements', note 30 May 1921, in Folder PP PO 224, Mundaneum, Mons.

27   Akira Iriye, *Cultural Internationalism and World Order* (Baltimore, MD: Johns Hopkins University Press, 1997), 73. See also Tomás Irish, 'Peace through History? The Carnegie Endowment for International Peace's Inquiry into European Schoolbooks, 1921–1924', *History of Education* 45, no. 1 (2016): 38–56.

28   Eckhardt Fuchs, 'The Creation of New International Networks in Education: The League of Nations and Educational Organizations in the 1920s', *Pedagogica Historica* 43, no. 2 (2007): 199–209.

29   Katherine Storr, 'Thinking Women: International Education for Peace and Equality, 1918–1930', in *Women, Education and Agency, 1600–2000*, ed. Jean Spence, Sarah Aiston and Maureen Meikle (Abingdon: Routledge, 2010), 168–86.

30   Chay Brooks, 'The Apostle of Internationalism: Stephen Duggan and the Geopolitics of International Education', *Political Geography* 49 (2015): 64–73.

31 Katharina Rietzler, 'From Peace Advocacy to International Relations Research: The Transformation of Transatlantic Philanthropic Networks, 1900–1930', in *Shaping the Transnational Sphere*, ed. Rodogno et al., 186.

32 Rietzler, 'From Peace Advocacy to International Relations Research', 187.

33 Georgina Brewis, *A Social History of Student Volunteering: Britain and Beyond, 1880–1980* (New York: Palgrave, 2014).

34 UIA, *Organisation internationale du travail intellectuel* (Brussels: UIA, 1921), 8.

35 'Organizing World's Intellectual Work: Union of International Association at Brussels Comprises 230 Members', *The New York Times*, 3 October 1921.

36 UIA, *Sur la Création de l'Université Internationale* (Brussels: UIA, 1920), 11.

37 UIA, *Sur la Création de l'Université Internationale*, 5 and 10.

38 Ibid., 17.

39 'Note no. 5555. 1927-05-2. Université Internationale. Cycle d'exposés fondamentaux', in box HLF 225, Mundaneum.

40 Glenda Sluga, *Internationalism in the Age of Nationalism* (Philadelphia, PA: University of Pennsylvania Press, 2013).

41 UIA, *Annuaire de l'Université Internationale 1922: Status – Programme – Organisation – Sessions* (Brussels: Palais Mondial, 1922), 3, 17.

42 'Université Internationale. IVme session: 15–30 juillet 1927' in box HLF 225, Mundaneum.

43 UIA, *Sur la Création de l'Université Internationale*, 10 and 12.

44 UIA , *Université Internationale: Cours et Conférence annoncés. Supplémet du 30 juillet au Programme du 3 juillet* (Brussels: UIA, 1920). 1. The following year, the number of such chairs rose to 23: UIA, *Annuaire de l'Université Internationale 1922*, 3.

45 Rayward, *The Universe of Information*, 225.

46 Ibid., 234–8. See also note 'L'Université Internationale et la Société des Nations', 1921, in box PP PO 224, Mundaneum.

47 'Programme des Cours et Conférences de la IIe Quinzaine', *La Vie Internationale* 6, no. 1 (1921): 153–7.

48 Account of the theosophical congress, including repeated references to Wadia's involvement, feature in no. 43 of the periodical *Le Message Théosophique et Social* (7 August 1924).

49 Rabindranath Tagore, 'Appel en faveur d'une Université Internationale' (brochure) in box PP PO 224, Mundaneum. Two French translations of texts by Tagore – 'L'Alliance de l'Orient et de l'Occident' and 'L'Avenir de l'Inde' – also featured in the International University files. On Visva-Bharati, see Kumkum Bhattacharya, *Rabindranath Tagore: Adventure of Ideas and Innovative Practices in Education* (Cham and Heidelberg: Springer, 2014), 57–74.

50 Margaret J. Phillips, 'A Critique of the Idea of World University', *Higher Education in Europe* 14, no. 3 (1989): 73.

51 Paul Otlet, 'Les Noirs et la Société des Nations', *La Patrie Belge*, 19 January 1919.

52 Paul Otlet to W. E. B. Du Bois, 20 April 1921, in W. E. B. Du Bois Papers, Series 1A. General Correspondence [hereafter: Du Bois Papers], in Special Collections and University Archives, University of Massachusetts Amherst Libraries. Available online: http://credo.library.umass.edu (accessed 26 July 2018).

53 'Programme des Cours et Conférences', 155; 'Calendrier-Horaire de la Quinzaine Internationale', *La Vie Internationale* 6, no. 1 (1922): 148–9.

54 Jessie Fauset, 'Impressions of the Second Pan-African Congress', *The Crisis* 23, no. 1 (1921): 14.

55 W. E. B. Du Bois, *The World and Africa: An Inquiry into the Part Which Africa Has Played in World History*, new edn (New York: International Publishers, [1947] 1965), 237.
56 Paul Panda Farnana to Du Bois, 31 May 1921 and 'Sur le Congrès Pan Africain: Suggestion de M. Paul Otlet', 3 June 1921, Du Bois Papers.
57 Du Bois to Otlet, 12 July 1921, Du Bois Papers.
58 UIA, *Annuaire de l'Université Internationale 1922*, 3.
59 Rita Hofstetter and Bernard Schneuwly, 'The International Bureau of Education (1925–1968): A Platform for Designing a "Chart of World Aspirations for Education"', *European Educational Research Journal* 12, no. 2 (2013): 215–30.
60 UIA, *Sur la Création de l'Université Internationale*, 8.
61 'Assemblée de l'Université Internationale', 26 August 1921 in box PP PO 224, Mundaneum.
62 'La Séance Russe', *La Vie Internationale* 6, no. 1 (1922): 177.
63 Marc Raeff, *Russia Abroad: A Cultural History of the Russian Emigration 1919–1939* (New York: Oxford University Press, 1990), 60–1.
64 'La Séance Russe', 178. On this library, see Alfred Erich Senn, 'Nikolai Rubakin's Library for Revolutionaries', *Slavic Review* 32, no. 3 (1973): 554–9.
65 For earlier instances of collaboration, see Rayward, *The Universe of Information*, 284. In 1922, Rubakin dedicated his large-scale *Introduction à la psychologie bibliologique* to Otlet (together with Adolphe Ferrière).
66 Daniel Laqua, 'Activism in the "Students' League of Nations": International Student Politics and Confédération Internationale des Étudiants', *The English Historical Review* 132, no. 556 (2017): 605–37.
67 UIA, *L'Université Internationale*, 6.
68 Julius Ernst Lips, *Die internationale Studentenbewegung nach dem Kriege ('La Confédération Internationale des Etudiants')* (Leizpig: Verlag Vivos Voco, 1921), 36.
69 Lips, *Die internationale Studentenbewegung nach dem Kriege*, 55–6.
70 CIE, *1922 Annuaire publiée par l'Office Centrale de la Confédération Internationale des Étudiants* (Ghent: Maison d'Éditions et d'Impressions, 1922), 24. See also 'Compte-rendu de la réunion de Bruxelles', *Le Monde Universitaire* (March 1921), 11.
71 UIA, *Annuaire de l'Université Internationale 1922*, 13.
72 National Union of Students of the Universities and University Colleges of England and Wales, *Report of the C.I.E. Council at The Hague, January 15–20, 1923* (London: NUS, 1923), 24.
73 Letters from the CIE to Halecki, 17 September 1923 and 16 October 1923 in folder PP PO 24/2 PO2 ('Palais Mondial 1924–25'), Mundaneum. See also Oskar Halecki, *Le Problème de l'Université Internationale: Rapport préliminaire soumis à la Commission de Coopération Intellectuelle (Sous-Commission Universitaire)*, 5 in 13 C, dossier 28370, doc. 34985, League of Nations Archives, United Nations Organization, Geneva (UNOG).
74 Ludmila Genttnerová, 'Clôture de la Troisième Quinzaine', 2 September 1922, in box PP PO 224, Mundaneum.
75 On the Maison des Étudiantes, see *Université de Bruxelles 1909–1934* (Brussels: Liber Memorialis, 1934), 226–7.
76 Letter from Giovanni Boccardi, Osservatorio Astronomico dell'Universita di Torino, 18 September 1922, in box PP PO 224, Mundaneum.
77 UIA, *Sur la Création de l'Université Internationale*, 5, 10 and 12; UIA, *L'Université Internationale*, 3.

78 UIA, *L'Université Internationale*, 4.

79 'Programme des Cours et Conférences', 153–7.

80 Rayward, *The Universe of Information*, 254.

81 'Palais Mondial. IIIe Quinzaine Internationale. Bruxelles 20 août – 3 September 1922' [bulletin no. 3 (17 August 1922), in box PP PO 224], Mundaneum.

82 Clarence Owens to Paul Otlet, 3 September 1922, in box PP PO 224, Mundaneum. On the mission that Owens formed part of, see 'Une importante mission commerciale américaine en Belgique', *L'Indépendance Belge*, 1 September 1922.

83 Letters by Clarence Owens of 1 December 1922 and 9 June 1923, in box PP PO 224, Mundaneum.

84 'Report of the International Trade Commission of the Southern Commercial Congress', *Congressional Record, Sixty-Seventh Congress, Fourth Session, 25 January 1923*, 10.

85 Charles Tardieu, 'L'Université internationale', *Le Figaro*, 20 July 1922.

86 Tardieu, 'L'Université internationale'. On Belgian foreign policy and internationalism, see Madeleine Herren, *Hintertüren zur Macht: Internationalismus und modernisierungsorientierte Außenpolitik in Belgien, der Schweiz und den USA 1865–1914* (Munich: Oldenbourg, 2000).

87 Barthélemy Raynaud, 'L'Université Internationale', *Journal du Droit International* 49 (1922): 205.

88 Rayward, *The Universe of Information*, 298.

89 Jean-Jacques Renoliet, *L'Unesco oubliée: la Société des nations et la coopération intellectuelle, 1919–1946* (Paris: Publications de la Sorbonne, 1999). See also Daniel Laqua, 'Transnational Intellectual Cooperation, the League of Nations, and the Problem of Order', *Journal of Global History* 6, no. 2 (2011): 223–47.

90 Cited in Zweig, *The Idea of a World University*, 33.

91 Letter by Paul Otlet, 7 September 1923, no. 13/30886/28370, in 'Université Internationale' (R1056), UNOG.

92 Halecki, *Le Problème d l'Université Internationale*, 2.

93 Dossier 28370 (see note 90) contains the responses from different governments.

94 Zweig, *The Idea of a World University*, 38.

95 'Programmes des Cours et Conférences', 153 and 157; UIA, *Annuaire de l'Université internationale 1922*, 32–42.

96 Zweig, *The Idea of a World University*, 45.

97 Ibid., 50.

98 John Eugene Harley, *International Understanding: Agencies Educating for a New World* (Stanford, CA: Stanford University Press, 1931), 238–50.

99 Daniel Gorman, *The Emergence of International Society in the 1920s* (Cambridge: Cambridge University Press, 2012), 193.

100 Leaflet 'Students' International Union' (1925), 13, in Subject File 'Youth/Students: Organizations N (ctd.) – S', Swarthmore Peace Collection, Swarthmore College.

101 Helen McCarthy, *The British People and the League of Nations: Democracy, Citizenship and Internationalism, c. 1918–1945* (Manchester: Manchester University Press, 2011).

102 Educational Institute of Scotland/World Federation of Education Associations, *World Education: proceedings of the first biennial conference of the World Federation of Education Associations held at Edinburgh, July 20 to July 27, 1925* (Edinburgh: World Federation of Education Associations, 1925), 412–21.

103 Patricia Clavin, 'Conceptualising Internationalism between the World Wars', in *Internationalism Reconfigured: Transnational Ideas and Movements between the World Wars*, ed. Daniel Laqua (London: I.B. Tauris, 2011), 1–14.

104 John Hellman, *The Communitarian Third Way: Alexandre Marc and Ordre Nouveau* (Montreal and Kingston: McGill-Queen's University Press, 2002).

105 Ferdinand Kinsky, 'In Memoriam: Alexandre Marc', *Publius* 30, no. 4 (2000): 169–72.

106 Alexandre Marc, 'Mission of an International University', *International Social Science Bulletin* 4, no. 1 (1952): 225–9.

107 Marc, 'Mission of an International University', 225.

108 Ibid., 226.

109 Jean-Francis Billon, 'The World Federalist Movements from 1945 to 1954 and European Integration', *The Federalist* 33, no. 1 (1991): 26–53.

110 Mark Mazower, *Governing the World: The History of an Idea* (London: Penguin, 2012), 233. On the debates of the Chicago Committee to Frame a World Constitution, see Or Rosenboim, *The Emergence of Globalism: Visions of World Order in Britain and the United States, 1939–1950* (Princeton, NJ: Princeton University Press, 2017), 168–208.

111 Zweig, *The Idea of a World University*, ciii and 31.

112 Ibid., 8.

113 Ibid., 74–7.

114 Ibid., 60.

115 Elise Boulding, *Building a Global Civic Culture: Education for an Interdependent World* (Syracuse, NY: Syracuse University Press, 1990), xvi. Boulding explicitly mentions Zweig's involvement and his later book in *Children's Rights and the Wheels of Life* (New Brunswick, NJ: Transaction Publishers, 1979), 39.

116 Bruce Lambert, 'Harold Taylor, Novel Educator and College President, Dies at 78', *The New York Times*, 10 February 1993.

117 Harold Taylor, 'Foreword' in Zweig, *The Idea of a World University*, vi.

118 Gene Maeroff, 'Japan in Big Offer for a UN College', *The New York Times*, 25 November 1973.

119 Harold Taylor, 'A University for the World', *The Phi Delta Kappan* 56, no. 1 (1974): 39.

120 Boulding, *Building a Global Civic Culture*, xvi.

121 Article 1 of the Charter of the United Nations University; adopted by the UN General Assembly on 6 December 1973 [resolution 3081 XXVIII].

122 Taylor, 'A University for the World', 41.

123 United Nations University, *2016 Annual Report* (Tokyo: UNU, 2017), 11 and 23.

124 United Nations University, *2016 Annual Report*, 25.

125 *Charter of the University of Peace*, Article 2, as featured in International Agreement for the Establishment of the University for Peace, based on resolution 35/55 of the General Assembly of the United Nations, 5 December 1980.

126 University for Peace website, https://www.upeace.org (accessed 10 April 2018).

127 *University for Peace: Report of the Secretary-General*, United Nations General Assembly, A/70/288, 5 August 2015.

128 Albert Castel, review of Michael Zweig, *The Idea of a World University*, in *History of Education Quarterly* 7, no. 4 (1967): 544.

129 Phillips, 'A Critique of the Idea of World University', 73.

Chapter 4

CARVING OUT A NEW ROLE: THE UIA
AFTER THE SECOND WORLD WAR

Nico Randeraad and Philip Post

After the death of its founders Henri La Fontaine in 1943 and Paul Otlet in 1944, it was uncertain whether the Union of International Associations would be able to resume its activities once the Second World War had ended. The only concrete step was the installation of Otlet's lawyer, Jules Polain, as provisional administrator in May 1945. La Fontaine's bequest provided funds to relaunch the Union, but there was no apparent urgency to spend the money. On the contrary, the court order appointing Polain contained the possibility of a total liquidation of the organization.[1]

The tide turned in the spring of 1948, after the Economic and Social Council of the United Nations (ECOSOC) commissioned UN official Lyman C. White to promote the participation of non-governmental organizations (NGOs). As part of his activities, White paid a visit to Brussels, where he sought to convince Polain and his associates that the Union could occupy a special place in the new global order of international organizations. He urged them to launch a new international journal and suggested that financial support from the United States might be available. Within a few months, the Union was brimming with initiatives. Four hundred questionnaires were dispatched to international associations. Georges Patrick Speeckaert was taken on as secretary and sent to America to lobby for the Union. In January 1949, the UIA's first *Monthly Bulletin* – featuring the recurrent promotional reference: 'founded in 1910' – was published.

It was clear that White's suggestions were taken seriously and greatly helped to revive the UIA. It proved, however, difficult for the Union to integrate effectively into the transnational scene of the post-war years. Whereas in this period, as Akira Iriye argues, transnationalism 'was being fortified with a strong organizational base', the Union struggled to acquire a sound financial basis and to find its place among the growing number of international (non-governmental) organizations.[2] The central aim of this chapter, therefore, is to find out why the UIA had such difficulties in (re-)establishing itself as a hub of international non-governmental organizations after the Second World War.

This core question leads us to take an inside-out view of the Union, reviewing its various initiatives and evaluating the role of the organization's leadership, but also to scrutinize – outside-in – the constraints that the national and international environment imposed on the Union. Our account, in other words, is a multisited, transnational history in which the UIA's institutional development, the interests of the Belgian state, the structuring effects of ECOSOC and the half-hearted response of private American foundations are the main topics. Between the end of the Second World War and the summer of 1948, the UIA was waiting to be brought back to life. Once it had regained strength, the Cold War had taken a firm grip on Europe and the world. This worked out badly for the UIA, which tended to portray its endeavours as apolitical and scientific. In the early post-war period, the UIA had neither the means nor the passion to enter into special relations with the countries behind the Iron Curtain. More generally, its contacts beyond the West were mostly indirect. It only established more effective collaborations with what has become known as the Global South after decolonization had gained ground.

The chapter first locates this case within the historiography of post-war internationalism. It then zooms in on the formative years 1948–52 when the Union reconstructed itself amid a parade of national and international actors, both individuals and organizations. We pay particular attention to the organization's quest for money. Finally, we highlight publications through which the Union tried to push history and science as allegedly neutral vehicles for its larger objectives. In the conclusion, we suggest that the difficulties facing the Union in the late 1940s and early 1950s had lasting effects on the 'survival journey' of the organization up until today.

Internationalism Revisited

A focus on internationalism bears the temptation to highlight success and concord across borders, yet it cannot ignore undeniable setbacks. The present-day world is, after all, hardly the utopia some internationalists had in mind for the 'peoples of all nations'. Rather than merrily write about the virtues of cooperation and doing-good, historians increasingly speak of alternative internationalisms – a heading that also covers non-liberal and 'dark' varieties.[3]

The UIA's re-appearance of the Union from 1948 onwards is an interesting case in this historiographical reorientation. Just as it was difficult for the Union to create a role for itself after the Second World War, it is not easy for scholars to place the Union now. It is remarkably absent from the old and new histories of post-war internationalism, except perhaps as the producer of knowledge about these organizations.[4] It clearly does not belong to the class of alternative, non-liberal internationalisms recent scholarship has focused on. However, whereas the Union's goals were firmly embedded in liberal-democratic ideas about global order, it was unable to benefit from the boom of reformist transnational activities in the late 1940s. This 'new internationalism', aptly described by Iriye, was characterized by the proliferation of international organizations, many of which were non-governmental, dealing with cultural exchange, peace, human rights, environmentalism and developmental assistance, while helping to forge a global community.[5] The UIA related to all of this, but only at a secondary level. Since its birth, it had wanted to be an information centre for what with the UN Charter came to be known as international 'non-governmental organizations'. Following the conventional definition of the term, the Union itself is also an NGO but, while transnational single-issue organizations and movements mushroomed after the war, the Union itself struggled to survive.

Researchers have emphasized different aspects when evaluating the nature of post-war internationalism. The Union does not play a prominent role in any of these accounts, but its vicissitudes speak to all of these scholarly perspectives. Akira Iriye has sensitized us to the importance of transnational relations, especially of persons, ideas, memories and cultures, as distinct from international relations and national interests in the traditional sense.[6] In his recent history of NGOs, Thomas Davies has highlighted a 'complex but broadly cyclical pattern of evolution' of transnational civil society from the Second World War until the present day.[7] Mark Mazower has underlined American realism with regard to international institutions such as the UN.[8] Glenda Sluga has brought back nationalism and national interests into the history of internationalism.[9] Wolfram Kaiser and Kiran Klaus Patel have called for taking into account 'multiple connections' when studying cooperation and competition among international organizations and NGOs in post-war Western Europe.[10]

When applying these lenses to the UIA, its precarious position becomes all the more evident. It was one of the many transnational organizations trying to carve out a role in an international order that saw the advance of the UN but was dominated by the United States. The Union sought to consolidate its political and juridical position by obtaining consultative status with ECOSOC, but remained toothless in the face of the hardening Cold War. In order to secure its finances, representatives of the Union came knocking on quite a few doors of affluent American foundations. At home, the Belgian state proved to be a rather unreliable supporter of the UIA. Whereas prominent politicians recognized the importance of keeping its headquarters in Brussels, the Union often came away empty-handed when asking for additional funding or suitable accommodation.

'Follow the actors' is one of the methodological directives that has emerged from the literature on transnational history. With no apparent interconnection, a similar approach has made an appearance in the study of NGOs in international relations (IR) literature. DeMars and Dijkzeul, for example, have sought to better understand the politics and practice of NGOs and, thereby, renew IR theory. Whereas we are less concerned with fine-tuning IR theory, we gratefully make use of their methodological imperative to 'follow the partners' (although we prefer 'actors') and of the interlinked conceptual touchstones: practice, bridging and power.[11] Through the practice of finding and connecting actors and by forming networks, NGOs try to bridge divides in world politics, such as the division between state and society, public and private, the national and international sphere and normative and material aspects of power dynamics. Without aspiring to accomplishing the entire research agenda of these IR scholars, we use their core concepts to write a critical history of the UIA in the immediate post-war period.

Accordingly, we follow a number of actors from within and outside the Union in the crucial period between 1948 and 1952. We foreground their hopes, aims, journeys and meetings in order to understand what they were achieving through their interactions or, at least as frequently, what they did *not* accomplish. 'Bridging', for that matter, is always a tentative endeavour, sometimes leading to increasing power but often also to failure. For our multisited history, we rely on multiple sources. The Union's publications are clearly not sufficient to understand what happened behind the scenes. In order to study the practices of international relations in and around the Union, we gratefully used the archives of the Union in Brussels. This allowed us to follow the activities of its long-term secretary-general Georges Patrick Speeckaert. We also gained better insight into the involvement of other protagonists, notably Paul van Zeeland and Aake Ording, through their personal archives in Louvain-la-Neuve and Oslo, and Oskar Leimgruber through the Swiss Federal Archives in Bern. It is plausible, of course, that relevant information about other actors is available in archives around the world.[12]

High Hopes and (Mildly) Bitter Fruits

During 1946–7, several Brussels-based international organizations – including the International Institute of Administrative Sciences and the (soon to be renamed) International Colonial Institute – resumed their activities. The ideas sustaining these bodies had remained vivid in various countries during the war, and their agendas seemed more pressing than that of the UIA, which needed an external impetus to get things going. The incentive for the UIA came from the UN, which in 1946 started to attend to the matter of consultative status of NGOs as stipulated by Article 71 of the UN Charter. This article enabled NGOs to participate in the activities of the UN and thereby enhanced their prominence in international relations. In May 1948, the first general conference of NGOs having consultative status with the UN was held in Geneva. The Union was conspicuous by its absence, which must have surprised Lyman C. White, then secretary of the NGO committee of ECOSOC.

White had obtained his PhD in 1933 from Columbia University, having written a doctoral thesis on 'The Structure of Private International Organizations' and devoted a few pages of his study to the Union. He had studied at the Graduate Institute of International Studies in Geneva in 1929–30 and, since then, had spent longer periods in Europe.[13] As he wrote in his thesis, the Union 'had practically ceased to exist as an organization grouping international organizations together' by the early 1930s.[14] He did, however, warmly welcome the UIA's purpose of furthering cooperation among international organizations, and mentioned that he would return to this subject matter 'in some later work'.[15] Back in 1933 he could hardly have foreseen that twelve years later – in a very different world – he would embark on a career in the Secretariat of the UN and directly affect the future of the Union.

In 1948, as secretary of ECOSOC's committee on NGOs, one of the organizations he talked to was the UIA, by then hardly more than an echo from the past. The founding fathers had deceased, and their successors did not know what course of action was most advisable in the new global order. White, however, understood the UIA's potential function as *trait d'union* for NGOs around the world. For the Union, White's visit was a wake-up call. On 28 July 1948, Jules Polain – in his capacity as the UIA's interim administrator – convened a provisional executive committee to resume its activities.

The composition of the Provisional Committee reveals that in 1948 the Union still largely relied on ideals from the past. The committee members were in their late fifties or older, and mostly represented the scientific internationalism of the interwar period. Polain (1892–1951) himself was an attorney in Brussels who had been active in the Centre Belge d'Études et de Documentation, established in 1941 to anticipate the end of German occupation and the post-war recovery of Belgium.[16] He was well connected to influential circles in Brussels that pursued strategies confirming or even bolstering the place of the Belgian capital in the world.[17] He asked the former Belgian prime minister Paul van Zeeland (1893–1973) to chair the committee, while Count de Jonghe d'Ardoye accepted to be interim secretary-general. Other committee members were prominent representatives of international organizations that, like the Union, had already established a seat in Brussels before the war. Octave Louwers (1878–1959) was secretary-general of the International Colonial Institute. Former Minister of Foreign Affairs and now ambassador Fernand Muûls (1892–1981) was a member of the Institute of International Law and the Institute of International Relations. Emile Vinck (1870–1950) was secretary-general of International Union of Local Authorities, whose earlier cooperation with the UIA is discussed in Wouter Van Acker's chapter. Edmond Lesoir (1874–1966) was secretary-general of the International Institute of Administrative Sciences, of which the only foreigner on the committee, chancellor of the Swiss Federation Oskar Leimgruber (1886–1976), was president.

New élan was needed to carry out the programme of rejuvenating the Union. First of all, Polain and Van Zeeland secured the support of the municipality of Brussels so that they could take up residence in the Egmont Palace, a prestigious building (today housing the Belgian Ministry of Foreign Affairs) where the organization would stay until the end of the 1950s. More importantly, Georges Patrick Speeckaert was recruited to serve as head of the secretariat. For a while, he combined this function with administrative secretary of the International Colonial Institute. In 1952, he was appointed to the higher-status role of UIA secretary-general – a position he would retain until 1970. Speeckaert, a devout Catholic, had studied law in Louvain, had been a prisoner of war in Germany, and had been active in the Resistance movement. As head of the Department of Social Services of the Red Cross, he had been committed to the rebuilding of Belgium after the war.[18]

Speeckaert's priority was finding domestic and international support for the UIA's activities. The preliminary planning included drawing up an inventory of its archives, preparing the revival of the *Annuaire de la Vie Internationale* (which would become the *Yearbook of International Organizations*), publishing a *Monthly Bulletin*, providing a calendar of international meetings and organizing a survey among international organizations. In order to secure continuity, the UIA needed to acquire new funds, but more importantly, it also had to formalize its relationship with the UN in order to be recognized as a player in the new international system. Everything, in short, depended on money and status. Annoyingly for the Union, the two were closely connected: when in November 1948 Speeckaert undertook a journey to Paris to meet Howard E. Wilson of the Carnegie Endowment for International Peace and then president of the Interim Committee of Consultative Non-Governmental Organizations (established by ECOSOC), in order to discuss possible financial support, he was told that a decision would only be taken once the Interim Committee had reached a conclusion about its consultative arrangement with the UN.[19] Without some form of UN recognition, it would be very hard to convince important foundations to make donations to the Union.

After his visit to Paris in November 1948, Speeckaert travelled to Geneva in December, accompanied by Polain, talking to representatives of the UN and non-governmental organizations. It became clear that they had better not beat the big drum. Bertram Pickard, attached to the Liaison Section Non-Governmental Organizations of the European Office of the UN, was not convinced that this was the right moment for the Union to start spreading its wings. He recommended that Speeckaert and Polain wait for the final report of the Interim Committee. In a note of December 1948, Pickard more forthrightly stated:

> The fact that the Union which had made so promising a start before World War I proved unable to fill this role between the World Wars suggests that a Centre in Brussels probably could not now be effective for this general purpose [i.e. general cooperation among NGOs]. In any case, this question of general cooperation between NGOs is already under careful consideration by the Interim Committee and it is important that no similar initiative be taken which would complicate this study.[20]

Pickard's note ended with the suggestion that the Union should not seek to become a representative body for international cooperation, but rather a study and publication centre independent from individual NGOs. As founding father and director of the Federation of Semi-Official and Private International Institutions Established in Geneva, Pickard was hardly a neutral observer, as his organization in some way constituted a rival to the Union. Yet his view carried weight in ECOSOC circles, and he eventually convinced others, including the UIA's cadre, to follow his line of reasoning. White too had to acknowledge that a cautious strategy was the more promising option, and that the Union had better concentrate on a role as service and information centre, as he wrote in a letter to Speeckaert in December 1948.[21]

Speeckaert kept close track of the developments within the Interim Committee. In the spring of 1949 he travelled to America to attend meetings of the committee at Lake Success in New York (where between 1946 and 1951 the headquarters of the UN was located). Wilson allowed Speeckaert to sit in on the meetings and to share the Union's views. Speeckaert understood what was expected and pointed out that, for the time being, the Union would limit its activities to 'documentation, information, study and publication'.[22] His talks with other UN representatives and members of NGOs in New York reinforced his opinion that the Union would have to develop into some kind of secretariat *for* NGOs rather than an official federation *of* NGOs.

The Interim Committee and the Union held each other in a tight grip: the Union felt ill-advised to step off the beaten track, whereas the committee was gradually drawn into the idea that it had to give the Union at least some sort of recognition. The two years following the Lake Success meeting were dominated by a carefully orchestrated negotiation process towards granting the Union consultative status with ECOSOC, which formally took effect on 18 September 1951.

At the second general conference of consultative NGOs (29 June to 2 July 1949), held in Geneva, Speeckaert and Polain got to know Aake Ording of Norway, who had prepared a personal memorandum on relations between NGOs. Later in July, Ording came to Brussels for an unofficial meeting with Speeckaert, Polain and Van Zeeland, and was joined by Howard Wilson of the Interim Committee, Max Habicht and Anne Winslow who, like Ording, had undertaken a study of the consultative process and inter-organization relationships of NGOs. Baron Hervé de Gruben, secretary-general of the Belgian Ministry of Foreign Affairs was also present, underlining the weight the Belgian government attached to manoeuvring the Union on the right track. The meeting focused on figuring out how a reorientation of the Union might result in an international service centre for and about NGOs – a plan that had been taking shape in Ording's head.

Between July 1949 and the end of 1950, the Union worked on updating its statutes from 1920, aligning its mission and organization with the post-war reality. At the General Assembly of February 1951, its official name became 'Union of International Associations. Service Centre for International Non-Governmental Organizations', which confirmed the approach laid out by the Interim Committee and Ording.[23] In the meantime, ECOSOC had rewarded the Union with some sort of formal recognition by expressing its 'appreciation of the value and usefulness of the *Yearbook of International Organizations* published by the Union of International Associations'.[24] More importantly, it decided not to give further consideration to the publication by the UN itself of a handbook concerning NGOs, thereby giving the Union – for the time being – a monopoly of this anchor-hold for its activities.

Despite the good news about the *Yearbook* and the promise of consultative status, the Union could have hoped to gain more from the Interim Committee. A section of Habicht and Winslow's report for the Interim Committee was withdrawn before the third general conference of consultative NGOs in June 1950. It was no accident that this was exactly the part dealing with an international service centre. Apparently, there were fears in Geneva that too close a collaboration between the

Interim Committee, the international NGOs and the Union in Brussels would weaken the central role intended for ECOSOC in the implementation of Article 71. It was fine for the UIA to get a piece of the cake, but evidently not more than that.[25]

For the UIA, international recognition was conducive to obtaining funding from the Belgian government. Although its relationship with the Belgian government had never been smooth, it was clear that the Union would not survive without state subsidies. Moreover, as the Union's supporters never tired of repeating, the organization greatly contributed to the international reputation of Brussels, which had suffered dramatically from the German occupation. La Fontaine's legacy and a few private donations helped to defray the costs of the Union's re-establishment, but if it had not been for a subsidy of 300,000 Belgian francs in 1950 – 65 per cent of the total budget in that year – the Union would have probably gone under.[26] Over the years that followed, the Belgian state continued to subsidize the Union, even though the amount slowly decreased and by the end of the 1950s its contribution to the overall resources was less than 10 per cent.

The Quest for International Funding

Although the Belgian government helped to keep the Union going in the early 1950s, the UIA aimed to stand on its own feet. Once the path to consultative status was sufficiently passable, the question of funding took centre stage. When Lyman White visited Brussels in 1948, he had already pointed to American resources that in his opinion could be tapped. Given the lack of investment capital in Europe for international non-governmental projects, it seemed indeed smart to try the transatlantic route. Ording thought he could play a key role in this quest for money. During the Second World War, he had spent much time in London, first as secretary to the board of directors of the Bank of Norway, then as division head of the Norwegian ministry of Supply and Reconstruction. In that capacity, he became involved in the UN Relief and Rehabilitation Administration (UNRRA). In 1947, he was appointed director of the United Nations Appeal for Children. Ording was therefore well versed in UN-coordinated international cooperation, when in 1949 the Interim Committee asked him to conduct a study on the relations between NGOs. His idea to create a service centre for international NGOs seemed to match the profile the Union had already begun to promote.

Below the surface, however, tensions and hostilities between Ording and the Union staff were simmering from the start. In his report for the Interim Committee, which Ording completed in May 1949 – so before meeting Speeckaert and others – he had not set high hopes for the Union. 'The Second World War', he wrote, 'destroying parts of its facilities, meant a serious setback for its work, and its location and limited organizational backing make the Union inadequate to solve alone those problems which have to be faced today.'[27] When, not long thereafter, he got in touch with the Union staff, 'prominent people and experts in the field' warned him against engaging with the organization, which 'was said to be out of date in its methods, too limited in its composition, and with little or no activity since the German occupation of its offices during the war'. Ording himself, however, thought at the time that there was sufficient common ground between them. He expected that 'the weaknesses and the limitations of the UIA as it then existed could be overcome' and that he could render useful services to that end.[28]

Ording strongly believed that the Union would have to raise its ambitions, and that he could be its front man. Even before the meeting of 20 July 1949 in Brussels between the members of the Interim Committee and the Union, he had drafted a rough outline of future cooperation, based on a conversation with Van Zeeland, in which he did not shy away from adding a touch of self-promotion. Whereas he was willing to concede that 'the facilities allready [*sic*] available and the work allready [*sic*] started by the Union' were most useful, they should be greatly increased, 'and that the contact, plans and support developed by Mr. Ording can be most usefull [*sic*] to this end'. He put himself forward as the ideal person to establish 'an international Committee of outstanding individuals' to sponsor and direct the work of the international service centre he had in mind, and 'to make special investigations as to the possibilities of financial support'.[29]

Encouraged by Van Zeeland's apparent support, Ording immediately set to work and began lobbying for his idea of Union wherever he went. He regularly contacted the Brussels headquarters, not so much to receive instructions but rather to lay out his own agenda. In October 1949 he wrote to Van Zeeland from Geneva, complaining that he had understood from Leimgruber – the Swiss member of the Union's Provisional Committee – that the latter was not in favour of trying to raise funds from private sources, exactly the opposite of what Ording had in mind.[30] As evidenced by his next steps, Ording ignored this opinion and continued his efforts to obtain funding, in particular in Scandinavia, if only 'through contributions from institutions and organizations in Norway, Sweden and Denmark to have financed my own work and travel during the next ¾ of a year'.[31]

In this part of the job, he succeeded brilliantly. In September 1950, he proudly sent in an overview of the subsidies he had collected over the past year, featuring sums from the Nobel Prize Committee and the Christian Michelsen Institute.[32] These subsidies were paid directly to Ording, and not to the Union. He assured Polain that every Norwegian Kroner had been used for the benefit of the centre. From the correspondence between Ording, mostly writing from Oslo, and both Speeckaert and Polain in Brussels during the period between September 1949 and October 1950, it appears that the latter two were keen on first settling affairs with the Belgian government (securing funding) and with the Interim Committee (preparing for international status), whereas Ording wanted to move on and immediately establish a sponsoring committee composed of highly reputable politicians. While Speeckaert was sometimes taken aback by Ording's activism, and was afraid that the outside world would think there were two Unions, Ording despaired of ever getting the Brussels base to advance.

Once the dust of the third general conference of consultative NGOs in June 1950 had settled and the support of the Belgian government was secured, Polain, Speeckaert and Van Zeeland became more willing to give Ording a chance. Funds were put aside for an allowance and a travel grant so that he could make his long-awaited journey to the United States. Habicht, who was becoming a trusted adviser of the Union's staff in Brussels, thought that this investment would pay itself back in due time.[33]

Whereas the UN and its agencies were amply funded by the United States, and European states could benefit from American support through the Marshall Plan, the hope of NGOs such as the Union mainly lay with obtaining private funding. In this field, American actors were leading, too. Christophe Verbruggen's chapter in the present volume has noted the UIA's earlier quest for support from the Carnegie Endowment for International Peace. After the Second World War, large philanthropic foundations continued to be an important source for financial backing for civil society efforts. At the same time, as Inderjeet Parmar, John Krige and Ludovic Tournès have shown, they were a key means of extending and consolidating American hegemony during the Cold War.[34] The 'Big Three' foundations (Carnegie, Rockefeller and Ford) were deeply involved in US foreign affairs, international relations, science, and peace and democracy initiatives – in particular if they served American interests. As noted earlier, two representatives of the Carnegie Endowment, Howard Wilson and Anne Winslow, played a prominent role in ECOSOC discussion on its work with NGOs.

Ording's first visit to the United States took place from 18 October to 8 December 1950, in a period of sharp international tension as a result of China's intervention in the Korean War and heavy losses of US and UN troops. He had been made secretary-general of the UIA, side by side with Polain, so that he could act with some authority. The 'most important goal for us to shoot at', was the Ford Foundation, Ording wrote.[35] The Ford Foundation, established in 1936, was about to expand its funding programme and had asked Paul Hoffman to become the new president. Ording happened to have met Hoffman earlier in 1950 in Oslo, when the latter was still the head of the Economic Cooperation Administration, the agency administering the Marshall Plan.

Despite his high hopes regarding the Ford Foundation, Ording visited a large number of UN staff, diplomats, politicians, trade union leaders, professors and businessmen. He had prepared a memorandum on the proposed service centre for international NGOs, emphasizing the importance of these organizations in the development of democracy and in the system of international relations that was taking shape:

> Democracy is the sum total of the activities of innumerable organizations representing all facets of man's life. On the national level this interplay of organized forces has reached a high degree of development. On the international level the development of democracy is contingent on a corresponding international evolution of cooperating social forces and groupings.[36]

He received a lot of well-intended advice and names of other people to get in touch with, but only a few of those he met were willing to talk about money, and all of them were dismissive. Joseph E. Johnson, president of the Carnegie Endowment and Lindsey F. Kimball, vice-president of the Rockefeller Foundation, made it very clear that their organizations had other priorities and that support for the Union was out of the question.

The Ford Foundation therefore seemed like Ording's best shot. He met with Hoffman in New York on 9 November. The future president (his appointment was not yet official) squelched Ording's plans in a few minutes. The Ford Foundation, Hofmann explained, was just then entering upon a strategy study, which was not expected to be completed before mid-1951.[37] And he added that the foundation was not out for exchange of factual information only: 'Propaganda or promotion may not be the right words but ... something of the kind is needed to expand our freedoms.'[38] Whether the UIA would ever be able to deliver on this, he left open, but between the lines he made perfectly clear that it would be difficult for the UIA to fulfil his criteria in the immediate future. The increasing threats of the Cold War required a bolder stance than the UIA was willing to adopt.

Ording, however, remained optimistic. Reflecting on what he had accomplished, he wrote to Brussels that he was 'leaving this country with the feeling that something substantial has really been achieved'. He admitted that he 'was not returning with cash in my pocket', but insisted that he was 'looking for long term and more serious solutions'.[39] In their responses to Ording, Speeckaert and Polain remained confident that his efforts would be rewarded, but they must have felt disillusioned by the poor results. Ording continued to try to get through to Hoffman and 'the American ... psychology in these matters', hoping that the Ford Foundation would eventually come across generously.[40] He did his best to address Hoffman's doubts regarding the UIA, and even alluded to the fear for the outbreak of another major war:

> In this case the program of the Center would need to go outside the limited field of services in techniques, administration and general information within the existing framework of slow growth. A dynamic program would have to be developed, aiming at the promotion of basic common purposes and at making the vast non-governmental structure an efficient means for winning democracy's world struggle for survival.[41]

Awaiting war or peace, Ording paid a visit to Britain to try his luck there. Again, he got in touch with politicians, administrators and businessmen, but he had to admit to Polain that 'the immediate financial results were surely humble indeed'.[42] He also liaised with UNESCO staff in Paris to make sure that their initiatives in the field of knowledge transfer would not cut the ground from under the Union's feet and to find out whether subsidies from its side were possible. As Speeckaert expected, at this early stage the attempts to attract UNESCO funding proved fruitless. The Union did, however, obtain consultative status with UNESCO in 1952.

To top the disappointing news about funding options, a letter of April 1951, from Hoffman himself, informed Ording that the Ford Foundation would not accede to the Union's request:

> Rightly or wrongly, we concluded that our first programs should be limited to projects which are aimed at contributing toward the solutions of crisis situations

in the world. In every case our endeavor is to see that these efforts will be of long-range benefit.

Hoffman kept the door slightly open by promising to have another look at the proposal at a later date, when the foundation's plans would be more fully developed.[43] It was true, on the one hand, that the Ford Foundation initially engaged itself heavily with concrete Cold War issues, in Europe and Asia, and that it prioritized American organizations.[44] On the other hand, the overview of funded projects in 1951 shows that several international organizations in the field of education and research did receive grants.[45] The UIA, however, was not thought to become a key player.

Ording persevered in the face of these setbacks. First of all, he secured some funding for himself from the Norwegian Parliament. Quite bluntly, he wrote to Polain that he was willing to transfer the money to Brussels to cover urgent expenses, but that in that case he would step down to seek employment elsewhere. If he could dispose of the money himself, he would continue his work for the centre.[46] Polain, whose health was failing rapidly, did not have much of a choice. He therefore allowed Ording to plan another visit to the United States. In December 1951, Ording went on another fundraising tour to New York. It appeared that Lyman White had worked out an independent proposal for the establishment of what he called an 'International Organization Service Office in New York City at the Headquarters of the United Nations'.[47] This idea corresponded with a plan that Elisabeth Mann Borgese, youngest daughter of Thomas Mann, had developed to organize a world congress of NGOs. Mann Borgese was involved with her husband, the antifascist exile Giuseppe Antonio Borgese, in the federalist Committee to Frame a World Constitution, and closely connected to Robert M. Hutchins, then associate director of the Ford Foundation.

Although Ording realized that the initiative of White and Mann Borgese might transcend the scope of the service centre he had in mind, he was thrilled by the fact that the Ford Foundation had reappeared on the radar. They sat down to draft a memorandum on the establishment of an INGO Foundation. Even when White stepped out of the project at the last moment, Ording did not waver and called in the help of Habicht, who happened to be in New York. While waiting for a first reaction from the Ford Foundation, Ording continued lobbying for a Union-style service centre, and met with political and business leaders to raise support. Shortly before New Year's Eve he returned to Norway, leaving further negotiations to Habicht.

Upon his return, he received the sad news of Polain's death, which left the Union's leadership in a temporary vacuum. In view of the growing uncertainty about the UIA's future, Ording had accepted a temporary job as member of the Norwegian Delegation to the General Assembly of the UN held in Paris early in 1952. While, for the time being, Ording retained his position as UIA secretary-general, the relations rapidly turned sour. The Ford Foundation declined the proposal of Mann Borgese, Habicht and Ording, which pulled the last plug out of potentially fruitful cooperation between Ording and the Union. Behind the scenes Van Zeeland tried to gather old loyal supporters to create a new basis for the Union. He wrote to Leimgruber that he had understood from Polain that the latter had grave doubts about Ording, owing to the fact that he had made no effective contribution to the Union, and that it became clearer and clearer that his efforts were focused on realizing his personal agenda.[48] Meanwhile, Ording felt that he was being sacrificed for the lack of new subsidies from outside Belgium. 'When things go well', he wrote to Mann Borgese,

> everyone is happy. When an effort fails there is always a need for a scapegoat. And those who are against the whole broader aspect of the NGO work, the congress a.s.o., have now taken the opportunity to launch their attack, based on the failure of the application to the Ford Foundation.[49]

Scapegoat for the Union's inner circle, tragic hero in his own eyes – in the summer of 1952 Ording accepted a position in Norway, and left the Union.

While the dissension between Ording and his colleagues in Brussels became quite personal at times, it boiled down to a fundamental difference of opinion as to what kind of organization the Union should aspire to be. Whereas Ording tried to curry favour with American funders and held that the UIA would have to become more audacious and dare to take a political stance, Speeckaert, Polain and the members of the Executive Committee judged the Union should stick to the role of provider of impartial and 'technical' information. With this, the UIA filled a niche, but not one that would attract a lot of political and financial support. After the rejections for American funding, it was clear to them that the organization should play to its proven strengths.

Advancing Internationalism

The Union was a small organization that had set itself a herculean task. During the years 1948–52 highlighted in this chapter, its Brussels secretariat employed only a few people: a part-time secretary-general, a part-time secretary, and three or four assistants and typists. In 1952, the Union opened offices in Geneva, London and Paris, but these were largely paper constructions staffed by people who had their main employment in other organizations. In Geneva, for example, the job was temporarily done by the lawyer Raoul Lenz, a collaborator of Habicht.

With this relatively small staff, the Union managed to bring off a surprisingly visible output. First and foremost, the *Yearbook of International Organizations*, for which the Union is widely known, neatly fitted in with the strategy of presenting itself primarily as a service centre. It was not always easy to gather the material that was needed for the yearbook, but at least it was an operation that the Union had some experience in and could carry out without having to take an overtly political stance. ECOSOC acknowledged the Union's lead in collecting solid information about NGOs around the world, and was glad not having to organize this from scratch or rely on inaccurate data. In 1948 and 1949 a Swiss editor independently published an *Annuaire des organisations internationales / Yearbook of International Organizations*, but this endeavour met with quite a bit of criticism. The 1950 edition came out in collaboration with the Union, which took full responsibility as from the 1951–2 volume onwards.

In terms of time investment and accountability, the publication of a monthly bulletin was arguably a more arduous task. The bulletin offered a platform to leaders and scholars of international organizations, allowing them to publicize the cause of international cooperation in the post-war world. In one of the first issues, for example, Lyman White made the case for peace 'through the promotion of the common interests of humanity, by organized international action.'[50] These types of appeals were evidently grist to the Union's mill. Through the periodical it hoped to continue pursuing its long-established policy of promoting knowledge transfer for the benefit of international associations and developing an 'international mentality'. The Union was keen to steer clear of politically sensitive issues, and thereby remained faithful to Otlet and La Fontaine's original message of how the exchange of neutral information could by itself lead to peace.

Between 1948 and 1952, two elements stood out in the editorial policy of the bulletin, which echoed the voices of Otlet and La Fontaine: the emphasis on the history of internationalism, in particular of the UIA itself, and the promotion of a science of international exchange. To start with the first, the recurrent reference to the foundation of the Union in 1910 in the header of the *Monthly Bulletin*, was a conscious choice to keep in touch with the origins of the organization. When the Union resumed its activities in mid-1948, the letter it sent to international associations started by highlighting the achievements in the first twenty years of its existence. The *Bulletin*'s first issue also referred to the historical model by explaining the vision of its founders as well as the ongoing relevance of their work. In 1951, the bulletin featured an article by E. A. De Bevere, principal of the International People's College in Denmark and a former collaborator of Otlet and La Fontaine. He held that their ideas had not lost their original significance and that the threat of 'twilight of civilization as we know it' could be averted by international associations, 'the active, dynamic, intellectual, moral and spiritual vanguard of humanity, which in the opinion of the Founders of the Union, they ought to be'.[51] Such high-flown discourse, typical of the international peace movement of the early twentieth century, continued to appeal to Speeckaert and others in the Union's inner circle.

At the same time, the Union needed practical objectives to justify and secure its existence. The ins and outs of international exchange, therefore, became another key field of interest. The *Bulletin* not only published numerous articles about individual NGOs, but also helped to develop a separate science of internationalism. How to organize international (scientific) congresses was an important element therein. One of Speeckaert's first actions as secretary was to systematize the data about international congresses the Union possessed, in order to quantify the advance of international gatherings and thereby prove the urgency of collecting and spreading information. From the first issue, the *Bulletin* included an 'International Congress Calendar', listing the main NGO and scientific congresses in the months to come.

Speeckaert quickly realized that knowledge about organizing international congresses constituted a niche for the Union, which could provide it with a special position in the international arena. As a follow-up to his overview of congresses, he presented a checklist for congress organizers and participants, because despite their diverging themes – as he wrote – 'from an administrative and technical point of view all congresses have a certain number of commonalities'.[52] This continued to be a spearhead of Speeckaert's internationalist agenda. In 1951, he invited Gerhard Dehne, then director of the German-American Trade Promotion Company and the first German to contribute to the *Bulletin*, to outline the technique of organizing an international congress.[53] The article explained in detail what organizers needed to do and what participants were entitled to expect, from reduced prices of tickets to a decent signposting at the congress venue.

The editorial policy to leave politics out and concentrate on technical issues was only successful up to a point. With hindsight, it is abundantly clear that in the first years of publication (from 1948 to the early 1950s), the *Bulletin* and its successors heavily leaned towards the Western world, and favoured cooperation within UN-defined boundaries. There were hardly any attempts to look behind the Iron Curtain. Moreover, the Global South, as we would now define it, only slowly entered into the picture. Once the new statutes were approved in 1951, the Union began to look more actively for members outside Western Europe.

On the one hand, the emphasis on science and technical skills surrounding international exchange followed almost naturally from the nineteenth-century idea of scientific universalism that had driven Otlet and La Fontaine. In this sense, the Union followed its long-established project of peace, however utopian it was. Whereas, as Mark Mazower argues, this programme continued to exert a certain attraction in the interwar years, it was no match for the hard realism of the Cold War.[54] On the other hand, the Union's shift to 'technical' expertise was a conscious choice, fitting in with the widespread claim to non-political knowledge that was meant to hold the world together despite the political cleavages that emerged after the Second World War.[55]

Conclusion

The short period 1948–52 that we have highlighted in this chapter is in many ways representative for the decades that followed. The search for a place on the international scene was carried forward with scarcely slackened fervour. One cannot say that the Union's leadership lacked stamina. In 1956, a few years after Ording had disappeared from the scene, the Union obtained a substantial subsidy from the Ford Foundation that kept it going for some time. In 1957, Speeckaert was the driving force behind the publication of a chronological list of *The 1,978 International Organizations Founded Since the Congress of Vienna*, 'admittedly not a novel', but nevertheless 'a history of human relations *par excellence*', as he put it in the introduction.[56] In 1960 and 1964, this overview was followed by two other 'offerings to the Muse of History', chronological lists of all international congresses in the periods 1681–1899 and 1900–14, still valuable sources for the historians of internationalism.[57]

This chapter has explored the ways in which the Union tried to carve out a distinct, allegedly non-political, role in a world full of tensions: tensions between international organizations, between states and their representatives, but also between personal visions of the role of the international sphere. On the one hand, the Union emphasized its 'technical' and supporting role, which came to the fore in studies on the history and present-day practice of international meetings, while on the other hand its board members and staff were campaigning for subsidies, and trying to strike deals with supranational organizations, governments and private, non-governmental organizations, including philanthropic foundations.

Seen through the lens of the UIA, transnationalism in the post-war settlement was clearly not a story of linear success. The Union was relatively disadvantaged, in particular with regard to subsidizers, as it did not have a specific cause to bring to the fore. As liaison office or clearinghouse, it had many competitors, and in many ways, it was crowded out by new initiatives linked to the UN. Without financial support from America the Union could not hope to grow substantially and, for example, open full-fledged offices in Geneva or New York. The old utopian goals of La Fontaine and Otlet had little chance of gaining mainstream support: after the Second World War, the heyday of this type of internationalism was definitely over. Nevertheless, the Union persisted, and managed to conquer and keep a special place on the global stage.

Notes

1   Archives de l'Université catholique de Louvain (Louvain-la-Neuve), Papiers de Paul Van Zeeland, inv. no. 73, Procès verbal de la réunion du comité exécutif provisoire qui s'est tenu le mercredi, 28 juillet 1948.

2   Akira Iriye, 'The Making of a Transnational World', in *Global Interdependence: The World after 1945*, ed. idem (Cambridge, MA: Belknap Press, 2014), 722.

3   See, for example, Daniel Laqua, *The Age of Internationalism and Belgium, 1880–1930: Peace, Progress and Prestige* (Manchester: Manchester University Press, 2013); Jessica Reinisch, 'Introduction: Agents of Internationalism', *Contemporary European History* 25, no. 2 (2016): 195–205.

4   See, for example, Margaret E. Keck, and Kathryn Sikkink, *Activists beyond Borders: Advocacy Networks in International Politics* (Ithaca, NY: Cornell University Press, 1998); John Boli and George M. Thomas, eds, *Constructing World Culture: International Nongovernmental Organizations since 1875* (Stanford, CA: Stanford University Press, 1999).

5   Akira Iriye, *Global Community: The Role of International Organizations in the Making of the Contemporary World* (Berkeley, CA: University of California Press, 2004), 37–59.

6   Iriye, 'The Making of a Transnational World'.

7   Thomas Davies, *NGOs: A New History of Transnational Civil Society* (London: Hurst 2014), 123.

8   Mark Mazower, *Governing the World: The History of an Idea* (London: Penguin, 2012), 214–43.

9   Glenda Sluga, *Internationalism in the Age of Nationalism* (Philadelphia, PA: University of Pennsylvania Press, 2013).

10 Wolfram Kaiser and Kiran Klaus Patel, 'Multiple Connections in European Co-operation: International Organizations, Policy Ideas, Practices and transfers 1967–92', *European Review of History* 24, no. 3 (2017): 337–57.

11 William E. DeMars, and Dennis Dijkzeul, eds, *The NGO Challenge for International Relations Theory* (London: Routledge, 2015), 5.

12 The Hoover Institution Archives at Stanford University, for example, possesses the Howard E. Wilson papers, which also cover the period he worked for the Carnegie Endowment.

13 Lyman C. White, *International Non-Governmental Organizations: Their Purposes, Methods and Accomplishments* (New Brunswick, NJ: Rutgers University Press, 1951), ix.

14 Lyman C. White, *The Structure of Private International Organizations* (Philadelphia, PA: George S. Ferguson, 1933), 239.

15 White, *The Structure of Private International Organizations*, 238.

16 Thierry Grosbois, 'Le Centre belge d'études et de documentation face à l'après-guerre en Europe (1941–1944)', in *Inventer l'Europe: Histoire nouvelle des groupes d'influence et des acteurs de l'unité européenne*, ed. Gérard Bossuat and Georges Saunier (Brussels: P.I.E.-Peter Lang, 2003), 197–222.

17 Laqua, *The Age of Internationalism and Belgium*, 211–15.

18 Union of International Associations Archives (Brussels), Etapes de la reprise d'activités de l'U.A.I., author and date unknown; Hommage à Georges Patrick Speeckaert, author unknown, 1971. We have made extensive use of the uninventoried archives of the Union of International Associations, which are kept at its headquarters in Brussels.

19 UIA Archives, Rapport des diverses visites faites à Paris les 12 et 13 novembre 1948.

20 Swiss Federal Archives (Bern), E2001E#1967/113#15737*, Union des associations internationals, Bruxelles (1949–51), B. Pickard, Tentative Memorandum on the Proposed Programme of Union of International Association (Brussels), 7 December 1948.

21 UIA Archives, letter from L. White to G. P. Speeckaert, 29 December 1948.

22 UIA Archives, report of Speeckaert about his trip to the United States, 28 April 1949.

23 In 1965 the Union returned to its original name, Union of International Associations, without any extension.

24 Resolution 334 B (XI) of the Economic and Social Council of the United Nations, adopted 20 July 1950 (UN Documents E/2489).

25 UIA Archives, letter from Ording to Speeckaert, 27 May 1950.

26 UIA Archives, 'Note sur l'Union des Associations Internationales et sa situation financière', undated [1960].

27 Arbeiderbevegelsens Arkiv og Bibliotek (Oslo), Aake Anker-Ording Papers, ARK-1025, D-L0104, A. Ording, *The Non-Governmental Organizations. Some Proposals for Immediate and Long Term Consideration* (1949), 2.

28 Aake Anker-Ording Papers, D-L0107, A. Ording, *Report to the U.I.A. Service Center* (1952), 2.

29 UIA Archives, letter from A. Ording to P. van Zeeland, 14 July 1949.

30 UIA Archives, letter from A. Ording to P. van Zeeland, 18 October 1949.

31 Ibid.

32 UIA Archives, letter from A. Ording to J. Polain, 27 September 1950.

33 UIA Archives, 'Situation de Mr Ording au sein de l'U.A.I', 7 September 1950.

34 Inderjeet Parmar, *Foundations of the American Century: The Ford, Carnegie, and Rockefeller Foundations in the Rise of American Power* (New York: Columbia University Press, 2012), 2; John Krige, *American Hegemony and the Postwar Reconstruction of Science in Europe* (Cambridge, MA: MIT Press, 2006) Ludovic Tournès, ed., *L'Argent de l'influence. Les fondations américaines et leurs réseaux européens* (Paris: Autrement, 2010).

35 UIA Archives, letter from A. Ording to J. Polain, 10 October 1950.

36 UIA Archives, 'Service Center for International Non-Governmental Organizations' (1950).

37 UIA Archives, notes on a conference with Paul Hoffman, 9 November 1950.

38 Ibid.

39 UIA Archives, letter from A. Ording to G. P. Speeckaert, 7 December 1950.

40 UIA Archives, letter from A. Ording to G. P. Speeckaert, 10 March 1951.

41 UIA Archives, A. Ording, Additional Notes on a Service Center for International Non-Governmental Organizations (1951), 1951, 13.

42 UIA Archives, letter from A. Ording to J. Polain, 2 April 1951.

43 UIA Archives, letter from P. Hoffman to A. Ording, 26 April 1951.

44 Alan R. Raucher, *Paul Hoffman. Architect of Foreign Aid* (Lexington, KY: University of Kentucky, 1985), 87.

45 *The Ford Foundation. Annual Report for 1951* (31 December 1951): 20–1.

46 UIA Archives, letter from A. Ording to J. Polain, 6 July 1951.

47 UIA Archives, letter from A. Ording to J. Polain, 15 December 1951.

48 UIA Archives, letter from P. van Zeeland to O. Leimgruber, 7 March 1952.

49 UIA Archives, letter from A. Ording to E. Borgese, 31 March 1952.

50 *Union des Associations Internationales. Bulletin mensuel*, July–August 1949.

51 *Union des Associations Internationales. Bulletin mensuel*, June–July 1951.

52 *Union des Associations Internationales. Bulletin mensuel*, June–July 1949.

53 *Union des Associations Internationales. Bulletin mensuel*, August–September 1951.

54 Mazower, *Governing the World*, 109.

55 Jessica Reinisch, 'Expertise Is Always Political', *Experts: Past, Present, Future*, 4 July 2017. Available online: https://expertspastpresentfuture.net/expertise-is-always-political-75ae2ac143b3 (accessed 19 November 2017).

56 *The 1,978 International Organizations Founded Since the Congress of Vienna. Chronological List* (Brussels: UIA, 1957), III.

57 The quote is from *Les Congrès internationaux de 1681 à 1899: Liste complète* (Brussels: UIA, 1960), 7.

Part II

THE UIA IN A WORLD OF
INTERNATIONAL ORGANIZATIONS

Chapter 5

BUILDING A 'NEW INTERNATIONAL ORDER': INTERNATIONAL WOMEN'S ORGANIZATIONS AND THE UIA

Sarah Hellawell

In May 1910, delegates from the International Council of Women (ICW) – an umbrella organization founded in 1888 – attended the World Congress of International Associations in Brussels, the formative gathering of the Union of International Associations. Although the purpose of the event was to study international associations in all its forms, the female delegates were not officially listed as congress 'adherents'. Indeed, only a handful of women were included on the list at all.[1] *La Ligue* – the journal of the Belgian League for Women's Rights (Ligue Belge du Droit des Femmes) – reported that women had been permitted to make observations in the congress section on social work, but that they had been excluded from the main committees.[2] The periodical also criticized the gathering's limited international make-up, as delegates were primarily drawn from Belgium, France and Switzerland. Nonetheless, *La Ligue* featured positive remarks on the congress: activists were pleased that the work of the women's movement had featured in the exhibition that accompanied the congress. Looking ahead, the ICW resolved to 'defend the questions in the interest of women' at future events by preserving and collecting documentation concerning women.[3]

This example draws attention to the limitations of internationalist ventures, even those that presented themselves as comprehensive. It highlights internationalism's gendered nature, which makes it all the more relevant to consider how female activists sought, and had, a voice within internationalist projects. Sidelined at the formative congress of the UIA, female internationalists did to some extent work with the Union. The ideals of internationalism appealed to the organized women's movement, whose members forged links across national borders to overcome their subjugation in national politics.[4] Transnational women's networks emerged in the nineteenth century in conjunction with the campaigns for abolition, temperance, peace and suffrage.[5] Leila Rupp has drawn attention to the ways in which international women's organizations both embodied and animated such networks.[6] While some international women's organizations, including the ICW, had been founded before the First World War, the interwar years saw a fresh 'surge of activism' at the international level.[7] Lobbying the League of Nations became a major feature of international women's activism, and the targeting of international institutions continued after the Second World War, with campaigners focusing on the newly created UN.[8]

In integrating the history of women's associations with the history of the UIA, this chapter contributes to the wider restoration of women to the narrative of international relations. A range of recent studies has shown how the involvement in transnational networks provided women with access to the international political sphere.[9] Members of international women's organizations engaged with different associations and networks in order to construct a world order that would include a prominent role for women. This chapter shows that at various points, cooperation with the UIA formed part of women's work towards this goal. Moreover, the chapter highlights several concerns that international women's organizations shared with the UIA: documentation, peace, intellectual cooperation as well as the quest for recognition by international institutions. In addressing these themes, the chapter also contributes to the wider literature on internationalism.

Documentation and the Women's Movement

In the 1970s, the Bibliothèque Léonie La Fontaine – featuring material on women, feminism, gender relations and sexuality – opened at the newly established University of Women (Université des Femmes) in Brussels.[10] Named after Belgian feminist Léonie La Fontaine (1857–1949), the library adopted the well-established method of preserving documentation on women as a form of political activism. Although there is no direct connection between the library and its eponym, its aims do overlap with those of La Fontaine herself and with the documentary work of the UIA's founders, namely the collection and preservation of information.

Born in 1857, Léonie La Fontaine was the younger sister of UIA co-founder Henri La Fontaine. Sharing feminist and pacifist ideals, Léonie and Henri collaborated on several ventures. For instance, both were founding members of the Belgian League for Women's Rights, established in 1892. From the outset, transnational connections with feminists in neighbouring countries – particularly France and the Netherlands – and with international women's organizations shaped the Belgian women's movement.[11] In 1906, Léonie co-founded the National Council of Belgian Women (Conseil National des Femmes Belges), the Belgian section of the ICW. Through her involvement in the ICW, she built connections with politically active women from Europe and North America as well as Australia, New Zealand and South America.[12] In 1909, with support from her ICW colleagues and Belgian women's associations, she established the Central Office of Documentation on Matters concerning Women (Office Central de Documentation pour les Questions concernant la Femme) – later known as the Central Office of Female Documentation (Office Central de Documentation Feminine, OCDF).[13] The OCDF became an important component of the

International Institute of Bibliography (IIB), established in 1895 by Henri La Fontaine and his collaborator, Paul Otlet.[14] Belgian women also played crucial roles in the associated International Office of Bibliography. Nonetheless, the OCDF's vision for the collection and preservation of information went beyond the scope of the IIB: documentation was considered a powerful political tool in the campaign for women's rights.

In 1898, Charles Sury, secretary of the International Office of Bibliography, compiled a catalogue of publications by Belgian female authors. The extensive list, which predated the establishment of the OCDF, comprised 977 titles, covering diverse subject areas – from religion, geography and language to medical science.[15] Writing in *La Ligue*, Léonie La Fontaine expressed her gratitude to Sury. As she noted, his bibliography would prove that women 'have had new and interesting ideas' and were 'capable of reasoning, of having a sane and clear opinion on all things'.[16] La Fontaine and the Belgian League for Women's Rights considered the bibliography an instrument to highlight the diverse intellectual contributions made by Belgian women.

At the international level, the ICW recommended that every national branch should 'form a Standing Committee of Information, with a Bureau of Information if possible, where statistics regarding the women of the country shall be collected and kept up to date'.[17] The ICW championed the IIB's work as part of the 'vast movement' to give value to documentation and knowledge.[18] In this context, the International Council emphasized the work of the OCDF. As well as encouraging its national sections to collect documentation, the ICW urged for the representation of women at IIB congresses so that they could 'defend the question of women's documentation'.[19] For these activists, documentation went some way to addressing the marginalization of women, particularly female thinkers and writers. Women's associations stressed the importance of including women in the work of constructing bibliographies and documentation centres, as well as collecting material relating to women.

In addition, many women's associations actively preserved their own record of activity to secure their place in the historical narrative. Early on, suffrage activists sought to recover the activity of women as well as produce histories of the suffrage movement, as women were mostly absent from mainstream histories.[20] Conscious of the value of keeping records for future activists and historians, early feminists established archives and collections. For instance, the Library of the London Society for Women's Service was established in 1926 to preserve the history of the British suffrage movement.[21] The Women's International League for Peace and Freedom (WILPF) provides us with another example of feminist documentation efforts. As will be discussed in the next section, WILPF had its roots in a 1915 peace congress and counted Léonie La Fontaine among its members. In the mid-1930s, American WILPF activists began to collect the papers of the organization's national sections and leading figures. In response, the British section urged its members to send relevant documents, so that its work would 'become better recognised'.[22] The initiative led to the creation of the Swarthmore College Peace Collection – a key archive for peace history research, which has also been shaped by the feminism of its founders.[23]

Meanwhile in Amsterdam, Dutch feminists Rosa Manus, Johanna Naber and Willemijn Posthumus-van der Goot established the International Archives for the Women's Movement (IAV).[24] The IAV was distinctly international in its focus and members of international women's associations sat on its advisory board. Part of its work involved publishing a *Yearbook of International Archives for the Women's Movement*, covering additions to the archive as well as recent publications.[25] The Dutch archive cooperated with other collections that shared its objective, including the Women's Service Library. Yet the IAV's aim was not just to preserve material relating to the women's movement, but to give 'the women's movement the *scientific basis* to which, as an important cultural movement, it is entitled'.[26] Like Léonie La Fontaine, the IAV's founders claimed that documentation provided the women's movement with legitimacy. Knowledge was considered a tool for securing equality.[27] IAV co-founder Rosa Manus shared Léonie La Fontaine's feminist–pacifist outlook: both were active in the network of international women's associations, particularly WILPF. This connection confirms, as Julie Carlier suggests, that there was significant transfer between the Belgian and Dutch women's movements, which helped to facilitate the creation of transnational networks.[28]

The documentation of matters concerning women was distinctly transnational and became an important feature of the work carried out by international women's associations, particularly the ICW and WILPF. As illustrated by the OCDF, the IIB's founders – who went on to establish the UIA – and international women's organizations had a shared interest in documentation, knowledge and international cooperation. However, women's archives, libraries and bibliographies were more than simply part of the broader international movement for documentation. Their establishment was inherently intertwined with feminist goals for equality. Yet for feminists such as Léonie La Fontaine, documentation was but one aspect of their activism.[29] Like the UIA's founders, many internationally active feminists turned their attention to the issues of war and peace upon the outbreak of war in 1914.

Women's Internationalism and Peace Activism

During the occupation of Belgium in the Great War, Léonie La Fontaine fled to Switzerland – then considered by many a centre of antimilitarism.[30] There, she became a founding member of the World Union of Women for International Concord. Initiated by the American Clara Guthrie Cocke, thirty-six other women were present at its formative meeting, including Marguerite Gobat, a Swiss feminist and pacifist.[31] The World Union asserted that a combination of 'rational thought, education and love' would secure permanent peace.[32]

Even before the war, peace had been a concern for many international women's associations.[33] Both La Fontaine and Gobat had long-held pacifist commitments and operated in similar pacifist circles before 1914 alongside members of their own families. Marguerite's father, Charles Albert Gobat, received the Nobel Prize for Peace in 1902 for his leadership of the International Peace Bureau (IPB). Henri La Fontaine worked closely with him. Both the IPB and Henri won the Nobel

Prize, in 1910 and 1913 respectively. Marguerite shared her father's pacifism and was the IPB's librarian in Bern, working alongside Léonie and Henri La Fontaine.[34] She was also an OCDF board member and helped to collect documentation and regularly contributed to the Belgian journal *L'International Féminin*.[35] For both Marguerite and Léonie, pacifism was intertwined with feminism. As well as being a leading figure in the Belgian women's movement, Léonie was a founding member of the Belgian section of the International Arbitration and Peace Association and attended gatherings of the Universal Peace Congress.[36] Despite their feminist–pacifist views, neither Gobat nor La Fontaine were present at the large women's peace congress held at The Hague in 1915, yet they later were involved with the women's peace association that emerged from it, namely WILPF.

The 1915 congress attracted approximately 1,200 delegates from twelve nations – primarily in Europe and North America – as well as messages of support from across the globe.[37] The event was by no means uncontroversial. The British *Daily Mail* described it as a 'feminine farce', exemplifying the ridicule that the event received in the press.[38] Nevertheless, some political leaders expressed their respect for the aims of the congress and the activities that resulted from it. It was decided at The Hague to send envoys to meet with heads of both neutral and belligerent states, who 'apparently, recognized without argument that an expression of the public opinion of a large body of women had every claim to consideration in questions of war and peace'.[39] On hearing the activists' proposals for a permanent peace based on international cooperation, Woodrow Wilson sent a telegram to the association expressing that its plan 'appeals both to my head and to my heart'.[40] The American president repeatedly met with one of the driving forces behind the congress, US social reformer Jane Addams.

UIA co-founder Paul Otlet endorsed the aims and methods of the 1915 congress. The British national section – which came to be one of WILPF's largest and most active branches – published Otlet's report titled *Levant l'étendard de l'action* (Raising the Standard of Action) in its 1915 edition of *Towards a Permanent Peace*.[41] His article described the main features of the Hague Congress, focusing primarily on the delegates' gendered, and at times feminist, critique of war. He reported the delegates' maternalist language, including the claim that women, as mothers, had a special interest and unique responsibility to prevent militarism and protect humanity.[42] As has been noted, Otlet's colleague Henri La Fontaine was an advocate of women's rights and peace. Otlet himself, however, was by no means an absolute pacifist or feminist: his link to peace and women's activism stemmed from his commitment to internationalism and intellectual cooperation. For Otlet, peace was the natural result of a better organization of international relations, and he therefore became an early supporter of the idea of a League of Nations.[43] Likewise, the 1915 women's congress called for a 'Society of Nations' – including a permanent international court of justice and an international conference to facilitate international cooperation – as the basis of a constructive peace.[44]

At The Hague, the delegates, who were predominantly suffragists, urged that women should 'share all civil and political rights and responsibilities on the same terms as men'.[45] In particular, they argued that women ought to be represented at the post-war peace conference and that the parliamentary franchise for women should be incorporated in the peace settlement. The congress impressed Otlet, who listed a group of thirty delegates as accomplished organizers and gifted orators, capable of working alongside male activists, politicians and diplomats. He concluded by acknowledging the role that women could play as a 'new factor in international relations'.[46]

Léonie La Fontaine and Marguerite Gobat were not the only women prevented from attending the congress. The war rendered travel to The Hague difficult. Only three British women managed to avoid the restrictions across the English Channel.[47] There were no French delegates present. Many French feminists remained nationally minded, supported the war effort and opposed the aims of the Hague Congress. As a result, French feminist pacifists were forced to step down from offices within national women's suffrage associations.[48] When five Belgian delegates arrived late, the Congress 'rose to its feet' to welcome them.[49] Despite these initial difficulties, supporters worked from 1915 onwards to establish national sections of the association. In 1915, Gobat co-founded a Swiss WILPF section, alongside Gertrud Woker and Clara Ragaz. In addition, she assisted with administrative work at the association's headquarters – *La Maison Internationale* – in Geneva and wrote for WILPF's journal, *Pax International*.[50] WILPF considered both its main goals – women's rights and peace – to be inherently international and it sought to organize women across national borders.[51] Moreover, the organization collaborated with a range of associations to lobby the League of Nations. Alongside the UIA and a range of international women's organizations, WILPF thus became part of the liberal internationalist circles that supported the League.

By 1919, WILPF received reports from fifteen national sections.[52] A Belgian national section had been created in 1915 by Eugenie Hamer and Marguerite Sarten.[53] Communication with Belgian supporters, however, was patchy. In 1920, the association reported that 'there had been a hiatus with our relations with Belgium'.[54] Despite her pacifism, Léonie La Fontaine initially had few links with the new transnational women's peace association. In the early 1920s, however, the UIA seems to have helped her establish formal links with WILPF. In September 1920, the UIA hosted its first *Quinzaine Internationale* (International Fortnight) at Palais Mondial in Brussels.[55] WILPF representatives were present at the *Quinzaine*. During her visit to Belgium over the course of the fortnight, French WILPF member Jeanne Mélin met with various members of Belgian women's associations. Reporting in WILPF's *Bulletin* 'that the Belgian chauvinism, so much exploited in the press, does not represent the feeling of the mass of the people', Mélin gauged support for the women's peace association.[56] Inspired by her meeting with Mélin, Léonie La Fontaine went on to establish a Belgian WILPF section in 1921. Based in Brussels, this small branch had the support of Léonie's brother, who regularly addressed its meetings.

In 1922, Lucie Déjardin, an activist in the Ligue des Femmes Socialistes, founded a second Belgian WILPF branch in Liège, drawing on women from more socialist circles than the seemingly 'bourgeois' Brussels branch.[57] Committed to internationalism, WILPF permitted more than one national section to affiliate to the association in an attempt to incorporate national minorities. There were also two WILPF sections in Switzerland: one based in Geneva, and the other at Arbon.[58] Likewise, both German and Czechoslovak branches operated in Czechoslovakia. Where multiple branches existed, members often addressed national concerns. For instance, Czechoslovakian members viewed 'the development of understanding between the nationalities in our own country' as 'the most important task'.[59] Despite the national priorities of these branches, internationalism and the building of a transnational association remained integral to the work of WILPF. Therefore, in 1923, Mélin and Catherine Marshall, a British WILPF member, assisted in the re-organization of a central Belgian section, of which Léonie La Fontaine became president.[60]

The Belgian WILPF section was particularly supportive of the UIA, partly because of Léonie La Fontaine's work with her brother and Otlet as well as their proximity to the Belgian centre of this international network. The branch took a vocal opposition to the Belgian government's decision to block the UIA's use of Palais Mondial, stating that 'all the international organizations have to protest against this restriction of former rights'.[61] In 1923, the French and Belgian sections spearheaded WILPF's contribution to a UIA project, known as *Les Cahiers de la Paix*.

Data Collection: Les Cahiers de la Paix

WILPF became well known for its 'fact-finding missions' as it sought to influence international relations through its 'meticulous collection' of data.[62] Several of its members undertook assignments and presented evidence to both national governments and the League of Nations. For instance, Edith Pye and Camille Drevet – WILPF members from, respectively, Britain and France – travelled around China and the Far East between October 1927 and June 1928 on WILPF business.[63] Missions like this were part of WILPF's efforts to raise the voice of women on matters relating to international relations. In this respect, WILPF shared the UIA's goals for documentation and internationalism. The association took up one of the UIA's ventures to conduct an 'enquiry-referendum' with the aim of drawing up a world constitution.

In 1923, members of the French WILPF section initiated the association's contribution to the UIA's *Cahiers de la Paix*. Many WILPF members were dissatisfied with the terms of the post-war peace settlement, which they regarded as a 'continuation of a state of war'.[64] They criticized the League of Nations as being controlled by a small group of diplomats and issued regular calls for a revision of the treaty. The association's vision of a 'New International Order' centred on the cooperation of the people of the world rather than the cooperation of nation-states. Similarly, the *Cahiers* project appealed to national and international associations – including cooperatives, trade unions, intellectuals, feminists, pacifists and religious groups – to record their complaints of the current international system and propose measures to secure more effective international reconstruction.[65] The campaign's aim was to create a true 'League of the Peoples', based on the cooperation of existing national and international associations to represent public opinion. Thus, WILPF's vision of a 'New International Order' and the UIA's *Cahiers* project overlapped considerably.

The project was inspired by the *Cahiers de doléances* of 1789, which allowed French people to record their complaints, with a view to placing grievances before the Estates-General. Likewise, the *Cahiers de la Paix* aimed to raise the voice of the people regarding the international order. For WILPF, the *Cahiers* project was a practical method of ascertaining public opinion and promoting the collaboration of international associations. Rather than call on individuals to write *Cahiers*, the leaders of WILPF's contribution suggested that associations should record their thoughts collectively, emphasizing the role that international associations should play in the construction of peace and international governance.[66] The completed *Cahiers* would be sent to the UIA headquarters in Brussels, where a world congress would be held to discuss the proposals and to establish plans to publicize the desire for a 'New International Order'. The campaign was a central aspect of WILPF's fourth international congress, held in Washington, DC, in May 1924.[67]

WILPF's participation in the *Cahiers de la Paix* venture has been dismissed as a utopian mission, assumed to be based on the 'avant-garde' thinking of French member Gabrielle Duchêne – one of the main instigators of WILPF's contribution.[68] Yet the project had wide support within WILPF: other French members – particularly Andrée Jouve and Jeanne Mélin – were instrumental to the campaign and WILPF's *Cahiers* commission comprised members of the German, British, Hungarian, US and Belgian sections.[69] While there were tensions surrounding the anti-capitalist stance expressed by more radical members such as Duchêne, WILPF members agreed on the role of education and international cooperation to secure peace. As a feminist–pacifist association, it emphasized the valuable role women could play in the field of international relations. WILPF's *Cahier* proposed that the international order be organized by an effective League and international court of justice. The association also advocated disarmament, free trade, the pooling of raw materials and the introduction of an international charter of labour to secure peace.[70]

The UIA received WILPF's *Cahier* as planned, but very little seems to have come of the initiative.[71] Indeed, discussion of the campaign quickly fades from WILPF reports, which came to be dominated by debates on the Dawes Plan of August 1924. Nonetheless, WILPF's enthusiastic support for the 'vast world referendum' demonstrates a connection between this international women's association and the UIA.[72] While concurring with the UIA's desire to see a reform to the international system, there was consensus within WILPF about the value of international associations to the 'organization of the peoples of the world so as to remove the causes of war'.[73] WILPF's proposals focused on the role of women in international relations and peace. WILPF members urged women 'to spread understanding and knowledge' on questions relating to international politics.[74]

Women's Internationalism, Intellectual Cooperation and the League

As the example of the *Cahiers* project demonstrates, international women's organizations such as WILPF valued the collaboration of associations operating at the international level. In particular, they emphasized that the League of Nations should play an active role in promoting such contacts. Likewise, Paul Otlet and Henri La Fontaine urged the League of Nations to include intellectual cooperation in its remit. Their plan for an intellectual branch of the League would incorporate much of the work conducted by the UIA and IIB, including the collection and organization of documentation, arranging international scientific congresses, standardization and education to promote internationalism.[75] Although their scheme for an intellectual League of Nations based in Brussels was not realized, it did prompt discussion within League circles. In 1922, the League's International Committee on Intellectual Cooperation (ICIC) was established, and in 1926, this body was complemented by the creation of an International Institute of Intellectual Cooperation.[76] During the interwar years, intellectual cooperation – both through these League bodies and through informal networks – was central to the goals of women's organizations and the UIA alike.

With its emphasis on the value of education for peace, intellectual cooperation appealed to the network of international women's organizations and provided a space for internationally organized women to engage with the League.[77] In 1927, the ICW celebrated the ICIC as 'perhaps the most important permanent contribution made by the League to the problem of human government', as it extended 'the range and meaning of politics'.[78] The ICW's education and peace committees discussed the ICIC's work, and the association initiated a liaison committee of international non-governmental organizations to support the League's work in this field.[79] Comprising thirty international associations, the committee held its annual meetings at either the Institute for Intellectual Cooperation in Paris or the League Secretariat in Geneva.[80] ICW's leading role in the liaison committee shows how women's organizations were active participants in the vibrant network of associations that cooperated with the League. Similarly, WILPF emphasized intellectual cooperation as a means to secure peace. In January 1929, the association's Conference on the Modern Methods of Warfare in Frankfurt promoted intellectual cooperation. Swiss WILPF member and chemist, Dr Gertrud Woker, took the lead in arranging this technical and scientific conference, which attracted the attention of the global community, including leading scientists and internationalists such as Albert Einstein, Paul Langevin and Romain Rolland.[81]

Women's organizations took a particular interest in the development of educational schemes aimed at promoting peace and international understanding. Laura Dreyfus-Barney, ICW vice-president, served on the League of Nations Sub-Committee of Experts on the Teaching of Youth, which was part of the ICIC.[82] Similarly, members of the Norwegian branches of the ICW, WILPF, the Teachers' Peace Society, the Federation of University Women and the Association of University Graduates for the League of Nations urged for a permanent centre to be created within the Institute for Intellectual Cooperation to promote world peace and international understanding through education.[83] Early on, WILPF campaigned for the modification of school curricula to promote the League. It thus engaged with an issue – namely textbook revision – that figured prominently in interwar cultural internationalism.[84] The British WILPF section produced a bibliography of textbooks 'for the enlightenment of public opinion'.[85]

This focus on education resonated with wider aspects of internationalist discourse in the interwar years: as Daniel Laqua's chapter in this volume has shown, the UIA engaged in its own educational ventures. Yet, as a women's organization, WILPF emphasized a gendered vision of education, arguing that 'the future of education lies in the hands of women'.[86] As well as permitting international women's organizations the space to promote issues such as education and peace, the arena of intellectual cooperation broadened their access to the international sphere.

Women's Internationalism in the UN Era

The end of the Second World War and the establishment of the UN opened a new era in international politics.[87] Many internationalist groups had to come to terms with the fact that the League of Nations had failed to secure peace. Yet at the same time, internationalism was no longer merely the utopian ideal of pacifists and intellectuals: there was widespread support for the newly created UN and its remit.[88]

In the second half of the 1940s, the principal international women's organizations as well as the UIA regrouped and took stock, having been forced to suspend the majority of their activities during the war.[89] There were notable changes in their leadership as key figures who had dominated the work of these organizations had passed away during the 1930s and early 1940s.[90] In addition, new organizations were formed, including the Soviet-backed Women's International Democratic Federation in December 1945.[91] Despite these changes, there was significant overlap and continuity in terms of the form, structure and pursuit of internationalist causes.

Women's organizations continued to assert their influence upon international relations, particularly in relation to the issue of citizenship.[92] Quick to resume its work, WILPF held its tenth international congress in Luxembourg in August 1946. The International Alliance of Women – another leading women's organization – followed suit a few days later, staging its first post-war congress in Switzerland. The following year, the ICW met in Philadelphia. WILPF continued to advocate 'peace and freedom by means of education' in this period.[93] In 1949, it relaunched its international summer schools – events that had been a prominent feature of WILPF's contribution to the study of international relations during the interwar years.[94] The meetings provided a space for internationally minded women to exchange knowledge and strengthen connections across national borders.

As discussed by Nico Randeraad and Philip Post in this volume, the UIA eventually resumed its activities in 1948–9, focusing on its role as a documentation centre.[95] Anne Winslow, editor for the Carnegie Endowment for International

Peace, played an active part in discussions that led to the redefinition of the UIA's role. At the time, she was already an expert in the study of NGOs. Later on in her life, she published widely on the role of women in international life, also examining their participation in the trade union movement and the International Labour Organization.[96] While Winslow's later interactions with the UIA were limited, she did contribute to its periodical in 1954. Her article focused on the work of the Carnegie Endowment's 'International Center', which was located opposite the UN headquarters in New York and housed the offices of thirty-eight non-governmental organizations. The Jane Addams Peace Association, which was part of WILPF's educational programme, had its offices in the Carnegie building. Women United for the United Nations – established in 1946 by American women to support the UN and international cooperation – also ran an information centre from these premises. Winslow's article for the UIA's journal thus indicated the links between the Carnegie Endowment and women's internationalism.[97]

More generally, however, personal connections between the UIA and international women's organizations were less apparent than they had been before the Second World War. One key reason was the redefinition of the Union's purpose, focusing on documentation rather than activism. That said, the UIA's periodicals – *Le Bulletin Mensuel* (1949–50), *NGO Bulletin* (1951–3), *International Associations* (1954–76) and *Transnational Associations* (1977–2005) – did cover the work of international women's organizations. For instance, they included details of meetings and congresses held by WILPF, the International Federation of University Women and the ICW.[98] They also discussed campaigns relating to women's issues, including the movement for the suppression of traffic in persons and the UN's International Women's Year held in 1975.[99]

The presence of such issues within UIA publications highlights the role of women's organizations within the wider world of non-governmental organizations and their interactions with the UN system. On the surface, the UN appears to have provided more opportunities for the international women's movement than the League had done.[100] Several women's organizations benefitted from consultative status with the UN's Economic and Social Council and there were more women present at the UN's formative meetings in San Francisco than there had been at the establishment of the League. Like the League's Covenant, the UN Charter affirmed the eligibility of women for positions on equal terms with men. Although women remained underrepresented within the UN bureaucracy, some individuals were able to take advantage of this opportunity. For example, Swedish WILPF member Alva Myrdal led the UN Department of Social Affairs between 1950 and 1955. Her role also highlights a wider issue: the particular contribution of women's organizations to meetings on 'social questions' in the UN's early work. For instance, the UIA's summary of UN activity in 1953 indicates that many international women's organizations attended the meetings of the Social Commission, including the IAW, ICW, International Federation of Business and Professional Women, International Federation of University Women and WILPF. This report also shows that many international women's organizations worked with the United Nations International Children's Emergency Fund (UNICEF).[101]

Nonetheless, women largely remained on the UN's peripheries during its formative years.[102] Moreover, not all female delegates at the UN considered themselves as representing their gender. For example, Ellen Wilkinson – the British Labour politician who had been a prominent figure in WILPF throughout the interwar years – did not want to be defined as a 'woman delegate' at San Francisco in 1945. As Laura Beers suggests, her decision to distance herself from this label might indicate her frustration with tokenism.[103] At the same time, women's organizations actively sought to increase the number of delegates to the UN General Assembly, picking up a cause that they had previously pursued in regard to the League. WILPF asserted that 'only complete cooperation of men and women as full equals in shaping and making decisions in the UN will bring about the fulfilment of the aims and principles laid down in the United Nations Charter'.[104]

In 1946, the UN resumed an international enquiry into the status of women that the League of Nations had launched in 1937. This League initiative had been a direct response to sustained pressure from the international women's movement and thus demonstrates the impact of campaigners' pre-war efforts. Aiming to collect data on women's position in the legal, economic and political spheres, this proposed survey bore similarities to activists' earlier documentation efforts: as early as 1912, Léonie La Fontaine's OCDF had initiated a questionnaire to 'make known the role of women in the economic and social life of different countries'.[105] Although the outbreak of war in 1939 disrupted the League's investigation, the plans marked an important step towards recognizing the transnational dimension of women's rights.

The UN's continuation of the League enquiry was led by a Commission on the Status of Women (CSW), which first operated as a sub-committee of the UN's Commission on Human Rights and then as a full commission of the United Nations Economic and Social Council.[106] Engaging with the UN's discussions about human rights and citizenship in the aftermath of the Second World War, the CSW focused on women's political equality by preparing a Convention on the Political Rights of Women, approved by the General Assembly in 1952.[107] As international NGOs with consultative status, women's associations were represented at meetings of the CSW. The commission dealt with issues that had long concerned feminists, such as the campaign for 'Equal Pay for Equal Work'. On this matter, women's organizations made some headway, as they contributed to the UN's Equal Remuneration Convention in 1951.

Cooperation between non-governmental international organizations as well as collaboration with the UN remained key features of both the work of the UIA and the international women's movement. In particular, the status of international associations at the UN was central to the UIA's immediate post-war work.[108] At the formative Conference of Consultative Non-Governmental Organizations, held in Geneva in May 1948, a study committee was established to consider the legal status of organizations with UN consultative status. The Conference aimed to ensure that non-governmental organizations were able to fully cooperate with the UN. Among the associations represented on the study committee were the Liaison Committee of Women's International Organizations and the UIA.[109] The Liaison Committee was an alliance of different associations; it had been founded in 1931 to advise the League of Nations on issues relating to women, such as the trafficking of women and children and the nationality of married women.[110] With offices in New York, Paris and Geneva, the Liaison Committee worked in collaboration with the UN, UNESCO and the ILO.

In the immediate aftermath of the Second World War – and hence around three years before the Geneva conference – the Liaison Committee of Women's International Organizations had published a history of its work, titled *An Experiment in Co-operation*. The pamphlet traced the group's activity, including its role in facilitating the cooperation of international women's associations, as well as its work with the League of Nations and its contributions to interwar intellectual cooperation. In some respects, the Liaison Committee and the UIA had similar aspirations, as both organizations attempted to facilitate the collaboration of international associations. Moreover, the Liaison Committee emphasized the role that women were to play in the new UN, demanding 'that women of the world shall share in the government of the world in order to ensure the peace and well-being of the world'.[111]

From the Old to the New: Peace Education, Activism and International Organizations

Well beyond the debates during the UN's early years, the activist and academic Elise Boulding promoted the work of transnational women's organizations to bring women out from the 'underside to become partners with men in shared spaces'.[112] Boulding was a peace activist and a renowned scholar in the field of peace education. She also was an Active Member of the UIA – with 'active membership' being a trustee-style category to which admission was granted by its General Assembly.

Boulding's early commitment to work for peace as both a campaigner and a researcher had been animated by her Quaker beliefs and by the events of the Second World War.[113] It was her participation in WILPF in the early 1940s that helped her 'to foster her connections to many, if not most, of the subsequent organizations in which she became involved', including the UIA and UN.[114] She went on to serve as international chair of WILPF between 1968 and 1972. In the later stages of her career, Boulding's commitment to both peace education and working with international organizations also manifested itself in her involvement in UNESCO's Cultures of Peace programme.[115]

Boulding first observed the workings of international organizations while living in Princeton with her husband during the early 1940s: Kenneth Boulding worked for the League of Nations' Economic and Financial Organization, which had moved from Geneva to Princeton in 1940.[116] It was during this time that she forged a close friendship with Alva Myrdal. During her long political career, Myrdal headed the UN's section on social welfare policy, sat in the Swedish parliament, served as Swedish ambassador to India, participated in the UN's Conference on

Disarmament and received the Nobel Prize for Peace in 1982.[117] Much like La Fontaine and Gobat in the early twentieth century, Boulding and Myrdal shared an interest in peace and internationalism. Both held prominent roles in the field of peace studies: Boulding was secretary-general of the International Peace Research Association from 1965 and Myrdal founded the Stockholm International Peace Research Institute in 1985. Thus, much like the earlier generation of WILPF members, the two women promoted the value of knowledge, research and education for both peace and women's rights.

Myrdal was a role model and mentor to Boulding, influencing her theories on the connection between grassroots activism and global civic culture.[118] For Boulding, the family was a microcosm of society, which allowed individuals – particularly women – to develop peacemaking skills, such as communication and mediation. Boulding articulated a feminist perspective on peacemaking and remained actively involved in WILPF throughout her life. In 1975, the UIA's periodical *International Associations* published her article on 'Female Alternatives to Hierarchical Systems, Past and Present'. In this piece, she argued that due to their prolonged subjugation, women had developed 'organizational techniques that work outside power structures'.[119] Like her WILPF forerunners, Boulding thus emphasized the importance of transnational women's networks to allow women to work within and beyond the male-dominated political sphere, as well as the valuable contribution they could make to peace. This article was but one of several pieces that she contributed to UIA publications. For instance, her report on 'The Family, the NGO and Social Mapping in a Changing World', which was prepared for a UNICEF Conference held in May 1969, also appeared in *International Associations*.[120]

Much of Boulding's published work focused on the past, present and future of international non-governmental organizations. In her 1988 book *Building a Global Civic Culture*, she traced the history of international non-governmental organizations, noting that 'the idea of globe-spanning associations of private citizens is scarcely a century old and is one of the most striking phenomena of the twentieth century. It is based on a new-old perception that humankind has common interests.'[121] One year prior to the publication of this monograph, Boulding had contributed an article for the UIA's journal, identifying her own contribution to peace education as part of the ongoing development from 'the era of the Old Internationalism' (1888–1939) to the 'New Internationalism in peace education' (1964–86). In doing so, Boulding linked the foundation of the UIA in 1910 and the International Peace Research Association in 1965 – of which she was a founding member – as part of the same 'exciting, popular concept' of internationalism.[122]

Boulding's lifelong commitment to peace research and international activism demonstrates the connection between the history of the international women's movement and the work of the UIA. Despite serving as WILPF's international chair during the so-called peak of 'second wave' feminism, Boulding suggested that 'none of the 1960s movements was really new',[123] thus stressing the longer history of international women's organizations and their engagement with the international sphere.

Conclusion

Taking the UIA as a starting point to trace connections and shared interests, this chapter has revealed both the opportunities and restrictions facing female internationalists. The histories of international women's organizations, the UIA, the League of Nations and the UN have developed side by side and, at times, intersected and overlapped. From the nineteenth century to the UN era, female internationalists have worked in their own organizations and in collaboration with international institutions, emphasizing women's roles in the collection of knowledge and documentation, peace and international cooperation. Just as WILPF collaborated with the UIA in 1924, Elise Boulding – who was active in both associations – remained committed to the building of a 'New International Order' through the cooperation of international organizations well into the 1980s.[124]

In 1945, the Charter of the UN set out its commitment to equal rights for women, seemingly testifying to the influence of women's associations on the development of international institutions.[125] Although women initially remained on the peripheries of the UN, the personal and political connections between female internationalists and the wider sphere of internationalism highlight the significance of international women's organizations. Shared interests in internationalism, peace, intellectual cooperation and the documentation of knowledge facilitated these connections and relationships. As this chapter has shown, women faced persistent obstacles in the field of international relations. However, the examples that have been discussed also highlight their perseverance and illustrate the nature of women's internationalism. The work of figures such as Léonie La Fontaine and Elise Boulding shows that this internationalism was partly sustained by the motivation to collect documentation on women's situation and to assert female authority on issues relating to war and peace.

Notes

1   Office Central des Associations internationales, *Revue des Congrès*, no. 1 (22 April 1910): 4; 'Le Congrés mondial des Associations Internationales', *La Ligue*, no. 3 (1910): 80; W. Boyd Rayward, *The Universe of Information: The Work of Paul Otlet for Documentation and International Organisation* (Moscow: VINITI, 1975), 179.
2   'Le Congrés mondial des Associations Internationales', 80.
3   Ibid., 81.
4   Pierre-Yves Saunier, *Transnational History* (Basingstoke: Palgrave, 2013), 25; Ann Taylor Allen, Anne Cova and June Purvis, 'International Feminisms', *Women's History Review* 19, no. 4 (2010): 493–501.
5   Janet Zollinger Giele, *Two Paths to Women's Equality: Temperance, Suffrage and the Origins of Modern Feminism* (New York: Twayne Publishers, 1995); Patricia Ward D'Itri, *Cross-Currents in the International Women's Movement, 1848–1948* (Bowling Green, OH: Bowling Green State University Popular Press, 1999); Margaret H. McFadden, *Golden Cables of Sympathy: The Transatlantic Sources of Nineteenth-Century Feminism* (Lexington, KY: University Press of Kentucky, 1999), 7.

6   Leila Rupp, *Worlds of Women: The Making of the International Women's Movement* (Princeton, NJ: Princeton University Press, 1997), 13.

7   Nitza Berkovitch, *From Motherhood to Citizenship: Women's Rights and International Organizations* (Baltimore, MD: John Hopkins University Press, 1999), 62; Karen Offen, *European Feminisms, 1700–1950* (Stanford, CA: Stanford University Press, 2000), 259.

8   Carol Miller, "'Geneva – the Key to Equality': Inter-War Feminists and the League of Nations', *Women's History Review* 3, no. 2 (1994): 219–45; Margaret E. Keck and Kathryn Sikknik, *Activists Beyond Borders: Advocacy Networks in International Politics* (Ithaca, NY: Cornell University Press, 1998), 56.

9   Glenda Sluga and Carolyn James, *Women, Diplomacy and International Politics since 1500* (Abingdon: Routledge, 2016); Helen McCarthy, *Women of the World: The Rise of the Female Diplomat* (London: Bloomsbury, 2014). See also Marie Sandell, *The Rise of Women's Transnational Activism: Identity and Sisterhood between the World Wars* (London: I.B. Tauris, 2015).

10 Caroline Verdier, 'Trajectories of Two Women's Libraries: A Comparative Study of the Bibliothèque Léonie La Fontaine and the Bibliothèque Marguerite Durand', in *Parcours des Femmes: Twenty Years of Women in French*, ed. Maggie Allison and Angela Kershaw (Bern: Peter Lang, 2011), 25.

11 Julie Carlier, 'Entangled Feminisms: Rethinking the History of the Belgian Movement for Women's Rights through Transnational Intersections', *Revue Belge de Philologie et d'Histoire* 90, no. 4 (2012): 1339–51; Julie Carlier, 'Forgotten Transnational Connections and National Contexts: An "Entangled History" of the Political Transfers that shaped Belgian Feminism, 1890–1914', *Women's History Review* 19, no. 4 (2010): 503.

12 International Council of Women, Quinquennial Reunion in Canada 1909. 5ICW/B/06, Women's Library, London School of Economics and Political Science.

13 Julie Carlier, 'Moving Beyond Boundaries: An Entangled History of Feminism in Belgium, 1890–1914' (PhD diss., Universiteit Gent, 2010), 454.

14 Rayward, *The Universe of Information*, 49.

15 Charles Sury, 'Bibliographie Féminine Belge: Essai de Catalogue des Ouvrages publiés par les Femmes belges de 1830 à 1897', *La Ligue*, no. 3 (1898): 60–1.

16 Léonie La Fontaine, 'Letter', *La Ligue*, no. 3 (1898): 60.

17 Oglive Gordon, 'The Formation and Growth of the International Council of Women', Quinquennial Reunion in Canada 1909, 16. 5ICW/B/06.

18 Office Central pour les questions concernant la Femme, 'Conseil international des femmes. Congrès Quinquennial Toronto 1909', 1, report in Mundaneum, Fonds Féminisme, Fonds Office central de documentation féminine (OCDF).

19 Office Central, 'Congrès Quinquennial Toronto 1909', 6.

20 Early feminists produced histories of women's work, such as Alice Clark, *Working Life of Women in the Seventeenth Century* (London: George Routledge & Sons, 1919); Barbara Drake, *Women and Trade Unions* (London: Labour Research Department, 1920). Others wrote accounts of the movement for votes for women, for example Ray Strachey, *The Cause* (London: George Bell & Sons 1928).

21 Jill Liddington, 'Fawcett Saga: Remembering the Women's Library Across Four Decades', *History Workshop Journal* 76, no. 1 (2013): 12.

22 WIL, *Monthly News Sheet* (November 1935): 5.

23 Wendy Chmielewski, 'Resources for Researching Opposition to WWI', paper presented at the 'Resistance to War' Conference, Leeds, UK, 18–20 March 2016. See

also Swarthmore College Peace Collection's brief history of the archive. Available online: http://www.swarthmore.edu/library/peace (accessed 27 October 2017).

24 Dagmar Wernitznig, 'Memory Is Power: Rosa Manus, Rosika Schwimmer and the Struggle about Establishing an International Women's Archive', in *Rosa Manus (1881–1942): The International Life and Legacy of a Jewish Dutch Feminist*, ed. Myriam Everard and Francisca de Haan (Leiden: Brill, 2017), 231.

25 Francisca de Haan, 'Getting to the Source. A "Truly International" Archive for the Women's Movement (IAV, now IIAV): From its Foundation in Amsterdam in 1935 to the Return of its Looted Archives in 2003', *Journal of Women's History* 16, no. 4 (2004): 153.

26 Archive IAV memorandum (April 1937) quoted in de Haan, 'Getting to the Source', 154.

27 Léonie La Fontaine, 'Letter', *La Ligue*, no. 3 (1898): 60; Lin McDevitt-Pugh, 'Coming Full Circle: A History of the IIAV's International Work', in *Traveling Heritages: New Perspectives on Collecting, Preserving and Sharing Women's History*, ed. Saskia E. Wieringa (Amsterdam: Askant, 2008), 131.

28 Carlier, 'Forgotten Transnational Connections and National Contexts'; see Mieke Aerts, 'Feminism from Amsterdam to Brussels in 1891: Political Transfer as Transformation', *European Review of History* 12, no. 2 (2005): 367–82.

29 Stéphanie Manfroid, 'Léonie La Fontaine (1854–1949): une femme dans l'aventure documentaire', *AIDA informazioni* 21, no. 1 (2003): 45.

30 Stéphanie Manfroid and Raphaèle Cornille, 'Women in Belgian History: Léonie La Fontaine, Feminist & Pacifist', *Women in Belgian History*. Available online: https://www.google.com/culturalinstitute/beta/exhibit/women-in-belgian-history/QQ8AfJxE?hl=en (accessed 27 October 2017).

31 Bruna Bianchi, 'Towards a New Internationalism: Pacifist Journals Edited by Women, 1914–1919', in *Gender and the First World War*, ed. Christa Hämmerle, Oswald Überegger and Birgitta Bader Zaar (Basingstoke: Palgrave, 2014), 181.

32 Acte de fondation de l'Union mondiale de la femme pour la concorde internationale (9 Février 1915). Ville de Genève, Bibliothèque publique et universitaire, MS. Fr. 9072.

33 International Council of Women, *Second Quinquennial Meeting* (1899). 5ICW/B/04; Heloise Brown, *The Truest Form of Patriotism: Pacifist Feminism in Britain, 1870–1902* (Manchester: Manchester University Press, 2003), 1.

34 'Office Central de documentation féminine', *L'International Féminin, Organe de la Société Belge pour l'Amélioration du Sort de la Femme* (Janvier 1913), 3.

35 OCDF, Inventaire des Documents Entrés, 1906–31 in Mundaneum, Fond Féminisme, OCDF; Carlier, 'Moving Beyond Boundaries', 455.

36 Léonie La Fontaine, 'Congrès de Stockholm', *La Ligue*, no. 4 (1910): 129.

37 Women's Peace Party, Report of the International Congress of Women, The Hague, 28 April–1 May 1915, 4.

38 'British Women and the Enemy', *Daily Mail*, 19 April 1915; Ingrid Sharp, '"A Foolish Dream of Sisterhood": Anti-Pacifist Debates in the German Women's Movement', 1914–1919', in *Gender and the First World War*, ed. Hämmerle et al., 201–2.

39 Emily Greene Balch, 'At the Northern Capitals', in *Women at The Hague: The International Congress of Women and its Results*, ed. Jane Addams, Emily Greene Balch and Alice Hamilton (Chicago: University of Illinois Press, 2003), 52.

40 Woodrow Wilson telegram to the ICWPP delegation at Paris (May 1919). WILPF microfilm collection at Northumbria University, reel 17.

41 Paul Otlet, 'Raising the Standard of Action', *Towards Permanent Peace* (WIL: London, 1915), 18.

42 Sarah Hellawell, 'Antimilitarism, Citizenship and Motherhood: The Formation and Early Years of the Women's International League (WIL), 1915–1919', *Women's History Review* 27, no. 4 (2018): 551–64.

43 Rayward, *The Universe of Information*, 206.

44 International Committee of Women for Permanent Peace, Resolutions produced at The Hague (1915), 8.

45 Women's Peace Party, Report of the International Congress of Women, 10.

46 Otlet, 'Raising the Standard of Action', 18.

47 Women's Peace Party, Report of the International Congress of Women, 4; see Sybil Oldfield, 'England's Cassandras in World War One', in *This Working Day World: Women's Lives and Culture(s) in Britain, 1914–1945*, ed. Sybil Oldfield (London: Taylor & Francis, 1994), 89.

48 Annika Wilmers, 'Pacifism, Nationalism and Internationalism in the French and German Women's Movements during the First World War', *Minerva: Journal of Women and War* 1, no. 1 (2007): 74.

49 Emmeline Pethick Lawrence, 'A Bond of Faith', *Towards a Permanent Peace* (London: WIL, 1915), 17.

50 For example, Marguerite Gobat, 'The Danger of Crystalization', *Pax International* 1, no. 7 (May 1926): 2.

51 British activists declared peace organizations 'inadequate unless they could find international expression'. See Emily Hobhouse, 'Foreword', *Bericht-Rapport-Report* (Amsterdam: ICWPP, 1915). SCPC, WILPF (DG043), Part II: Reel 141.1.

52 WILPF, Report of the International Congress of Women, Zurich, 12–17 May 1919, 2.

53 Women's Peace Party, Report of the International Congress of Women, 10.

54 WILPF, *Bulletin of the Women's International League for Peace and Freedom* (December 1920), 13.

55 Rayward, *The Universe of Information*, 221–8.

56 WILPF, *Bulletin of the Women's International League for Peace and Freedom* (December 1920), 13.

57 WILPF, *Bulletin* (February 1922). See also Daniel Laqua, *The Age of Internationalism and Belgium, 1880–1930: Peace, Progress and Prestige* (Manchester: Manchester University Press, 2013), 129.

58 Marguerite Gobat, 'Proceedings', Report for the Fourth Congress of the Women's International League for Peace and Freedom, 19.

59 Maria Aull, 'Proceedings', Report for the Fourth Congress of the Women's International League for Peace and Freedom, 8.

60 Lucie Déjardin, 'Proceedings', Report for the Fourth Congress of the Women's International League for Peace and Freedom, 5.

61 WILPF, *Bulletin* (November 1923–February 1924); Rayward, *The Universe of Information*, 251.

62 Laura Beers, 'Advocating for a Feminist Internationalism between the Wars', in *Women, Diplomacy and International Politics since 1500*, ed. Glenda Sluga and Carolyn James (New York: Routledge, 2016), 205.

63 Camille Drevet and Edith M. Pye, *Report of the W.I.L.P.F. Delegation to China* (Geneva: WILPF, 1928).

64 'Les Cahiers de la Paix', *Bulletin of the Women's International League for Peace and Freedom* (March–April 1923), 26.

65 'Les Cahiers de la Paix'.

66 Ibid.

67 WILPF, Report of the Fourth Congress of the Women's International League for Peace and Freedom.

68 Emmanuelle Carle, 'Women, Anti-Fascism and Peace in Interwar France: Gabrielle Duchêne's Itinerary', *French History* 18, no. 3 (2004): 299.

69 Isabelle Vahe, 'Jeanne Mélin (1877–1964): une féministe radicale pendant la Grande Guerre', in *French and Francophone Women Facing War*, ed. Alison Fell (Oxford: Peter Lang, 2009), 97.

70 WIL, *Monthly News Sheet* (July 1924), 3.

71 Ibid.; Rayward, *The Universe of Information*, 261.

72 'Les Cahiers de la Paix', *Bulletin of the Women's International League for Peace and Freedom* (March–April 1923), 26.

73 WIL, *Monthly News Sheet* (July 1924): 3.

74 Lotte Heller, 'Political Aspects of a New International Order', *Report of the Fourth Congress of the Women's International League for Peace and Freedom*, 53.

75 Paul Otlet, 'On the Organisation of Intellectual Work within the League of Nations: Report and Resolution presented by the Union of International Associations', 157–9.

76 Daniel Laqua, 'Transnational Intellectual Co-operation, the League of Nations, and the Problem of World Order', *Journal of Global History* 6, no. 2 (2011): 227.

77 Joyce Goodman, 'Women and Intellectual Co-operation', *Paedagogica Historica* 48, no. 3 (2012): 357.

78 ICW, Outline of Address on International Intellectual Cooperation (Geneva, 1927). 5ICW/C/02/03.

79 ICW, Education Committee Resolution (1927). 5ICW/C/02/03.

80 Report of the Activities of the International Council of Women since the last Council Meeting, Dubrovnik 1936 (ICW: Brussels, 1938), 20–1. 5ICW/B.

81 WILPF, *Pax International* (February 1929): 3–4.

82 Laura Dreyfus-Barney, 'Peace through Intellectual Co-operation', *International Council of Women Bulletin* (February 1933), 8. 5ICW/P/01.

83 'Norway and Peace through Education', *International Council of Women Bulletin* (January 1926): 2.

84 Akira Iriye, *Cultural Internationalism and the World Order* (Baltimore, MD: The John Hopkins University Press, 1997), 73.

85 WIL, Annual Council Meeting Minutes, 30–31 October 1919, 13.

86 WIL, 'The Kingsway Hall Meeting', *Towards Permanent Peace* (1915), 22.

87 Thomas Davies, *NGOs: A New History of Transnational Civil Society* (London: Hurst, 2014), 124.

88 Glenda Sluga, *Internationalism in the Age of Nationalism* (Philadelphia, PA: University of Pennsylvania Press, 2013), 80.

89 For instance, branches in fascist regimes closed. The German WIL branch struggled to meet from 1933 onwards and leading German WIL members, Anita Augspurg and Lida Gustave Heymann, went into exile in Switzerland. See Emmeline Pethick Lawrence, *My Part in a Changing World* (London: Victor Gollancz, 1938), 329.

90 UIA pioneers Henri La Fontaine and Paul Otlet died in 1943 and 1944, respectively. Léonie La Fontaine died in 1949 and prominent members of the IAW, ICW and WILPF passed away, including WILPF president Jane Addams (d.1935); British WIL president Helena Swanwick (d.1939); Dutch feminist Rosa Manus (d.1942); German feminist Dr Anita Augspurg (d.1943); and Swiss WILPF member Marguerite Gobat (d.1937).

91 Offen, *European Women*, 386–7; Celia Donert, 'Women's Rights in Cold War Europe: Disentangling Feminist Histories', *Past and Present*, supplement 8 (2013): 180.

92 Glenda Sluga, '"Spectacular Feminism": The International History of Women, World Citizenship and Human Rights', in *Women's Activism: Global Perspectives from the 1890s to the Present*, ed. Francisca de Haan, Margaret Allen, June Purvis and Krassimira Daskaolva (Abingdon: Routledge, 2013), 54.

93 UIA, 'XIth International Congress of WILPF', *Bulletin Mensuel* 1, no. 5 (May 1949): 79.

94 Jan Stöckmann, 'Women, Wars, and World Affairs: Recovering Feminist International Relations, 1915–39', *Review of International Studies* 44, no. 2 (2018): 234.

95 UIA, 'Statuts revisés de l'U.A.I', *Bulletin Mensuel* 2, no. 11 (1950): 252.

96 Anne Winslow, *Women, Politics, and the United Nations* (Westport, CT: Greenwood Publishing, 1995); Carole Riegelman Lubin and Anne Winslow, *Social Justice for Women: the International Labour Organization and Women* (Durham, NC: Duke University Press, 1990).

97 Anne Winslow, 'The Carnegie Endowment International Center', *International Associations* 6, no. 2 (1954): 72–6.

98 'Programme of Coming Congresses', *Bulletin Mensuel* 1, no. 5 (May 1949): 78; Vibert Douglas, 'The International Federation of University Women and Scholarly Research', *Bulletin Mensuel* 2, nos. 8–9 (1950): 192; Baronne Pol Boël, 'Le Conseil International des Femmes', *Bulletin Mensuel* 2, no. 10 (1950): 215.

99 L. D. Potter, 'The International Bureau for the Suppression of the Traffic of Persons', *International Associations* 6, no. 2 (1954): 77; Helvi Sipilä, 'Les ONG au Service de la Femme', *International Associations* 27, nos. 6–7 (1975): 339.

100 Madeleine Herren, 'Gender and International Relations through the Lens of the League of Nations (1919–1945)', in *Women, Diplomacy and International Politics since 1500*, ed. Glenda Sluga and Carolyn James (New York: Routledge, 2016), 183.

101 UIA, 'Inter-Governmental Decisions of Interest to NGOs', *NGO Bulletin* 5, nos. 6–7 (1953): 271–81.

102 Paula F. Pfeffer, '"A Whisper in the Assembly of Nations": United States' Participation in the International Movement for Women's Rights from the League of Nations to the United Nations', *Women's Studies International Forum* 8, no. 5 (1985): 469.

103 Laura Beers, *Red Ellen: The Life of Ellen Wilkinson, Socialist, Feminist, Internationalist* (Cambridge, MA: Harvard University Press, 2016), 403–5.

104 WILPF, 'Women in the United Nations', Resolutions passed at the Eleventh International Congress, Copenhagen, 15–19 August 1949.

105 Questionnaire No.11 (October 1912), OCDF preparatory documents and leaflets in Mundaneum, Fonds Féminisme, OCDF.

106 'United Nations Commission on the Status of Women', *Yearbook of International Organisations*. Available online: https://uia.org/s/or/en/1100064295 (accessed 31 July 2018).

107 Jaci Eisenberg, 'The Status of Women: A Bridge from the League of Nations to the United Nations', *Journal of International Organizations Studies* 4, no. 2 (2013): 13–16.

108 'La reprise des Travaux de l'U.A.I', *Bulletin Mensuel* 1, no. 1 (1949): 3.

109 UIA, *Bulletin Mensuel* 1, no. 5 (1949): 72.

110 Susan Zimmermann, 'Liaison Committees of International Women's Organizations and the Changing Landscapes of Women's Internationalism, 1920s to 1945', *Women and Social Movements, International* (Alexandria, VA: Alexander Street Press, n.d.); Barbara Metzger, 'Towards an International Human Rights Regime during the Inter-War Years: The League of Nations' Combat of Traffic in Women and Children',

in *Beyond Sovereignty: Britain, Empire and Transnationalism, c. 1880–1950*, ed. Kevin Grant, Philippa Levine and Frank Trentmann (Basingstoke: Palgrave, 2007), 73; Ellen Carol DuBois, 'Internationalizing Married Women's Nationality: The Hague Campaign of 1930', in *Globalizing Feminisms, 1789–1945*, ed. Karen Offen (Abingdon: Routledge, 2010), 215.

111 Liaison Committee of Women's International Organizations, 'An Experiment in Co-operation, 1925–1945' (*c.* 1945), 16. 7AMP/F/08/06.

112 Elise Boulding, *The Underside of History: A View of Women Through Time* (New York: Sage, 1992), 335.

113 'Elise Boulding, Peace Scholar, Dies at 89', *New York Times*, 1 July 2010.

114 Mary Lee Morrison, 'The Life and Work of Elise Boulding: Honouring Women as Peacemakers', *Affilia: Journal of Women and Social Work* 21, no. 2 (2006): 178.

115 Mary Lee Morrison, *Elise Boulding: A Life in the Cause of Peace* (Jefferson, NC: MacFarland, 2005), 136.

116 Patricia Clavin, *Securing the World Economy: The Reinvention of the League of Nations, 1920–1946* (Oxford: Oxford University Press, 2013), chapter 8.

117 'Alva Mrydal, Nobel Woman, Dies in Sweden at 84', *New York Times*, 3 February 1986.

118 Elise Boulding, *Cultures of Peace: The Hidden Side of History* (Syracuse, NY: Syracuse University Press, 2000), 110.

119 Elise Boulding, 'Female Alternatives to Hierarchical Systems, Past and Present', *International Associations* 27, nos. 6–7 (1975): 340.

120 Elise Boulding, 'The Family, the NGO and Social Mapping in a Changing World', *International Associations* 21, no. 11 (1969): 549.

121 Elise Boulding, *Building a Global Civic Culture: Education for an Interdependent World* (Syracuse, NY: Syracuse University Press, 1988), 35.

122 Elise Boulding, 'Peace Education as Peace Development', *Transnational Associations* 39, no. 6 (1987): 321–2.

123 Boulding, *The Underside of History*, 308.

124 Boulding, 'Peace Education as Peace Development', 325; WILPF's Fourth International Congress focused on the theme of building a 'New International Order'.

125 Sluga, 'Women, Feminisms and Twentieth-Century Internationalisms', 82; Donert, 'Women's Rights in Cold War Europe', 178.

Chapter 6

LEGITIMIZING THE TRANSNATIONAL ASSOCIATIVE EXPERT: THE UNION INTERNATIONALE DES VILLES AND THE UIA

Wouter Van Acker

International organizations seek to build legitimacy both within and beyond the nation-state, and it is vital to understand this process when analysing the forms of transnational governance that emerged in the early twentieth century. The UIA and the International Union of Cities (Union Internationale des Villes, UIV) were early arrivals onto this new global scene, which quickly became more populated and subdivided. The case of these two organizations allows us to study the mechanisms through which different bodies sought recognition for their specific domain.[1] At its foundation in 1910, the UIA aimed to unite the increasing number of specialized transnational ventures and create a platform for discussing their shared interests and concerns. The UIV was established three years later, viewing the concerns of cities and municipalities as its core business. Like the UIA, it has remained active to the present day: during the interwar period, it was known as the International Union of Local Authorities, and in 2004 it became the World Organization of United Cities and Local Governments after a fusion with the Federation of United Cities.

This chapter investigates the ways in which the UIV used its interactions with the UIA to position itself as an authoritative international organization in an increasingly complex field of international power formation. Legitimacy is a contested concept, which has received substantial attention, particularly in the field of political sociology.[2] Rather than proposing a single definition of legitimacy, this chapter will, successively, consider the UIV's social, scientific and political legitimization and the way in which it was connected to the UIA. Despite their different dynamics and roles, there were intersections and parallels between the UIV and the UIA in terms of their social construction, their methods and spaces for organizing and disseminating information as well as their critical positioning within a geopolitical sphere dominated by nation-states.

Social Legitimacy: *The UIV as 'Associative Expert'*

In the late nineteenth century, a new and influential sociological actor surfaced at the crossroads of knowledge and action: 'the association' or, as Yves Lochard and Maud Simonet-Cusset have called it, 'the associative expert'.[3] An increasing number of associations emerged in the judicial, professional and scientific fields, based on professionalization and specialization processes that manifested themselves in the establishment of new university courses, training schools, professional codes of ethics, licences and credential boards. If 'the expert' claimed particular knowledge based on areas of professional practice, 'the association' accumulated a body of knowledge or expertise, organizing a space of sociability where such knowledge was transmitted to its members.[4] The emergent social role of the association was not merely a matter of assembling and mobilizing knowledge: from the outset associations were committed to a political project of 'associationism' or affiliate activism.[5] Being affiliated with an association implied sharing a commitment to certain values with its members.

In 1901, the French 'Law of Associations' provided a legal basis for citizens to set up non-profit associations. Although in Belgium similar legislation was only approved in 1921, the country was the first to accord civic status to international associations with 'scientific objectives', based on a law issued in 1919 – a measure that owed much to the UIA's campaigning on this matter.[6] Such legislation further stimulated the foundation of national and international associations, introducing an intermediary body between the state and civil society. It is within this context of an emergent global civil society – or 'international life', as Otlet and La Fontaine called it – that the creation of the UIV and the UIA as legitimate 'associations of associations' must be situated.

Emile Vinck, a senator for the Belgian Workers' Party, was the driving force behind the first International Congress of Cities, which met in Ghent in 1913 and led to the UIV's creation. In organizing this event, Vinck pursued three goals: to formalize the study of questions concerning municipal governance principles into a comprehensive science of the city; to assemble a community of experts; and to facilitate the public exchange of information on these questions. In this undertaking, he was assisted by the Art Nouveau architect and professor of architecture at the Belgian Academy of Fine Arts, Paul Saintenoy, and by UIA co-founder Paul Otlet. Vinck, Saintenoy and Otlet jointly served as secretaries-general of the first congress. Their work was backed by major political figures, with Emile Braun, the mayor of Ghent, and Gérard Cooreman, president of the Chamber of Representatives, presiding over the event.[7]

Vinck hoped that the congress would formalize links between the national associations in which cities and municipalities had started to group themselves, and that this would help to systemize the exchange of information on urban governance. Such associations had emerged in various German states as early as 1860; an umbrella organization, the Deutscher Städtetag, was founded in 1905. In Great Britain, there was the Association of Municipal Corporations (1872); in Switzerland, the Union des Villes Suisses (1897); in Italy, the Associazione dei

Comuni Italiani (1901); and in the Netherlands, the Vereeniging van Nederlandsche Gemeenten (1912).[8] Along with his work towards the 1913 congress, Vinck also made preparations to establish a Belgian Union of Cities and Municipalities to join the cast of these national organizations. Furthermore, he desired to make the central office of this Belgian organization operate as an international bureau of municipal information, analogous to existing offices in Berlin and Zurich.

The proposed organizational model for the UIV – an international association of associations of cities – resembled that of the UIA, which was an umbrella organization for international associations. Organized on the occasion of the 1913 Ghent world's fair, the first International Congress of Cities took place from 15 to 18 June – only five weeks after the second World Congress of International Associations, which had assembled representatives from 169 international associations and twenty-two governments. Vinck's organizational scheme for the new international association was directly informed by the studies and advice he received from his colleagues heading the UIA – Paul Otlet, Henri La Fontaine and Cyrille Van Overbergh. By 1913, all three were able to claim legitimacy as internationally recognized experts on the phenomenon of associations, both through their scholarly work and practical commitment. Otlet had established his reputation through the International Institute of Bibliography (IIB), which maintained transnational links with many associations, societies and institutes for the development of a central bibliographic repertory and documentary encyclopaedia. La Fontaine, as president of the International Peace Bureau, played an important role in bringing together various pacifist associations. Van Overbergh was an active member in the Ligue Démocratique Belge, a coordinating association for the Catholic workers' movement that received important stimuli through the *Rerum Novarum* encyclical of 1891.[9]

The UIA provided the organizers of the 1913 Congress of Cities with the infrastructure and expertise to set up and manage international associations. The UIA's central office at the Rue de la Régence – located in the building complex of the Royal Museums of Fine Art – offered to host the UIV secretariat. The new association thus gained a postal address as well as access to a collective library of more than 75,000 volumes and to a rich archive of documentation on international organizations. Furthermore, the UIV was invited to develop a section on urbanism for the UIA's International Museum. Last but not least, Vinck and his colleagues were able to draw on the IIB's 'services of documentation', which UIA publications presented as one benefit of cooperation with the Union. These services comprised the collection and processing of facts on urban developments.[10] At the 1913 congress, Otlet had put forward the idea of an international municipal information office – echoing a proposal he had made at the 1910 International Congress of Administrative Sciences. After the Ghent congress had ratified Otlet's plan, the documentation centre was developed within the UIA headquarters.

The UIA's expertise in setting up an international association and the information services provided by the IIB were of direct interest to the community of city associations, as the latter sought to establish an international network that transcended national boundaries and that would acquire social legitimacy as an organization. Meanwhile, at a personal level, this cooperation legitimized Vinck and Otlet's authority as secretaries-general – at least in this initial phase. According to Max Weber, any power needs to legitimize itself as 'deserved', as it offers an advantage.[11] The present case shows how the UIA's legitimacy reflected on, and could be reinvested in, a new international body that sought to acquire a degree of trust from a heterogeneous international community.

Scientific Legitimacy: The International Construction of Urban Expert Knowledge

The 'performative construction of expert knowledge' – a notion formulated by Eric Engstrom – was crucial in the development of international networks.[12] Phillip Wagner has applied Engstrom's concept to the community of urban planners, tracing the development of 'international expert networks' in this field for the period between 1900 and 1960. As Wagner has shown, this process involved contestation – based on professional, political and national divides alongside claims of scientific-technical universality.[13]

The 1913 Congress of Cities sought to construct this sort of scientific legitimacy through the systematic study of all problems faced by municipalities and cities. In the words of Vinck, this endeavour meant learning how these problems 'presented themselves in different countries, which solutions had been found or proposed, and which principles certified by experience could claim to be representative of the architecture of cities, municipal sociology and the administration of municipalities'.[14]

In order to constitute such a comprehensive 'municipal science', the congress was divided into two sections: a first one, chaired by Saintenoy, dealing with 'the construction of cities' (or 'urban planning', as we now understand it), and a second one, chaired by Vinck, which examined the 'organization of municipal life' (or 'urban governance', as we would call it today). The two sciences were considered complementary in that the latter covered the more theoretical field of urban sociology, whereas the former was described as 'applied sociology', or urban sociology put into practice. Comparisons were made with the mind–body divide that characterized the interdisciplinary relationship between psychology (science of the mind) and physiology (science of the body). These notions were in line with the sociological ideas propounded at Brussels-based bodies such as the Société des Études Sociales et Politiques and the Institut des Sciences Sociales. Otlet and La Fontaine were involved in these sociological circles, and so was Vinck.[15]

The 'third' congress section consisted of the Comparative Exhibition of Cities, which Otlet had curated and which the delegates visited on the first day. Located in a hall linked to the Brussels pavilion on the world's fair exhibition grounds, the exhibition included the Cities and Town Planning Exhibition, staged by the urban sociologist and urban planner Patrick Geddes.[16] Geddes's travelling exhibition was complemented by material from the UIA's International Museum (Figure 6.1), showing 'graphical documents on the issue of the organization of

Figure 6.1 Illustrations concerning the development of areas around railway stations, to which a session was devoted at the International Congress of Cities in Ghent (1913). *Source:* Scan Mundaneum-batch-3-052, 'Affiches' collection, Paul Otlet papers, Mundaneum, Mons.

municipal life and municipal services'.[17] Through the UIA, Otlet also arranged for the contributions from the Chicago Welfare Association, the association 'Le Plus Grand Bruxelles', a museum for trade and industry in the German city Hagen and from the city councils of Ghent, Antwerp, Liège, Lier and Ypres.

The show also included printed copies of the utopian plan for a World Centre of Communication, which Hendrik Christian Andersen and Ernest Hébrard had developed. Andersen had presented this scheme to the UIA's 1913 congress. With Andersen's consent and the UIA's support, Otlet adopted this project, envisaging the construction of a 'Cité Mondiale' or international district in Brussels. Otlet's lecture 'A Grandiose Plan for an International City' at the first Congress of Cities initiated a tireless campaign for the idea of the Cité Mondiale, which the UIA would continue to support during the interwar period.[18]

As part of the exhibition, the UIA and IIB set up a library and reading room where a selection of fundamental works and journals on town planning was at the visitors' disposal. Most of these materials produced or assembled by the UIA, including a section on child welfare provided by the Chicago Welfare Association, were arranged to be sent off for the International Exhibition in Lyon starting in May 1914.[19] The French Radical politician and mayor of Lyon Edouard Herriot hoped to claim greater authority within the organization and wanted to host the second UIV congress in his city – a plan that was prevented by the outbreak of the First World War.

The activities of the UIV's documentation centre were not so much interrupted as reoriented as a result of the war. Between 1914 and 1918, the UIV had its temporary seat in The Hague. And with urban planners instead of municipal civil servants taking the lead, the documentation centre was conceived – in line with Otlet's theory of documentation – as a loose-leaf *Encyclopaedia of Cities and Civic Art*.[20] This publication comprised elaborate guidelines for the production of the encyclopaedia, and it was meant to serve as a major instrument for all those involved in planning the reconstruction of war-ravaged areas. As suggested by the Belgian town planner Louis Van der Swaelmen, the work was to be divided and carried out by a group of experts appointed by the scientific or artistic authorities of each nation.[21] UIV leaders were convinced that the organization's network would provide it with the expertise and knowledge to prepare an international aid programme. In this vision – as illustrated by Figure 6.2 – the UIV turned into a sort of relief organization dedicated to studying 'the reconstruction of cities destroyed or damaged by the war ... in Belgium'.[22] After the war, the Dutch–Belgian Committee of Civic Art in The Hague handed over its collection of documentation to the UIV headquarters in Brussels – the first step in executing the UIV's ambition to provide a publicly consultable 'depot of documentation' on municipal affairs.

The field that the UIV claimed as its domain of expertise changed after the war, partly in response to the expanding milieu of what Pierre-Yves Saunier has termed the 'Urban Internationale'. This was an environment 'where ways of judging, apprehending and acting on the city were defined, where expertise and professional legitimacies were created, where knowledge and disciplines were constructed, and where profiles of politicians responsible for urban issues were modified'.[23] In the interwar years, a variety of international organizations organized congresses and other events dedicated to planning and urban problems.[24] Some of these bodies had been founded before the war: the standing committee of the International Housing Congresses had been organizing congresses from 1889 onwards, while the International Congresses of Administrative Sciences (Congrès Internationaux des Sciences Administratives, CISA) had been launched in 1910 to discuss theoretical and technical issues concerning local and national administrations.[25] In 1913, the International Garden Cities and Town Planning Association (later, International Federation for Housing and Town Planning, IFHTP) was created in London.[26] Further bodies emerged during the 1920s: the Congrès International de l'Organisation Scientifique, founded in 1925, promoted the application of the methods of 'scientific management' within private and public institutions; and the Congrès International d'Architecture Moderne (CIAM), founded in 1928, advocated the cause and principles of modernist architecture and urban planning.

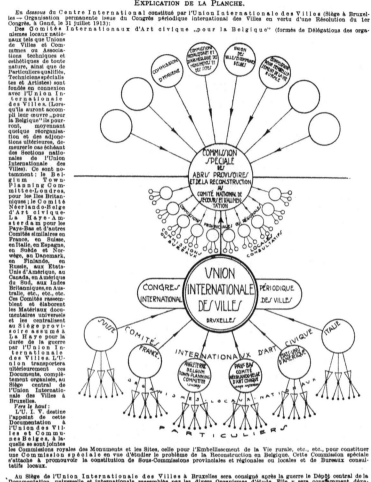

ORGANISATION DE LA COOPÉRATION INTERNATIONALE A L'ÉTUDE DE LA RECON-
STRUCTION DES CITÉS DÉTRUITES OU ENDOMMAGÉES PAR
LA GUERRE DE 1914 EN BELGIQUE.

EXPLICATION DE LA PLANCHE.

Figure 6.2 Louis Van der Swaelmen, 'Organization of International Cooperation to Study the Reconstruction of Cities Destroyed or Damaged by the War of 1914 in Belgium'. *Source:* Louis Van der Swaelmen, *Préliminaires d'art civique mis en relation avec le 'cas clinique' de la Belgique* (Brussel: CIAUD/ICASD, 1980), 113.

In this period, urban planners and architects showed greater interest in joining associations that represented their profession, notably the IFHTP and later CIAM, than in the UIV. UIV's strategic reprofiling during the interwar years was a concurrent development. It cast itself as the principal international organization that had local government and administration as its core business. As Renaud

Payre has argued, the UIV now sought to establish itself as 'the "intermunicipal" market of reform' for municipal government.[27]

Writing to Otlet in 1919, Vinck stated that he 'saw only disadvantages in an announced meeting of the supporters of the Union Internationale des Villes'.[28] It would require inviting a lot of members, who might then claim the power and potentially override the vision and structure set up by its founders. 'We have not advanced enough', Vinck wrote, 'to be able to show these Sirs really interesting realizations.' Moreover, he said, 'such a conference cannot give us any more power than we possess at this moment'.[29] Instead, he preferred to gather informally during the conference linked to the Exhibition of Reconstruction in 1919 in Brussels, to which the members of the UIV were invited, and to hold a preparatory meeting for the organization of a second World Congress of Cities. This meeting eventually took place in September 1920, coinciding with the UIA's *Quinzaine Internationale* (international fortnight) and the inaugural session of its International University, which Daniel Laqua discusses in the present volume. During two weeks of conferences and related events, an 'urbanism and municipalism' section – featuring town planners and municipal delegates from Britain, France, Italy, Japan, Spain, Norway, Denmark, Luxembourg and the Netherlands – provided the framework for discussing the reactivation of the UIV.[30] Stefan Couperus and Shane Ewen have traced the UIV's internal dynamics in this period and shown how Vinck, Henri Sellier, the socialist mayor of the Parisian suburb of Suresnes, and the Dutch socialist alderman from Amsterdam, Florentinus Marinus Wibaut, assumed the lead as they agreed to stage a preparatory conference in Paris.[31] This event took place in 1922 and was followed in 1924 by the second UIV congress in Amsterdam, which formally re-established the UIV, or International Union of Local Authorities (IULA), as it was increasingly called.

After its re-establishment, the UIV's documentation centre further pursued its goal to 'furnish its members with all the information that may be useful for the administration of their municipality'.[32] Vinck and his partners initially drew up an 'analytical bibliography of studies and information on municipal questions'.[33] Relevant articles from 198 specialized journals were cut out, glued onto separate cards and classified in the UIV's 'vast archive on municipal questions'. These initial efforts would have been impossible without the support of the UIA–IIB institutional complex. This was followed by an 'analysis of what seems to be essential in municipal matters' in these articles and by a preparation of brief summaries. From 1921 until the outbreak of the Second World War, these abstracts were published in a bibliographical section entitled 'Les Tablettes Documentaires Municipales' in the UIV's journals: *Le Mouvement Communal* (1919–2008), *Les Tablettes Documentaires Municipales* (1921–5, 1930–2), *Les Sciences Administratives* (1925–7), *L'Administration Locale* (1927–39), and *Les Tablettes Documentaires à l'usage des administrations publiques* (1937–9).[34] After 1924, support for these publications came not so much from the UIA, which lost influence both nationally and internationally, but from the IIB, which continued to grow. Although Otlet saw a new generation take over the reins of the IIB, the institute's leadership recognized the sales potential of the Universal Decimal Classification (UDC) for the field of administration.

Due to its information services, the post-war UIV/IULA served as a clearing house on urbanization, habitation, sewerage, lighting and heating, hygiene, and transportation and communication technology, as far as these matters concerned municipal councillors, civil servants or local officials. Each page of the 'Tablettes Documentaires' contained about ten abstracts, indexed with codes using Otlet and La Fontaine's UDC, which allowed each municipality to construct a bibliographical reference tool or a collection of study files. In practice, this series largely adopted the model of the *Encyclopaedia of Cities* developed by Otlet and Van der Swaelmen during the war. It contributed to the UIV's scientific legitimacy and provided the basis for gathering support for the role that the UIV sought to play on the geopolitical stage.

Critical Legitimacy: Bureaucracy versus the State

Sellier, Wibaut and Vinck were all urban socialists, linked to the international movement that has been dubbed 'socialist municipalism' or, somewhat jestingly, 'gas and water socialism'.[35] This movement promoted the 'socialization' of the means of production in order to gain greater municipal autonomy. Socialist municipalism was an important tendency within the UIV. Although the UIV should not be equated with it, the development of municipal corporations and civil services as buttresses of the financial and administrative autonomy of municipalities and cities was one of the organization's main ideological objectives. In the face of growing state interventionism, this agenda contributed significantly to the UIV's *critical legitimacy*. In the case of international organizations, this form of legitimacy is obtained to the extent that they seek to rebalance the distribution of power and resources, empowering those that tend to be marginalized in political decision-making processes.[36]

Many powers or privileges that cities wanted to appropriate belonged to national governments, which began to play a more active role in providing measures designed to improve the general welfare of their citizens.[37] Problems such as social mobility, employment and health did not just concern individual cities but were national in scope: they had as great an impact on the national well-being as on the well-being of any locality. Claims of responsibility for carrying out these reforms were therefore made at both local and national levels. The power play between these levels of government produced different results in different countries, but in general, cities remained dependent on financial support from central government, which meant that it was difficult to prevent the growth in state control over municipal income and expenditure. The autonomy of cities was conditioned by this wider relationship. By carrying the struggle for greater urban autonomy to an international level, and by appealing, in the face of growing nationalism, to a new democratic world order in which cities would play a greater role, the UIV gained much critical legitimacy.

Many urban authorities decided to take over services from the private sector and deliver them themselves, as a result of which municipal autonomy was strengthened.[38] In order to coordinate the expanding provision of services, radical administrative reform was necessary.[39] As noted by Pierre Rosanvallon, new bureaucratic power structures emerged in France in the 1880s capable of representing general civil interests following an ideology of a 'corporatism of the universal'.[40] Similarly, in 1890s America 'the idea of legitimacy vested in objective administrative power' came out of the discontentment with parties and the longing for management of public affairs.[41] The general ideal of the administration became that of a well-oiled machine that would steer the services' new range of duties in the right direction. As Max Weber pointedly observed, bureaucracy became the new machinery for controlling the societal forces unchained by the industrial revolution.[42]

Patrizia Dogliani has shown how the UIV's contestation of the domination of nation-states was entwined with the political project of left-wing European socialists.[43] She sees the UIV's inception partly as the result of the impulse which the 1900 Paris congress of the Second International gave towards the creation of an autonomous municipal movement. Discussions of municipal action at the Paris congress – promoted by members of the Belgian Workers' Party, including Jules Destrée, Emile Vandervelde and Vinck – led to a resolution that portrayed municipal services as 'embryos of a collectivist society'. The influence of socialist reformers during the UIV's early years was decisive but diluted over the years as it became increasingly 'an association of national and local institutions rather than a movement of opinions, individuals and professions', in which socialist municipalists were not always in the majority.[44]

In the 1920s and 1930s, the agenda of the UIV congresses was increasingly dominated by an interest in technical questions of municipal administration and local government. As Renaud Payre has observed, this diffuse field of study between science, politics and administration was tagged with a variety of names, such as 'the art of the town councillor', 'municipal Taylorism' or 'the science of local government'; and it aimed 'to systematise practical knowledge of local government in order to maximise the efficiency of its organisation and legitimise its call for greater autonomy'.[45] Oscar Gaspari has shown that in this period, national governments increasingly frustrated the efforts of those UIV activists who hoped to gain recognition for the political and institutional role of towns on the international stage: governments restricted the freedom of cities to develop their municipal organizations, and they claimed a monopoly on international political and institutional relations.[46] Stefan Couperus has extended these conclusions. He has shown how internal cleavages as well as unfavourable relations with the League of Nations meant that transnational municipalism as a means of elevating the level of municipal services and administrative routines was favoured over the earlier utopian-political project of a 'World League of Cities'.[47]

Even so, the UIV's increased focus on practical and technical aspects of local municipal administration was not apolitical, as the field of expertise covered by the municipal civil services enjoyed a certain degree of independence from the state and, through its development, promoted a critical reform of the state apparatus. This shift in the UIV's critical agenda manifested itself in its increased collaboration with CISA.[48] In the face of growing state interventionism and rising nationalisms, radical opposition against the agencies of state administration was restrained within the milieu of the UIV, and this opened the path for the ideological rapprochement between UIV and CISA/IISA members, as both groups addressed the organization of administration and bureaucratic management of civil services.[49]

Paul Otlet's activism covered both the UIV and CISA/IISA. He successfully promoted the classification scheme and documentary methods associated with the IIB and UIA within various administrations, drawing on the communication networks of the UIV, CISA and the International Association of Accountancy.[50] At the first International Congress of Administrative Sciences in 1910, Otlet and Johan Zaalberg, city manager of the Dutch community Zaandam and director of the Dutch records management office,[51] demonstrated the benefits of the UDC tables for the organization of municipal archives and the system of files or 'dossiers'.[52] In 1922, the Dutch records management office became part of the main office of the Dutch Association of Municipalities (Vereniging van Nederlandse Gemeenten or VNG) under Zaalberg's direction. Zaalberg facilitated the adoption of the IIB's UDC system, including the documentation tools of the cabinet with folders, but adjusted the IIB's tools for the use of municipal administration. The 'Zaalberg method' was implemented in practically all Dutch municipalities and became known as the 'Code VNG' or 'Basic Archival Code'. In Belgium, the Union of Cities and Municipalities, which was directed by Vinck, and the IIB continued to promote the UDC for administrative purposes at least until 1955, when the tables of a UDC variant for administrative purposes – the 'national decimal classification' – were published.[53] The UIV's journal widely publicized the IIB's classification system and its benefits for the management of administrative documentation in Europe or, what we would call today, 'records management' in municipal administrations.

At the second International Congress of Administrative Sciences, held in Brussels in 1923, Otlet presented an extensive report, *Manuel de la Documentation Administrative*. The Belgian Union of Cities and Municipalities distributed this document at the congress; some of its ideas were visualized in schemas, first in an exhibit linked to the event and then in a 1926 atlas (Figure 6.3). In his paper, Otlet elaborated on the idea that each administration should have 'a central documentation office' or 'intelligence bureau' that was to be like a great modern factory:

> The large modern factory has been able to record minute by minute all that happens in its numerous services. … At all levels of the administrative hierarchy, it is therefore necessary to have 'command posts' positively taking inspiration from examples of industry and transport, but especially by creating what is necessary for the administration, based on the idea of public service resting on principles of science and democracy.[54]

Otlet conceived all documentation, officials, committees and councils as part of 'one documentary organism' that was 'to enable the immediate retrieval of what

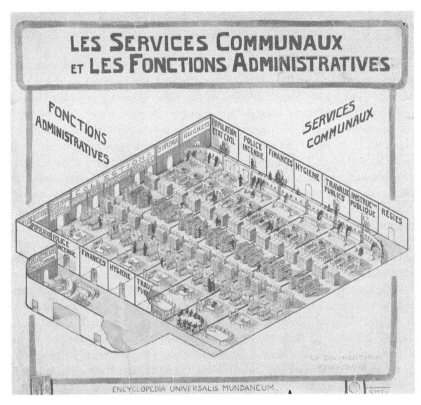

Figure 6.3 Paul Otlet, 'Municipal Services and Administrative Functions', possibly exhibited at the CISA congress of 1923 and featured with other illustrations of the theories of Fayol in his Atlas Administrative (1926). *Source:* Scan MUND-xxxxxx42_2008_0001_ MA, 'Affiches' collection, Paul Otlet papers, Mundaneum, Mons.

is of interest in the acting government',[55] a centralist scheme which he grounded in the then dominant management theories of Taylorism and Fayolism.[56] The theory of scientific management that the American engineer Frederick Taylor had developed was based on an inductive analysis of labour productivity. Taylor extended his proposals for rationalization and economic efficiency to a new corps of civil servants.[57] By contrast, Fayolism – the theory of business administration developed by French mining engineer Henri Fayol – put greater emphasis on management processes and procedures in creating a corps of professional civil servants. Fayol had elaborated his ideas in *L'Incapacité industrielle de l'État* (1921) and *La Doctrine administrative dans l'État* (1923) and gave a keynote lecture at the 1923 CISA meeting.[58] At the same event, Otlet argued that these new principles of (scientific) management, which had already been applied in industry and commercial enterprises, urgently needed to enter into the documentary work of municipal administrations. His presentation at the 1923 CISA congress therefore concluded with the recommendation that CISA should develop an 'International

Office of Administrative Documentation' analogous to and in collaboration with the UIV's documentation office, acting as a mediator between its different national sections.[59]

Such a CISA documentation office finally became a reality in 1930 when, at its fourth congress in Madrid, CISA was transformed into the IISA on the initiative of Oskar Leimgruber, vice-chancellor of the Swiss Federation. Albert Devèze, a Belgian Minister of State, was active in turning the Brussels-based CISA secretariat into the institute's seat. He promised offices in the Belgian capital and offered a large subsidy to IISA.[60] In his paper to the 1930 congress, Otlet further pushed the UDC system and documentary methods developed by the IIB for the use of records management, and he reiterated his idea of a central IISA documentation office, which was adopted in the final resolutions.[61] In 1934, the UIV and IISA co-founded a committee to study how the organization and dissemination of information about public administration services could be improved. In 1936, they collaborated in organizing three 'round table' conferences in Zurich, Berlin and Warsaw about the education of civil servants.[62] In 1937, the permanent secretariats/documentation offices of the UIV and IISA merged in Brussels and, one year later, joined with the secretariat of the IFHTP.[63] The fact that only strictly technical matters were discussed at the UIV's final pre-war conferences – held in Paris (1937) and Glasgow (1938) – reveals the programmatic evolution that the UIV experienced during the interwar period. It shows how its specialization in matters of local civil service and municipal administration reinforced the autonomy of bureaucratic structures. What is less apparent, however, is that this process of forging a strong and independent administration restructured the democratic legitimacy of local government.

Conclusion: Shifting Spaces of Representation

As applied to international organizations, legitimacy relates to the consent of a body of specialists whom the organization claims to represent, and the justification of what sort of normative field it asserts to cover through collective expertise.[64] Both in the social construction of its audience and stakeholders, and in the assumption of a particular normative framework, the input of expert reason which the UIA–IIB complex claimed to cover was instrumental for the legitimization of the UIV/IULA. But besides 'to whom' and 'for what', legitimacy also relates to the question *where* an international organization is legitimate: the recognition of particular transnational spaces that it occupies as well as critical opposition to other spaces of decision-making. As depicted by Otlet in Figure 6.4, the major challenge for the 'organization of international life' was the reconciliation of the functional logic of international associations and the territorial logic of governments. What is particularly interesting in the case of the UIV–UIA relationship is how these associations carved out transnational representational spaces whose borders were demarcated in critical opposition to the traditional geography of geo-politics monopolized by the nation-state.

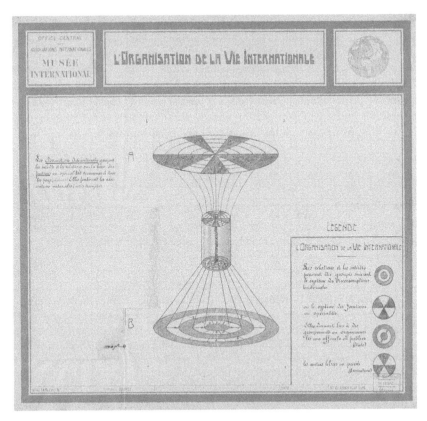

Figure 6.4 Paul Otlet, 'The Organization of International Life' (1912). *Source:* Scan MUND-00011582_2008_0001_MA, 'Affiches' collection, Paul Otlet papers, Mundaneum, Mons.

In the same way that global civil society can be considered to exist apart from, against, in support of, in dialogue with, in partnership with *and* beyond the nation-state,[65] the UIV and UIA's relationship with nation-states was in practice multi-faceted and unstable. As early information societies, the physical space they occupied was state property or territory, such as their central office or headquarters, library, and documentation centre, situated within the Cinquantenaire palace in Brussels – a prestigious monumental building commemorating the fiftieth birthday of the foundation of Belgium.[66] Likewise, the spaces for the creation and distribution of the UIV's journals and UIA bulletins and sites of their congresses belonged to or were made accessible by the state.

On an ideological level, however, the UIA and UIV successfully circumscribed a new cosmopolis by associating on an international level the new figure of the rational expert, who dedicated his life to a particular area of knowledge and who was quickly gaining ground on and next to the politician. Building on processes of professionalization and bureaucratization, the members federated by the UIA and UIV – respectively specialists and their associations, and officials and their administrations – had acquired their authority on the basis of their expertise. As Max Weber pointed out, this process contrasts with the way in which politicians develop claims to legitimacy.[67] It is precisely the potential geopolitical force of this parapolitical field of the expert which makes the UIV and UIA so interesting for the history of global civil society. As ruling became increasingly impossible without consulting professional commissions, bureaucracies and expert organizations, the cosmopolis of the UIV consisted of nothing less than an associative information 'network' running through the 'iron cage' of local authorities.[68]

Notes

1 On Paul Otlet's involvement in the UIV, see Wouter Van Acker, 'Een geografie van de informatienetwerken in de stedelijke beweging: het informatiemodel van Paul Otlet (1868–1944) voor de Union Internationale des Villes', *Stadsgeschiedenis* 3, no. 2 (2008): 122–42.

2 Achim Hurrelmann, Steffen Schneider and Jens Steffek, *Legitimacy in an Age of Global Politics* (Basingstoke: Palgrave, 2007); James Brassett and Eleni Tsingou, 'The Politics of Legitimate Global Governance', *Review of International Political Economy* 18, no. 1 (2011): 1–16; Steven Bernstein, 'Legitimacy in Intergovernmental and Nonstate Global Governance', *Review of International Political Economy* 18, no. 1 (2011): 17–51; Furio Cerutti, 'The Deeper Roots of Legitimacy and Its Future', *Review of International Political Economy* 18, no. 1 (2011): 121–30; David Beetham, *The Legitimation of Power* (Basingstoke: Macmillan, 2013).

3 Yves Lochard and Maud Simonet-Cusset, 'L'Expertise associative comme question sociologique', in *L'Expert associative, le savant et le politique*, ed. Yves Lochard and Maud Simonet-Cusset (Paris: Éditions Syllepse, 2003), 7–14.

4 Corinne Delmas, *Sociologie politique de l'expertise* (Paris: La Découverte, 2011).

5 Jacques Ion, 'Modes d'engagement et savoirs associatifs: petit coup d'oeil dans le rétroviseur' in *L'expert associative, le savant et le politique*, ed. Yves Lochard and Maud Simonet-Cusset (Paris: Éditions Syllepse, 2003), 21–6.

6 European Commission, 'Study on Volunteering in the European Union: Country Report Belgium'. Available online: http://ec.europa.eu/citizenship/pdf/national_report_be_en.pdf (accessed 20 March 2018). UIA, 'International Associations under Belgian Law'. Available online: https://uia.org/belgianlaw (accessed 20 March 2018).

7 Anon., *Congrès International de l'art de bâtir des villes: Gand 1913* in Paul Otlet papers, box UIV PO 31, Mundaneum, Mons.

8 Jean-Luc Pinol, Guy Burgel, Odile Goerg, Xavier Huetz de Lemps and Marc Boone, *Histoire de l'Europe urbaine*, vol. 2: *De l'Ancien Régime à nos jours: expansion et limite d'un modèle* (Paris: Seuil, 2003), 152–9.

9 Emmanuel Gerard, *De christelijke arbeidersbeweging in België 1891–1991* (Leuven: Universitaire Pers Leuven, 1991).

10 Office Central des Associations Internationales, *L'Union des Associations Internationales. Constitution du Centre International. Congrès Mondial. Office Central. Musée International. Documenational Universelle* (Brussels: Union des Associations Internationales, 1912), 20.

11 Max Weber, *Economy and Society: An Outline of Interpretive Sociology* (Berkeley, CA: University of California Press, [1922] 1978), 214.

12 Eric J. Engstrom, *Figurationen des Experten: Ambivalenzen der Wissenschaftlichen Expertise im Ausgehenden 18. und frühen 19. Jahrhundert* (Frankfurt am Main: Peter Lang, 2005).

13 Phillip Wagner, *Stadtplanung für die Welt? Internationales Expertenwissen 1900-1960* (Göttingen: Vandenhoeck & Ruprecht, 2016), 13–14.

14 *Premier Congrès International et Exposition Comparée Des Villes: Documents Préliminaires* (Brussels: Union internationale des villes, 1913), 6.

15 Wouter Van Acker, 'Sociology in Brussels, Organicism and the Idea of a World Society in the Period before the First World War', in *Information Beyond Borders. International Cultural and Intellectual Exchange in the Belle Époque*, ed. W. Boyd Rayward (Aldershot: Ashgate, 2013), 143–68. See also Boyd Rayward's contribution in this volume.

16 Wouter Van Acker, Michiel Dehaene and Pieter Uyttenhove, 'Tussen stedenbouw en stadsbestuur: De stedententoonstelling van Patrick Geddes en het internationaal stedencongres', in *Gent 1913: op het breukvlak van de moderniteit*, ed. Wouter Van Acker and Christophe Verbruggen (Heule: Snoeck, 2013), 154–69.

17 *Premier Congrès International et Exposition Comparée Des Villes*, xviii–xx. On Otlet's campaign for the Cité Mondiale, see Wouter Van Acker and Geert Somsen. 'A Tale of Two World Capitals: The Internationalisms of Pieter Eijkman and Paul Otlet', *Revue Belge de Philologie et d'Histoire* 90, no. 4 (2012): 1389–409; Wouter Van Acker, 'Universalism as Utopia: A Historical Study of the Schemes and Schemas of Paul Otlet (1868–1944)' (PhD diss., Ghent University, 2011), Chapter 7 on the Cité Mondiale; Giuliano Gresleri and Dario Matteoni. *La Citta' Mondiale: Andersen, Hébrard, Otlet, Le Corbusier* (Venice: Marsilio Editori, 1982).

18 Hendrick C. Andersen, 'Un centre mondial: projet de Cité Internationale', *Proceedings of the World Congress of International Associations, 2nd session, Ghent-Brussels, 15–18 June 1913* (Brussels: Union des Associations Internationales, 1913), Paul Otlet, 'Un Projet grandiose de Cité Internationale', in *Premier congrès international et exposition comparée des villes* (Brussels: Union internationale des villes, 1913), also published in *La Vie Internationale* 4 (1913): 53–8.

19 'UIA – Exposition Urbaine Lyon 1914', Box 92, UIA Archives, Manuscript Section, Hoover Institution at Stanford University. See also Pierre-Yves Saunier and Renaud Payre. 'A City in the World of Cities: Lyon and Municipal Associations in the 20th Century' in *Another Global City: Historical Explorations into the Transnational Municipal Moment 1850-2000*, ed. Shane Ewen and Pierre-Yves Saunier (Basingstoke: Palgrave, 2008), 69–85.

20 UIV / Comités internationaux d'art civique 'Pour La Belgique', *Encyclopédie des Villes et de l'Art Civique*, vol. 1 (Brussels/Leiden: UIV / Société d'éditions A. W. Sijthoff, 1916); UIV / Comités internationaux d'art civique 'Pour La Belgique', *Encyclopédie des Villes et de l'Art Civique: programme-tables des matières*, vol 2: *Commentaire des principes fondamentaux d'urbanisation et guide analytique pour l'étude comparée des 'standards' expérimentaux universels réalisés en application du dernier état des connaissances internationales relatives à l'urbanisme – aménagement, extension, construction et organisation des cités* (Brussels and Leiden: UIV/Société d'éditions A. W. Sijthoff, 1917); Paul Otlet, Louis Van der Swaelmen, Hendrik Petrus Berlage, Th. J. Cuypers, and Henri Evers, *Encyclopédie des Villes et de l'Art Civique: Rapport introductif au gouvernement belge* (Brussels/Leiden: UIV/Société d'éditions A. W. Sijthoff, 1917).

21 Louis Van der Swaelmen, *Préliminaires d'art civique mis en relation avec le 'cas Clinique' de la Belgique* (Brussel: CIAUD/ICASD, [1916] 1980), 113.

22 Van der Swaelmen, *Préliminaires d'art civique mis en relation avec le 'cas Clinique' de la Belgique*, 113.

23 Pierre-Yves Saunier, 'Sketches from the Urban Internationale, 1910–1950: Voluntary Associations, International Institutions and US Philanthropic Foundations', *International Journal of Urban and Regional Research* 25, no. 2 (2001): 382.

24 Helen E. Meller, 'Philanthropy and Public Enterprise: International Exhibitions and the Modern Town Planning Movement, 1889–1913', *Planning Perspectives* 10 (1995): 295–310; Pierre-Yves Saunier, 'La toile municipale aux XIXe et XXe siècles: un panorama transnational vu d'Europe', *Urban History Review* 34, no. 2 (2006): 163–76; Pierre-Yves Saunier, 'Reshaping the Urban Internationale: The US Foundations and International Organisation in Municipal Government, Planning and Housing 1920s–1960s', paper presented at the conference *Philanthropy and the City: An Historical Overview, New York, 2000.* Available online: http://rockarch.org/publicatio ns/conferences/saunier.pdf (accessed 24 April 2018).

25 On the former, see Saunier, 'Sketches from the Urban Internationale', 383. On the latter, see Renaud Payre, 'L'Etat vu d'en haut: la réforme de l'Etat au sein des espaces internationaux de la science administrative dans l'entre-deux-guerres', *Revue française d'administration publique* 4, no. 120 (2006): 651–66.

26 Michael Alexander Geertse, 'Defining the Universal City: The International Federation for Housing and Town Planning and Transnational Planning Dialogue 1913–1945' (PhD diss., Vrije Universiteit, Amsterdam, 2012).

27 Renaud Payre, 'A l'École du gouvernement municipal: les congrès de l'Union Internationale des Villes de Gand (1913) à Genève (1949)', in *Administrer la ville en Europe (XIXe–XXe siècles)*, ed. Bruno Dumons and Gilles Pollet (Paris: L'Harmattan 2003), 112.

28 Emile Vinck to Paul Otlet, 6 August 1919, in Paul Otlet papers, UIV PO 31, Mundaneum.

29 Ibid.

30 H. J. D. Revers, *IULA 1913–1963: The Story of Fifty Years of International Municipal Co-Operation* (The Hague: Martinus Nijhoff, 1963), 28–9.

31 Stefan Couperus and Shane Ewen, 'Whose "Urban Internationale"? Intermunicipalism in Europe, c. 1924–36: The Value of a Decentred, Interpretive Approach to Transnational Urban History', in *Cities Beyond Borders: Comparative and Transnational Approaches to Urban History*, ed. Nicolas Kenny and Rebecca Madgin (Aldershot: Ashgate Publishing, 2015), 149–72.

32 Emile Vinck, 'L'Union des Villes et l'Exposition de la Reconstruction', *La Cité* 1, nos. 4–5 (1919): 57–8.

33 'Documentation des services publics par les Tablettes Documentaires', *Le Mouvement Communal*, no. 5 (1923): 2.

34 On the UIV's different journals, see Renaud Payre and Pierre-Yves Saunier, 'Municipalités de tous pays, unissez vous! L'Union Internationale des Villes ou l'internationale municipale (1913–1940)', *Amministrare* 30, nos. 1–2 (2000): 221.

35 Patrizia Dogliani, 'European Municipalism in the First Half of the Twentieth Century: The Socialist Network', *Contemporary European History* 2, no. 4 (2002): 573–96.

36 This definition is based on Erla Thrandardottir, 'NGO Legitimacy: Four Models', *Representation* 51, no. 1 (2015): 107–23 and Patrice Duran, 'Légitimité, droit et action publique', *L'Année Sociologique* 59, no. 2 (2009): 303–44.

37 Pinol et al., *Histoire de l'Europe urbaine*, 171–9.

38 Michèle Dagenais, Irene Maver and Pierre-Yves Saunier, *Municipal Services and Employees in the Modern City: New Historic Approaches* (Aldershot: Ashgate, 2003).

39　Renaud Payre, 'L'État vu d'en haut: la réforme de l'Etat au sein des espaces internationaux de la science administrative dans l'entre-deux-guerres', *Revue française d'administration publique* 4, no. 120 (2006): 651–66.

40　Pierre Rosanvallon, *Democratic Legitimacy: Impartiality, Reflexivity, Proximity* (Princeton, NJ: Princeton University Press, 2011), 38. Rosanvallon borrows this expression from Pierre Bourdieu.

41　Rosanvallon, *Democratic Legitimacy*, 37.

42　James R. Beniger, *The Control Revolution: Technological and Economic Origins of the Information Society* (Cambridge, MA: Harvard University Press, 1986), 6.

43　Dogliani, 'European Municipalism', 584–5.

44　Ibid., 586.

45　Renaud Payre, 'The Science That Never Was: "Communal Science" in France, 1913–1949', *Contemporary European History* 11, no. 4 (2002): 534.

46　Oscar Gaspari, 'Cities against States? Hopes, Dreams and Shortcomings of the European Municipal Movement, 1900–1960', *Contemporary European History* 2, no. 4 (2002): 597–621.

47　Stefan Couperus, 'In between "Vague Theory" and "Sound Practical Lines": Transnational Municipalism in Interwar Europe', in *Internationalism Reconfigured: Transnational Ideas and Movements between the World Wars*, ed. Daniel Laqua (London: I.B. Tauris, 2011), 67–89.

48　Denis Moschopoulos, 'The International Institute of Administrative Sciences: Main Stages of its History', *International Review of Administrative Sciences* 71, no. 2 (2005): 197–215.

49　On the first congresses of CISA see also Renaud Payre, 'Une République mondiale de l'administration? Circulations internationales, sciences de gouvernement et réforme administrative (1910-1945)', *Revue internationale de politique comparée* 23, no. 1 (2016): 39.

50　David A. R. Forrester, 'European Congresses of Accounting: A Preliminary Review of their History', *An Invitation to Accounting History. Glasgow* (1998). Available online: http://www.cs.trinity.edu/rjensen/readings/history/forrester/c06EuropeanCongress esAccounting.htm (accessed 13 April 2018).

51　Nico Randeraad, 'Een etalage van bestuurlijke vernieuwing. De tentoonstelling op gemeentelijk administratief gebied in 1906', *Amstelodamum* 82 (1995): 149.

52　Bernard Mantel, 'Zaalberg in Zaandam', in *Van Code tot Community*, ed. Ivo Klamer, Diane Schöller and Ad van Heijst (Rijswijk: Factor-i, 2008), 14–25.

53　Joris Vanderborght, 'De NDC, weg ermee? Een kennismaking. NDC en archief' *Bibliotheek- en Archiefgids* 82, no. 6 (2006): 11–15.

54　Paul Otlet, *Manuel de la Documentation administrative. I. Principes Généraux. Rapport présenté au IIe Congrès international des Sciences Administratives* (Brussels: Union des Villes et Communes Belges, 1923), 19.

55　Otlet, *Manuel de la Documentation administrative*, 4.

56　For a discussion by Otlet of the doctrine of 'Taylorism' and 'Fayolism' in relation to his ideas of documentation, see Paul Otlet, 'La Technique générale de l'Action', *Chimie et Industrie* 2, no. 3 (1924): 592–8.

57　On Taylorism and the impact of Taylorism in France, see George G. Humphreys, *Taylorism in France 1904-1920: The Impact of Scientific Management on Factory Relations and Society* (New York: Garland, 1986); Judith A. Merkle, *Management and Ideology: The Legacy of the International Scientific Management Movement* (Berkeley, CA: California University Press, 1980), 158–71.

58   Stéphane Rials, *Administration et organization, 1910–1930: De l'organisation de la bataille à la bataille de l'organisation dans l'administration française* (Paris: Beauchesne, 1977). On the practical impact of these ideas, see Alain Chatriot, 'Fayol, les fayoliens et l'impossible réforme de l'Administration durant l'entre-deux-guerres', *Entreprises et histoire* no. 34 (2003): 84–97.

59   Otlet, *Manuel de la Documentation administrative*, 93.

60   Stefan Fisch, 'Origins and History of the International Institute of Administrative Sciences: From Its Beginnings to Its Reconstruction after World War II (1910–1944/47)', in *IIAS/IISA Administration & Service 1930–2005*, ed. Fabio Rugge and Michael Duggett (Amsterdam: IOS Press, 2005), 39–40.

61   Paul Otlet, *Sur les Possibilités pour les entités administratives d'avoir à tout moment leur situation présentée documentairement* (Brussels: Institut International de Bibliographie, 1930).

62   Payre, 'L'Etat vu d'en haut', 662.

63   Stefan Couperus, *De Machinerie van de stad: stadsbestuur als idee en praktijk, Nederland en Amsterdam 1900–1940* (Amsterdam: Aksant, 2009), 134.

64   Sarah Lister, 'NGO Legitimacy: Technical Issue or Social Construct?', *Critique of Anthropology* 23, no. 2 (2003): 175–92.

65   Simone Chambers and Jeffrey Kopstein, 'Civil Society and the State', in *The Oxford Handbook of Political Theory*, ed. Anne Phillips, Bonnie Honig and John S. Dryzek (Oxford: Oxford University Press, 2008), 362–81.

66   See also Geary and Randeraad on uses of information in interwar international organizations: Michael Geary and Nico Randeraad, 'Information Processes and International Organizations (1910–1940)', in *The Politics of Information: The Case of the European Union*, ed. Tannelie Blom and Sophie Vanhoonacker (Basingstoke: Palgrave, 2014), 34–48.

67   For Max Weber's two lectures 'Science as Vocation' (1917) and 'Politics as Vocation' (1919), see David Owen and Tracy B. Strong, eds, *The Vocation Lectures / Max Weber*, trans. Rodney Livingstone (Indianapolis, IN: Hackett, 2004), 1–94.

68   For the image of the 'iron cage', or 'stahlhartes Gehäuse', see Max Weber, *The Protestant Ethic and the Spirit of Capitalism*, trans. Talcott Parsons (New York: Scribner, [1905] 1930).

Chapter 7

HISTORIANS AND INTERNATIONAL ORGANIZATIONS: THE INTERNATIONAL COMMITTEE OF HISTORICAL SCIENCES

Matthias Middell and Katja Naumann

The history of historiography offers at least three narratives about the relationship between historians and internationalization. The first underlines historians' close relation with nation-states by emphasizing their role in legitimizing accounts of national origins as well as the benefits they gained from doing so. The picture of historians as nation builders – inventing traditions and insisting on national difference – continues to nourish a steady stream of books.[1]

The second approach presents historians as part of their national community, but focuses on both cooperation and competition in the presentation of national histories. In this context, cooperation includes mutual inspiration in the development of methodologies, use of materials, institutionalization and professional behaviour. Competition encompasses the observation of others as well as claims of superiority. Congresses are one platform where such competition is staged.[2] Another field is constituted by academic journals, with their reviews and bibliographical notes, which include and exclude.[3] Karl Dietrich Erdmann's study about the international congresses of historians since the late nineteenth century provides a detailed overview of the dialectics of competition and cooperation. Written in the twilight of the Cold War period, it portrays the discipline as coming to terms with nationalism and East–West rivalry by stepping towards international organization.[4] What he called an 'ecumenical' association in 1987 became a 'global community' in the English version of 2005.[5]

The latter characterization refers to a third type of writing the history of historiography – one that does not focus on the national origin of individual historians or the national context of their work. Instead, it emphasizes the formation of transnational or even transregional scholarly communities, shaped by shared research interests. Be it the history of gender or of revolutions, the history of the state or of economies, of culture or of science – the number of historiographical studies that trace the development of ideas and concepts regardless of the authors' origins is growing and reflects the transformation of scholarly working conditions. Historians have become more mobile; digitization makes archival material more widely available; and subjects increasingly have to be addressed by multisited scholarship. Transregional examinations often require collective expertise and thus necessitate collaboration.

This chapter investigates internationalism among historians and thus offers a distinct perspective on the subject matter of this book. The Union of International Associations promoted the notion that the world was becoming increasingly integrated, and that international congresses and international organizations were one manifestation of this development. The chapter's initial sections consider the extent to which historians participated in this process, while noting the limits of their internationalism. We show how scholars within a specific discipline related to the aims pursued by the UIA – mostly without getting involved in the latter's activities. The discussion thus highlights attitudes, constellations and dynamics in professional and academic communities that the UIA was confronted with when promoting internationalism. The later sections shift to historians' engagement with global perspectives, both in the context of international congresses and the development of transregional communities. As a whole, the chapter relates the history of historiography to wider questions surrounding scientific internationalism and the emergence of global civil society.

Historical Congresses and the History of Internationalism

As many contributions to the present volume illustrate, historians have analysed international organizations in manifold ways. Yet their own community's road to international organization largely remains in the dark – notwithstanding Erdmann's book. To some extent, their path maps on to the wider history of internationalism. The first international congress of historians took place in Rome in 1898, and hence in a period that, as Bob Reinalda's figures in this book show, had seen a growth in international congress activity. After a rupture in transnational contacts during the First World War, the renewal of transnational bonds led to the creation of the International Committee of Historical Sciences (Comité International des Sciences Historiques, CISH) in 1926.

These developments seemingly fit the narrative espoused by the UIA. Indeed, in 1910, the Union's 'Table of International Organization' listed the historical congresses' discussions on cartography alongside other international classification and standardization efforts.[6] The UIA's periodical and the second edition of its *Annuaire de la Vie Internationale* subsequently featured the International Congress of Historical Sciences among several events that were seen to constitute 'international life'.[7] Nonetheless, little contact existed between historians and the UIA, for two reasons. First, although historians met several times from 1898 onwards, they did not initially aim to form an international association. Accordingly, there were no headquarters to which Henri La Fontaine and Paul Otlet could have turned in their quest for information. Secondly, the intent to document internationalism did not resonate widely among historians. As their early congresses demonstrated, the vast majority of historians believed much less in the universal collection of knowledge as practised by La Fontaine and Otlet in the International Institute of Bibliography since 1895. To the contrary, they were convinced of the necessity to put general history into perspective through knowledge of the particular.

Most participants of the first international meeting of historians in Rome came from Western and Central Europe, and the history of Antiquity was their main focus. Participating scholars who specialized in ancient Rome may have been attracted by the location rather than by the prospect of contributing to the wider professionalization of their field. But, all limitations aside, a point of departure for further gatherings was established.

The attitudes towards subsequent cooperation differed enormously. For instance, French scholars viewed the Parisian world exhibition of 1900 as an opportunity to represent their work by hosting an international congress. Most German colleagues saw no gains from joining an international association, as they considered their country as leading the discipline. Nevertheless, historians slowly developed a practice of gathering internationally to present and compare research findings and to support their discipline's professionalization. Creating a proper organization was not on their mind. The logistics of the individual congresses remained in the hands of local organizers, who mobilized funding from local universities and national governments. These scholars usually did not outline research problems that required a permanent organization. Of course, historians benefitted from international regulations protecting intellectual property and they travelled by trains for which other organizations started to coordinate technical standards. Historians had some contact with the emerging world of international organizations and they looked with interest at diplomats with whom they interacted through local patterns of sociability. But in the development of practices for their own profession, historians trusted more in the proximity to national politics (and funding opportunities) than in any international cooperation.

Such attitudes can partly be explained by the context of their work. The organization of archives and access to their wealth was directly related to state administration, and most archival research was exercised by scholars from the respective nations. When using foreign documents and accessing archives abroad, scholars mobilized private contacts and networks. Congresses offered the opportunity for such personal encounters and the visit of monuments and capitals of foreign powers. It seems that historians were as mobile as other political, academic and entrepreneurial elites while feeling less of a need for an organization. To most of them, national historical narratives were nothing to negotiate and regulate across borders.

Only a minority prioritized scholarly exchange, support across borders and the vision of universal history. The so-called Lamprecht controversy had exploded in the 1890s about the question of cultural versus political history, but the controversy's more important second part dealt with the question of whether universal history was in conflict with the standards of the profession.[8] In 1908, Leipzig-based historian Karl Lamprecht tried to use the tribune of the international historical congress in Berlin to promote his idea of universal history,[9] which had parallels to La Fontaine and Otlet's internationalist vision. Among other things, he planned to invite scholars from non-European regions to teach German students about their homes and he advertised the collection of material from across the world. Being an excellent networker across Europe and the Atlantic, Lamprecht suffered from his isolation among his German colleagues. Accident or not, at the time when his lecture was scheduled at the Berlin congress, delegates were enticed to attend a royal reception in Potsdam.[10]

In short, historians met internationally but the majority did not share the UIA's internationalist agenda. While internationalists started to develop their own historical narratives about a connected world, the most prominent representatives of the historical profession saw international congresses primarily as a platform for staging national superiority. Despite such limitations, these activities tied in with the wider history of internationalism. For example, in discussing international congress practices, Paul Otlet cited the historians' 1908 congress in Berlin as a 'model' in using a designated bureau to provide auxiliary services for delegates – from travel and postal arrangements to a hairdresser.[11] Successful congresses certainly required both organizational and diplomatic skills. Participation levels suggested that many historians recognized the need for transnational dialogue and self-organization.

Matters changed in the wake of the First World War. The infamous declaration of German professors supporting their government's war goals sent shock waves through the world of scientific internationalism. It interrupted communication between German and French historians, while Belgian scholars were frustrated by the lack of support from their German peers after the attack on their country. The war years saw dramatic ruptures in personal relations and friendships, for example between Lamprecht and the leading Belgian historian Henri Pirenne. Other historians began to collect material documenting war crimes committed by the opposing side and seeking to whitewash their army from the accusation of war atrocities. Yet the conflict was also a time of growing interest in the activities and thoughts of colleagues from across the border. Some historians argued for peace and reconciliation, although most of them remained in the 'trenches', observing the other side with hostile attention. The development of historiography in the 1920s and 1930s cannot be understood without its deep embossing by the experience of war.

The situation was therefore unfavourable to any kind of international(ist) association organizing future collaboration among historians. In this respect, circumstances seemed to contradict the optimism with which the UIA outlined the future of internationalism in 1921.[12] At the same time, historians were aware that the war and the explosion of violent nationalism had undermined basic assumptions of their profession. The four years of mass killing had destroyed the imagined superiority of European civilization, and the destruction of whole regions had undercut the success stories told about the genesis of European nations.[13] These developments enabled the growing influence of the United States and other non-European countries.[14] The world of international organizations was reordered within the framework of the League of Nations, where expertise was considered to be the basis for liberal internationalism.[15] Moreover, in some ways, the exclusion of German historians from scholarly communication and organization until the mid-1920s facilitated steps towards a political and methodological renewal of international historiography.[16] Scholars of the older generation, including Henri Pirenne in Belgium and Henri Berr in France, used their networks to facilitate the move towards a new social and economic history that was transnational and comparative in its approach.[17] At the end of the decade, this development found its intellectual centre in the French journal *Annales d'histoire économique et sociale*.

The Inner Workings of an International Organization

Discussions at the fifth International Congress of Historical Sciences in Brussels in 1923 had planted the idea of a more permanent body that would sustain future collaboration, also between the meetings. In May 1926, CISH was founded in Geneva. The UIA was not directly involved, but its inception resonated with the Union's support for transnational intellectual cooperation in this period. Moreover, history featured within the wider agenda of academic exchange at the International University sessions which Daniel Laqua discusses in the present volume.[18] Two years after its foundation, CISH held its first congress in Oslo. Marc Bloch's seminal lecture on comparative history set the tone, suggesting that cross-border cooperation would be to the advantage of the profession as a whole: it would allow historiography to develop a sense for peacekeeping and the mutual understanding of different cultures, and it would help to overcome the limitations of purely national history writing by systematically mobilizing the resources of historians abroad.[19]

This section analyses CISH as an international non-governmental organization that meets the definitional criteria set out by the UIA. The Union's classification scheme treats CISH as a 'federation of international organizations' (Type I-A) and as having 'international organizations as members' (Type II-y).[20] CISH was indeed built on national committees and, for a long time, such national representations had the power to decide who would enter the scene. Even joint initiatives such as presentations by scholars from different countries or even continents (as they became more regular after 1945) remained largely dependent on national resources and on the support by leading scholars of specific nations. Similar constraints applied to activities such as the preparation of bibliographic information. Only later on did CISH allow for member organizations that are international in their approach and membership. Tellingly, these are called 'affiliated organizations', as if of secondary rank. At least until the early 2000s, members were accepted to most of these thematic (rather than national) member organizations only when representing a country. The situation differs from country to country, but in most of them, national organizations decide how the respective national historiography might be represented at CISH level.

Following wider transformations in the world of international organizations after the Second World War, the United Nations Scientific, Educational and

Cultural Organization (UNESCO) has helped to nourish a network of bodies and initiatives fostering academic professionalism and interdisciplinarity. CISH has shown some interest in opportunities for collaboration, for example through membership in UNESCO's International Council for Philosophy and Human Sciences, which was launched in 1949.[21] As shall be discussed later, CISH members also became involved in writing world history or the history of regions such as Africa, partly under the auspices of such international bodies. This engagement, however, arose from the individual initiatives rather than from a programmatic decision within CISH.

Over the twentieth century, CISH has developed into a large organization with almost one hundred member organizations, both national and international; yet its relationship with other international bodies remains weak. The regular congresses demonstrate a lively interest in making CISH a platform for encounters and collaborative work. At the same time, its relative remoteness from the general development of internationalism remains. For example, it is left to an organizationally independent 'network of concerned historians' under the leadership of Antoine de Baets to defend historians who come under attack for political reasons.[22] Such human rights issues, resonating with the endeavours of other NGOs, are not absent from the agenda of CISH's general assemblies, but they remain in the background.

In contrast to many other international organizations, CISH has not seen the need to further professionalize its own administration. Governance is rather decentralized; members of the board and the general secretary work on a voluntary basis. The main task – the preparation of the next congress – is mainly left to local organizers who are often subsidized by national, regional and/or local institutions. It is therefore difficult to identify a special culture among the members of the secretariat – a subject that Bob Reinalda addresses in this volume.[23]

The publication of congress proceedings had long been secured by the same mechanism: it remained in the hands of the local organizers. When this method went into crisis (because subsidies were skyrocketing and/or the delay of manuscript submission went beyond an acceptable limit), publication activities simply stopped. There are publications from individual panels or participants, but many of these articles appear without mentioning CISH. This has not always been the case – take, for example, the involvement of CISH in the preparation of major world and continental histories.[24]

The annual bulletin, which was meant to inform member organizations about developments within CISH, disappeared in the early twenty-first century. The website provides standard information and the financial circumstances do not allow for the recruitment of a permanent editorial staff. Worse even, the bulletin never made it to the individual members but was distributed only to the member organizations and thus depended on their distributive capacities. One can argue that the decentralized administration makes the organization's performance a direct function of its presidents, general secretaries and other personalities on its board, and that this had advantages in times of competing nationalism and bloc confrontation. National funding agencies supported the model because it secured some influence on the representation of national historiography in the international realm.

In terms of relations to UIA or other protagonists of internationalism, CISH has shown little interest to learn from other actors in global civil society how to increase its visibility and how to attract individual membership or large funding for new tasks. It is therefore no wonder that the links between UIA and CISH are thin: limited to CISH being listed in UIA's *Yearbook of International Organizations* (with many sub-organizations of CISH being part of the list of seemingly independent organizations); and limited to CISH having a place in the matrix of academic professional organizations established by and connected to UNESCO. The latter has been recently revivified by recent world congresses in the social sciences and the humanities. This may lead to more interaction in the future, due to projects such as a new global history edited by the International Council for Philosophy and Human Sciences.

Conceptualizing Global Connectivity before 1945

Both the UIA and CISH exemplify aspects of scientific internationalism, which has helped to create spaces for the circulation and documentation of ideas and practices.[25] When approaching CISH from this perspective, two dimensions become apparent: on the one hand the institutional aim of maintaining an international organization through changing times; and on the other hand the question of how historians' research has addressed matters of global connectivity (of which the emergence of international organizations was a manifestation). The following two sections will address the latter issues.

From the beginning, historical congresses brought together both nationalists and cosmopolitans.[26] The former recognized the possibility of demonstrating their nation's superiority or defending it against representatives of other national historiographies. The latter saw congresses as an instrument of mutual understanding and of contributing to world-historical imaginations.[27] The writing of history is subject to a tension between these two approaches. On the one hand, every historical account, especially with the ambition to be original or to make a general argument, contextualizes – explicitly or implicitly – its subject in large-scale historical processes. On the other hand, when historians turned their occupation into an academic profession and established history as a scientific discipline, many concentrated on one aspect of the past, the formation and growth of the (mainly Western) nation-state, sidelining other dimensions of social and cultural organization.[28] As Gilbert Allardyce has noted, they marginalized the world at large, long-distance interactions and exchanges, as well as the global condition:

> As the practice of history became professional, the practice of world history became identified with amateurism. The new history defined itself against the old, and apprentices in the vocation, reared on specialized research, learned

to hold world history in suspicion, as something outmoded, overblown, and metahistorical. Whoever said world history, said amateurism.[29]

Early on, CISH became an arena for negotiating the worldliness of historical narratives and, closely linked to that, the positioning of this professional group towards the global condition. Terms such as 'Weltpolitik' or 'Weltwirtschaft' entered the vocabulary in the late nineteenth and early twentieth centuries.[30] While world history was debated at the congresses in Paris (1900) and Berlin (1908), scepticism vis-à-vis the perceived amateurishness of world history writing prevailed across the community. Convinced that only smaller-scale topics would allow for the ideal of an archive-based 'complete investigation', most historians hesitated to open their field in a way that would address contemporary experiences of globalization.

There were, however, at least three noteworthy counter-tendencies. First, as minoritarian as it may have been, a historiographical strand that insisted on the tradition of world history, dating back at least to the period of Enlightenment, continued into the nineteenth and twentieth centuries. Individuals such as Henry Thomas Buckle and Lord Acton, Kurt Breysig and Karl Lamprecht as well as the group around Henri Berr and the *Revue de synthèse* felt inspired by the wave of increasing global connections to intensify efforts towards a new world history. The audience followed them – the years around 1900 were the golden hour for publishers of world histories.[31]

Secondly, in parallel to professional historiography, academic disciplines such as area studies and anthropology emerged, investigating world regions largely neglected by their colleagues from history and social science departments. At many places, a wall was erected between anthropology and the social sciences: the former mainly dealing descriptively with the extra-European world while the latter analysed Western societies. Yet gazes across these walls were still necessary, especially for historians studying empires and colonial expansion. At some universities, contacts across the separated study of 'us' and 'them' were the rule, not the exception.[32]

A third counter-tendency was the reinterpretation of national history by authors who aimed at positioning their own nation in the broader theatre of global connections and competitions, using implicit comparisons to create/invent patterns of superiority and inferiority. While they would not have characterized themselves as world historians – on the contrary, they fought bitterly against colleagues who identified with the field of world history – their works were interventions in a debate about the 'global condition'.[33]

International congresses were a place for debates on how to realize world history. By the start of the twentieth century, new concerns meant that the role of the ancient world or medieval times as a source of analogies no longer were at the centre of the debate.[34] The congresses in 1900 (Paris) and 1903 (Rome) took inspiration from universal exhibitions and gave space to approaches from other disciplines. Intense debates occurred over the role and possibility of applying Comte's positivist paradigm to history.[35] The Romanian historian Alexandru Xenopol had introduced it by presenting his main thesis on his country's daco-roman origins;[36] and Ferdinand Brunetière developed a model for cultural comparison at the opening of the Paris congress, arguing in favour of a 'European literature as *tertium comparationis* for Italian, Spanish, French, English and German literature'.[37] German historian Ludwig Dehio submitted a contribution on similarities between the appropriation of the French Gothic style in both England and Germany – an early attempt to deepen the debate on comparison by integrating the problem of intercultural transfers.[38] While such efforts to address questions of European culture were celebrated as a productive congress outcome, the non-European world was quasi-absent from the debates, with the remarkable exception of the French legal historian Emile Louis Marie Jobbé-Duval, who argued in favour of integrating colonial institutions into the comparison of legal configurations.[39]

The central figure in the organizational committee was Henri Berr, who did not play a major role in the history congresses after 1900 but, with his idea of a historical synthesis, became one of the most influential organizers for the interdisciplinary embeddedness of French historiography.[40] He published a series of books under the title *L'Evolution de l'humanité* that can be characterized as a new and largely convincing attempt to reconcile the ambitions of universal interpretation and professionalism in historical research. His series impelled the most innovative writers from the first generation of the French Annales school to contribute original essays on world-historical questions.[41] Tellingly, Berr later developed connections with the world of interwar internationalism, working with UNESCO's forerunner, the Paris-based International Institute of Intellectual Cooperation. His role in this respect indirectly linked him to Paul Otlet and Henri La Fontaine, who had championed the creation of dedicated League structures for cultural and academic exchange.[42]

It was Henri Pirenne who took the lead for a new push to comparative history as an intellectual consequence of the First World War at the 1923 congress in Brussels.[43] For the first time, a subsection was devoted to modern and contemporary history of the colonies.[44] Pirenne also had links to the UIA's founders. In 1913, he was on the organizing committee for the congress section of the Ghent world's fair, which also included the second World Congress of International Associations. The UIA's periodical *La Vie Internationale* subsequently printed his speech.[45] Furthermore, in the 1920s, both Pirenne and La Fontaine were members of the Belgian Committee on Intellectual Cooperation, which supported the League of Nations' cultural and academic activities. The examples of Berr and Pirenne hence illustrate how efforts to venture beyond the national lens in historiography could combine with a wider involvement in internationalism. Moreover, as Daniel Laqua's chapter in the present volume has shown, while Pirenne called for historical comparison in the early 1920s, a strand on 'comparative national studies' also figured within the UIA's scheme for an International University in this period.

Following Berr and Pirenne's earlier efforts, Marc Bloch formulated the fundamentals of modern comparative history as the methodological basis for scientific world history research in his opening lecture at the Oslo congress of 1928.[46] He noted that comparative history demanded a high degree of professionalism and cautioned against attempts to overemphasize it as the key in historical explanations. Moreover, he acknowledged that the construction of units of comparison and the formulation of criteria that one might use for comparative purposes would unavoidably be influenced by one's own historical culture. Bloch emphasized that historians comparing two or more social phenomena had to take into account the relationships between them and not only look for differences. Selecting comparative history as the topic for his appearance on the international scene was a well-calculated symbolic act. At the same time, he claimed the heritage of the earlier Lamprecht controversy, discussing Max Weber's approach to historical sociology as well as following in Pirenne's footsteps.

The congresses following the Oslo meeting were mainly concerned with increasing tensions in Europe rather than with problems of world history. The first gathering of historians after the end of the Second World War – held in Paris in 1950 – was organized as a sort of general overview on what the historical discipline in Europe had achieved so far. Such an overview seemed necessary after years of interrupted contact.

Beyond Eurocentricity

After 1945, the new world order became a point of departure for new types of activities among historians. Decolonization, as announced in Nehru's *Glimpses of History* (1934), as well as Cold War competition started to dictate the agenda. Eurocentric positions became the target of ever-stronger criticisms and the inclusion of a 'Near and Far East', of Latin America, and of Africa was being championed – even within an organization as Eurocentric as CISH. This development had two dimensions: one was the discovery of the non-Western world as a topic of historians' deliberations and new coalitions with area studies; the other was the recognition of historiographies emerging in newly independent countries. UNESCO began a collective effort towards a history of mankind by activating a global community of historians. At the same time, both Soviet and North American historians started to produce their own narratives on world history, which were discussed at the 1965 congress – productive, despite being pursuits in competition.

The ten-volume *Vsemirnaja Istoria* (1955–65) had its origins in 1920s Russia, having been planned by Michail Pokrovskij, a key figure in early Marxist historiography. However, Pokrovskij and his successor Nikolaj Michajlovic Lukin fell out of favour under Stalin. Shortly before his arrest in 1938, Lukin had determined the topics for thirty volumes and found the first authors. On the eve of the Second World War, five volumes were in progress and one on the French Revolution had been published. After the war, the project continued under a different banner. The Academy of Sciences decided to reduce it to ten volumes and placed it under the direction of Evgenij Zhukov. From the beginning, the history of the non-European world played a major role in Russian historiography. Now it gained additional weight. Zhukov had studied Japanese Studies at the Department of Near Eastern Languages and Civilizations in Leningrad and in 1941 had gained a doctorate in Japanese history from Moscow University. For three years, he worked as a professor of Asian history; shortly thereafter, he assumed the leadership of the Pacific Institute (Tichookaanski Institut) at the Academy of Sciences and was named deputy director of the Academy's Institute for History.[47] Between 1942 and 1945, Zhukov had been a member of the Institute of Pacific Relations (IPR), which addressed political, economic and social processes in the Pacific region while being closely connected to internationalist milieus. On the one hand, the IPR acted as a think tank on American foreign policy and was supported by US philanthropic foundations, whose support for internationalist ventures Christophe Verbruggen's chapter in this volume has explored. On the other hand, the IPR also served as a network of academic experts. Quite rightly, Tomoko Akami has characterized the studies undertaken there as a 'forerunner of area studies'.[48]

Zhukov and his colleagues wanted to move away from the homogenizing concept of 'civilization' and shatter the containers that the term and concept of 'civilization' demarcated. Zhukov's lecture at the 1960 CISH congress in Stockholm shows that he saw his project as only being half-realized. He asserted that it led to the opposite of universal history because it divided humanity. If one wanted to advance the unifying aspects and commonalities, the first step would be to retrace the specific developments of individual nations. In this respect, the world history written now could not describe in detail the path of all nations to the extent that would have been required. For the time being, Zhukov concluded, one should hold to the rule that where empirical knowledge on integrative processes was lacking, one needed to outline national, geographic and historical particularities instead of establishing uniformity and synchronicity in a deductive manner.[49]

Ongoing and long-lasting conceptual engagement characterized another initiative in this period: the world histories edited between 1952 and 1975 by the International Commission for a Scientific and Cultural History of Mankind (SCHM). This project was launched and funded by UNESCO.[50] As with Zhukov's venture, many of its goals proved difficult to realize. Lucien Febvre had been asked to outline the concept for a new history of mankind in opposition to traditional universal histories, yet many of his ambitious objectives remained unfulfilled.[51] However, the venture did succeed in producing a non-Eurocentric world history since all UNESCO member states had the option of participating. Historians from non-European nations made good use of this provision. By the time the project was finished, approximately 300 scholars, educational experts and politicians from over 50 countries had participated. In this respect, Febvre's original prerequisite of wide collaboration had been met: he deemed it essential that the largest possible number of scholars and scholarly organizations from around the world collaborate in order to accumulate the knowledge needed for a truly global historical exploration.

The dynamics of an institutionalized debate between agents from all regions of the world shattered consolidated narratives and epistemological certainties. Eurocentric views were explicitly and persistently challenged, not by single voices but by a collective. After the declarations of independence in Asia and Africa, membership in UNESCO increased. The balance of power changed, bringing about a more global orientation, so that the attention on the North–South divide noticeably gained priority over the East–West conflict. The topical and regional focus of the SCHM project increasingly turned towards non-Western pasts in their linkages to contemporary processes of decolonization. Especially the fifth and sixth volumes, dealing with the nineteenth and twentieth centuries, reflected the rising interest in Asia, Africa and Latin America. All of these regions were discussed repeatedly and in detail, with India, China and Japan receiving the greatest attention. Without question, this was partly a result of the competition between the Soviet and US participants, with each side using the charge of Eurocentrism to justify its viewpoints. It was possible to do so because the same criticism had become the central topos in the interventions of non-European scholars, who from the project's initial planning stages to the final editorial comments actively engaged in preventing this new 'world history' from excluding large parts of the world's past.

Admittedly, the pleas for a more balanced treatment of non-European history were often associated with the effort to represent one's own national perspective and thus had markedly nationalist intentions. Numerous agents from 'smaller countries' conceived the SCHM as a podium from which they could articulate their interpretations of the world's past to an international audience. They used their (often recently gained) political sovereignty and membership in UNESCO to demand coverage of their national history. Thus, national history figured often more prominently in the discussions about the volumes than transnational processes and world-historical developments.

All in all, the debates about Eurocentric interpretations and diverging viewpoints produced a process of negotiation that led to an in-depth questioning of the theoretical assumptions of the SCHM. In particular, it became clear that the universalist notion of world history, in which one paradigm is applied to all regions of the world, could not be realized. Moreover, the number of comments received on every volume, each of which exceeded 1,000 pages in length, demonstrated the impossibility of giving equal representation to every culture. In the end, 411 comments from all over the globe were referenced in the introductions and footnotes. The idea of an unbiased interpretation, free from any political and cultural baggage, had proven to be a myth – indeed a highly problematic and powerful one.

Consequently, various mechanisms were developed in order to allow for an open debate. Since expectations could not be met, increasingly the SCHM was not perceived as the final blueprint for world history but rather as one step in a transnational debate about world history, which was necessarily linked to its time and to be continued in the future. Therefore, the published volumes included criticisms of the project's initial universalist notion. Insights gained from this project soon spread to other historiographical contexts, as evidenced by discussions at the CISH congresses of 1960 and 1965.

A third wave of interest emerged in the United States in critical response to modernization theory and the narrative of 'first in Europe, then elsewhere'. William H. McNeill's 1963 book *The Rise of the West* in particular marked the beginning of a wider debate and acceptance of world history in US academia. At the centre of its analysis were historical processes that had influenced regions, continents and civilization as a whole. Although based upon the established notion of diffusion, McNeill was one of the first scholars who presented contacts between people from distant places and different cultures as a core dynamic of historical change and who considered influence as having mutual effects. In an impressive way, he showed that the exposure to 'foreign' traditions had led people to borrow, appropriate and adapt ideas, skills, and technologies, bringing about an interdependent and constantly changing world.[52] The book, McNeill's later writings and his many curriculum-related efforts provided much of the inspiration that drew professional historians to global historical studies. As Patrick Manning states, his 'orderly synthesis of civilizational connections made it possible for historians to consider world history as academically feasible, and not simply philosophically speculative. Henceforth, study of world history could grow by itself, if slowly.'[53]

The CISH experienced a broadening of its geographical vision and cultural sensitivity, too. Already at its second post-war congress, held in Rome in 1955, a panel on colonialism and colonial constellations was given prominence by being placed in the section on methodology and general problems. A section on Latin America addressed relations between metropole and colony. While some participants presented such relations as a unidirectional impact of the European powers on the colonies, others argued with regard to the Spanish example for reciprocal impact and adaption. It was no coincidence that the Latin American example was addressed first. The source problem, so often discussed in these early years with regards to Africa, seemed less of an obstacle to the delegates. A second reason for the preference given to the region was the possibility of analysing both colonialism and decolonizing efforts with the distance of the professional historian, looking back at events that had happened at least one and a half centuries ago. The background, however, was of course the ongoing movement towards independence and an end of colonial dominance in both Asia and Africa.

The Stockholm congress of 1960 introduced a new structure that required reports to the congress to be no longer only chronological but also by continent.[54] This gave the non-Western world, often heavily underrepresented in reports on modern and contemporary history, a regular place at subsequent congresses. Several national committees reacted to this development by suggesting panels on world history problems. For instance, at the 1965 congress in Vienna, panels addressed 'Methods of Universal History Writing' and 'Evolution and Revolution in World History'.

While the Stockholm congress provided the opportunity to present ongoing projects of writing world histories, five years later in Vienna, the American Louis Gottschalk spoke on the historiography of world history up to the beginning of the twentieth century. His lecture formulated the cornerstone of a timely global interpretation – the rejection of the civilizing and Eurocentric position and the support for collective works. Additionally, there were sessions on decolonization, with papers on the socio-economic transformation in states that had recently become independent, and on the role of political mass movements in India. A discussion of sources on precolonial Africa also figured on the agenda. In a heated debate on periodization, different approaches towards the role of Africans in African history came to the fore.[55] While the session rejected an opinion that saw the history of Africa mainly structured by colonial interventions, the time was not yet ripe for a wider acceptance of the proposal to establish an International Commission for African History.[56]

Subsequent gatherings further promoted the inclusion of different world regions: the number of CISH panels and papers on African, Asian and Latin American affairs steadily increased. In this respect, CISH reflected trends beyond the historical profession: for instance, in assessing non-governmental organizations and 'their contribution to a new world order' in 1981, the UIA noted a wider process of diversification within such organizations.[57] Yet within CISH, this geographical and cultural broadening occurred within certain boundaries, as highlighted by the representation of scholars from the Global South. Only 8 out of 159 presentations at the Stockholm congress of 1960 were by scholars from outside Europe and the US. By the time of the 1985 congress, held in Stuttgart, their number had increased to a mere 26, compared to 156 colleagues from the Global North.[58]

How did the consideration of wider perspectives manifest itself after the end of Cold War and at the dawn of an age that has often been framed in terms of globalization? As programme committees decided upon major themes some two or three years before the congress, it comes as little surprise that the CISH congress of 1990, held in Madrid, did not mark a major shift. The programme of the 1990 congress as well as the subsequent one in Montreal shows an ever-increasing diversification of topics – from gender to technology, from medicine to food – and, as such, mirrored an ongoing trend towards specialization. For many such topics, mobilizing the expertise of historians from across the world would have been desirable, but world history was not the primary focus.

The 1990s gatherings in Spain and Canada prepared the ground for wider discussions that finally started in Oslo (2000), addressing the role to be played by world or global history as a new yardstick, a new interpretative framework or, potentially, a new master narrative for the historian's craft. The stakes became clear when Patrick O'Brien welcomed a large audience to one of the major themes of the Oslo congress, under the title 'Perspectives on Global History: Concepts and Methodologies / Mondialisation d'Histoire: concepts et méthodologie'. What would replace the established but now-outdated historiographical landscape that was based upon the Cold War-born bipolar structure? Was there a North American hegemony at the horizon that was approaching under the label of global history?

The proposal to take the public debate on globalization as the central axis of any interpretation of the past, present and future was confronted with two major questions: would the new field recognize its many sources of inspiration and, as a consequence, its many features and possible answers to common questions or would it come with a sort of devaluation of formerly important ways of thinking and writing history? Or, to put it differently: would the historians' most global organization be able to say farewell to its traditional setting (as expressed in both its intellectual and organizational framework) and would they place questions on the role of history in a globalizing world at the centre?

Conclusion

Other contributions in the present book have shown how documentation about international organizations can shape perceptions of 'global civil society'. As members of international organizations and transnational actors in their own right, historians can be construed as part of the latter. At the same time, stimuli to broaden the lens beyond national frameworks have meant that historians increasingly engage with global processes in their research. This endeavour involves tracing connectivity and exchange in ways that go beyond the UIA's project of covering such developments through organizational data.

As we have tried to demonstrate, there is a long historiographical tradition that has focused on universal, world and global history. But more is at stake. It is about a world where the number of actors who contribute to the production of history multiplies. The time of professionalism is not over, but its former features are challenged by notions such as Mode 2 science or civic science. For an organization that represents professional historians across the planet, this challenge translates into the necessity to establish a dialogue with the co-producers of history. The new project of a history of humankind proposed by the multidisciplinary International Council for Philosophy and Human Sciences invites such a dialogue and may conclude a long period of splendid isolation.

So far, CISH has opened itself towards such new trends without transforming its structure. The tension between an organization promoting increasingly global perspectives on the past and its own structure that at least partly relies on the old features of internationalism comes increasingly obvious. It remains an open question into which direction CISH will develop. But CISH's long history suggests that it will, on the one hand, stick to its specificities and on the other will be further driven by historiographical tendencies to venture beyond its traditions.

Notes

1 Stefan Berger, *Writing the Nation: A Global Perspective* (Basingstoke: Palgrave, 2007); Stefan Berger and Chris Lorenz, *Nationalizing the Past: Historians as Nation Builders in Modern Europe* (New York: Palgrave, 2010). For a recent discussion of the literature in this field, see Eric Storm, 'A New Dawn in Nationalism Studies? Some Fresh Incentives to Overcome Historiographical Nationalism', *European History Quarterly* 48, no. 1 (2018): 113–29.

2 Gerald Diesener and Matthias Middell, eds, *Historikertage im Vergleich* (Leipzig: Leipziger Universitätsverlag, 1996).

3 Matthias Middell, ed., *Historische Zeitschriften im internationalen Vergleich* (Leipzig: Leipziger Universitätsverlag, 1999).

4 Karl Dietrich Erdmann, *Die Ökumene der Historiker: Geschichte der Internationalen Historikerkongresse und des Comité International des Sciences Historiques* (Göttingen: Vandenhoeck & Ruprechet, 1987).

5 The English edition, edited by the then CISH president Jürgen Kocka, was not a simple translation but extended the story of the organization to the end of the twentieth century: Karl Dietrich Erdmann, *Toward a Global Community of Historians: The International Historical Congresses and the International Committee of Historical Sciences 1898–2000* (New York: Berghahn, 2005).

6 Congrès mondial des Associations Internationales, *Tableau de l'organisation internationale: éléments existants* (Brussels: Bureau Central des Associations Internationales, 1910).

7 Office Central des Associations Internationales, *Annuaire de la Vie Internationale 1910–1912* (Office Central: Brussels, 1912), 2157–8; 'Troisième Congrès international des sciences historiques', *La Vie Internationale* 2, no. 11 (1913): 284–5.

8 Georg Iggers, 'The "Methodenstreit" in International Perspective: The Reorientation of Historical Studies at the Turn from the Nineteenth to the Twentieth Century', *Storia della Storiografia* 6 (1984): 21–32; Lutz Raphael, 'Historikerkontroversen im Spannungsfeld zwischen Berufshabitus, Fächerkonkurrenz und sozialen Deutungsmustern: Lamprecht-Streit und französischer Methodenstreit der Jahrhundertwende in vergleichender Perspektive', *Historische Zeitschrift* 251, no. 1 (1990): 325–63.

9 Karl Lamprecht, 'Die kultur- und universalgeschichtlichen Bestrebungen an der Universität Leipzig. Vortrag gehalten auf dem Internationalen Historikerkongreß zu Berlin am 11. August 1908', *Internationale Wochenschrift für Wissenschaft, Kunst und Technik* 2 (1908): 1141–50.

10 Both Hans Helmolt, a disciple of Lamprecht, and the French François Simiand lamented the relative marginality of Lamprecht's presentations in a session on literature and oriental cultures: *Jahrbuch der Görresgesellschaft* 30 (1909): 219–22, as well as *Revue de Synthèse* 17 (1908): 223.

11 Paul Otlet, 'L'Organisation internationale et les Associations internationales', in Office Central des Institutions Internationales', *Annuaire de la Vie Internationale 1908–1909* (Brussels: Office Central, 1909).

12 'Les Conceptions et le Programme de l'Internationalisme', *La Vie Internationale*, fasc. 26, no. 1 (1921): 99–110.

13 For a brilliant summary of the crisis, see Rolf Petri, *A Short History of Western Ideology: A Critical Account* (London: Bloomsbury, 2018).

14 This is particularly highlighted in Adam Tooze, *The Deluge: The Great War and the Remaking of Global Order 1916-1931* (London: Penguin, 2014).

15 Daniel Laqua, ed., *Internationalism Reconfigured: Transnational Ideas and Movements Between the World Wars* (London: I.B. Tauris, 2011).

16 Peter Schöttler, '"Désapprendre de l'Allemagne": Les Annales et l'histoire allemande pendant l'entre-deux-guerres', in: *Entre Locarno et Vichy: les relations culturelles franco-allemandes dans les années trente*, vol. 1, ed. Hans-Manfred Bock, Reinhardt Meyer-Kalkus and Michel Trebitsch (Paris: CNRS Éditions, 1993): 439–62.

17 This is discussed in greater detail by Peter Schöttler, 'Henri Pirenne, un historien européen entre l'Allemagne et la France', *Revue Belge de Philologie et d'histoire* 76, no. 4 (1998): 875–83 and idem, 'Henri Berr et l'Allemagne', *Revue de Synthèse* 117, nos. 1–2 (1996): 189–203. On Berr bridging the gap between the debates about world history before and after the First World War, see also Lucien Paul Victor Febvre, Gilles

Candar, and Jacqueline Pluet-Despatin, eds, *De la Revue de Synthèse aux Annales: Lettres à Henri Berr, 1911–1954* (Paris: Fayard, 1997).

18 The programme for the International University of 1921 included subjects such as Japanese history, contemporary developments in Russia and in diplomacy: 'Programme des Cours et Conférences de la IIe Quinzaine', *La Vie Internationale* 6, no. 1 (1921): 153–7.

19 Marc Bloch, 'Pour une Histoire comparée des sociétés européennes', *Revue de synthèse historique* 46 (1928): 15–50.

20 'International Committee of Historical Sciences (ICHS)', *Yearbook of International Organizations*, Available online: https://uia.org/s/or/en/1100063975 (accessed 24 July 2018).

21 On this body, see Chloé Belloc, 'La Création du Conseil international de la philosophie et des sciences humaines: idéal et réalité d'un engagement scientifique et intellectuel, 1947–1955', *Relations Internationales*, no. 130 (2007): 47–63.

22 'Network of Concerned Historians'. Available online: http://www.concernedhistorians .org/content/home.html (accessed 12 March 2018).

23 'Biographical Dictionary of Secretaries-General of International Organizations'. Available online: https://www.ru.nl/fm/iobio (accessed 12 March 2018); Bob Reinalda, ed., *Routledge History of International Organizations from 1815 to the Present Day* (London: Routledge, 2009).

24 Katja Naumann, 'Mitreden über Weltgeschichte – die Beteiligung polnischer, tschechoslowakischer und ungarischer Historiker an der UNESCO-Scientific and Cultural History of Mankind (1952–1969)', in *Verflochtene Geschichten: Ostmitteleuropa*, ed. Frank Hadler and Matthias Middell (Leipzig: Leipziger Universitätsverlag, 2010), 186–226.

25 On this phenomenon, see, for example, Anne Rasmussen, 'L'Internationale scientifique 1890–1914' (PhD diss., École des Hautes Études en Sciences Sociales, Paris 1995).

26 A draft of statutes for these meetings circulating since 1898 insisted on the aim to debate all questions of international history both jointly and polemically. See Erdmann, *Die Ökumene der Historiker*, 26.

27 Erdmann's study features extensive discussion of the motivations behind organizing congresses and participating in them.

28 Stefan Berger, *Constructing the Nation Through History* (Basingstoke: Palgrave, 2012).

29 Gilbert Allardyce, 'Toward World History: American Historians and the Coming of the World History Course', *Journal of World History* 1, no. 1 (1990): 23–76, esp. 23–4. A similar observation about the distance taken by professional historians to the world history synthesis is made by Lutz Raphael, *Geschichtswissenschaft im Zeitalter der Extreme: Theorien, Methoden, Tendenzen von 1900 bis zur Gegenwart* (Munich: C.H. Beck, 2003), 197, who concludes that interest in world history came close to a total decline.

30 Jürgen Osterhammel, *Die Flughöhe der Adler: Historische Essays zur globalen Gegenwart* (Munich: C.H. Beck, 2017), 42–53 coined the term 'globalification' ('Globalifizierung' in German) to describe the (incrementally growing) influence of border-crossing perspectives on existing discursive formations. While this has been a particularly intense process over the past two to three decades, we can observe a similar interest in transregional and potentially global connections at the turn from the nineteenth to the twentieth century.

31 Hartmut Bergenthum, *Weltgeschichten im Zeitalter der Weltpolitik: Zur populären Geschichtsschreibung im wilhelminischen Deutschland* (Munich: Peter Lang, 2004).

32 An important role was played by anthropogeography on the one hand and by Wilhelm Wundt's *Völkerpsychologie* on the other.

33 Charles Bright and Michael Geyer, 'Benchmarks of Globalization: The Global Condition, 1850–2010', in *A Companion to World History*, ed. Douglas Northrop (Chichester: Wiley-Blackwell, 2012): 285–300.

34 Robert Evans and Guy Marchal, eds, *The Uses of the Middle Ages in Modern European States: History, Nationhood and the Search for Origins* (Basingstoke: Palgrave, 2011).

35 On Henri Berr's role in this orientation of the congress, see Agnes Biard, Dominic Bourel and Eric Brian, eds, *Henri Berr et la culture du XXe siècle* (Paris: Albin Michel, 1997); Martin Siegel, 'Henri Berr's Revue de Synthese Historique', *History and Theory* 9, no. 3 (1970): 322–34.

36 Alexandru Xenopol, *Les Principes fondamentaux de l'histoire* (Paris: 1899).

37 Ferdinand Brunetière, 'La Littérature européenne', *Annales du Congrès de Paris* 2 (1900): 5–9.

38 Ludwig Dehio, 'Einfluß der französischen auf die deutsche Kunst im 13. Jahrhundert', *Annales du Congrès de Paris* 2 (1900): 140–1.

39 Matthias Middell, 'Weltgeschichtsschreibung zwischen Jahrhundertwende und Erstem Weltkrieg in der europäischen Historiographie', *Periplus: Jahrbuch für Außereuropaforschung* 18 (2008): 95–126.

40 Laurent Mucchielli, 'Aux Origines de la nouvelle histoire en France. L'évolution intellectuelle et la formation du champ des sciences sociales (1880–1930)', *Revue de Synthèse* 116, no. 1 (1995): 55–98. On the background of French historiography prior to the First World War: Pim den Boer, *History as a Profession: The Study of History in France, 1818–1914* (Princeton, NJ: Princeton University Press, 1998).

41 Étienne Anhim, Romain Bertrand, Antoine Liliti, and Stephen Sawyer, *The Annales and the Tradition of World History* (Paris, 2012). Available online: http://annales. ehess.fr/index.php?/parcours-historiographiques/247-table-ronde-histoire-globale (accessed 17 March 2018).

42 Daniel Laqua: 'Transnational Intellectual Cooperation, the League of Nations, and the Problem of Order', *Journal of Global History* 6, no. 2 (2011): 245.

43 Marc Boone, Claire Billen and Sarah Keymeulen, eds, *Henri Pirenne (1862–1935): A Belgian Historian and the Development of Social and Historical Sciences* (Brussels: Fondation Jan Dhondt, 2011); Peter Schöttler, 'Henri Pirennes Kritik an der deutschen Geschichtswissenschaft und seine Neubegründung des Komparatismus im ersten Weltkrieg', *Sozial.Geschichte* 19, no. 2 (2004): 53–81.

44 *Compte rendu du Ve Congrès des Sciences Historiques Bruxelles 1923,* ed. G. de Marez and F.-L. Ganshof (Brussels: 1923), 166–83.

45 'Discours du président du Comité belge de réception, M. le professeur Henri Pirenne', *La Vie Internationale* 3, no. 5 (1913): 561.

46 Bloch, 'Pour une histoire comparée', An English version is available in: Marc Bloch, *Land and Work in Medieval Europe* (London: Routledge, 1967), 44–76.

47 S. L. Tikhvinskii, 'An Historian of Encyclopedic Knowledge, Editor and Educator', *Herald of the Russian Academy of Sciences* 77, no. 5 (2007): 497–500.

48 Tomoko Akami, *Internationalizing the Pacific: The United States, Japan and the Institute of Pacific Relations in War and Peace, 1919–1945* (London: Routledge, 2002), 13–15.

49 Rapports, *XI International Congress of Historical Sciences*, vol. 1, Methodology, Stockholm (1960): 74–88.

50 Until recently, this world history project was only briefly noted in the literature
    and then was presented as a failed venture. Only rarely has the SCHM received a
    more favourable appraisal. Poul Duehdahl argued that 'it was the first attempt at
    overcoming Eurocentrism after World War II': Poul Duedahl, 'Selling Mankind:
    UNESCO and the Invention of Global History 1945–76', *Journal of World History* 22,
    no. 1 (2011): 101–33. See also Paul Betts, 'Humanity's New Heritage: UNESCO and
    the Rewriting of World History', *Past and Present* 228, no. 3 (2015): 249–85.

51 Febvre had suggested a 'non-political world history' and an account of the 'great
    stages of interchange of borrowing' that followed transcultural exchanges across
    time. In reconstructing encounters, such a history was to encompass 'everything
    that circulated from one group to the other'. Yet already in 1950, Febvre's design had
    been narrowed. Soon afterwards, the arrangement for the individual volumes had
    changed and the regions of the world were treated separately. See Katja Naumann,
    'Avenues and Confines of Globalizing the Past: UNESCO's International Commission
    for a "Scientific and Cultural History of Mankind" (1952–69)', in *Networking the
    International System: Global Histories of International Organizations*, ed. Madeleine
    Herren (Heidelberg: Springer, 2014), 187–200.

52 William H. McNeill, *The Rise of the West: A History of the Human Community*
    (Chicago: University of Chicago Press, 1963). See also William H. McNeill, 'The Rise
    of the West after Twenty-Five Years', *Journal of World History* 1, no. 1 (1990): 1–21;
    Patrick Manning and William H. McNeill, 'Lucretius and Moses in World History',
    History and Theory 46, no. 3 (2007): 428–45.

53 Manning and McNeill, 'Lucretius and Moses in World History', 428.

54 Rapports, *XI International Congress of Historical Sciences*, vol. 2: *Histoire des
    Continents*, Stockholm (1960).

55 Rapports, *XIIe Congrès International des Sciences Historiques*, vol. 2: *Histoire des
    Continents*, Vienna (1965): 177–232. For the discussion, see Actes, *XIIe Congrès
    International des Sciences Historiques*, Vienna (1965): 311–26.

56 Actes, *XIIe Congrès International des Sciences Historiques*, Vienna (1965): 324. It was
    only in 1976 that the CISH accepted the Association of Historiens Africains as an
    affiliated organization, which became an internal commission in 1989.

57 Vladimir Hercik, 'International Voluntary Associations: Their Contribution to a New
    World Order', *Transnational Associations* 33, no. 5 (1981): 295–6.

58 Erdmann, *Toward a Global Community*, 267.

Part III

EXPLORING THE UIA'S PUBLICATIONS AND DATA

Chapter 8

THE UIA AND THE DEVELOPMENT OF INTERNATIONAL RELATIONS THEORY

Thomas Davies

There is a widespread misperception in English language literature on international relations (IR) that 'it was the carnage of the First World War, and the desire to avoid its horrors again, that gave birth to the discipline of International Relations in 1919 at Aberystwyth, United Kingdom'.[1] Although there is a growing body of English language scholarship on the development of IR theorizing in the years immediately prior to the First World War, it has focused primarily on authors based in Great Britain and the United States.[2] The contribution of continental European thinkers in this period, especially the founders of the Union of International Associations, is an area that deserves much greater attention.[3]

The UIA's influence in the study of IR has generally been considered in terms of its role as a source of data on international governmental and non-governmental organizations.[4] This viewpoint was shared by UIA president Franco A. Casadio, who wrote in 1970 that 'the UIA has played a twofold part in the study of international relations': (i) provision of 'basic information about the international community' and (ii) delineating 'definitions or descriptions, ... classifications, ... and tendencies'.[5] While this chapter does acknowledge the UIA's role as a source of data and definitions, it draws attention to another aspect of its work, namely the broader theorization of the international sphere. The UIA's contribution encompasses a vast array of topics, including, inter alia, global civil society, globalization, international integration, international organization, peace studies, supranational democracy and transnational relations.

This chapter commences by noting early contributions by UIA founders Paul Otlet and Henri La Fontaine to debates on international order. It also assesses the influence of their ideas and activities in the interwar era. The discussion then shifts to the UIA's role in regard to later theorization, including the transnationalism debates of the 1970s and the global civil society debates of the post-Cold War era.

Paul Otlet and Henri La Fontaine – A Panoply of Prescience?

Paul Otlet has sometimes been regarded as the person who coined the term 'mondialisation', the French word for 'globalization'. The latter word long preceded its English counterpart, which was popularized in the 1980s. While Otlet did indeed use the term both in the UIA's journal *La Vie Internationale* and in his 1916 peace plan, 'mondialisation' in fact has an even longer provenance.[6] Nevertheless, Otlet and La Fontaine's writings appear to have foreshadowed many aspects of today's globalization debates.

Preferring to use the term 'globalism' ('mondialisme'), Otlet and La Fontaine's many publications before the First World War outlined an array of factors by which they believed the world was becoming increasingly integrated.[7] For instance, in 1912, the two Belgians remarked upon the integrative effects of progress in transport and communications such as the railway and electrical telegraphy, economic developments such as global exchange of goods and globalized division of labour, international political cooperation on diverse issues, and the emergence of 'global thought', among many other factors.[8] Such comments seemed to anticipate the disaggregation of technological, economic, political and ideational drivers elaborated in post-Cold War discussions of globalization.[9]

Otlet and La Fontaine were most influential in respect of their contribution to the study of international organizations in world politics. Although building on the work of earlier authors who were also involved in the establishment of the UIA – notably Cyrille Van Overbergh and Alfred Fried – Otlet and La Fontaine helped to establish many of the core typological distinctions among international organizations taken forward to the present day in the study of IR.[10] This approach includes distinguishing international organizations on the basis of possessing five characteristics: members in multiple countries; openness to members from additional countries; objectives that reach beyond the boundaries of a single country; non-profit goals; and a permanent institutional structure.[11] They further pioneered the distinctions between intergovernmental organizations, non-governmental organizations, and hybrid international organizations by disaggregating 'official' organizations consisting of government members from 'free' organizations consisting of voluntary memberships and 'mixed' organizations with both government and private members.[12]

A particular strength of Otlet and La Fontaine's analysis was their consideration of the role of non-governmental organizations in processes now known as 'global governance'.[13] Among the features they highlighted was the way in which the roles of non-governmental organizations included proposing international standards that governments would later adopt – a process now known as 'norm entrepreneurship'[14] – citing examples such as the campaign against human trafficking.[15] They further elaborated on what is today known as 'global private governance',[16] which refers to the way in which certain non-governmental organizations – such as sport federations – set and enforce their own sets of international standards.[17] In this respect, Otlet developed an interesting distinction between the contrasting bases of legitimacy of states and private organizations in international governance:

representation of 'territorial interests' in the case of the former, and of 'professional economic and scientific specialism' in the case of the latter.[18]

At the time when Otlet and La Fontaine made their most significant intellectual contributions to the study of international relations – namely in the years immediately preceding and during the First World War – issues such as national self-determination were prominent features of intellectual discourse.[19] The 'inalienable and imprescriptible right' of nations to 'dispos[e] freely of themselves' was a subject that Otlet took up in his wartime peace plan, which, like other contemporaneous schemes, envisaged the creation of a 'confederation of states'.[20] His plan is significant as an early example of demanding an international guarantee for 'the natural and imprescriptible rights of human beings, namely, individual liberty and security, liberty of conscience, religious freedom, and the right of its public exercise, religious toleration, and inviolability of domicile and of property'.[21] Otlet stressed that these should apply to 'all races' and that 'no-one may be disturbed on account of his language or origin, nor from these causes be subject to intolerant, discourteous, or disrespectful treatment'.[22] He also called for IR of 'the rights of indigenous sovereigns and the authority of indigenous chiefs'.[23] In his respect for the rights of non-Europeans, Otlet's work contrasted with the racial prejudices that characterized much US-based work on international relations in this period.[24] Another contrast with many of his contemporaries was Otlet's call for international recognition of the rights of international associations and of their 'civil personality' – a demand that is being reiterated in the twenty-first century.[25]

Otlet and La Fontaine's plans for international associations were among the most ambitious to have been put forward. Prior to the First World War, their writings on international associations envisaged their ever-greater integration and harmonization. Their self-interest, and that of the Belgian state, was intimately entwined with these plans, since they envisaged the UIA and its Brussels base as a 'world center ... harmonizing the ... program and ... work ... of all the international associations in a federated body'.[26] Daniel Laqua has observed that, for Belgium, serving as a centre 'managing internationalism offered a solution to the country's perceived shortcomings, namely its short history of independent statehood, its limited military power and apparent lack of international prestige'.[27]

As the pioneering chronicler of internationalism Francis Lyons argued, Otlet and La Fontaine's vision of a world integrated through a federation of international associations, put forward in the years immediately preceding the First World War, belies an extraordinary remoteness from the realities of the context in which they wrote.[28] In subsequent years, a recurrent trend among many liberal IR theorists has been to concentrate their focus on apparently integrative dimensions of world politics, while underestimating the accompanying fragmentary processes.[29] Regrettably, it seems unlikely that this pattern will be broken: reflecting in 2007 on the previous half-millennium of liberalism, Michael Howard observed, 'Sadly little seems to have changed, either in the aspirations of the liberal conscience, or in their unintended results.'[30]

The UIA and the Infrastructure of IR Studies

Although the most remarkable dimension of Otlet and La Fontaine's work in the study of international relations consists of their intellectual contribution, they can also be considered pioneering in the development of some of the infrastructure through which international relations has been studied. This includes their role in assembling journals, congresses, research and educational institutions, and – best known of all – their data.

Accounts of the development of IR journals have generally commenced with discussions of the *Journal of Race Development*, which was launched in the United States in 1910 and was transformed into the *Journal of International Relations* following the First World War: for some, this constituted 'the first IR journal'.[31] The problem with such an account is that at the outset the *Journal of Race Development* was not concerned with international relations as currently understood, but instead with 'the problems which relate to the progress of races and states generally considered backward in their standards of civilization'.[32] By contrast, the UIA's first journal, *La Vie Internationale*, was launched in 1912 with goals far more closely resembling those of the later study of international relations: it aimed from the outset to be the first periodical to consider 'the ideas, facts and organizations that constitute international life' as a distinct field of study from 'international law, the pacifist movement, … science and technology, commerce and industry, statistics and sociology', each of which had pre-existing journals considering international problems within their particular domains.[33] *La Vie Internationale* was a significant outlet for articles on a wide array of international problems, including, inter alia, international organizations, interstate relations, diplomacy, transnational relations, anarchy, international law, international statistics, international economics, international history, and general theories of world politics.[34] Its contributors included a diverse spectrum of scholars from multiple fields, including Irving Fisher, Denys P. Myers, David Starr Jordan and Wilhelm Ostwald.[35] Although a number of these authors included eugenicists, the contents of this journal were far less oriented around the racist debates of comparable endeavours in the United States at the time, or the imperialist debates of the Round Table movement in the United Kingdom.[36] The journal's lasting influence, however, was limited by its failure to continue for long after the First World War, with the final issue being published in 1921.

Prior to the First World War, the UIA was also significant for its convening of congresses at which problems of international relations were discussed. While the UIA's 1910 and 1913 congresses of international associations served many wider political and social objectives, one focus was dissemination and exchange of research and ideas concerning international life, with an especial but not exclusive focus on international associations, both public and private. Numerous papers considering the various aspects of international life were assembled for these congresses and published by the UIA in extensive volumes, now held in a handful of research libraries around the world.[37]

Subsequent World Congresses of International Associations were held by the UIA until 1927, but those which followed the First World War were of far lesser significance than those that preceded the conflict. In the early 1920s, a more notable educational endeavour of the UIA was its effort to develop to what it claimed to be the world's first 'international university'.[38] Alongside much bolder ambitions such as 'uniting, in a movement of higher education and universal culture, the universities and international associations', it aimed also to 'enable a proportion of students to complete their education by initiating them into the international and comparative aspects of all great problems'.[39] Efforts towards international education were far from unprecedented and had been central to the pre-war work of organizations such as the International Association of Academies, the Universal Scientific Alliance, and the Society of International Studies and Correspondence, to name just a few.[40] However, the UIA was among the first organizations following the First World War to organize summer schools on international relations topics, bringing together academics and students from many countries at a series of *Université Internationale* events from 1920 to 1927. As Laqua claims, 'The *Université Internationale* never attained the significance and permanency that its founders had hoped for.'[41] More enduring were to be the summer schools organized by rivals such as the International Federation of League of Nations Societies, which launched its internationalist 'cours Ruyssen' in 1925,[42] and by the British League of Nations Union, whose Geneva summer school transformed into the Geneva Institute of International Relations in 1924.[43]

It was as a research establishment that the UIA was to make its most profound contribution, however, building on the reputation that had previously been achieved by the remarkable work of the International Institute of Bibliography in the development of information science.[44] As Pierre-Yves Saunier has shown in the present volume, the UIA's work undertaken in the collection of data on international associations – as commenced in the pre-war *Annuaires de la Vie Internationale* – has become the most widely (and often uncritically) utilized resource for those endeavouring to undertake statistical analyses of international organizations in world politics.

The *Annuaires* produced by Otlet and La Fontaine were widely referenced in significant works on international organization of the early twentieth century. In his 1915 study of *The Rise of Internationalism*, John Culbert Faries described the *Annuaires* and *La Vie Internationale* as 'invaluable compendiums' which formed the basis of a very significant proportion of the material cited throughout his volume.[45] More influentially, Leonard Woolf took forward Otlet and La Fontaine's analyses of international associations in his 1916 treatise on *International Government*.[46] He adopted their definition of the distinguishing characteristics of international organizations, and he – like so many later authors – adopted without criticism UIA data on international organization numbers in support of his claims with respect to their scale and reach.[47]

The work undertaken in the *Annuaires* and *La Vie Internationale* continued to be influential in writings on international organization after the First World War. Pitman Potter's well-known *Introduction to the Study of International Organization* made extensive reference to the statistical data and categories established by Otlet and La Fontaine in its discussion of 'private international associations'.[48] Similarly, the pioneer student of international non-governmental organizations Lyman C. White built on Otlet and La Fontaine's work in disaggregating the organizational, financial, and structural dimensions of private international associations.[49] However, for White the principal source of data on international organizations was the *Handbook of International Organisations* produced by the League of Nations which by the 1930s had succeeded the *Annuaires de la Vie Internationale* as the principal reference point for students of international organizations, whether public or private.[50]

White regarded the UIA as an interesting effort to create a 'super-international organization' itself comprised of international organizations, yet noted that by 1933 that it was being considered 'of little importance'.[51] Its role as an international research and educational institution had been superseded by the work of the League of Nations Secretariat, which produced the *Handbook*, and of the International Committee on Intellectual Cooperation and International Institute of Intellectual Cooperation, which undertook greatly more extensive work to bring together 'intellectuals' from around the world than the UIA could ever have hoped to achieve.[52] The UIA's role in the development of the study of international relations was also overshadowed by other developments after the First World War, for instance the establishment of new university departments such as those at Aberystwyth University and the London School of Economics and Political Science, new institutions of higher education in international relations such as the Graduate Institute in Geneva, and new international relations think tanks such as the Council on Foreign Relations and Chatham House.[53] Whereas the pre-war study of international relations had been dominated by amateurs such as Otlet and La Fontaine, following the First World War it was increasingly professionalized and instead dominated by endowed professorships in the field such as those occupied by Alfred Zimmern, the first Chair of International Politics at Aberystwyth in 1919–21 and subsequently at Oxford from 1930 to 1944.[54]

During the Second World War, the intellectual work of the UIA was to be further constrained by its incorporation into the German Central Congress Office in 1940, following the Nazi occupation of Belgium. According to Madeleine Herren, the UIA under German control was 'intimately ... involved in enquiries into, and repression of, international organizations', making extensive efforts to secure information on international associations and their members around the world for dissemination to the authorities.[55] In the later years of the Second World War, the UIA published a journal entitled *Bulletin des Associations Internationales* containing articles in French and German. This publication is indicative of the limited scope for intellectual enquiry on international relations in the context in which it was published. Although the journal had a number of superficial commonalities with its precursor, *La Vie Internationale*, such as being dedicated to publishing 'original articles' that 'contribute to the development of discussions about the international associations', its scope was now circumscribed only to consider 'international problems excluding any political or religious activity'.[56] The contents of the three issues published in 1943–4 were therefore restricted to an extraordinarily anodyne collection of papers on a limited range of topics in the arts and sciences, many of which were of little relevance to the study of world politics.

The UIA and Cold War IR

Following the Second World War, the refounded UIA established in 1949 a new journal – simply entitled the *Monthly Review* – with a focus closer to the original purposes of the institution, but now appealing especially for communications from other international associations 'which they think might be of interest to other associations'.[57] Although at first carrying fewer articles on the study of international relations than *La Vie Internationale*, the pages of this journal and its successors (the *NGO Bulletin* from 1951 to 1953, *International Associations* from 1954 to 1976, and *Transnational Associations* from 1977) were to offer during the first decades of the Cold War a significant outlet for academic research into transnational relations at a time when the now North American-dominated study of world politics was preoccupied with state-centric so-called realist approaches.[58]

The *Monthly Review* helped to relaunch the UIA's reputation as a centre for the exchange of ideas and research on international non-governmental organizations, publishing, for instance, the work of Lyman C. White on the contribution of these organizations to 'peace by pieces' by enabling cross-border cooperation in a wide array of issue areas.[59] White's article aimed to provide a nongovernmental counterpart to the earlier studies by David Mitrany of the 'functional approach' by which international organizations are understood to help to bring about peace through facilitating cooperation in specialist issue areas.[60]

In subsequent years, the UIA's journals became an important outlet for the dissemination of functionalist research. One of Mitrany's most influential papers – 'An Advance in Democratic Representation' – was first published in *International Associations* in 1954,[61] while Charles Merrifield published in the same journal his 'fresh look at the theory of functional development' in the same journal a dozen years later.[62] Mitrany's study – and another by White the preceding year[63] – provided early analyses of what would half a century later become known as the study of democracy in global governance – the problems and prospects for democratic representation in decision-making beyond the national level.[64] For White and Mitrany – like Zimmern before and many others following the end of the Cold War[65] – non-governmental organizations offered a potential mechanism to compensate for the democratic deficit at the international level.[66]

Beyond its journal's role as a significant forum for transnational research in the first decades of the Cold War – and thus at a time when the field was marginalized – the revived UIA also had some influence on international thought through the writings on the topic of its officers, most notably Georges Patrick Speeckaert, who continued Otlet and La Fontaine's work on the classification and quantification of international associations and congresses.[67] The successor volumes to the *Annuaires de la Vie Internationale* – the *Yearbooks of International*

Organizations – were also a core source for studies of transnational organizations such as Jean Meynaud's 1960 volume on international pressure groups.[68] Prior to the publication of this volume, Meynaud worked with the UIA and UNESCO in a study group concerning NGOs, and in the subsequent decade the UIA aimed towards 'reforming university teaching on the subject of international relations'.[69]

Accompanying the détente of the late 1960s and early 1970s, North American political science regained interest in non-state actors in world politics, with pre-eminent IR journal *International Organization* publishing in 1971 an influential volume on transnational relations edited by Robert Keohane and Joseph Nye.[70] Like Woolf and Potter's work half a century earlier, the principal source of quantitative data and classifications of transnational actors, especially for non-governmental organizations, in this volume was the UIA's *Yearbook of International Organizations*.[71] Subsequently the work of a number of students of transnational relations such as Louis Kriesberg and Elise Boulding was to appear in the pages of *International Associations*, alongside that of scholars of intergovernmental organizations such as Chadwick Alger.[72] More than two decades before Margaret Keck and Kathryn Sikkink were to espouse the concept of 'transnational advocacy network', Anthony Judge and Kjell Skjelsbeck used the pages of this journal to put forward in 1972 an agenda for research into 'transnational association networks'.[73]

From the late 1960s onwards, a growing array of datasets based on the UIA *Yearbook* was being produced.[74] Johan Galtung, the principal founder of the Peace Research Institute Oslo, appointed Skjellsbaek in 1967 to work on an IGO–NGO dataset partly derived from the *Yearbook* as a component of his early work in the development of peace studies.[75] Galtung saw participation in the intellectual work of the UIA as an integral component of his efforts to advance peace studies. Similarly, David Horton Smith, the principal founder of the Association for Research on Nonprofit Organizations and Voluntary Action (ARNOVA), collaborated with the UIA in seeking to pursue the development of the study of voluntary associations, which he now terms 'voluntaristics'.[76] Both Galtung and Smith, alongside other leading scholars such as Alger and Executive Secretary of the Society for International Development Andrew Rice, participated in the UIA's 1972 Milan congress on 'the philosophy of non-governmental organization'.[77]

Over the subsequent two decades, the UIA and its journal served as a centre for discussion not only of transnational relations and voluntary associations, but also of wider fields including peace studies, development studies and the re-emerging study of globalization.[78] While the data contained in the *Yearbook* (and to a lesser extent the *International Congress Calendar* that had been launched in 1960) continued to be viewed as an invaluable resource for researchers into international governmental and non-governmental organizations, other initiatives of the UIA in this period, such as the project launched in 1972 to develop an *Encyclopedia of World Problems and Human Potential* and the extensive efforts towards furthering network analysis by Anthony Judge, were not to achieve as warm a reception as had been hoped for. The American Library Association, for instance, described the *Encyclopedia* in 1987 as 'a problematic monument to idiosyncrasy, confusion and obfuscation': 'the context, arrangement, and absolute anarchy of the inclusiveness make this volume useless as a reference tool.'[79] In the closing years of the Cold War, therefore, the UIA was primarily of significance to the academic community as a data repository on international associations and secondarily as an outlet for scholarship from a range of backgrounds, but it was not as influential as it had previously been in setting new trends.

The UIA and Global Civil Society

Following the end of the Cold War, the removal of the bipolar superstructure and the apparent achievements of 'civil society' in the revolutions of 1989–91 encouraged students of IR to consider the potential for the development of 'global civil society'.[80] For one of the first to discuss the topic, Elise Boulding, speaking in 1989, 'the 18,000 globe-spanning, boundary-crossing peoples' associations technically known as international nongovernmental organizations but usually referred to as NGOs, represent the global civil society'.[81] Her source, not surprisingly, was the *Yearbook of International Organizations*, the data and categories of which were adopted without critique in her study on 'building a global civic culture', which viewed INGOs as playing a central set of roles in the process.[82]

The notion of 'global civil society' was a significant opportunity for the UIA, which added a subtitle to the *Yearbook* – 'guide to global civil society networks' – at the turn of the millennium.[83] At the same time, this volume became one of the principal bases for the measurement of global civil society by the Centre for the Study of Global Governance at the London School of Economics and Political Science, which put together a series of annuals of Global Civil Society from 2001 to 2012.[84] The objective of these volumes – to document the emergence of 'global civil society' – echoed the goals of Otlet and La Fontaine in producing the *Annuaires* a century before. Both emerged during periods of great optimism regarding international progress, and both were to be cut short by the shattering of these illusions over the subsequent years.[85]

During the 1990s and early 2000s, the pages of *Transnational Associations* provided an outlet for research into global civil society. As with the transnational relations debate of the 1970s, the global civil society conversations of the 1990s and 2000s were in part disseminated through this journal, which carried contributions by Ronnie Lipschutz, Jan Aart Scholte, Lester Salamon, Helmut Anheier, Peter Waterman, Francis Fukuyama and Steve Charnovitz, among other prominent authors.[86] The editor of *Transnational Associations*, Paul Ghils, made contributions to this debate, especially to definitional aspects,[87] as did Anthony Judge whose reflections often involved much greater critique of the limitations of data and the uncivility of many transnational actors than many academic IR authors on global civil society at the time were prepared to acknowledge.[88]

The resurgence of academic interest in what was now labelled global civil society brought renewed interest in the UIA's publications and data.[89] However, it also resulted in the development of competitor journals to *Transnational Associations*, which ceased publication in 2005. Academic journals such as *Global Governance* (established in 1995), *Globalizations* (published from 2004), and especially *Global Networks* (published from 2001) provided new outlets for academic research into transnational associations, international organizations, globalization, and global civil society, but in more traditional academic formats.[90]

In the second decade of the twenty-first century, global civil society is characterized by two significant developments that are problematic for the UIA. The first is the wave of digitally mediated transnational social movements lacking formally institutionalized structures of mobilization, ranging from the Arab uprisings through to the Occupy movements, which Manuel Castells has labelled 'networks of outrage and hope'.[91] While some have tried to study transnational social movements using UIA data,[92] this data fails to capture the numerous non-hierarchical and non-institutionalized dimensions that are paramount in today's transnational social mobilizations. This is a long-standing problem with UIA data, but while a focus on formal organizations and congresses spoke comparatively effectively to broader perceptions of the components of what Otlet and La Fontaine termed 'international life' in the early-twentieth-century 'age of internationalism', as well as during the 'NGO moment' of the later twentieth century, the weaknesses of such an approach are more apparent in the present day as perceptions of transnational social mobilization have changed.[93]

The second pre-eminent development in global civil society in recent years has been the growing significance, variety and scale of transnational civil society activities beyond the Western European and North American contexts.[94] UIA data, however, has tended to be far richer in relation to its coverage of European and North American developments than it has been in respect of those in other regions, a problem which was recognized by Johan Galtung as far back as the UIA's 1972 Milan congress on the 'philosophy' of NGOs.[95]

Conclusion

Although most commonly recognized in the IR literature as a source of data on international governmental and non-governmental organizations, the UIA is equally notable for its role in the development of theory in IR. Otlet and La Fontaine are especially noteworthy for their role in delineating definitional and structural characteristics of international non-governmental organizations. They also studied the interactions between these organizations and intergovernmental bodies, and such a perspective remains influential in discussions of global governance in the present day. As we have seen, their successors were also to play a part in the development of understandings of transnational relations and global civil society. The UIA has further served as a congress convenor, publisher and research partner for IR scholars for much of its existence, in addition to its better-known role as a data provider.

Although some of its staff, such as Anthony Judge, have cast a critical eye on what is now known as global civil society, all too commonly UIA data has been used by IR scholars to justify excessively optimistic assertions concerning the prospects for global civil society, which have been repeatedly shattered by subsequent events. In the present day, the organization is also at risk of obsolescence if it is unable to address the twin issues of the rise of non-institutionalized transnational social mobilization, and the expansion of transnational civil society beyond the Western European and North American contexts with which it is most familiar.

Notes

1 Alan Collins, 'Introduction: What is Security Studies?', in *Contemporary Security Studies*, ed. Allan Collins (Oxford: Oxford University Press, 2013), 1.
2 See, for example, David Long and Brian C. Schmidt, eds, *Imperialism and Internationalism in the Discipline of International Relations* (Albany, NY: State University of New York Press, 2005), and Duncan Bell, *Reordering the World: Essays on Liberalism and Empire* (Princeton, NJ: Princeton University Press, 2016).
3 Jan Stöckmann – in his article 'Nationalism and Internationalism in International Relations, 1900–1939', *History Compass* 15, no. 2 (2017): 1–13 – highlights the importance of research beyond the British and US contexts in this period but does not refer to the work of the UIA. The role of the UIA in the study of non-governmental organizations in IR before the First World War is investigated in Thomas Davies, 'Understanding Non-Governmental Organizations in World Politics: The Promise and Pitfalls of the Early "Science of Internationalism"', *European Journal of International Relations* 23, no. 4 (2017): 884–905.
4 For a discussion of this, please see the chapter by Pierre-Yves Saunier in this volume.
5 Franco A. Casidio, 'The Place of the Union of International Associations in the Study of International Relations', in *Union of International Associations, 1910–1970: Past, Present, Future* (Brussels: Union of International Associations, 1970), 12–13.
6 On Otlet and the origins of the term 'mondialisation', see Vincent Capdepuy, '1904, la mondialisation selon Pierre de Coubertin', 2014. Available online: http://blogs.histoir eglobale.com/1904-la-mondialisation-selon-pierre-de-coubertin_3828 (accessed 13 September 2017).
7 See, for example, Paul Otlet and Henri La Fontaine, 'La Vie internationale et l'effort pour son organisation', *La Vie Internationale* 1, no. 1 (1912): 9–34. On Otlet's globalism, see also Wouter Van Acker, 'Sociology in Brussels, Organicism and the Idea of a World Society in the Period before the First World War', in *Information Beyond Borders: International Cultural and Intellectual Exchange in the Belle Époque*, ed. W. Boyd Rayward (Farnham: Ashgate), 158.
8 Otlet and La Fontaine, 'La Vie internationale et l'effort pour son organisation', 9–11.
9 These are put forward for instance in Jan Aart Scholte 'Global Civil Society', in *Globalization: Critical Concepts in Sociology. Volume 3: Global Membership and Participation*, ed. Roland Robertson and Kathleen E. White (Abingdon: Routledge, 2003), 287.
10 On Van Overbergh, see Wouter Van Acker, 'Sociology in Brussels', 143–68; on Fried, see Daniel Laqua, 'Alfred H. Fried and the Challenges for "Scientific Pacifism" in the Belle Époque', in *Information Beyond Borders*, ed. Rayward, 181–200.
11 Paul Otlet, 'L'Organisation internationale et les associations internationales', in *Annuaire de la Vie Internationale, 1908–1909*, ed. Office Central des Institutions Internationales (Brussels: Office Central des Institutions Internationales, 1909), 37–8.

12 Otlet, 'L'Organisation internationale et les associations internationales', 46. For a discussion of present-day understandings of distinguishing features of nongovernmental organizations, see Peter Willetts, *Non-Governmental Organizations in World Politics: The Construction of Global Governance* (Abingdon: Routledge, 2011).

13 On this theme, see also Davies, 'Understanding Non-Governmental Organizations in World Politics'.

14 Martha Finnemore and Kathryn Sikkink, 'International Norm Dynamics and Political Change', *International Organization* 52, no. 4 (1998): 887–917.

15 Otlet, 'L'Organisation internationale et les associations internationales', 47.

16 Walter Mattli and Tim Buthe, 'Global Private Governance: Lessons from a National Model of Setting Standards in Accounting', *Law and Contemporary Problems* 68, no. 3 (2005): 225–62.

17 Otlet, 'L'Organisation internationale et les associations internationales', 86.

18 Ibid., 35.

19 Promotion of national self-determination as a solution to war was the primary concern of the Union of Nationalities, modelled on the Union of International Associations – see D. R. Watson, 'Jean Pélissier and the Office Central Des Nationalités, 1912–1919', *The English Historical Review* 110, no. 439 (1995): 1191–206.

20 Paul Otlet, 'A World Charter', *The Advocate of Peace* 79, no. 2 (1917): 44.

21 Otlet, 'A World Charter', 44.

22 Ibid.

23 Ibid.

24 On racism in early-twentieth-century US study of international relations, see Robert Vitalis, *White World Order, Black Power Politics: The Birth of American International Relations* (Ithaca, NY: Cornell University Press, 2015).

25 Otlet, 'A World Charter', 44. On present-day demands for international legal recognition of non-governmental organizations, see Erla Thrandardottir and Vincent Charles Keating, 'Bridging the Legitimacy Gap: A Proposal for the International Legal Recognition of INGOs', *International Politics* 55, no. 2 (2018): 207–20.

26 Union of International Associations, *The Union of International Associations: A World Center* (Brussels: Union of International Associations, 1914), 5–7.

27 Daniel Laqua, *The Age of Internationalism and Belgium, 1880–1930: Peace, Progress and Prestige* (Manchester: Manchester University Press, 2013), 21. On the role of Belgian interests, see also Madeleine Herren, *Hintertüren zur Macht: Internationalismus und modernisierungsorientierte Außenpolitik in Belgien, der Schweiz und den USA* (Munich: Oldenbourg, 2000); and Wouter Van Acker and Geert Somsen, 'A Tale of Two World Capitals: The Internationalisms of Pieter Eijkman and Paul Otlet', *Revue Belge de Philologie et d'Histoire* 90, no. 4 (2012): 1389–409.

28 F. S. L. Lyons, *Internationalism in Europe, 1815–1914* (Leyden: A. W. Sythoff, 1963), 369.

29 On the dialectics between globalization and fragmentation, see Ian Clark, *Globalization and Fragmentation: International Relations in the Twentieth Century* (Oxford: Oxford University Press, 1997). For an analysis of the fragmentary dynamics of liberal internationalism, see Beate Jahn, *Liberal Internationalism: Theory, History, Practice* (Basingstoke: Palgrave, 2013).

30 Michael Howard, *War and the Liberal Conscience* (London: Hurst, 2008), viii.

31 Robert Vitalis, 'Beyond Practitioner Histories of International Relations: Or, the Stories Professors Like to Tell (About) Themselves', in *What's the Point of International*

Relations?, ed. Synne L. Dyvik, Jan Selby and Rorden Wilkinson (Abingdon: Routledge, 2017), 100.

32   George H. Blakeslee, 'Introduction', *Journal of Race Development* 1, no. 1 (1910): 1.

33   Paul Otlet and Henri La Fontaine, 'Premiers Mots', *La Vie Internationale* 1, no. 1 (1912): 5–6.

34   Electronic copies of each issue of *La Vie Internationale* are available online at: https://uia.org/journals (accessed 23 February 2018).

35   Irving Fisher, 'De la Nécessité d'une Conférence internationale sur le Coût de la vie', *La Vie Internationale* 3, no. 12 (1913): 295–311; Denys P. Myers, 'La Concentration des Organismes Internationaux Publics', *La Vie Internationale* 4, no. 10 (1913): 97–122; David Starr Jordan, 'Ce que l'Amérique peut enseigner à l'Europe', *La Vie Internationale* 4, no. 15 (1913): 5–25; Wilhelm Ostwald, 'Théorie des Unités', *La Vie Internationale* 4, no. 16 (1913): 113–63.

36   On the Round Table, see Andrea Bosco, *The Round Table Movement and the Fall of the 'Second' British Empire (1909–1919)* (Newcastle: Cambridge Scholars Publishing, 2017).

37   Union des Associations, Internationales, *Congrès Mondial des Associations Internationales, Bruxelles, 9–11 Mai 1910* (Brussels: Office Central des Institutions Internationales, 1911); Union des Associations, *Congrès Mondial des Associations Internationales, Gand-Bruxelles, 1913* (Brussels: Office Central des Institutions Internationales, 1914).

38   This claim is reiterated at Union of International Associations, 'UIA's History'. Available online: http://www.uia.org/history (accessed 12 October 2017).

39   Union of International Associations, *International University* (Brussels: Union of International Associations, 1920), 1.

40   Thomas Davies, *NGOs: A New History of Transnational Civil Society* (New York: Oxford University Press, 2014), 47.

41   Daniel Laqua, 'Activism in the "Students' League of Nations": International Student Politics and the Confédération Internationale des Étudiants, 1919–1939', *The English Historical Review* 132, no. 556 (2017): 621.

42   Thomas R. Davies, 'Internationalism in a Divided World: The Experience of the International Federation of League of Nations Societies, 1919–1939', *Peace & Change: A Journal of Peace Research* 37, no. 2 (2012): 246.

43   Daniel Gorman, *International Cooperation in the Early Twentieth Century* (London: Bloomsbury, 2017), 53.

44   On this theme see, inter alia, W. Boyd Rayward, ed., *European Modernism and the Information Society: Informing the Present, Understanding the Past* (Aldershot: Ashgate, 2008).

45   John Culbert Faries, *The Rise of Internationalism* (New York: W. D. Gray, 1915), 180.

46   Peter Wilson, *The International Theory of Leonard Woolf: A Study in Twentieth-Century Idealism* (Basingstoke: Palgrave, 2003), 223.

47   Leonard Woolf, *International Government: Two Reports* (New York: Brentano's, 1916), 166–7.

48   Pitman B. Potter, *An Introduction to the Study of International Organization* (New York: The Century Co., 1922), 289–301.

49   Lyman Cromwell White, *The Structure of Private International Organizations* (Philadelphia, PA: George S. Ferguson Company, 1933), 324.

50   White, *Structure of Private International Organizations*, 15.

51   Ibid., 237 and 239.

52   Daniel Laqua, 'Transnational Intellectual Cooperation, the League of Nations, and the Problem of Order', *Journal of Global History* 6, no. 2 (2011): 223–47.

53   On Aberystwyth, see Brian Porter, ed., *The Aberystwyth Papers: International Politics, 1919-1969* (London: Oxford University Press, 1972); on the London School of Economics, see Harry Bauer and Elisabetta Brighi, eds, *International Relations at LSE: A History of 75 Years* (London: Millennium Publishing Group, 2003); on Chatham House and the Council on Foreign Relations, see Inderjeet Parmar, 'Anglo-American Elites in the Interwar Years: Idealism and Power in the Intellectual Roots of Chatham House and the Council on Foreign Relations', *International Relations* 16, no. 1 (2002): 53–75. For German developments, see Katharina Rietzler, 'Philanthropy, Peace Research, and Revisionist Politics: Rockefeller and Carnegie Support for the Study of International Relations in Weimar Germany', *Bulletin of the German Historical Institute* 5 (2008): 61–79.

54   D. J. Markwell, 'Sir Alfred Zimmern Revisited: Fifty Years On', *Review of International Studies* 12, no. 4 (1986): 279–92.

55   Madeleine Herren, '"Outwardly … an Innocuous Conference Authority": National Socialism and the Logistics of International Information Management', *German History* 20, no. 1 (2002): 85.

56   Union of International Associations, *Bulletin des Associations Internationales* 1, no. 1 (1943): 4.

57   Union of International Associations, *Monthly Review* 1, no. 1 (1949): 2.

58   Electronic copies of the UIA's journals are available online: https://uia.org/journals (accessed 23 February 2018). On realism in the context of the Cold War, see Michael Cox, 'Hans J. Morgenthau, Realism and the Rise and Fall of the Cold War', in *Realism Reconsidered: Hans J. Morgenthau and International Relations*, ed. Michael Williams (Oxford: Oxford University Press, 2007), 166–94.

59   Lyman C. White, '"Peace by Pieces": The Role of Non-Governmental Organizations', *Monthly Bulletin* 1, no. 7 (1949): 103–7.

60   On Mitrany's functional theory, see David Long and Lucian Ashworth, 'Working for Peace: The Functional Approach, Functionalism and Beyond', in *New Perspectives on International Functionalism*, ed. Lucian Ashworth and David Long (London: Palgrave, 1999), 1–26.

61   David Mitrany, 'An Advance in Democratic Representation', *International Associations* 6, no. 3 (1954): 136–7.

62   Charles Merrified, 'A Fresh Look at the Theory of Functional Development', *International Associations* 18, no. 12 (1966): 723–6.

63   Lyman C. White, 'Non-Governmental Organizations and Democracy', *NGO Bulletin* 5, no. 11 (1953): 437–42.

64   On democracy in global governance, see Jan Aart Scholte, 'Civil Society and Democratically Accountable Global Governance', *Government and Opposition* 39, no. 2 (2004): 211–33.

65   On Zimmern's discussion of democracy in global governance, see Thomas Richard Davies, 'A "Great Experiment" of the League of Nations Era: International Nongovernmental Organizations, Global Governance, and Democracy Beyond the State', *Global Governance: A Review of Multilateralism and International Organizations* 18, no. 4 (2012): 405–23.

66   This is noted in Steve Charnovitz, 'The Emergence of Democratic Participation in Global Governance (Paris, 1919)', *Indiana Journal of Global Legal Studies* 10, no. 1 (2003): 58–9.

67   Georges Patrick Speeckaert is perhaps best known for his volume, *Les 1978 Organisations internationales fondées depuis le Congrès de Vienne* (Brussels: Union of International Associations, 1957), but he also published extensively on transnational associations in the UIA's journal.

68   Jean Meynaud, *Les Groupes de pression internationaux: esquisse d'un cadre de recherche* (Paris: Fondation Nationale des Sciences Politiques, 1960).

69   Georges Patrick Speeckaert, 'A Glance at Sixty Years of Activity (1910–1970) of the Union of International Associations', in *Union of International Associations, 1910– 1970*, 47.

70   Themed journal issue on 'Transnational Relations in World Politics', ed. Robert O. Keohane and Joseph S. Nye, Jr.: *International Organization* 25, no. 3 (1971).

71   See especially Kjell Skjelsbaek, 'The Growth of International Nongovernmental Organization in the Twentieth Century', *International Organization* 25, no. 3 (1971): 420–42.

72   Louis Kriesberg 'International Nongovernmental Organizations and Transnational Integration', *International Associations* 24, no. 11 (1972): 520–5; Elise Boulding, 'Network Capabilities of Transnational Religious associations', *International Associations* 26, no. 2 (1974): 91–4; Chadwick F. Alger, 'Decision-Making in the United Nations', *International Associations* 24, no. 10 (1972): 460–5.

73   Anthony J. N. Judge and Kjell Skjelsbaek, 'Trans-National Association Networks (TANs)', *International Associations* 24, no. 10 (1972): 481–6. On the later concept of 'transnational advocacy networks', also called TANs, see Margaret E. Keck and Kathryn Sikkink, 'Transnational Advocacy Networks in International and Regional Politics', *International Social Science Journal* 51, no. 159 (1999): 89–101.

74   Anthony Judge, 'The Associative Society of the Future' (1979). Available online: https ://www.laetusinpraesens.org/docs/assfut.php (accessed 14 October 2017).

75   PRIO, 'Kjell Skjelsbæk'. Available online: https://www.prio.org/People/Person/?x=5332 (accessed 14 October 2017).

76   Johan Galtung, 'Peace Proposals as Science and Art', *International Associations* 24, nos. 8–9 (1972): 408–10; David Horton Smith, 'Future Trends in Research on Voluntary Action', *International Associations* 24, nos. 8–9 (1972): 397–400.

77   Geneviève Devillé, 'Milan 1972: la philosophie de l'organisation nongouvernementale', *International Associations* 25, no. 3 (1973): 147–62.

78   On globalization, see for example Guy Marchand, 'Le Mondialisme, force politique', *Transnational Associations* 32, no. 2 (1980): 88–91.

79   American Library Association, *Booklist* 83:698, January 1987. Part of this quotation is also to be found on the Wikipedia entry for the volume (accessed 14 October 2017).

80   Ronnie D. Lipschutz, 'Reconstructing World Politics: The Emergence of Global Civil Society', *Millennium* 21, no. 3 (1992): 389–420.

81   Elise Boulding, 'The Dialectics of Peace', in *The Dialectics and Economics of Peace*, ed. Elise Boulding and Kenneth Boulding (Fairfax, VA: Center for Conflict Analysis and Resolution, George Mason University, 1990), 6.

82   Elise Boulding, *Building a Global Civic Culture: Education for an Interdependent World* (Syracuse, NY: Syracuse University Press, 1990), 35–55.

83   Union of International Associations, *Yearbook of International Organizations 2000- 2001: Guide to Global Civil Society Networks* (Munich: K. G. Saur, 2000).

84   On the use of UIA data to measure global civil society, see Helmut Anheier, 'Measuring Global Civil Society', in *Global Civil Society 2001*, ed. Helmut Anheier, Marlies Glasius and Mary Kaldor (Oxford: Oxford University Press, 2001), 221–30.

85 Beset with the tarnishing of its reputation through acceptance of funds in 2009 from the Gaddafi International Charity and Development Foundation, the Centre was closed by the LSE ostensibly due to 'a shift in research priorities': 'LSE Global Governance to Close on 31 July 2011'. Available online: http://www.lse.ac.uk/website-a rchive/newsAndMedia/newsArchives/2011/07/globalgovernance.aspx (accessed 14 October 2017).

86 Ronnie D. Lipschutz, 'Learn of the Green World: Global Environmental Change, Global Civil Society and Social Learning', *Transnational Associations* 45, no. 3 (1993): 124–38; Jan Aart Scholte, 'Globalisation and Social Change', *Transnational Associations* 50, no. 1 (1998): 2–11; Lester Salamon, Helmut K. Anheier et al., 'The Emerging Sector Revisited: A Summary', *Transnational Associations* 51, no. 1 (1999): 9–28; Peter Waterman, 'Globalisation, Civil Society, Solidarity', *Transnational Associations* 46, no. 2 (1994): 66–85; Francis Fukuyama, 'Social Capital and Civil Society', *Transnational Associations* 55, no. 3 (2003): 162–72; Steve Charnovitz, 'Trans-Parliamentary Associations in Global Functional Agencies', *Transnational Associations* 54, no. 2 (2002): 88–91.

87 See, for instance, Paul Ghils, 'Les Images de la société civile', *Transnational Associations* 43, no. 1 (1992): 14–21; and Paul Ghils, 'La Nouvelle Agora: genèse de la société civile transnationale', *Transnational Associations* 51, no. 4 (2000): 173–80.

88 See, for example, Anthony J. N. Judge, 'NGOs and Civil Society: Some Realities and Distortions', *Transnational Associations* 46, no. 3 (1995): 156–80; and Anthony J. N. Judge, 'Interacting Fruitfully with Un-Civil Society', *Transnational Associations* 48, no. 3 (1997): 124–32.

89 For a review of work using UIA data, see Elizabeth Bloodgood, 'The Yearbook of International Organizations and Quantitative Non-State Actor Research', in *The Ashgate Research Companion to Non-State Actors*, ed. Bob Reinalda (Farnham: Ashgate, 2011), 19–34.

90 *Global Governance: A Review of Multilateralism and International Organizations* (ISSN 1075-2846); *Globalizations* (ISSN 1474-7731); *Global Networks: A Journal of Transnational Affairs* (ISSN 1471-0374).

91 Manuel Castells, *Networks of Outrage and Hope: Social Movements in the Internet Age* (Cambridge: Polity, 2012).

92 Jackie Smith and Dawn Wiest, *Social Movements in the World-System: The Politics of Crisis and Transformation* (New York: Russell Sage, 2012).

93 I am grateful to the editors for this point. On the 'age of internationalism', see Laqua, *The Age of Internationalism and Belgium;* and on the 'NGO moment', see Kevin O'Sullivan, 'Humanitarian Encounters: Biafra, NGOs and Imaginings of the Third World in Britain and Ireland, 1967–70', *Journal of Genocide Research* 16, nos. 2–3 (2014): 299–315.

94 Some pioneer examples are studied in Matthew Hilton, *Prosperity for All: Consumer Activism in an Era of Globalization* (Ithaca, NY: Cornell University Press, 2009).

95 Johan Galtung, contribution to the 1972 Milan congress on 'the philosophy of non-governmental organization', *International Associations* 25, no. 3 (1973): 159.

Chapter 9

EVERYTHING ONE WANTS TO KNOW ABOUT INTERNATIONAL ORGANIZATIONS? A CRITICAL BIOGRAPHY OF THE *YEARBOOK OF INTERNATIONAL ORGANIZATIONS*, 1909–2017

Pierre-Yves Saunier

Those searching online for a current directory of international organizations will invariably come across the *Yearbook of International Organizations* edited by the UIA. Over the years, its publisher has repeatedly assured potential readers that this is the reference work they are looking for. For instance, a promotional brochure from 2011–12 describes the UIA as 'a non-profit, independent, apolitical, and non-governmental institution' that operates 'in the service of international associations', undertaking such work 'since its foundation in 1907'. The leaflet extolls the *Yearbook*'s virtues: 'The approach is scientific, the result is quality. The information presented by the UIA is structured, comprehensive and concise.'[1]

Statements of objectivity, independence, continuity and comprehensiveness are expected from any reference work, but the *Yearbook* and its publishers have shown a particular gusto for such claims. In the 1990s, its US distributor hailed it as 'the most complete source of information on international bodies available *anywhere*' and cited a review proclaiming, 'Here's everything you could possibly want to know about international organizations.'[2] Such brazen statements have attracted little scrutiny. Commentators and scholars largely seem to take the comprehensiveness, accuracy, coverage and consistence of the UIA's volumes for granted. Consider the *Yearbook of Civil Society* series, until recently the flagship of the Global Civil Society Programme at the London School of Economics. It relies heavily on the raw data and statistical visualizations of the *Yearbook of International Organizations* to assess, chart and map the rise and evolution of international non-governmental organizations (INGOs).[3] But it does not comment about the data itself. We need to contrast this stance with Daniel Laqua's comment that the UIA's founders 'sought to validate their efforts by demonstrating the extent of "international life" – and in so doing, generated data that has informed the work of subsequent generations.'[4] This self-fulfilling prophecy often goes under the radar: the *Annuaire de la Vie Internationale* – published before the First World War and acknowledged as a forerunner of the *Yearbook* – was part and parcel of an attempt to organize, strengthen and support international life.[5]

This sends us back to the claim about the UIA being 'apolitical' and its work 'scientific'. In fact, the organization's internationalism was a political project that championed a specific version of global order, and it was defended as such by its founders and subsequent leaders. The scientific investigation of internationalism that they claimed to pursue was meant to prove that international life expanded and mattered, and that their political internationalism was rooted in an objective observation of the world. The registration and categorization of organizations itself has been, and remains, a political project that embodies and shapes world views.[6] Choices as to publication language – notably the switch to English in the 1950s – cannot be understood as apolitical either. The promotional material also stresses 'independence' – yet for decades, and in the very pages of the *Yearbook*, the UIA emphasized its close links with the United Nations Organization and its agencies. Furthermore, the 2011–12 brochure implicitly suggests that the observation and registration of 'international civil society' has been going on since 1907 – which does not mesh with the patchy and uneven publication record of the *Yearbook* and its forerunners. Another descriptor, 'non-profit', places the Union out of the materialistic realm, on a par with the disinterested international organizations it purports to document. Yet, with a subscription fee of between € 2,200 and 2,600 for the last three editions, the *Yearbook* is also a commercial product. All claims made in the UIA's promotional material thus beg for critical interrogation.

This chapter starts from a series of questions that emerge from my perception of contrasts between public presentation and liminal historical knowledge, between widespread usage and limited critical appraisal. What is the *Yearbook*'s publication history, and why did its style and substance change over time? What were the aims and methods of these data-gathering attempts, and how were they connected to a project of building up what was called 'internationalism' at the beginning of the twentieth century, and 'transnational civil society' or 'global civil society' in the early twenty-first century? Why were third parties interested by the identification and classification of international organizations that got involved in the publication of the *Yearbook* and predecessors? Who were the readers of the *Annuaire* and *Yearbook*, and how did they use these works? I will strive to answer these questions, assembling a critical biography of the *Yearbook* and other directories associated with the UIA, examining their production, diffusion and reception.

Publishing Directories of International Organizations

The *Annuaire* emerged from a series of actions and reflections launched in the late 1890s by the Belgians Paul Otlet and Henri La Fontaine. The two men sought to foster coordination and collaboration between international organizations based in Brussels, including those of their own creation (International Office of Bibliography, International Institute of Bibliography).[7] Otlet's notes suggest that the idea crystallized in the summer of 1905, as he sketched the creation of a 'central body' that would 'group together and develop the existing or to be created international institutions'.[8] The tasks of this *organisme* comprised the publication of *annuaires* (yearbooks) with a mission to document international scientific congresses, libraries, institutes and publications.[9] Backed up by La Fontaine, Otlet discussed his ideas with several individuals. As noted in Boyd Rayward's contribution to this book, one of them was Cyrille Van Overbergh, an eminent civil servant with responsibilities for higher learning, sciences and the arts as well as a protagonist of the sociological milieu to which Otlet and La Fontaine belonged.[10] The other was Ernest Solvay, the leading private sponsor of scientific institutions in Belgium.[11] The latter's note of rejection, which indicted the vagueness and excessive remit of the project,[12] was compensated by the commitment of the former. Otlet and Van Overbergh pushed ahead in 1906, intertwining the idea with other endeavours.

The Office Central des Institutions Internationales (Central Office of International Institutions) was created in 1907. That year, Van Overbergh published a survey of a new sociological phenomenon: the international association.[13] Its findings were based on a three-page questionnaire sent to ninety-seven international bureaux, unions and societies – almost exclusively in Europe and overwhelmingly in French-speaking countries. Alfred Fried, who had edited an *Annuaire de la Vie Internationale* since 1905, likely provided the addresses for recipients of the questionnaire. Yet the connection with Fried was more than practical: Fried and the leaders of the Central Office shared a passion for bibliography, a commitment to peace activism and the vision of an increasingly interdependent planet.[14] For them, the growing number of international associations and congresses was both proof and promise of that interdependence. Accordingly, a practical science of internationalism was needed to document and support this growth and help to 'organize the world', to use Fried's motto. As the vector for this practical science, the four men considered transforming Fried's volume, with its uneven entries about international associations, into a systematization of Van Overbergh's detailed survey of international associations' organization, rules and activities. The resulting contract between Fried, La Fontaine and Otlet stipulated that the Central Office would assemble, print, sell and distribute the *Annuaire* each year from 1908 onwards, while Fried would keep the property of the title and receive an honorarium for his editorial contribution.[15]

The Central Office – transformed into the UIA in 1910–11 – printed editions of the *Annuaire* for 1908–09 and 1910–11, portraying them as vehicles for the UIA's 'permanent enquiry into international organization'.[16] They were published in French, like Fried's previous editions, but whereas the latter had between 160 and 250 pages, the former were hefty volumes of respectively 1,551 and 2,652 pages, providing information on about 300 and 500 organizations respectively. What remained similar was the distribution of organizations between 'official international life' – bureaux, unions and conferences borne out of agreements between governments – and 'private international life', that is, international associations. The new *Annuaire* had detailed entries for all: several pages packed with statutes, board and committee members, incomes and expenses, documentary and artefact collections. It also contained chapters documenting the work of the Central Office and the editors' take on international life. The research was not done in-house: in line with the notion of a permanent survey, and in view of the Office's limited resources, the *Annuaires* relied on the organizations' self-reporting by way of questionnaires.

The increased content of the 1910–11 edition was made possible by a 15,000 US dollar grant (75,000 Belgian francs) from the Carnegie Endowment for International Peace, provided in December 1911 for the year 1912. The Carnegie Endowment was just beginning its operations, and had decided to support selected peace organizations in Europe – a development that is also being discussed in Christophe Verbruggen's contribution to this volume.[17] Carnegie funding was a boon to the meagre resources of the Office, amounting to 90 per cent of its 1912 income.[18] Otlet and La Fontaine underlined that it was nowhere near their initial request of no less than 75,000 US dollars, but took great care to send one of the first copies of the new and expanded *Annuaire* to Nicholas Murray Butler, the Endowment's president.

The 1912–13 edition of the *Annuaire* was never published. With Otlet and La Fontaine having left Brussels early in the war, a small team kept on working under Van Overbergh.[19] In the string of letters whereby he and Otlet begged for the Endowment's continued support, La Fontaine wrote in April 1915 that the new *Annuaire* had been 'nearly completed and half of it was printed last July. It could have been published in November.'[20] Yet minutes of the meetings in Brussels make it clear that work was still ongoing, to a point where, as of October 1916, material grew so large that two volumes would have been necessary. In light of its limited resources, the Brussels team shifted gear and considered publishing a compact 300-page version, nicknamed '*Annuaire-résumé*'. Chapters for the *Annuaire-résumé* were being edited in spring 1917 when everything stalled: UIA resources had been strained beyond breaking point. When activities resumed after the war, neither the 1918–19 minutes of the Union's bureau meetings, nor the many letters sent to the Carnegie Endowment to solicit funding, suggest that Union leaders considered the publication of this material, or any new edition of the *Annuaire*, as a future milestone. The Union's 'formidable tasks' lay elsewhere.

Otlet and La Fontaine's priority was to find a place for the Union within the new family of international organizations that developed after the Armistice, including inter-Allied associations and the League of Nations. This concern to liaise with the League was at the origin of a new directory of international organizations. In 1919–20, Inazō Nitobe, under-secretary of the League, was in charge of connecting with international associations as the fledgling League Secretariat was eager to make sense of its environment. After his first visit to Brussels, he saw the pre-war *Annuaire* as a navigation tool within the world of private associations and asked Otlet and La Fontaine to revise their list of associations for the use of League staff and delegates to the League Assembly.[21] The subsequent correspondence offers no hints of a joint League–UIA endeavour to revive the *Annuaire*. Nor was the *Annuaire* anywhere in the plan that the Union sent to the League when La Fontaine and Otlet tried to counter the French proposal for the creation of a bureau for international intellectual work.[22] Instead, the 1919 list of associations became the foundation for the League's own work in publishing a directory of international organizations.

In 1921, the League's 'International Bureaux' section published the *Répertoire des organisations internationales/Handbook of International Organisations*, which it expanded in subsequent editions. The *Répertoire/Handbook*, alternatively issued in French and English, or both, was a smaller in-octavo volume, which grew from 167 pages in 1921 to some 500 in the late 1930s. Unlike the UIA's earlier *Annuaire*, it did not carry editorial chapters. It did, however, feature informative sections about the League and encompassed private and governmental international organizations. Its compact entries, from a few lines to one page, compiled essential information, as in Figure 9.1.

For the League Secretariat, documenting international groups went beyond the mere implementation of Article 24 of the Covenant and its brief to collect information about international offices established by treaties between

---

COMITÉ INTERNATIONAL D'ÉTUDES DES ASSOCIATIONS CATHOLIQUES D'INFIRMIÈRES.
INTERNATIONAL COMMITTEE OF CATHOLIC ASSOCIATIONS OF NURSES.
INTERNATIONALE ARBEITSGEMEINSCHAFT DER KATHOLISCHEN PFLEGEORGANISATION.

Siège : Paris (XVe), 15, rue Tiphaine.
Date de fondation : 1928.
But : Etudier et promouvoir la coopération entre les Associations nationales d'infirmières catholiques.
Membres : Sont membres du Comité, les Associations catholiques d'infirmières, nationales ou régionales, qui répondent au double caractère professionnel et catholique. Sont membres adhérents, les Associations dont le caractère professionnel ou catholique ne serait pas encore assez affirmé.
Associations membres en : Allemagne, Autriche, Belgique, Royaume-Uni, Canada, Etats-Unis d'Amérique, France, Suisse.
Associations membres adhérents en Argentine, Espagne et Italie.
Direction : Un comité composé de :
Présidente : Mlle D'AIROLES (France).
Vice-présidentes : Mlle VAN DER RYDT (Belgique), Frau BREUER (Allemagne), Mrs. GLANVILLE et Miss HEALY (Royaume-Uni).
Secrétaire : Miss MACKINTOSH (Royaume-Uni).
Trésorière : Mlle NODET (France).
Directeur spirituel : R. P. GARESCHE (Etats-Unis d'Amérique).
Finances : Cotisations des associations nationales et adhérentes au prorata de leurs membres. Budget annuel, moyenne : 6.000 francs.
Travaux : Congrès tous les quatre ans.
Résumé historique : Les principales activités du Comité international ont consisté : 1º à susciter la fondation d'associations catholiques d'infirmières dans les divers pays, entre autres, en Suisse, Autriche, Espagne où les pourparlers ont abouti; en Argentine, Colombie, Pologne où se poursuivent les pourparlers; 2º à poursuivre le perfectionnement technique des infirmières religieuses et laïques, notamment création d'une commission internationale de perfectionnement technique créée au Vatican en faveur des religieuses.
Le premier congrès a eu lieu à Lourdes en 1933; le second aura lieu à Londres en 1937. Un Congrès supplémentaire à Rome en 1935.
Publications officielles : Bulletin bi-annuel publié en français, anglais, allemand.

Figure 9.1 Extract from the League of Nations' *Handbook of International Organisations*. *Source: Répertoire des organisations internationales (associations, bureaux, commissions, etc.)* (Geneva: Société des Nations, 1936), 197.

governments. It was a matter of identifying the League's supporters, constituency and partners beyond national governments. As the League's procedures and apparatus were being developed, representatives and members of international associations were asked to contribute. Moreover, many of them did not wait for invitations from Geneva and began to press for their causes by targeting the new institutions. Within this context, it was vital to know who was who and who made what.[23] The *Handbook* answered this need, and during the interwar years it served as a low-intensity tool for international governance.[24] The UIA had no connection to the publication of these volumes, save for providing the 1919 list that was used by League people to send questionnaires for the 1921 *Handbook* (self-reporting was still the method for collecting information). Despite subsequent UIA claims that the League's publication 'prevented' the Union to resume the *Annuaire*'s publication after the Great War,[25] no mentions of such a project can be found while Otlet and La Fontaine focused on projects such as the Musée International, the Quinzaine Internationale, the Université Internationale and the Cité Mondiale.[26]

The Second World War seriously affected all the organizations created by La Fontaine and Otlet.[27] The latter was ousted from his leadership positions in 1941, despite his attempts to entice German authorities to support its work. As noted in Christophe Verbruggen's chapter, the Union itself was taken over by the Nazi apparatus, as many other international associations in occupied Europe.[28] The UIA's library and files were raided by occupation authorities, destroyed or brought to Germany to be used by the Deutsche Kongress-Zentrale, a governmental agency in charge of managing German participation into international associations and meetings.[29] With La Fontaine and Otlet having died in 1943 and 1944, the post-war UIA was very much an empty shell, unable to be a protagonist in the organization of a new international order. As Nico Randeraad and Philip Post have shown in the present volume, it was only at the beginning of 1948 that a provisory committee took the decision to revive its activities, thanks to a bequest by La Fontaine. By then, others had already taken the initiative in terms of directories of international organizations.

Two Swiss journalists, Marcel Henchoz and René-Henri Wust, created a society to publish a directory whose first edition was published in Geneva in the spring of 1948.[30] This *Annuaire des organisations internationales / Yearbook of International Organizations* was presented as a guide for all those who had to find their bearings in the new and teeming international life. Entries with generic information covered the new United Nations Organization and its agencies, as well as older intergovernmental unions and 'non-governmental organizations'. It alternated between French and English, matching the language in which the information was collected. The quality was uneven: the volume captured organizations created as recently as 1947, but many old organizations were not included and many entries were hardly documented.

The new publication boldly claimed to be the first to offer a synthesis of increasing relationships between nations, as embodied in international organizations. It did not acknowledge *Annuaires* or *Handbooks*. This edition was followed by a second one in 1949, with 650 international organizations described. The third edition, in 1950, was still under the copyright of Henchoz and Wust's society, but the UIA appeared as a co-editor.[31] This agreement had been announced to the readers of

the *Bulletin de l'Union des Associations Internationales* in January 1950, following a
teaser in December 1949.[32] Yet, when it was published in June 1950, with 980 pages
and entries for 1,000 organizations, the organization of the volume and the coverage
of the entries were not significantly different from the previous edition – save for
the addition of a Universal Decimal Classification number for each organization, in
true UIA fashion. No traces have been found of further negotiations between the
two parties, but in August 1951 the UIA's periodical announced that the *Yearbook*
was now the 'sole property' of the Union.[33] A new editorial process was presented
in the same article, and trumpeted in subsequent advertisements carried by the
Union's *Bulletin* as in Figure 9.2: the material would initially be collected by the
Union through questionnaires, and sent to the Non-Governmental Organizations

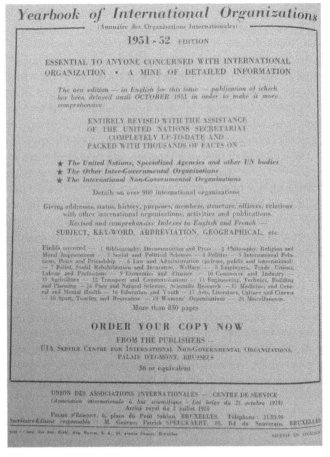

Figure 9.2 Advertisement for the *Yearbook of International Organizations* in the UIA's
NGO Bulletin (1951). *Source: NGO Bulletin* 3, 8–9 (1951), backmatter. N.B.: at the time,
'international non-governmental organizations' and 'non-governmental organizations'
were often used synonymously in UN parlance.

section of the UN Secretariat for revision and additions. When published, in August 1951, the 1951–2 edition amounted to 1,224 pages. It included 345 additional international organizations and was much better documented.

This new *Yearbook* embodied the UIA's reinvention under the aegis of intergovernmental organizations. Between 1949 and 1950, the Union's committee worked with representatives of the Interim Committee/General Conference of the Consultative Non-Governmental Organizations at the United Nations, liaised with UN officials in charge of NGOs and built strong connections with members of the Economic and Social Council of the United Nations (ECOSOC). In 1949, Aake Ording, a Norwegian member of the UN staff, was assigned to examine a new programme and structure for the UIA.[34] Results began to emerge one year later. In July 1950, the General Conference of Consultative Non-Governmental Organizations formally expressed its interest in transforming the UIA into a service centre for INGOs.[35] This was the emphasis of Ording's plan, whose report listed the technical tasks such a centre would fulfil, including 'to collect and distribute information on international NGOs, through a Bulletin, a Handbook and otherwise'.[36]

Ording followed his scheme from inception to its adoption in UN meetings – a process that is discussed in greater depth in Nico Randeraad and Philip Post's chapter.[37] In July 1950, ECOSOC adopted a resolution that sanctioned the scheme as it thwarted the project of a UN-made handbook on non-governmental organizations. Instead, it asked the UN secretary-general to rely on the UIA's *Yearbook*, and to cooperate with the latter, firmly installing Ording's scheme on the UN side.[38] The Union itself revised its statutes and published them in November 1950. There was a new name ('Union of International Associations. Service Centre for International Non-Governmental Organizations') and a new governing structure where representatives from intergovernmental and non-governmental organizations were prominent. There were specific missions too, including to '1) collect information about international, non-governmental, nonprofit making Organizations; 2) place this information in the bands [*sic*] and at the disposition of all interested persons and to ensure its distribution'.[39]

This UN-driven reinvention needs to be understood in light of Article 71 of the UN Charter, which called for 'suitable arrangements for consultation with non-governmental organizations' as part of the ECOSOC's operations – a scheme soon replicated with specialized UN agencies. As a result, the list of associations requesting or obtaining consultative status quickly swelled.[40] A minor element in this wider process, the *Yearbook* was necessary for the UN to steer its relations with other international organizations. It became the touchstone of the new UIA, whose redefined governance and brief ensured that it would provide services to the UN and to INGOs, and cooperate with the UN in publishing the *Yearbook*.[41] This entailed constraints that have shaped the content of the *Yearbook* until today: the definition of criteria for inclusion in consultation with ECOSOC officials;[42] the obligation to include in the *Yearbook*, regardless of other criteria, every INGO that received consultative status with the UN (a heavily politicized process during the Cold War);[43] and the coverage of both IGOs and INGOs alongside one another. But it also gave the Union a status as publisher of a directory with strong connections to the core of the international system. This role was valued, cherished and protected as a monopoly.[44]

Until 1980, the Union published the *Yearbook* every two years, save for a three-year gap between the 1951–2 and 1954–5 editions. Except three editions in French, the other fifteen used English, sometimes with a supplementary index in French or other languages. Despite the growth in the number of entries, the individual entries kept the same framework over time.

Eyvind Siegfried Tew and Anthony Judge were the two UIA staff members who shaped the Union's *Yearbook* publication during this period. From his obituaries, we can gain some glimpses of Tew's background: coming from a Quaker family and being a seasoned traveller as well as a speaker of many different European languages (plus Esperanto), this British citizen spent the war years as a cryptographer for the British intelligence service. He was brought into the *Yearbook* set-up for copy-editing work by Peter Hunot, H. G. Wells's former secretary and an advocate for world government, who edited the 1951–2 edition. In 1956, a Ford Foundation grant made it possible to hire Tew on a permanent basis. He settled down in Brussels in October 1956 as editor of the *Yearbook* and other UIA publications until 1975. Anthony Judge is an Australian who was born in Egypt in 1940 and grew up in Zimbabwe.[45] Judge's first contact with the Union was in 1961–3, when he worked as an intern assistant-editor for the *Yearbook*.[46] Five years later, aged 28, he returned as a consultant while finishing his MBA thesis at the University of Cape Town. He was then hired by the Union, editing its periodical *Transnational Associations* from 1969 to 1978, and in parallel developing computer-based resources that fuelled the *Yearbook* and other UIA publications. Judge became the major editorial force in the *Yearbook* after 1980 and occupied different executive positions within the UIA. These *Yearbook* editors – just as the Union's successive general secretaries (Georges Patrick Speeckaert, 1950–70; Robert Fenaux, 1970–85) – were not major internationalist authors in the vein of Otlet and La Fontaine, but their trajectories and their writings, including the *Yearbook*'s forewords, underline that they were just as dedicated to the cause of cooperation through international organization.

In-house publishing stopped in 1981 with the *Yearbook*'s nineteenth edition, co-published by the UIA and the International Chamber of Commerce. This one-off collaboration may have been connected with difficulties for the Union to edit and distribute the *Yearbook* on its own, as suggested by its next move. The venture with the Chamber of Commerce having been found unsatisfactory,[47] Judge asked Karl Saur, whose company had been distributing UIA publications in Germany since 1974, whether he would add the publication of the *Yearbook* to their joint activities. From 1983, the *Yearbook* was published by the Munich-based firm and reinvented in style and substance. Its size incrementally augmented with successive editions. This expansion partly followed the increase in the number of international organizations included in the *Yearbook*, but it chiefly resulted from a clear desire to create a gamut of products.

New volumes added to the ones that described international organizations according to the framework established by the *Handbook* (location, foundation, aims, activities, finance, members, etc.). From the 1983–4 edition, there appeared a geographic volume listing organizations by places (membership and secretariats) and a subject volume arranging organizations by subjects, completed by a bibliographic volume in 1995–6, and finally a volume of data analysis (statistics and visualizations) with the 2001–2 set. From 1994 to 2008, the *Yearbook* was also published on CD-ROM (including a French version and some segments in Spanish and German), and in 2004 it went online. This growth in size and sophistication of data presentation was made possible by the 1972 decision to shift data management from the filing cabinet to the computer.[48] The transition materialized first in the printing production process, later in indexation and visualization, and eventually in the diffusion of the *Yearbook* itself. The contract with Saur and the computerization also resulted in other publications derived from *Yearbook* data: specialized directories of international organizations in Africa and the Arab world (1984–5), a *World Guide to Religious and Spiritual Organizations*, a *Who's Who in International Organizations* from 2007 (later included in the *Yearbook* set) and more remotely the *Yearbook of World Problems and Human Potential*.[49] Although the imprint of K. G. Saur Verlag was bought in 1987 by Reed International, sold to the Gale Group by the now Reed-Elsevier firm in 2000 and again to De Gruyter in 2006, the contract with the Union was maintained.

The title changed hands again in 2011: since then, it has been published by Brill-Nijhoff, without any salient change to the presentation and organization of the work. The *Yearbook* is now one of the assets showcased in presentations of Brill's portfolio,[50] among a number of series and periodicals connected to public international law, human rights, humanitarian law and international relations. This might have been the reason for the publishers' interest in this reference work on international organizations, and this brings our attention to its trajectory as a commercial product.

Distributing Directories of International Organizations

In 1950, a footnote in the *Bulletin of the Union des Associations Internationales* mentioned that copies of the *Annuaire* were still available for sale. They could be obtained for 300 Belgian francs a piece, or 500 for the two editions, plus postal fees.[51] There are no clues that customers rushed for the occasion, but it sounds surprising that the Union or its printer still held copies of the *Annuaire* some forty years after its publication. One of the scarce archival clues about the distribution of the *Annuaire* is a 1929 buying order found in Paul Otlet's correspondence.[52] The sender was the World Peace Foundation, a pacifist body connected to Tufts University in Massachusetts. Trying to trace this specific copy reveals that the current World Peace Foundation does not have an online library catalogue, which illustrates the difficulties of appraising the presence of the *Annuaire* in private libraries. The other clue is a note scribbled by a League of Nations employee in 1919: 'I am told that there are only three copies of this in England, and we are trying to borrow a copy from one of the owners.'[53]

The library trail can be pursued further, though. As of April 2016, print copies of the *Annuaire* can be found into 101 public libraries in Europe and North America according to WorldCat.[54] Whether or not the *Annuaire* was bought by the public libraries who now hold it, when exactly, or whether other library copies of those big volumes with a fragile binding were discarded, owing to bad conditions or obsolescence, is not known. Likewise, we do not have any clues about the associations, diplomatic services, individual scholars and activists that may have obtained a copy of the *Annuaire*.

Can we appraise the dissemination of the *Annuaire* in the light of such limited information? The only tack for those 101 copies in public libraries is provided by the invoices of the printer who worked for Central Office in 1913: Oscar Lamberty bound exactly 202 volumes of the 1910–11 *Annuaire*, in two runs, which added to a previous batch of six copies that were sent to very important personalities.[55] Thus, the *Annuaire* fares well when its presence in public libraries fares is compared to the print run of its first edition.[56]

Library catalogues provide other yardsticks through comparison with other volumes belonging to the internationalist sphere. One is the second edition of the *Handbuch der Friedensbewegung* (1911–13). Written by one of the *Annuaire's* authors, Alfred Fried, this specialized directory of the pacifist movement can be retraced to 126 libraries covered by WorldCat. Nicholas Murray Butler's *The International Mind*, published in English in 1912, is now on the shelves of some 400 WorldCat libraries around the world and Frédéric Passy's *Pour la paix* (1909) in 102. *L'Internationalisme scientifique*, a survey of scientific international organizations written by Otlet and La Fontaine's Dutch rival Pieter Eijkman, also published in French in 1911, is present in sixty-nine of these libraries. Conversely, there are only some forty hits for the *Annuaire du mouvement pacifiste* for the years 1910 to 1913, a yearbook published in Bern by the International Peace Bureau where La Fontaine was a major character. Such comparisons suggest that the *Annuaire* may not have found its way onto libraries shelves as often as pacifist bestsellers in English, but reached a robust presence when compared to other directories of international life or to pacifist essays in French. It also compares well with the *Handbook* published by the League of Nations during the 1920s and 1930s, with respectively sixty-two WorldCat hits for the English 1921 edition and twenty-four for the French one.

I might be chasing the wrong rabbit, though. If Otlet and La Fontaine papers do not include sales figures, customer lists or complaints about postal deliveries, this is not merely the result of archival mishaps. A note sheet of the budget of the Office Central between 1907 and 1911 leaves a telling blank in the line 'vente de l'*Annuaire*' for the 'income' column.[57] Otlet and La Fontaine openly stated their position in their 1911 memorandum to the trustees of the Carnegie Endowment: 'It was necessary to distribute a great number of complimentary [*Annuaire*] copies to persons and institutions which would have been obliged to buy the publication.'[58] As La Fontaine later wrote, the *Annuaire* belonged to 'the category [of publications for which] it is impossible to rely on the usual publishers, and which can find buyers in sufficient numbers to cover their expenses only after several years of publication. Besides, they ought to be free of any mercantile concern, inadequate with the greatness of the movement they have to serve.'[59] True to such views, the 1912 report only included figures on 'possible' and 'indispensable' expenses, but none about income.[60] In addition to this elision of commercialization, the very conception of the *Annuaire* was barely conducive to it. Conceived as a 'permanent inquiry' about international associations, the *Annuaire* was to include 'as many documents as possible.'[61] This did not set the table for a regular, predictable and marketable publication. The absence of subscription campaigns, save for the first edition, as well as the absence of commercial advertisements in the *Annuaire* confirm the impression: selling the *Annuaire*, or even covering its costs, was not a priority.

Conversely, the post-1945 *Yearbook* was conceived as a commercial venture. This was conspicuous in the typesetting of the first edition, with its many advertisements. Local advertisements such as those in Figure 9.3 suggest that it

Figure 9.3 Advertisements in the UIA's *Yearbook of International Organizations* (1948). *Source: Annuaire des organisations internationales/ Yearbook of International Organizations* (Geneva: Société de l'Annuaire des Organisations Internationales, 1948), 279.

targeted people who, having come to Geneva to join international organizations, sought information on that sphere of activity, or about services and goods serving the needs of visiting individuals and expatriated families.

After returning to the UIA, the *Yearbook* maintained its identity of a practical volume to be sold to 'people in governmental and private positions of responsibility', 'all those in the diplomatic, governmental and intergovernmental services' as well as 'the sociologist, researcher, specialist and officer of international NGOs'.[62] The revamped Union – now conceived as a service centre – marketed the *Yearbook* as a sober, reliable and easy-to-get product. Editorial statements about international cooperation were left to other UIA publications, while efforts were made to reach out to potential customers: the 1952 thank-you note for the forty-eight newspapers and journals that had published a review of the 1951–2 edition shows that the Union did not spare on review copies.[63] Advertisements were also published, with a consistent series in the journal *International Organization* beginning in 1952.[64] The journal, created in 1947 by the aforementioned World Peace Foundation, was a place of convergence for researchers, officials and activists who believed in the new structure of international organization and who sought information about its development, and thus a well-chosen outlet for *Yearbook* advertisements. Besides other scientific journals in international relations, the UIA and its distributors also targeted the periodicals of the American Library Association from the early 1950s. In different languages and for different audiences, these advertisements invariably emphasized the patronage of intergovernmental organizations and their contribution to the robustness of the information, together with the practicality of the volume (see Figure 9.4). To get hold of this appealing volume, a wide array of methods of payment was offered – from transfers to UIA bank accounts in six different countries to subscription through post offices or UNESCO book coupons.[65] The new *Yearbook* was to be bought, and the Union attended to it earnestly.

Appraising the results of this commercial drive is deceptive. Locating the *Yearbook* in WorldCat is a quagmire: the publication has been catalogued in too many different fashions, serial or isolated holding of the title cannot be distinguished, and the development of the online subscription puts the cherry on the headache. All in all, no accurate figures can be established, but one edition or the other can be found in hundreds of libraries across the world, suggesting that it has effectively reached out to the 'sociologist and researcher'. Diplomats also seem to have had access to the *Yearbook*: the 1949 and 1951–2 *Yearbook* copies I consulted came by inter-library loan from the Department of External Affairs of Canada, while the 1950 edition in the library of Université Laval was a gift from the French General Consulate of Quebec.

Was it enough for the *Yearbook* to cover its expenses, or even be profitable for its mother house? Consistent sales figures are not available: older numbers have still to be found in UIA archives, and recent ones are considered confidential by the Union.[66] Nonetheless, incidental sources of information suggest that the *Yearbook* was not an instant or permanent bestseller, but nonetheless became the major asset in the UIA catalogue. A first snapshot captures the 1951–2 edition,

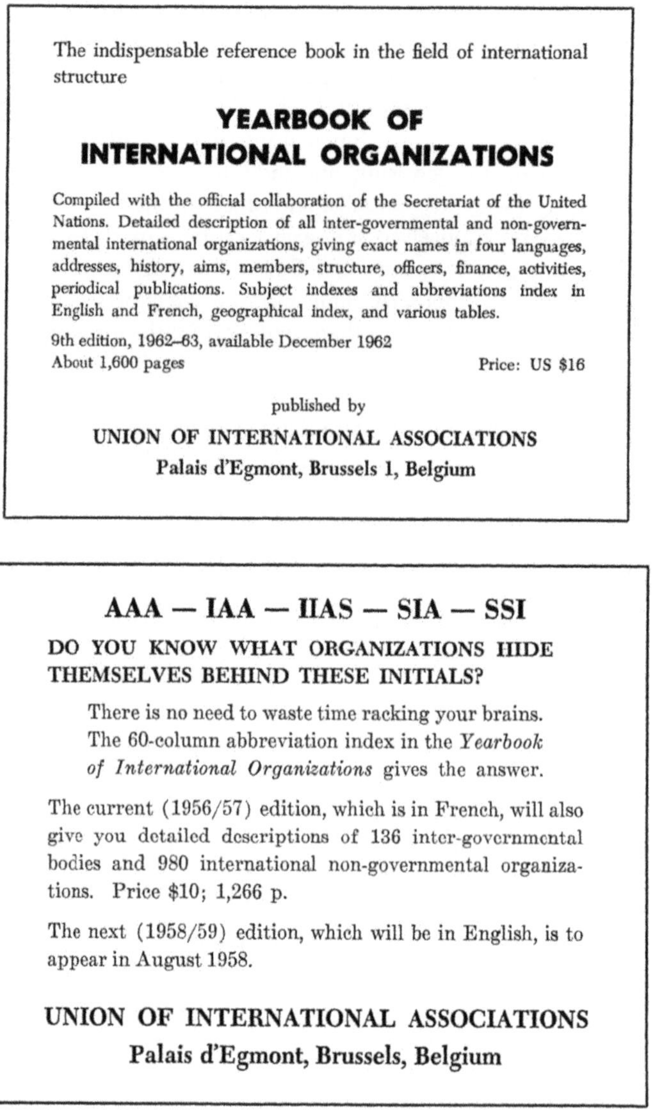

The indispensable reference book in the field of international structure

YEARBOOK OF
INTERNATIONAL ORGANIZATIONS

Compiled with the official collaboration of the Secretariat of the United Nations. Detailed description of all inter-governmental and non-governmental international organizations, giving exact names in four languages, addresses, history, aims, members, structure, officers, finance, activities, periodical publications. Subject indexes and abbreviations index in English and French, geographical index, and various tables.

9th edition, 1962–63, available December 1962
About 1,600 pages   Price: US $16

published by

UNION OF INTERNATIONAL ASSOCIATIONS
Palais d'Egmont, Brussels 1, Belgium

AAA — IAA — IIAS — SIA — SSI

DO YOU KNOW WHAT ORGANIZATIONS HIDE THEMSELVES BEHIND THESE INITIALS?

There is no need to waste time racking your brains. The 60-column abbreviation index in the *Yearbook of International Organizations* gives the answer.

The current (1956/57) edition, which is in French, will also give you detailed descriptions of 136 inter-governmental bodies and 980 international non-governmental organizations. Price $10; 1,266 p.

The next (1958/59) edition, which will be in English, is to appear in August 1958.

UNION OF INTERNATIONAL ASSOCIATIONS
Palais d'Egmont, Brussels, Belgium

Figure 9.4 Advertisements for the *Yearbook of International Organizations* (1958 and 1962), featured, for instance, in the IR journal *International Organization* 12, no. 2 (1958) and 16, no. 4 (1962). *Source:* Union of International Associations.

thanks to a grant application that the UIA filed with the Ford Foundation in July 1954. Secretary-general Speeckaert mentioned a 5,000 US dollar deficit for that edition, insisted on the extreme difficulty of covering the 1954–5 edition's costs, and warned that the next couple of editions would likely end up in deficit, jeopardizing the UIA's very existence.[67] His next grant application suggests that

Speeckaert had over-dramatized the situation – or misjudged the Ford Foundation grant-making criteria: the 1954–5 edition had been 'more than self-supporting' according to an assessment of early 1956.[68]

This, however, was not the beginning of a soaring sales trend, as we can gather from another vantage point in the late 1960s. In addition to his 1968 report about the use of computer data-processing methods at UIA, Anthony Judge studied the activities, image and organization of the Union, including markets and competitors. His conclusion pinpointed the pivotal role of the *Yearbook*: 'The UIA has one very good publication on which its reputation and income has been built, namely the *Yearbook of International Organizations*. The production of this and improvement in its quality is the most important activity of the UIA.'[69] This appraisal was supported by the UIA's financial reports. They confirmed the Union's difficulties during the 1950s, when support from governments dwindled – especially from Belgium.[70] The Union's balance sheet was in the red between 1957 and 1961, recouped debts between 1962 and 1965 and returned to net profit in 1966. In addition to a three-year grant from the Ford Foundation that kept the organization afloat in 1956–8, it was the growth of publication sales that put the Union back on its feet. Or, more accurately, the growth of *Yearbook* sales. Combined with low editorial cost, an increased print run and a rising price delivered a growing profit.[71] This was not the case with other UIA publications: between 1958 and 1968, the *Yearbook* was profitable all but two years, for a grand total three times superior to the magazines of the Union, which were its second source of income – and its major source of expenditure. Balance sheets leave no doubt that the Union survived thanks to the *Yearbook* (English) editions, which paid for its other activities.

Using material from the Union's distribution department, Judge broke down the sales of the 1966–7 edition by country/continent and by type of buyer.[72] Among identified buyers, the largest portion were in the United States (30 per cent) and 78 per cent came from five countries (United States, France, United Kingdom, Belgium, Switzerland). Distribution by type suggests that the *Yearbook* actually reached the constituencies claimed by the 1951–2 introduction: one-third of identified sales was made to governmental and intergovernmental bodies, another third went to libraries – chiefly in the United States – while 21 per cent were sold to private organizations (mostly commercial and airline firms, but also travel agents and congress bureaux). Geographical comparison with the 1954–5 *Yearbook* shows that the increase had taken place in countries and regions that were at the core of the new international order (the North Atlantic world) or were joining it (Africa, Asia) while it failed to attract buyers in the communist block: the *Yearbook* thrived in the parameters of a Cold War context. The 1966–7 figures also showed that, while INGOs made for most of the organizations covered in the *Yearbook*, they only contributed a little segment of its identified customers (5 per cent of that total, less than airline companies). If that weak presence was to be confirmed by more complete information about buyers, the *Yearbook* diffusion would certainly contrast sharply with the UIA's aim to be a 'service centre' for INGOs. According to Judge, and besides their financial limitations, many INGOs were reluctant to buy a volume for which they provided content: they saw the

Table 9.1 Sales data on the *Yearbook of International Organizations*, 1952–67

Yearbook edition	Print run	Number sold	Price in Belgian francs
1952–3	3,000	3,000	350
1954–5	3,000	3,000	500
1956–7	2,750	2,750	500
1958–9	3,500	3,500	580
1960–1	3,250	3,150	700
1962–3	4,500	4,100	700
1964–5	4,500	4,150	800
1966–7	5,500	4,800 (ongoing)	880

Source: Anthony Judge, 'Report of a Preliminary Investigation of the Possibility of Using Computer Data Processing Methods', Appendix I, exhibit 21a. Available online: http://www.laetusinpraesens.org/uia/docs/thesis/appen/apprep_all.pdf (accessed 30 April 2018).

Union as a profit-making Belgian body with pretentions to organize INGOs and teach them what to do.[73]

This failure to tap into the INGOs segment was one of the weaknesses identified by Judge, together with the fact that the Union had not maintained a satisfactory sales information system, that its publications in general were under-advertised and that there was no systematic attempt to develop sales despite the increased interest in international affairs.[74] To Judge, this was alarming because a growing number of specialized directories and registries competed with the *Yearbook* in different segments of the market.[75] Besides a counterfeiting publication,[76] a more serious potential danger existed: *The Europa Yearbook*, published every year, identified organizations absent from the Union's *Yearbook*, provided information in much greater detail, included national organizations of international relevance, and was distributed in retail outlets. Moreover, it obviously drew some of its content from the *Yearbook* pages. The total number of entries was still very inferior to that of the *Yearbook* – but if its publishers decided to expand their scope, then the Union's flagship might be in trouble, Judge warned. This seemed particularly problematic as little could be done to discourage a private publisher from walking on the Union's turf.

Undeterred by the recent disappointing direct mail campaign for the last edition (15,000 leaflets sent, nine order forms returned), Judge insisted that rising sales over the previous ten years showed that demand was robust and growing. Sales of the *Yearbook* were expandable if appropriate changes were made: a better connection with the *Yearbook*'s information providers, an active search for correct, improved or missing information about international organizations, serious market research and sales analysis, new forms of advertisement, a larger staff, a wider remit to cover national organizations and a shrewd diversification plan – a *Yearbook* published every year and specialized directories that would prevent any newcomer to 'split the market'. Even the poor quality of the volume's cover called for improvement. In his final recommendations, Judge pushed the envelope further: 'The UIA should consolidate and cease production of all publications whose utility, readership or sales are unsatisfactory. It should concentrate on selling and improving the services related to the *Yearbook of International Organizations*.[77] Given priority, the *Yearbook* would be the best tool for fulfilling what he deemed the best prospect for the Union at large: its work as a facilitator in 'bond formation within the world-system', weaving formal and informal links between international organizations.[78]

The continuously increasing size, content and price of the *Yearbook* suggest that it has remained the bread and butter of the Union's visibility, revenues and activities until today. Some hints show that the Union ran into cash flow problems in the mid-2000s, and the proposed solution was increased subscriptions to the *Yearbook*.[79] In the absence of a robust series of sales figures, though, one can only speculate about the evolution of print and online subscriptions, and the impact of new rival publications since 1968. According to WorldCat, the volume on international organizations that Gale Research added to its *Encyclopedia of Associations* in 1984 is now present in more US libraries than the *Yearbook*.[80] Anyhow, the *Yearbook*'s gauge of enduring success might lie elsewhere: in its usage.

Using Directories of International Organizations

Directories of international organizations are barely credited with shaping the world views of their readers the way that encyclopaedias or dictionaries are. Only the occasional librarian mentioned that the *Yearbook* played a pivotal role in his training.[81] No clues have been found either about its daily use at airline companies and travel agencies, in governmental departments or in intergovernmental organizations. Yet, just as any other directory, the *Yearbook* was certainly often flicked through to find a telephone number, the name of an officer, or the aims of an organization. In his endorsement of the *Yearbook*, Wallace Atwood – director of the office of international relations at the US National Academy of Sciences and a member of the UIA's executive council – claimed that the volume stood 'at his fingertips' and saved him 'hundreds of hours' when looking for accurate and current information on the organizations he had to deal with.[82]

Besides such passing mentions, specific users have left more durable traces: scholars and activists interested in the causes of peace, internationalism and international organization. Platforms of digitized academic journals can be used to recover their usage.[83] They provide a sample which, although overdetermined by digital availability, suggests how the *Annuaire* and *Yearbook* have been reviewed and cited. A systematic analysis of the pieces that mentioned these volumes shows that they have been used in three major ways: as a beacon pointing to the world's future, a certificate of accuracy for facts and numbers, and a pool of data to assess trends and patterns in international organization.

While digitized journal collections only offer the briefest of mentions regarding the *Annuaire*'s very first editions, the complimentary copies of the Central Office's 1908–1909 edition did reach a select number of go-betweens. These included protagonists of the peace movement where Fried, La Fontaine and Otlet were household names. Among those, none was more sanguine than William Stead, the English journalist and social reformer who – among other fiercely fought causes – advocated women's rights, peace and the superiority of the Anglo-Saxon race.

> When I opened the box and took out the book I felt as if I had suddenly come into the possession of King Solomon's magic carpet, which enabled me to fly far into the future. … When you read its pages you seem to be witnessing the erection of a new world. … An enormous multitude of forces are creating a new body in the shape of a highly complex international organization, and they are informing it with a new soul – the Conscience of Humanity. This is the greatest of all the miracles of our time, the almost automatic evolution of one harmonious World State out of the multitudinous jarring congeries of national states which constitute the armed anarchy of this planet.

Stead's words, whose original place of publication I was unable to locate, were quoted in a couple of occasions by US pacifists.[84] The *Annuaire* was also hailed in other journals with pacifist or internationalist leanings (*Isis, American Journal of International Law, Revue internationale de droit privé*). The 'magic carpet' still flew after the Second World War, with the 1951–2 *Yearbook* edition being tagged in *World Affairs* as 'an eloquent testimonial to the way in which men of good will by international organization are implementing understanding on the basis of mutual interest and need throughout the world'.[85] Much more recently, the opening note of a publication emanating from the American Society of International Law mentioned (wrongly) that the non-existence of an annual of international organizations 'until 1957' was a sign that the number and importance of international organizations had been insignificant up to that point.[86] The *Yearbook* and its growing content have thus been interpreted as a record of current trends in the international order, a 'weighty evidence (in both senses of the term) of how trans-frontier cooperation has been speeding up'.[87] This analogon, which was also embedded in editorial texts within the *Yearbook* itself, made it possible for reviewers to vouch for the world's evolution towards integration and cooperation. Such mentions, which often appeared in journals committed to the project of international organization or 'peace research', were nonetheless quite limited: they appeared in only a handful of the forty-two reviews I identified in scientific journals. Most of them addressed the *Yearbook* on a different plane.

The most frequent qualification for the *Yearbook* was that of 'reference' – a tag that the earlier *Annuaire* had hardly received. Some reviewers undergirded the *Yearbook* with flowery metaphors, the most frequent being that of an international maze/labyrinth that the *Yearbook* helped modern Theseus to navigate. Most of them were more concise and insisted that the book was 'useful', 'comprehensive', '*vollständigste*', 'impressive', '*précieux*', '*wertvoll*', 'reliable', 'authoritative': 'the standard guide' for all those who needed to identify, characterize or locate an international organization or the international organizations in a given domain. When the reviewer for *World Affairs* mentioned that the 1962–3 edition had 'the density and compactness of a good telephone directory', he might not have written tongue-in-cheek.[88] Its growing status as a reference volume from the mid-1950s was enhanced by its presence in the 'research tips' or 'selected bibliographies' sections published by journals in international law or politics, and later by citations in scientific articles.

The *Yearbook* thus became the place where lawyers, political scientists, sociologists, geographers, historians and other scholars found certified information about international organizations. By contrast, the earlier *Annuaire* had had no such status – both because of its limited circulation and because the discipline of international relations was only just emerging in the 1920s and 1930s.[89] Footnotes that cited the *Yearbook* as their source of factual information became frequent after 1960. How many international organizations currently exist? How many INGOs deal with anthropology? Which countries are members of the European Broadcasting Union? How far do intergovernmental organizations include African countries? How many multinational companies have a subsidiary in Sri Lanka? Which INGOs hold consultative status with UN agencies? How large is the budget of a specific association? Do memberships of Taiwan and the People's Republic of China in international organizations overlap or exclude one another? Until today, researchers from many disciplines have relied on the *Yearbook* for answers to such questions, using it as a proxy for actual statutes of specific international organizations, a source of precise information on organizations and a spring of accurate numbers. The *Yearbook* has been treated as an authoritative voice in such matters. For instance, when a lecturer in law at the University of Salzburg found a contradiction between Russian sources and the *Yearbook* as to the membership of the Chamber of Commerce of the Uzbek Socialist Republic within the Afro-Asian Organization for Economic Co-operation, he ultimately relied on the *Yearbook*.[90]

Reliance on the *Yearbook* became stronger when researchers tried to assess the changing number of international organizations, beginning in the late 1960s. A 1968 article by political scientist Edward Miles may have been the first to compare different editions of the *Yearbook* to this end.[91] In the process, he referred to the *Yearbook* as the 'official count' of international organizations. Subsequent scholars also adorned the *Yearbook* and its predecessors with official or semi-official status, and cited its ties with the UN and the League of Nations as a certificate of its accuracy.[92] They referred to the 'United Nations and the Y*earbook of International Organizations*' section, which has invariably been included in every edition of the *Yearbook* from the 1951–2 to the 2011–12 edition.[93] This section astutely quoted a League document of 1921 and the aforementioned 1950 ECOSOC resolution to suggest official collaboration. It thus provided the *Yearbook* with a varnish of officialdom, even though it was only in 2007 that the Union signed an official agreement with an intergovernmental organization regarding the identification of INGOs.[94]

The treatment of the *Yearbook* as an authoritative source was not limited to numbers and information: it extended to the definitions and categories that shaped these numbers. As for any directory, the editorial team had to decide which organizations to include or omit. The decision had to be ad hoc, because there existed no official definition. For a long time, UN texts themselves did not go further than saying that an INGO was an organization not established by intergovernmental agreements.[95] The *Yearbook*'s content was thus defined by specific criteria, established in accordance with UN staff – likely in the mid-1950s. These criteria were only made explicit in the 1968–9 edition: seven major characteristics decided whether non-governmental organizations were 'genuinely international' and could be included in the *Yearbook*.[96] Until the 1976 edition, this, for instance, altogether excluded organizations whose activities, budget and membership did not cover at least three countries. After 1976, such organizations could be included in the *Yearbook* but under different and shifting categories separated from 'genuinely international' organizations: the tag from the early 1980s was 'internationally oriented national organizations', whose number was comparable to the number of 'genuinely international' organizations, and in the 1990s new classes were created to accommodate emergent and 'non-conventional' types of organizations (networks and virtual groups, religious orders, governmental and non-governmental bodies connected to intergovernmental organizations).[97]

In almost every article I have found where *Yearbook* data has been used, authors have conflated the number of existing INGOs with the content of the *Yearbook*, and even more narrowly with the *Yearbook*'s category of 'genuinely international bodies'. This suggests how far the categorization of the *Yearbook*'s, and its content, have been framing the perimeter of most studies.[98] Only a handful of the identified 172 articles which have used figures or lists from the *Yearbook* include any acknowledgement of the 'seven aspects' used for inclusion and exclusion as 'genuine international bodies' and the consequences of such criteria for the research parameters, questions and conclusions. While it seems likely that most scholars were aware of the *Yearbook*'s limitations, they did not articulate their concerns: their choice to work with what they had seems to have muted the critical appraisal of their main source.

Just two articles about INGOs mentioned complementary research to establish lists of organizations in a given field.[99] One of these explained that the list of human rights organizations compiled from the *Yearbook* yielded 225 'genuinely international' INGOs, before conversations with activists, the use of additional printed sources as well as the inclusion of relevant 'internationally oriented national organizations' mentioned in the *Yearbook* raised the number to a total of 325 organizations to which the research questionnaire was eventually sent. Yet, even these two articles did not question the *Yearbook*'s definitions and categories. Only two other scholarly articles seem to have done so.[100] Most significantly, sociologist Evelyn Bush insisted that the *Yearbook*'s definitions hindered a satisfactory identification of religious groups active in the domain of human rights for two main reasons. Firstly, the *Yearbook*'s association with the institutional needs of the UN, as well as the criteria ruling inclusion in the *Yearbook* and its 'genuinely international organizations' category, tended to sideline smaller, informal INGOs with a financial or membership gravity centre in one or two countries whereas it over-represented organizations that enacted the organizational and normative principles shared by the UN and the UIA. Secondly, the *Yearbook*'s classification assumed that religion and secular contributions to civil society and international life were different by nature, with compassion and rationality being respectively the chief motivation for action. Through a comparison between the data from the *Yearbook* and the online Human Rights Directory (www.hri.ca), Bush concluded 'that research using the *Yearbook* … is indeed biased toward the more powerful organizations in the human rights field', and that the *Yearbook* 'religious organizations' category did not adequately capture the growth of religion-motivated organizations engaging public issues such as human rights.[101] Her points ring true when bearing in mind the publication's wider history and context: the UIA's commitment to support organized internationalism through its publication and the arrangement with the UN that shaped the criteria for inclusion.

The next question, then, is to evaluate how far research on international organizations has relied on the *Yearbook*. Indeed, researchers did not only use the *Yearbook* as a source for lists, facts and figures. International relations specialists and sociologists have also given it prominence as a source of data for their quantitative approaches.[102] Within the sample of scholarly articles used for this chapter, and notwithstanding the sample bias, this peaked at two moments in time and in connection with specific disciplinary communities on the US social sciences scene. Firstly, between 1968 and 1980, it was chiefly American scholars of international relations who developed quantitative approaches based on *Yearbook*'s data as they tried to figure out the path to world order through international organization. Other disciplines chipped in, the very first article of that cluster being signed by a development sociologist.[103] INGOs were part of the picture,[104] but specialists working on intergovernmental organizations clearly led this first phase. Twelve out of nineteen articles using *Yearbook* data dealt exclusively with intergovernmental organizations.[105]

A second cluster appeared in the late 1990s, focusing on the place and role of international associations in globalization. Two strands of social scientists – whose work still dominates the field today – contributed to that spike. The first strand comprised specialists of transnational social movements such as Jackie Smith and Kathryn Sikkink.[106] The second group featured researchers who endorsed the global neo-institutionalist approach of US sociologist John Meyer and strived to establish the dynamics and genealogy of 'world society': they mined the *Yearbook* for data on INGOs, seam after seam, following its initial exploitation by John Boli and George Thomas. Within this large set of articles, the *Yearbook* is treated, in Jackie Smith's words, as 'the most comprehensive, annual census of international associations'.[107]

In both clusters, *Yearbook* data fuelled different types of quantitative tools. Some were modest but widely adopted: counts of environmental INGOs per country to estimate pressure for environmental compliance in different countries;[108] creation rates of INGOs to trace the growing or diminishing strength of 'world discourse' within a specific subject domain;[109] country membership in IGOs and INGOs to assess the political autonomy of postcolonial states;[110] country participation in INGOs to index support and incentives to 'world order' and international cooperation in different nations;[111] and the logging of national memberships in INGOs to estimate 'linkage to world society'.[112] Together with the latter, 'shared membership score' – which measure a country's membership in IGOs or INGOs as recorded in *Yearbook* entries – have frequently been used ever since Robert C. Angell's introduction of the score in the late 1960s.[113] A whole metrology was thus derived from the *Yearbook* and its data, some of it being described as 'standard measure'.[114] *Yearbook* data also fed into analytical statistics: scholars counted keywords in INGO names and descriptions,[115] analysed membership figures,[116] drew from the 'NGO relations' section of the *Yearbook* to estimate the density of international civil society,[117] or mapped the geographical repartition of secretariats offices.[118] Those with a knack for more sophisticated quantitative analysis used *Yearbook* data to create dependent, independent or control variables about INGOs as they implemented regressive analysis or event history analysis to understand the development of international organization at large, or international organizations' development in one domain after the other.[119] The references in all these articles make it clear that the data extracted and coded from the *Yearbook* – alongside the indicators or variables it helped to build – was exchanged among individuals and generations of researchers.[120] The *Yearbook* and its data became part of a toolkit that circulated between collaborators, among colleagues and from masters to disciples, helping to create a research milieu. The reliance on *Yearbook* data extended beyond North America: when the London School of Economics team began to publish its *Global Civil Society Yearbook* in 2001, its researchers calculated a 'membership density index' for each country, based on the membership information of the *Yearbook* INGOs entries. More generally, their claim that INGOs were the embodiment of global civil society relied heavily on the *Yearbook* and its content – thus reproducing the justification loop installed by Fried and friends.[121]

How much has this reliance and presence led scholars to ponder the representativeness, consistency and accuracy of the data collected by the UIA and featured in the *Yearbook*? Here, a distinction needs to be made between researchers who used data about IGOs and data about INGOs. Canadian political scientist Michael Wallace and his US colleague David J. Singer, who assembled data about intergovernmental organizations between 1815 and 1964, were openly critical about the information provided by the *Annuaire*, the *Handbook* and the *Yearbook*. Vagueness of information, inaccuracies in the *Annuaire*, chronological publication gaps for the *Handbook*, as well as incomplete information and inconsistency of rules for the *Yearbook* provided sufficient grounds for caution. More generally, they could not abide by the unspecified and inconsistent criteria for inclusion and the limited verification of information:

> It was clear that different rules had been used from year to year or even from page to page. In general, it seemed that the editors had largely permitted the organizations to categorize themselves as well as to define their own founding date, membership, and so forth. ... Such a procedure, of course, is not conducive to uniformity and comparability.[122]

For these reasons, Wallace and Singer's 'Correlates of War' project incorporated additional data from many other sources. *Yearbook* data was again verified and complemented with other sources when this dataset was expanded in the early 2000s.[123] Despite the fact that, until the 2000s, scholars relied on *Yearbook* data to study shared membership in IGOs after 1964,[124] quantitative indicators about IGOs have usually been built from the expanded and corrected data of the 'Correlates of War' project.

The situation is quite different in the literature on INGOs, where *Yearbook* data reigns supreme. John Boli and George Thomas fashioned the crown with their original statement that the *Yearbook* data was 'adequate for meaningful analysis' because of semi-official status of the *Yearbook*, continuous contact with 13,000 organizations, and annual revision and addition of information by UIA staff.[125] The very same year, Jackie Smith also endorsed *Yearbook* data, insisting on the use of various sources by the *Yearbook* staff in order to identify and characterize INGOs.[126] Such endorsements invite us to return to the Union's collection method. From Fried's first *Annuaires* to the current edition of the *Yearbook*, information has come from the organizations themselves by way of questionnaires. Both the origins of the *Annuaires* in the survey technique and the limited resources of the UIA conspired to leave it to international organizations to provide information. These questionnaires have never been included in the *Yearbooks*, but some can be found in archives.[127]

The articles that I have consulted do not confront the questions that arise from this situation. How many INGOs have been able to commit enough staff's energy, competence and time to complete the UIA's questionnaires sent by the Union? What has been the response rate for these surveys, especially when the updating of an existing entry was required? To what extent have organizations provided up-to-date and accurate facts or figures about such sensitive matters as membership distribution by country, budget amount or connections to other international organizations, considering the likely consequences for both their inclusion in the *Yearbook* and their public image? What has been the capacity of the *Yearbook* editorial team to fact-check this information or to complete questionnaire items that were not filled by the organizations? How far were UIA staff members able to chase organizations that had not yet been included in the *Yearbook* or to follow up with organizations that did not return questionnaires? These questions are important to appraise the coverage, accuracy and consistency of the *Yearbook*'s content – and, consequently, of the data researchers derived from it. They are not part of the critical apparatus of the articles in my sample, though.

Answers to these questions are scarce. Some clues, however, are offered by the 1968 'Judge report' and by the appendixes published in the *Yearbook* since 1983–4. From the former, we learn that 'the quality cannot be controlled because the UIA only includes what it gets and does not make, or cannot make, extensive efforts to improve the quality of individual entries'.[128] Judge blamed this incapacity to upgrade data quality on the lack of mechanisms for searching missing or additional information; the poor quality of existing files at UIA; the dearth of staff and time to gather information from external sources; the belatedness of questionnaire campaigns; and the costs involved in modifying existing text between different editions.[129] The UIA's shoestring operation was taking its toll. Judge's conclusion was stern: data for many organizations was insufficient, the accuracy of information was diminishing and chances to reverse this development were complicated by the *Yearbook*'s principle to only include information approved by the organization concerned.

This remained a constant challenge, as confirmed by appendixes present since the 1983–4 edition, chiefly the 'Editorial Problems and Policies' section. It acknowledged the under-reporting of INGOs that did not fit with the 'genuinely international' category and the fact that some organizations did not want to provide information on their budget or other items they deemed confidential. Some appendixes claimed that editors did their best to corroborate inflated statements and claims, but the method for collecting and publishing information remained unchanged: 'The guiding principle has been to portray the organization as it sees itself usually from its own documents. ... The editors cannot verify the claims made in documents received.'[130] Although the wording and location changed slightly between editions, these caveats have been repeated over time between 1981 and 2015. The *Yearbook*'s 'Warning' section, published since the 1986–7 volume, notes that '[the] final evaluation of the information presented here must be left to the users of this volume'.[131] As with insurance contracts clauses written in small fonts, we may not have paid enough attention to this warning. More recently, the *Yearbook* has presented, for the first time, an evaluation of its data collection process: the 2014–5 edition includes a (discreet) mention that the annual questionnaire to INGOs has had a response rate of 35 to 40 per cent – as such, it hardly amounts to an annual comprehensive census.[132]

Conclusion

Having considered the chain that has been presented here – from production to consumption of the *Yearbook* and other directories of international organizations – I argue that their value has been overstated. Overstated by the UIA itself, and its publishers, who have staged a narrative of continuity, objectivity and consistency that leaves no place for the more tumultuous history of discontinuity, activism, institutionalization and difficulties of the *Annuaire*, *Handbook* and *Yearbook*. Overstated by us scholars, who have largely accepted and used the *Yearbook* as an official or semi-official source of comprehensive, accurate and fine-tuned fact and data pool. This stance has been at its strongest for data concerning INGOs that political scientists and sociologists have been using in the last twenty years or so, especially through quantitative approaches to civil society.

What's next? Evelyn Bush's remarks about the biases embedded within the *Yearbook* do not seem to have been fully taken aboard yet. As of February 2018, her 2007 article has only been cited three times in the journals available on JSTOR, four times according to Web of Science, and only one of the forty-seven citations mentioned in Google Scholar acknowledges or follows up on her analysis of the *Yearbook*'s data.[133] This is the case although, as early as 2007, John Boli and David Brewington pointed readers to Bush's piece in order to assess 'general problems and limitations that are bound to afflict any data source of this nature'.[134] Interestingly, Boli and Brewington's piece included an unprecedented critical appraisal of *Yearbook*'s data: UIA's 'seven rules' used for inclusion were explicitly mentioned, as well as the availability rate of the information used in the chapter (membership numbers, for instance, were only available for 51.3 per cent of the organizations studied).[135] It was, to my knowledge, the first time that qualifications of the *Yearbook*'s INGOs data were made public.

Other clues suggest that INGOs researchers are developing a more critical take on the *Yearbook*. Elizabeth Bloodgood and Hans Peter Schmitz have underlined that this most common source for quantitative data on INGOs has been problematic for 'the definition of INGOs which affects the conceptual assumptions shaping the dataset and the number of INGOs reported' and that 'a large part of the more detailed information is plagued by missing values, as UIA relies on self-reporting'.[136] They follow these remarks with a panorama of the attempts by NGO scholars to build their own ad hoc databases, using but not being bound by *Yearbook* material, and tailored to their research questions. It remains to be seen whether the insights of scholars like Bush or Bloodgood will blossom into a thorough critical examination, or if the *Yearbook*, in the absence of other easily accessible cross-sector options for INGOs data, is too unique to be failed.

Notes

Several people have been very generous in helping me write this chapter: *grand merci* to Christoph Verbruggen, Stéphanie Manfroid, Daiana Torres, Gregory Meyer, Michele Hiltzik, Elisabeth Bloodgood, Davide Rodogno and Daniel Laqua.

1   The brochure was online on the website of publisher Brill-Nijhoff until July 2017 and can now be viewed at https://www.dropbox.com/s/gtyqxkdqj1uglgl/Brill%20yearbook%20promotional%20material%202011.pdf (accessed 1 August 2018).
2   *Reference & User Services Quarterly* 38, no. 1 (1998).
3   Published between 2001 and 2012, beginning with Helmut Anheier et al., eds, *Global Civil Society 2001* (Oxford: Oxford University Press, 2001). See 'Global Civil Society Knowledge Base'. Available online: http://www.gcsknowledgebase.org (accessed 3 July 2017).
4   Daniel Laqua, 'Alfred H. Fried and the Challenges for "Scientific Pacifism" in the Belle Époque', in *Information Beyond Borders: International Cultural and Intellectual Exchange in the Belle Époque*, ed. W. Boyd Rayward (Farnham: Ashgate, 2014), 182.
5   Anne Rasmussen, 'L'Internationale scientifique 1890–1914' (PhD diss., École des Hautes Études en Sciences Sociales, Paris, 1995); W. Boyd Rayward, *The Universe of Information: the Work of Paul Otlet for Documentation and international Organization* (Moscow: VINITI, 1975).
6   Patrick Tort, *La Raison classificatoire* (Paris: Aubier, 1989).
7   See Rasmussen, 'L'Internationale scientifique', ch. 5 and Rayward, *The Universe of Information*, ch. 7.

8	Otlet, 9 août 1905, 'Chemise I. La fondation de l'UAI. A. Origines-historiques-membres. 1 Origines', box 242, Papiers Otlet, Mundaneum archives, Mons (hereafter: 'PO, Mundaneum').

9	Folder 'Septembre 1905. Congrès mondial' in 'Chemise 1. La fondation de l'UAI ... 1 Origines', box 242, PO, Mundaneum.

10	Wouter van Acker, 'Sociology in Brussels, Organicism and the Idea of a World Society in the Period before the First World War', in *Information Beyond Borders,* ed. Rayward, 143–68.

11	Nicolas Coupain, 'Ernest Solvay's Scientific Networks: From Personal Research to Academic Patronage', *The European Physical Journal Special Topics* 224, no. 10 (2015): 2075–89; Andrée Despy-Meyer and Didier Devriese, eds, *Ernest Solvay et son temps* (Brussels: Archives de l'Université Libre de Bruxelles, 1997).

12	Solvay to Otlet, 17 September 1905, Folder 'Septembre 1905. Congrès Mondial' in 'Chemise 1. La fondation de l'UAI ... 1. Origines', box 242, PO, Mundaneum.

13	Cyrille Van Overbergh, 'L'association internationale', *Le Mouvement Sociologique international* 8, no. 3 (1907): 615–927 and *L'Association internationale* (Brussels: De Witt, 1907).

14	Laqua, 'Alfred H. Fried'.

15	Convention entre M. A. Fried, et MM. La Fontaine et Otlet, 218 D6 O6, Papiers Personnels Henri La Fontaine, Mundaneum, Mons (hereafter HLF, Mundaneum). '1905.08.04' has been handwritten on the document, but the content refers to the 1907 edition of the *Annuaire.* Laqua, 'Alfred Fried' details the convention between the three men.

16	*Annuaire de la Vie Internationale 1910–1911* (Brussels: Union des Associations Internationales, 1913), 42.

17	Butler to La Fontaine, 15 December 1911, Series III Division of Intercourse and Education, Subseries B, vol. 178, Carnegie Endowment for International Peace Records, Butler Library, Rare Books and Manuscripts Library, Columbia University, New York City (hereafter CEIP, Columbia). Another 15,000 dollars were granted by the Endowment in April 1913, amidst Endowment trustees' growing irritation in front of aggressive attempts by European peace societies to receive more funds.

18	'Rapport présenté par l'Office des Associations internationales à la Carnegie Endowment for International Peace', November 1912, III, B, 178, CEIP, Columbia.

19	Minutes of the meetings of the administrative committee of the Union between 1915 and 1919, boxes 315–19, Union des associations internationales 1910–37, Germany Deutsche Kongress-Zentrale 1870–1943, Hoover Institution Archives, Stanford University. For the origins of that collection, Madeleine Herren-Oesch '"Outwardly ... an Innocuous Conference Authority": National Socialism and the Logistics of International Information Management', *German History* 20, no. 1 (2002): 67–92.

20	La Fontaine to Haskell, 28 April 1915, CEIP, Columbia.

21	Nitobe to Otlet, 6 September and 11 October 1919, 'List of international bureaux etc', Registry Files 1919–27, R 1004, Archives de la Société des Nations, Geneva. The translated index was published as *Liste des Unions, Associations, Institutions, Commissions, Bureaux Internationaux, etc. List of International Unions, Associations, Institutions, Commissions, Bureaux, etc., publiée par la Société des Nations – League of Nations, établie par l'Union des Associations Internationales,* London, His Majesty's Stationery Office, 4 November 1919.

22	Takashi Saikawa, 'From Intellectual Co-operation to International Cultural Exchange: Japan and China in the International Committee on Intellectual Co-Operation of the

League of Nations, 1922–1939' (PhD diss., Universität Heidelberg, 2014), ch.1 and esp. p. 28.

23 Helen McCarthy, *The British People and the League of Nations: Democracy, Citizenship and Internationalism, c.1918–1945* (Manchester: Manchester University Press, 2011); Jean Michel Chaumont, *Le Mythe de la traite des blanches: Enquête sur la fabrication d'un fléau* (Paris: La Découverte, 2009).

24 Other repertories were published at the time: one example is a competing handbook on international cultural organizations published in Japanese and English by the Japanese government. See Madeleine Herren, Martin Rüesch and Christiane Sibille, *Transcultural History: Theories, Methods, Sources* (Berlin: Springer, 2012), 39.

25 Georges Patrick Speeckaert, 'A Glance at Sixty Years of Activity (1910–1970) of the Union of International Associations', in *Union of International Associations, 1910–1970: Past, Present, Future* (Brussels: Union des Associations Internationales, 1970), 32 and 35.

26 Van Acker, 'Universalism', ch. 7 and 8.

27 Françoise Lévie, *L'homme qui voulait classer le monde: Paul Otlet et le Mundaneum* (Brussels: Les impressions nouvelles, 2006), ch. 14.

28 Mark Mazower, *Governing the World: The History of an Idea* (London: Penguin, 2012), ch. 6.

29 Herren 'Outwardly ... ', esp. 72–3 and 82–6.

30 Wust took up journalism after the war, during which he was a close collaborator of Général Guisan. He had been a member of the far-right party Union Nationale in the 1930s. See Luc Van Dongen, *La Suisse face à la Seconde Guerre mondiale, 1945–1948, émergence et construction d'une mémoire publique* (Geneva : Société d'histoire et d'archéologie de Genève, 1997), 144 and 178.

31 UIA secretary-general Georges Patrick Speeckaert later wrote that the Geneva publishers approached the Union: 'Ouvrages de référence sur les organisations et réunions internationales', *Bulletin des bibliothèques de France* 5, no. 11 (1960): 7.

32 'We shall hope to publish quite soon, a Hand-book with remarks on the organisations actually active at the moment': 'Statistical and Chronological Table of International Organisations', *Bulletin Mensuel* 2, no. 10 (1949): 155.

33 'Échos du centre de service UAI', *NGO Bulletin* 3, nos. 6–7 (1951): 180–1.

34 Speeckaert, 'A Glance', 34.

35 'The Third Conference of Consultative Non-Governmental Organizations', *Bulletin Mensuel* 2, nos. 8–9 (1950): 189.

36 Aake Ording 'In the Service of International Progress', *Bulletin Mensuel* 2, no. (1950): 144–6.

37 In 1950 and 1951, Ording applied for grants by the Ford Foundation for turning the UIA into a 'service center for INGOs'. Ford Foundation memos mention Ording's 'extreme aggressiveness' in this occasion. 'Union of International Associations. Summary & background statement', 19 November 1954, Ford PA 05600305, reel 0509, section 4, Ford Foundation Papers, Rockefeller Archive Center, Tarrytown (hereafter FFP, RAC).

38 Resolution 334, part B, United Nations, *Economic and Social Council Records, 5th Year, 11th Session, Supplement n°1 Resolutions*, p. 81 (available through Unbisnet.un.org). No official agreement was ever signed following this resolution.

39 'Revised Statutes for the UIA', *Bulletin Mensuel* 2, no. 11 (1950): 252–6.

40 Cf. the growing list of organizations with consultative status in *Yearbook of the United Nations* in 1946–7, 1947–8 and 1948–9.

41 Actual cooperation, in the form of revision of entries by UN staff, disappeared from advertisements with the 1962–3 edition, while the annual UN *Report of the Secretary General on the Work of the Organization* dropped the ritual mention of cooperation between the UN and the Union after 1976. Every *Yearbook* edition since 1951–2 has highlighted UN endorsement.

42 Anthony Judge, 'Report of a Preliminary Investigation of the Possibility of Using Computer Data Processing Methods', appendix 1 'Analysis of Internal and External Factors Which May Influence the Future of the Organization', exhibit 38, p. 1. All the documents written by Judge and used in this chapter are available on his website (www.laetusinpraesens.org), and were downloaded in November 2015.

43 First mention in 'Types of Organization', *Yearbook of International Organizations 1978* (Brussels: Union of International Associations, 1979).

44 In November 1952, the 1953 edition of the *Répertoire des organisations scientifiques internationales* was being finalized by UNESCO when the UIA secretary launched a campaign of direct and indirect political pressures to persuade UNESCO to terminate that publication and instead provide a subsidy to the Union for the *Yearbook*. See correspondence in 061 A 01 UIA/31, 'Yearbook of International Organizations, Yearbook of International Organizations edited by Union of Intern. Associations, Bureau of general services', Registry and Mail Division, Index of Inactive Correspondence Files, Series 1946–56, Archives de l'UNESCO, Paris.

45 Himself being reluctant to answer further questions, Anthony Judge's trajectory is reconstructed from his publications and his Wikipedia entry. He left the Union in 2007.

46 'The Union of International Associations: A Profile', *World Union – Goodwill* 2, no. 3 (1962): 40–3. *World Union – Goodwill* was published in India by followers of Sri Aurobindo and his 'word union' project.

47 Anthony Judge, 'Sharing a Documentary Pilgrimage. UIA/Saur Relations 1982–2000', July 2001.

48 Anthony Judge, 'Information Culture of the Union of International Associations, a Historical Review', 4 February 2005.

49 The latter resulting from a joint endeavour launched in 1972 with the Mankind 2000/ Humanity 2000 group, see Jenny Andersson, *The Future of the World: Futurists, Futurology, and the Post Cold War World* (Oxford: Oxford University Press, 2018).

50 Presentation by Brill representative for Eastern Europe, Russia, June 2013. Available online: http://slideplayer.com/slide/4665450 (accessed 3 July 2017).

51 'Bibliographie des Annuaires des Organisations Internationales', *Bulletin mensuel* 2, nos. 6–7 (1950): 162.

52 Otler to Wouters, 30 April 1929, folder 56, box 918, PO, Mundaneum.

53 Lloyd to Leak, 17 July 1919, R1004, Registry Files 1919–27, League of Nations Archives, Geneva. In 1926, another League memo clarified that there had only been two copies in England, one in the Foreign Office and one elsewhere.

54 The URL for WorldCat is http://www.worldcat.org. As with other serials, the *Annuaire*'s identification is difficult because of catalogues' confusion or lack of precision regarding the presence of one or both the two editions. Moreover, WorldCat only aggregates a limited numbers of public libraries catalogues, with uneven coverage of and within countries, and has a strong bias for university libraries. These searches were made in April 2016.

55 'Facture au 31 décembre 1913', 218 D3 SD 1-58, HLF, Mundaneum.

56   Not much can be done of the national or regional distribution of holdings because their presence or absence is biased by the multiple filters embedded into WorldCat.

57   'Recettes 1907–1911', 218 D3 SD 1-25, HLF, Mundaneum.

58   'Note', appended to La Fontaine to Scott, 30 April 1911, Series III Division of Intercourse and Education, Subseries B, vol. 178, CEIP, Columbia.

59   'Rapport sur l'Office central des associations internationales présenté à la Carnegie endowment for international peace' (21 October 1912), 6, in Series III, Division of Intercourse and Education, Subseries B, vol. 178, CEIP, Columbia.

60   The back matter is rarely included in the digitized version available from the Union's website, but no insert with information for obtaining the *Annuaire* is present between 1912 and 1914. This would only happen in the first post-war issue of the journal, in 1921.

61   'Rapport sur la situation de l'Union', *La Vie Internationale* 1, no. 2 (1912): 312.

62   'Introduction', *Yearbook of International Organizations, 1951–1952* (Brussels: Union of International Associations, 1952), 11.

63   'Échos de l'UAI centre de service', *NGO Bulletin* 4, nos. 8–9 (1952): 314.

64   Advertisements have been found through the search engines of several platforms for digital versions of scientific journals (see below). Digitalization does not always include non-editorial pages (whence a bias for US journals, for JSTOR carries them and HeinOnline does not).

65   *NGO Bulletin* 3, nos. 6–7 (1951), backmatter.

66   Correspondence of this researcher with UIA, December 2015.

67   Georges Patrick Speeckaert to Shepard Stone, 19 July 1954 and 16 September 1954, PA 05600305 reel 0509 section 4, FFP, RAC.

68   'The development of the UIA's resources coming from its publications', PA 05600305 reel 0509 section 4, FFP, RAC.

69   Judge, 'Report of a Preliminary Investigation', appendix 1: 'Analysis on internal and external factors which may influence the future of the organization', 101.

70   Judge, 'Report of a Preliminary Investigation', appendix 1 and appendix 1 exhibits 30 to 33.

71   The flip side was a financial low every two years, between editions of the *Yearbook*, and a shrinking cash flow during the months pending publication of the new edition.

72   Judge, 'Report', appendix I, exhibit 21. Note that figures are not comprehensive or coherent.

73   One may also wonder why INGOs would have trusted the content of a volume when their own self-reporting was left unchecked.

74   Judge, 'Report' (Appendix 1), 34.

75   Those published by the Library of Congress in 1962 (science organizations) and by the International Council of Voluntary Agencies in 1967 (development organizations) were considered hostile and most damaging.

76   Heinz Adamczyk et al. eds, *Handbuch der internationalen Organisationen* (Berlin: Dietz Verlag, 1967) [The German Union Library Catalogue only includes a 1969 version.]

77   Judge, 'Report' (Appendix 1), 114.

78   Diagnoses, statements and directions in this report seem to have been partly a blueprint for Judge's action during his following four decades of editorial work and supervision for the Union.

79   Anthony Judge 'UIA Survival: Separate Siamese Twins?', 30 January 2005.

80   Note that Gale became the publisher of the *Yearbook* in the early 2000s.

81 Louis-Jacques Lyonette, 'In Memoriam: Adolf Sprudzs', *International Journal of Legal Information* 31, no. 2 (2003): xxxvi–xxxvii.

82 'Foreword', *Yearbook of International Organizations 1958–1959* (Brussels: Union of International Associations, 1958), 9.

83 Explicit mentions of *Annuaire* and *Yearbook* have been searched systematically in Academic Search Complete, SocIndex, PAIS Archive, Sociological Abstracts, Academic on File, JSTOR, Web of Science, Hein on Line, Persée, Cairn (available at the Université Laval library). The search for mentions of the *Annuaire* returned a few dozen hits, and a few hundreds for the *Yearbook*. Major biases derive from the remit of these resources and glitches in digitization. Online search did not return every relevant article, when compared with Chadwick F. Alger 'Research on Research: A Decade of Quantitative and Field Research on International Organizations', *International Organization* 24, no. 3 (1970): 414–50. Secondly, results are overwhelmingly from journals in French and English, and published in the United States. Note that a systematic search of monographs and collections of essays was excluded for lack of digital platforms allowing the full-text exploration of coherent series of books over time.

84 A. W. Allen, 'International Peace through Enlightened Self-Interest', *The Advocate of Peace* 73, no. 2 (1911): 42; Lucia Ames Mead, *Swords and Ploughshares or the Supplanting of the System of War* (New York: Putnam, 1912), 56.

85 Elmer Louis Kayser, 'Books', *World Affairs* 115, no. 3 (1952): 92.

86 *Studies in Transnational Legal Policy* 31 (1999): 1.

87 *Civilisations* 14, no. 4 (1964): 414.

88 *World Affairs* 126, no. 2 (1963): 150.

89 Only twelve footnotes refer to the *Annuaire* as a source of information. The *Annuaire* was acknowledged, though, in the first systematic book-length academic studies of international organizations, such as John C. Faries, 'The Rise of Internationalism' (Ph.D. diss., Columbia University, 1915) and Lyman C. White, *The Structure of Private International Organizations* (Philadelphia, PA: George S. Ferguson, 1933).

90 Henn-Jüri Uibopuu, 'International Legal Personality of Union Republics of U.S.S.R.', *The International and Comparative Law Quarterly* 24, no. 4 (1975): 834.

91 Edward Miles 'Organizations and Integration in International Systems', *International Studies Quarterly* 12, no. 2 (1968): 196.

92 See, for example, John Boli and George M. Thomas, 'World Culture in the World Polity: A Century of International Non-Governmental Organization', *American Sociological Review* 62, no. 2 (1997): 174.

93 This section disappeared in the first editions published by Brill. The mention of cooperation between the UN and the Union resurfaced in the 2014–15 edition, in a more discreet phrasing.

94 The agreement stipulated that the Union would manage UNESCO NGO section's database.

95 ECOSOC, Resolution 288 (X), 27 February 1950. Subsequent ECOSOC resolutions did establish some criteria for awarding consultative status, but they did not define INGOs as such.

96 'What Kind of Organizations Are Included', *Yearbook of International Organizations 1968–1969* (Brussels: Union of International Associations, 1969), 11–12.

97 The table 'Phases and Emphases of International Organization Data Series' allows us to appraise reallocation of organizations among new types ('Before you start' section in the 2014–15 edition of the statistics and visualization volume).

98 Including Boli and Thomas, 'World Culture', 174, whose section about the *Yearbook* and INGOs data was reprinted as chapter in their influential co-edited volume *Constructing World Culture* (Stanford, CA: Stanford University Press, 1999).

99 Jackie Smith, Ron Pagnucco and George A. Lopez, 'Globalizing Human Rights: The Work of Transnational Human Rights NGOs in the 1990s', *Human Rights Quarterly* 20, no. 2 (1998): 379–412; Corinne Lennox and Anna-Maria Biro, 'Introductory Study: Civil Society organisations and the International Protection Regime for Minorities', *International Journal of Minority and Group Rights* 18, no. 2 (2011): 135–60.

100 Evelyn L. Bush, 'Measuring Religion in Global Civil Society', *Social Forces* 85, no. 4 (2007): 1645–65. Patricia Bromley also described the 'well-known weaknesses' of the *Yearbook* but stopped there ('The Rationalization of Educational Development: Scientific Activity among International Nongovernmental Organizations', *Comparative Education Review* 54, no. 4 (2010): 577–601.

101 Bush, 'Measuring', 1657.

102 For a survey of statistical studies of non-state actors and their conclusions, see Elizabeth Bloodgood, 'The *Yearbook of International Organizations* and Quantitative Non-State Actor Research', in *The Ashgate Research Companion to Non-State Actors*, ed. Bob Reinalda (Farnham: Ashgate, 2011), 19–33.

103 Ruth C. Young, 'Structural Approach to Development', *The Journal of Developing Areas* 2, no. 3 (1968): 363–76.

104 Kjell Skjelsbaek, 'The Growth of International Nongovernmental Organization in the Twentieth Century', *International Organization* 25, no. 3 (1971): 420–42.

105 Michael Wallace and J. David Singer, 'Intergovernmental Organization in the Global System, 1815–1964: A Quantitative Description', *International Organization* 24, no. 2 (1970): 239–87.

106 Both researchers used the *Yearbook* to constitute their data base, and cooperated to code data.

107 Jackie Smith and Dawn Wiest, 'The Uneven Geography of Global Civil Society: National and Global Influences on Transnational Association', *Social Forces* 84, no. 2 (2005): 629.

108 Andrew B. Whitford and Karen Wong, 'Political and Social Foundations for Environmental Sustainability', *Political Research Quarterly* 62, no. 1 (2009): 190–204.

109 See, for example, Yong Suk Jang, 'The Worldwide Founding of Ministries of Science and Technology, 1950–1990', *Sociological Perspectives* 43, no. 2 (2000): 247–70.

110 Ruth C. Young, 'Political Autonomy and Economic Development in the Caribbean Islands', *Caribbean Studies* 16, no. 1 (1976): 86–114.

111 See the research by Robert C. Angell, esp. *Peace on the March: Transnational Participation* (New York: Van Nostrand Reinhold, 1969). When discussing Angell's conclusions, other researchers have relied and continue to rely on *Yearbook* data: Michael P. Sullivan 'International Organizations and World Order: A Reappraisal', *The Journal of Conflict Resolution* 22, no. 1 (1978): 105–20; Bruce Russett, John R. O'Neal and David R. Davis, 'The Third Leg of the Kantian Tripod for Peace: International Organizations and Militarized Disputes, 1950–85', *International Organization* 52, no. 3 (1998): 441–67.

112 John W. Meyer, Patricia Bromley and Francisco O. Ramirez, 'Human Rights in Social Science Textbooks: Cross-National Analyses, 1970–2008', *Sociology of Education* 83, no. 2 (2010): 121. The measure was established in John Boli, Thomas A. Loya and Teresa Loftin, 'National Participation in World-Polity Organization', in *Constructing World Culture*, ed. Boli and Thomas, 50–77.

113   The 'shared membership' score is used as a proxy for commitment or influence
        of a country and its citizens in the international system or in international
        social movements. See Robert C. Angell, 'An Analysis of Trends in International
        Organizations', *Peace Research Society International Papers* 3 (1965): 185–95. Note
        that this piece was not available for the sample used in this study.

114   Meyer et al., 'Human Rights', 121.

115   David John Frank, in his single or co-authored pieces 'Science, Nature, and the
        Globalization of the Environment, 1870–1990', *Social Forces* 76, no. 2 (1997): 409–35;
        'The Individualization of Society and the Liberalization of State Policies on Same-
        Sex Sexual Relations, 1984–1995', *Social Forces* 77, no. 3 (1999): 911–43, 'The Global
        Dimensions of Rape-Law Reform: A Cross-National Study of Policy Outcomes',
        American Sociological Review 74, no. 2 (2009): 272–90.

116   Mark J. Schafer, 'International Nongovernmental Organizations and Third World
        Education in 1990: A Cross-National Study', *Sociology of Education* 72, no. 2 (1999):
        69–88; Kiyoteru Tsutsui and Christine Min Wotipka, 'Global Civil Society and the
        International Human Rights Movement: Citizen Participation in Human Rights
        International Nongovernmental Organizations', *Social Forces* 83, no. 2 (2004):
        587–620; Jackie Smith and Dawn Wiest, 'The Uneven Geography of Global Civil
        Society', *Social Forces*, 84, no. 2 (2005): 621–52.

117   Jackie Smith. 'Characteristics of the Modern Transnational Social Movement Sector'
        in Jackie Smith, Charles Chatfield and Ron Pagnucco, eds, *Transnational Social
        Movements and Global Politics: Solidarity beyond the State* (Syracuse, NY: Syracuse
        University Press), 42–58.

118   Howard Ramos, James Ron and Oskar N. T. Thoms, 'Shaping the Northern Media's
        Human Rights Coverage, 1986–2000', *Journal of Peace Research* 44, no. 4 (2007):
        385–406.

119   Jason Beckfield, 'Inequality in the World Polity: The Structure of International
        Organization', *American Sociological Review* 68, no. 3 (2003): 401–24.

120   This was also true for the large databases that used *Yearbook* data and have been
        subsequently used by many researchers. 'Correlates of War', now considerably
        expanded and available at www.correlatesofwar.org, was started by political scientists
        Michael Wallace and J. David Singer in the 1960s. The 'Transnational Social
        Movement Organization Dataset, 1953–2003', made public under the aegis of the
        Inter-university Consortium for Political and Social Research, was created in 2003–5
        by sociologists Jackie Smith and Dawn Wiest.

121   Helmut Anheier, 'Measuring Global Civil Society', in *Global Civil Society 2001*, ed.
        Anheier et al., 221–4; Helmut Anheier and Sally Stares, 'Introducing the Global Civil
        Society Index', in *Global Civil Society 2002*, ed. Anheier et al. (New York: Oxford
        University Press, 2002), 241–54.

122   Wallace and Singer, 'Intergovernmental Organization in the Global System', 245.

123   Jon C. Pevehouse, Timothy Nordstrom, and Kevin Warnke, 'The COW-2
        International Organizations Dataset Version 2.0', *Conflict Management and Peace
        Science* 21, no. 2 (2004): 101–19.

124   See, for example, Charles W. Kegley Jr. and Llewellyn D. Howell, 'The Dimensionality
        of Regional Integration: Construct Validation in the Southeast Asian Context',
        International Organization 29, no. 4 (1975): 997–1020; Harold K. Jacobson, William M.
        Reisinger and Todd Mathers, 'National Entanglements in International Governmental
        Organizations', *The American Political Science Review* 80, no. 1 (1986): 141–59.

125   Boli and Thomas 'World Culture', 174.

126 Smith, 'Characteristics of the Modern Transnational Social Movement'.

127 Questionnaires for editions from the 1950s are featured in '*Yearbook of International Organizations* edited by Union of Intern. Associations', Bureau of General Services, Registry and Mail Division, 'Index of Inactive Correspondence Files', Series 1946–56, 061 A 01 UIA/31, UNESCO Archives, Paris. For an example, see https://www.dropbox.com/s/3pihk0cv176u2rd/questionnaire_1954.pdf (accessed 3 August 2018).

128 Judge, 'Report of a Preliminary Investigation', appendix 1 'Analysis of International and External Factors', 51.

129 Ibid., 53.

130 *Yearbook of International Organizations 1997–1998*, vol. 5 (Munich: K.G. Saur Verlag 1997), 1777.

131 *Yearbook of International Organizations 2014–2015*, vol. 1A (Leiden: Brill, 2015), x.

132 *Yearbook of International Organizations 2014–2015*, vol. 5, 444.

133 Stephanie A. Limoncelli, 'What in the World Are Anti-Trafficking NGOs Doing? Findings from a Global Study', *Journal of Human Trafficking* 2, no. 4 (2016): 316–28.

134 John Boli and David V. Brewington 'Religious Organizations', in *Religion, Globalization and Culture*, ed. Peter Beyer and Lori Gail Beaman (Leiden: Brill, 2007), 206.

135 Boli and Brewington, 'Religious Organizations', I, 207.

136 Elizabeth A. Bloodgood and Hans Peter Schmitz, 'The INGO Research Agenda: A Community Approach to Challenges in Method and Theory', in *Routledge Handbook of International Organization*, ed. Bob Reinalda (Abingdon: Routledge, 2013), 73.

Chapter 10

LOOKING FOR INFORMATION ON INTERNATIONAL SECRETARIATS: DIGGING DEEPER INTO THE *YEARBOOK OF INTERNATIONAL ORGANIZATIONS*

Bob Reinalda

This contribution focuses on international secretariats, organs of intergovernmental organizations (IGOs) and international non-governmental organizations (INGOs) and their executive heads. Craig Murphy has calculated that in 1910 multilateral conferences convened by the secretariats of IGOs began to outnumber the conferences called at the invitation of heads of states and their governments.[1] It was exactly in this period that the UIA began its work for documentation. The chapter digs into the data gathered by the organization, drawing on material in its *Yearbook of International Organizations*, the *Yearbook*'s predecessors and the UIA journal, published with different titles between 1912 and 2005.[2] In doing so, it examines the UIA's knowledge of secretariats of both types of international organizations (IOs), the representation of the world of IOs in UIA publications as well as the UIA's own position in the field.

Although IGOs are created and controlled by states, their role and status have developed beyond that of being their 'agents'. Having an agency of its own may result from the activities and authority of an IGO's secretariat and from the roles that experts and INGO representatives play within the organization. While many articles and books have been written on IGOs, few have actually examined the bureaucracy itself.[3] Secretariats of IGOs are hierarchically organized bodies that take care of continuity of the organization, seek to devote themselves to its objectives and purposes and, given the awareness of path dependency, function as institutional memories of the IGO's undertakings. Secretariats run the headquarters and represent the IGOs both vis-à-vis states and vis-à-vis other international actors. The major constraints to leadership by the IGOs' executive heads are political (the conflicts and alignments between member states), organizational (the quality of the IGO's bureaucracy) and financial (the lack of resources). Opportunities for leadership result from the expertise that IGO secretariats have at their disposal and from the use of the organizations' platform to find support from other international actors and to act as a public voice for the views and values of IGOs.

Ernst Haas was one of the first scholars to apply theories of bureaucracy and organizational growth to explain how IGOs acquire independence from their environment of states. He found that both internally directed management and externally oriented political pursuit were crucial for leading a secretariat.[4] Robert Cox and Harold Jacobson opened the 'black box' of IGO decision-making, tracing the influence of executive heads as well as other segments of the bureaucracy.[5] In line with principal-agent theory and historical institutionalism, Frank Biermann and Bernd Siebenhüner explicitly discern between member states, which are actors within the IGO, and the international bureaucracy or secretariat, which is a semi-autonomous actor within the IGO. They see the secretariat as a 'hierarchically organized group of civil servants who are expected to act following the mandate of the organization and the decisions of the assembly of member states'.[6] Jörn Ege and Michael Bauer similarly argue for an explicit distinction between the political and the administrative, with member-state representatives as the political branch and the bureaucracy as the administrative branch.[7]

The internal management of INGOs deserves much closer attention. As Liesbet Heyse has argued, publications on the internal operations of NGOs are too descriptive and prescriptive in nature. Her approach focuses on the outcomes of decision-making processes by studying governance structures, leadership styles and particular management practices. She also discusses the pressure on NGOs to professionalize, linked to the need for greater efficiency, performance and accountability.[8] Jutta Joachim has noted the institutionalization and formalization effects of NGO engagement in IGOs, linked to the move of NGOs from critical outside agents towards partners in IGO decision-making.[9]

This chapter sheds fresh light on IO secretariats by drawing on UIA data. It initially discusses the evolution of international secretariats, which provided the context for the UIA's documentary work. The subsequent two sections examine the competitive relationship between the UIA and the League of Nations Secretariat as well as surveying the available UIA data on IOs, international meetings and secretariats between 1840 and 1944. The final sections shift to the post-1945 period, in which the *Yearbook* became an important source for quantitative non-state actor research.[10] In this context, it also traces wider UIA engagement with the role of both IGO and INGO secretariats.

Emergence and Growth of International Secretariats since 1815

IGOs were subject to institutional dynamics from the very beginning. The oldest IGO, the Central Commission for the Navigation of the Rhine (1815), was not designed as an independent regulatory institution, but, once established, it adopted a path-dependent logic, gradually gaining competence and independence and developing its own, still functioning bureaucracy. The European Commission of the Danube, set up as a temporary body in 1856, also showed path dependence and turned into a permanent organization, which appointed and paid its own officials.[11]

From the 1860s, a series of multilateral conferences on specific trans-border issues resulted in the establishment of so-called public international unions (PIUs) with permanent secretariats. The PIUs responded to the expansion of modern capitalism and technology, which did not take much notice of national borders, as steamships, the telegraph and intellectual property rights illustrate.[12] At the time, the secretariat of a PIU was referred to as 'central office' or 'bureau'. It acted as an intermediary between governments and carried out specific administrative duties in line with its *règlement* – an agreement that, unlike the constitution, could be adapted to changed circumstances. Initially, secretariat duties were chiefly practical and informational, yet several bureaux were entrusted with more active powers of administration, such as doing research, preparing conferences and even exerting arbitral functions. The initial tendency was to locate the bureaux in small neutral states, notably Switzerland and Belgium.[13] Member states debated the bureau's location and the required qualities of its director, who had to be a person of intellectual and moral standing. If the secretariat was to be based in the country of the last conference, its staff had to be replaced every time, which was soon regarded as unpractical, whereas a fixed location raised questions about surveillance.[14] Some PIUs set up governing boards, while others left the general supervision to the government of the country where the PIU was located. This, however, created the practice of confining major positions to Swiss or Belgian subjects. Another drawback was that this model prevented the bureau from communicating directly with its member governments. Both arguments informed later decisions to depart from this model and re-establish organizational autonomy.

This early period was characterized by a degree of experimentation. The Permanent Commission of the International Institute of Agriculture provided an example of organizational failure, because its members were directly responsible to their governments and the staff was hardly multinational.[15] With the responsibility for the institutions' day-to-day running and the growth of functions, the position of director was upgraded to director-general. Organizations strengthened, because states selected capable leaders with organizational and diplomatic capacities who were aware of the organization's institutional memory. By 1910, the PIUs had acquired roles such as agenda-setting, which had previously been the domain of state representatives.[16] Eighty per cent of the PIUs survived the First World War, largely due to leadership by their executive heads in a situation of disrupted international relations.[17]

Before the war, the growth in private organizations with transnational connections was related to enhanced means of communication and to the emergence of social groups with the time, education and resources to participate in such activities. The system of multilateral conferences had an open character: activists who had established transnational advocacy networks travelled to conferences that had been initiated by governments – and, in turn, governmental representatives attended privately initiated conferences. Non-governmental attendance was appreciated because of the expertise and understanding the private organizations brought to the debates. While debate rather than action was the rule, NGOs developed relations with both governments and international secretariats.

The design of the League of Nations Secretariat in 1919 marked a crucial turn, as it established the new principle of 'international civil servants serving the IGO'. One position in the debate among the founders followed the experience of the inter-Allied war councils of 1917–19 and favoured a secretariat based on a few national officials who would be loyal to and be paid by the major member states. However, this principal-agent model of the war councils was rejected in favour of the establishment of a truly 'international secretariat', whose members had to distance themselves as far as possible from national ties and devote themselves solely to the League's purposes. They needed to be capable individuals with broad vision and flexible minds and would be paid by the organization. This 'international secretariat' became the dominant model for IGOs, with a unitary staff, multinational in composition, headed by a secretary-general (or similar title), responsible to the IGO and functioning independently of national governments.[18] The new model included room for the establishment of relations with internationally active NGOs.

Setting up the League Secretariat was a journey into unexplored territory. Appointments were made by the League, and only after the administrative need had arisen. However, the League's secretary-general Eric Drummond chose carefully, since appointees had to be acceptable to their home governments. Senior positions were earmarked for nationals of leading states and many positions were occupied by persons of the same nationality. Smaller states were thus excluded, and national preferences remained present in this international body. Drummond's successor in 1933, Joseph Avenol, brought the Secretariat closer to French bureaucratic procedures: more top-down, more coordination and less scope for staff initiative. When Frenchman Albert Thomas became director of the International Labour Office in 1919, he transformed the Office into a strong secretariat. Given the support of the workers in the tripartite organizational structure, Thomas secured within the various bodies a position for the director like that of a minister introducing and defending proposals in parliament. His successor in 1932, Harold Butler – a former British civil servant – changed the leadership style, because he believed that the governing body, rather than the director, should be formulating policies.[19] As this example illustrates, IGO secretariats often rested on bureaucratic traditions brought in by the first executive head but were further shaped by mixing with other traditions.

The UIA and the League of Nations Secretariat

As one of the main providers for data on the number of IGOs and INGOs, the UIA's role in capturing the development of international society deserves attention. Two elements seem significant, namely the UIA's vision of IOs and its competition with the League of Nations, which, like the UIA, felt the need to gain an overview of public and private international actors. This section discusses the position of the

UIA, whereas the subsequent one provides available UIA data on IOs, international meetings and secretariats between roughly 1840 and 1944.

From 1907, Henri La Fontaine and Paul Otlet's Central Office of International Institutions sought to enhance cooperation between private international associations and to serve as a documentation centre. In 1910, the Central Office became the secretariat of the newly founded UIA. INGOs were the UIA's grassroots, with 137 INGOs and forty-three governments attending the 1910 UIA world congress and 169 INGOs and twenty-two governments the 1913 congress. In 1914, the UIA combined 230 INGOs, almost half the total number registered at the time (see Table 9.1).

As Pierre-Yves Saunier discusses in this volume, the Central Office cooperated with Austrian peace activist Alfred Fried in publishing two editions of its *Annuaire de la Vie Internationale* (1908–9, 1910–11), covering both intergovernmental ventures and 'private international life'. These publications provided extensive profiles of IOs, featuring legal and practical information about objectives, means and composition of bodies. Moreover, in 1912 the UIA published a *Liste des associations internationales* with addresses. Its journal *La Vie Internationale*, which was launched as a series of individual publications ('fascicules') in 1910 and appeared regularly between 1912 and 1914, featured visions and elaborations of international secretariats by Fried and Denis Myers.[20]

The years 1907–14 proved an ambitious beginning for UIA activities, but the First World War cut this momentum. During the war, Otlet developed a vision of the confederation's secretariat that resembled the war councils' principal-agent model rather than the 'international secretariat' model of the League of Nations.[21] Nonetheless, the UIA lobbied for a League of Nations, considering Brussels as the ideal 'world city' and the UIA as a relevant institution for intellectual cooperation. Otlet and La Fontaine attended the Paris Peace Conference in January 1919 but experienced several disappointments. The League, as it ultimately emerged, bore little resemblance to the organization the two Belgians had envisioned, both in terms of the model for its secretariat and the choice of Geneva as host city.[22]

While the UIA never gained the role and recognition that it had aspired to, it did cooperate with the League in documenting the activities of IOs. With 'the kind assistance' of La Fontaine and Otlet, the League produced a *Liste des unions, associations, institutions, commissions, bureaux internationaux, etc.* in 1919. The Secretariat used this list to send out a questionnaire, thus establishing its own relations with these IOs.[23] In 1921, the League published its own *Handbook of International Organisations*, followed by *Supplements* with changes of addresses and other information.[24] Although a memorandum by Drummond had recognized the UIA's track record in 1921,[25] the League Secretariat's subsequent documentation activities effectively rendered the Union's efforts redundant. The UIA published another issue of *La Vie Internationale* in November 1921, but between 1922 and 1938, the League's *Quarterly Bulletin of Information on the Work of International Organizations* replaced much of the UIA's work in this field.

The League and the UIA cooperated on the *Code des Voeux Internationaux* (1923), covering 1,216 resolutions adopted at 151 international meetings, and the UIA published its *Tableau de l'organisation internationale* (1924). Moreover, Otlet elaborated a detailed classification of both public and private IOs in ten main fields.[26] However, by the second half of the 1920s, the UIA increasingly seemed unable to meet its wider aspiration of playing an active role in organizing other bodies.[27]

Meanwhile, the League continued its own documentation activities. Its *Handbooks* of 1921, 1923 and 1925 contained detailed descriptions of the League Secretariat and the International Labour Office in both French and English, featuring information on bodies, sections and executive heads, followed by descriptions of the League's commissions and technical organizations in French. The League thus circulated essential information about the newly created secretariats. The evolution of the League Secretariat was extensively analysed in Egon Ranshofen-Wertheimer's well-known book *The International Secretariat*, published in anticipation of the creation of the UN Secretariat.[28] Felix Morley, who studied the League Secretariat during the 1930s, regarded its lower grades as a civil service and its upper grades as a political cabinet.[29] The subtitle of Helen Moats's study from this period reads similarly: 'International Civil Service or Diplomatic Conference?'[30] The Secretariat was further discussed by the Royal Institute of International Affairs at Chatham House, London. This work resulted in the informative pamphlet *The International Secretariat of the Future* (1944). Having chaired the Chatham House discussions, Eric Drummond supported the strengthening of the secretary-general's political role and argued that the previous entanglement of the office and major member states had to end: the new secretary-general should preferably come from a small state.[31]

The League's administrative experience was not analysed by the UIA, but played a role in the new way of thinking about cooperation between states that David Mitrany introduced in the field of international relations studies.[32] Rather than starting with the design of federal arrangements, as had happened at the end of both world wars, he preferred 'functional' arrangements that applied specialized technical knowledge to specific transnational issues. Nowadays James Salter, the first director of the League's Financial and Economic Organization, is seen as an influence on Mitrany's functionalism and on international public administration.[33]

Numbers of IOs, International Meetings and Headquarters, 1840–1944

Although La Fontaine and Otlet continued their documentary work on IOs, unlike others, they hardly evaluated the League of Nations' organizational development. The fact that League activities in some ways replaced the work of the UIA may help explain why the *Yearbooks of International Organizations* do not provide numbers of IOs for the years between 1909 and 1951. Moreover, the number of INGOs they list for 1909 seems rather small (176).

Trying to narrow this data gap, I combined information from the *Annuaires*, *Handbooks* as well as later UIA publications. The first result is Table 9.1, which provides the trend between 1905 and 1936. It suggests that the total number of IOs

Table 10.1 Numbers of IOs, based on *Annuaires* and League *Handbooks*
(*Répertoires*), 1905–36

Publication	Total number of IOs	Numbers of IOs registered in the publication	Numbers of IGOs	Numbers of INGOs
Annuaire (Fried), 1905	202		59	143
Annuaire (UIA), 1908–9	380	*217*	*41*	*176*
Annuaire (UIA), 1910–11		*412*	*41*	*371*
Known in November 1912 (*Annuaire UIA*, 1910–11, Préface)	510			
Liste (UIA), 1912	503			
Liste (League), 1919	469		64	405
Handbook (League), 1921		*313*	*25*	*288*
Handbook (League), 1923		*354*	*28*	*326*
Tableau (UIA), 1924	553			
Handbook (League), 1925		*488*	*25*	*463*
Handbook (League), 1936		*633*	*40*	*593*

Source: 'Bibliographie des annuaires des organisations internationales', *UIA Monthly Review* 2, no. 6–7 (1950): 162. Numbers in italics refer to IOs registered in that publication (as counted by the author). Unitalicized numbers refer to numbers given in the source.

grew from 202 in 1905 to 633 in 1936. The table differentiates between IGOs and INGOs, with 371 INGOs listed in the *Annuaire* of 1910–11 – a significantly higher number than the 176 mentioned in the *Yearbooks*. The number of IOs for 1912 (503) is identical with what Francis Lyons later considered to have been the total of such organizations on the eve of the First World War. Having assessed several sources – including a 1957 publication by UIA secretary-general Georges Patrick Speeckaert – he concluded that this sum broke down into 37 IGOs and 466 INGOs (Table 10.1).[34]

The League's *Handbooks* used the widest possible interpretation of the term 'international bureau' (also associations, commissions, congresses and unions) and focused on permanent organizations (or at least holding periodical meetings). Reference to League-related PIUs was minimal (four in 1925, six in 1936), because most PIUs objected to being placed under the League's direction. The League clustered INGOs in fifteen policy fields. Organizations that were deemed primarily 'national' institutions – including the Carnegie Endowment for International Peace and Nobel Foundation – were excluded.[35]

Further numbers on IGOs and INGOs that help to narrow the *Yearbook* data gap between 1909 and 1951 are available in Table 10.2, which provides information on five-year periods, with for instance 68 IGOs and 813 INGOs in the period 1925–9. The table shows the increase of international meetings, IGOs and INGOs between 1850 and 1944. It is based on the 1970–71 *Yearbook*, which used data from both the UIA and from the Correlates of War (COW) project. This combination of the two datasets by the UIA is rare and should receive more attention, given the use and status of COW data in international relations literature.[36] Comparison shows similar trends, but also differences. Variations between the two datasets are linked

Table 10.2 Numbers of international meetings, IGOs and INGOs (five-year periods), 1850–1944

Time Period	Int. meetings during period	IGOs according to UIA	IGOs according to Wallace & Singer (COW)	INGOs
1850–4	10	1	2	6
1855–9	15	3	3	10
1860–4	38	4	3	16
1865–9	57	9	6	25
1870–4	79	12	7	33
1875–9	156	14	9	50
1880–4	150	17	11	61
1885–9	236	19	17	90
1890–4	291	22	21	125
1895–9	363	24	23	163
1900–1914	602	29	30	224
1905–9	749	33	44	355
1910–14	976	37	49	467
1915–19	83	45	53	518
1920–4	1399	56	72	650
1925–9	1828	68	83	813
1930–4	1935	73	87	941
1935–9	1720	79	86	1038
1940–4	-	92	82	1084

Source: Table 5 in *Yearbook of International Organizations, 1970–1971* (Brussels: UIA, 1971), 882. For the UIA, IGOs and INGOs are the 'cumulative total created, excluding dissolutions', while for Wallace and Singer IGOs are 'total in existence'.

to the underlying criteria and the inclusion of some bilateral organizations by the COW project.[37]

Table 10.2 also lists international conferences related to the process of international organization, with numbers growing from twenty-five in the 1850s to 1,059 in the 1910s and 3,655 in the 1930s. Notwithstanding some variations, the *UIA Monthly Review* of 1949 presented roughly similar numbers of international conferences and congresses between 1840 and 1939.[38] In the UIA periodical *International Associations*, Geneviève Devillé indicated the geographical development of international meetings, starting with two international meetings taking place in two European cities in 1858. This number subsequently rose to twenty-three meetings in fifteen European cities (representing eight countries) in 1883; 132 meetings in fifty-three European cities (sixteen countries), four North American cities and three South and Central American cities in 1908; and 325 meetings in seventy European cities (twenty-four countries), nine North American cities, one South American city, three North African cities and one Asian city in 1933.[39]

UIA sources offer little information about IO secretariats prior to the late 1940s. Table 10.3 provides IO headquarters locations by continent in roughly ten-year periods. In 1930, Europe still clearly dominated – indeed, the gap with

Table 10.3 Location of IO headquarters by continent, 1850–1930

Year	Total	Africa	America North	America South/Central	Asia	Europe	Pacific
1850	6					6	
1870	34		2			32	
1880	67	1	7			59	
1890	117	1	11	1		104	
1895	208	1	17	2	2	186	
1906	294	1	18	3	2	270	
1912	437	1	15	3	1	417	
1921	321	1	19	2	2	297	-
1926	397	-	24	3	1	369	-
1930	705	1	29	5	4	669	-

Source: Yearbook of International Organizations, 1970–1971 (Brussels: UIA, 1970), 880.

Table 10.4 Numbers of officers of IGOs and INGOs in 1954, 1956 and 1958

	1954	1956	1958	1958* men	1958* women
IGOs	683	771	851	751	20
(number of IGOs)	(120)	(130)	(147)	(130)	(130)
INGOs	6,209	7,642	9,024	6,873	352
(number of INGOs)	(1,008)	(1,056)	(1,326)	(1,056)	(1,056)

*Source: Schedule 1 in Yearbook of International Organizations, 1962–1963 (Brussels: UIA, 1962), 15; * 'Officers and Staff of International Organizations in 1958', International Associations 10, no. 9 (1958): 652.*

North America had substantially widened over the years. In terms of country-by-country distribution, 183 IOs had their seats in France in the mid-1930s, 140 in Switzerland, seventy-eight in the United Kingdom and seventy-seven in Belgium.[40] Geographical data as presented in Tables 10.3 and 10.4 (covering the period 1951–2011) further reveal the dominance of certain regions and may add to the debate about the recruitment of professional staff. Such information is instructive, given the ongoing debates within the UN system regarding the geographical distribution of staff and the dominance of nationals from Europe and North America.[41]

The UIA and the United Nations Secretariat

During the occupation of Belgium in the Second World War, German forces moved many of the books, journals as well as documentary material that La Fontaine and Otlet had collected to Berlin. Both men passed away (in 1943 and 1944) and the UIA came to a standstill, although it published three issues of a *Bulletin des Associations Internationales* (1943–4). It was not until 1948 that the

UIA resumed its activities. In May 1948, the UIA's Provisional Committee attended the first conference of INGOs having consultative status with the UN Economic and Social Council (ECOSOC). Article 71 of the UN Charter specifies that ECOSOC may make suitable arrangements with NGOs that are concerned with matters within its competence. Adopting the UN's terminology, the Provisional Committee substituted the term 'association with a private character' by 'NGO'. In the present volume, Nico Randeraad and Philip Post have traced the UIA's post-war development, its interaction with the UN system and the decision to rebuild the Union as an information centre.

In March 1948, ECOSOC had called for the compilation of a list of IGOs, aimed at gaining an overview, but also showing awareness of possible duplication and dispersal of efforts. Officials at the UN Secretariat recognized the UIA's potential and, in July 1950 the ECOSOC Committee on NGOs adopted a resolution that noted the UIA's work and its involvement in the new *Yearbook*, which had been relaunched by two Swiss journalists. The ECOSOC Committee did not favour a separate UN publication and suggested that the UN secretary-general offer the UIA 'as much information and cooperation as possible'. ECOSOC's first president, Ramaswami Mudaliar, praised the *Yearbook* as 'excellent' and supported the resolution, which ECOSOC adopted unanimously.[42] In 1953, the ECOSOC Committee expressed its appreciation of the *Yearbook*, also voicing the hope that the UIA's work would become better known and that its continuation would be secured.[43] In November 1955, UN secretary-general Dag Hammarskjöld proposed that if ECOSOC were to undertake a general examination of the structure of IGOs, it should adopt the *Yearbook* as its basic document.[44]

The new *Yearbook* reflected the calls for information on both IGOs and INGOs by UN bodies, with a focus on what were termed 'conventional' IOs (since 1981 referred to as types A to D): federations of membership organizations (the UN) and universal, intercontinental and regionally defined membership organizations. The second group of 'other international bodies' mentions, among others, 'emanations' and 'organizations of special form' and the third group of 'special types' also covers 'dissolved organizations' and 'multilateral treaties'. UIA definitions of IGOs and INGOs closely accord with UN definitions.[45] Anthony Judge's overview article in the *Yearbook* (first published in 1978 and later updated) reviews the complete range of IOs,[46] while Section 1.4 in *Yearbook* 2015–16 outlines the long-term development of editorial policies.[47]

The legal status of INGOs has been a long-standing UIA concern, with a first convention drafted by the Institute of International Law in 1910 and another by the UIA's 1913 congress. The 1910 draft was revised in 1923. The issue was taken up again in 1948, but an ECOSOC Study Committee did not consider proposals based on this earlier work acceptable because INGOs would have been placed under too strict control by ECOSOC. It prepared a preliminary agreement, but saw its work hampered by the unwillingness of INGOs to give serious consideration to the draft and the issues raised by it. A UIA attempt to gain UNESCO acceptance of a draft convention on the facilitation of INGO activities failed in 1959–60. INGOs were more successful in the Council of Europe, which formulated guidelines for granting consultative status to NGOs in 1954 (revised in 1972), and in 1985 adopted the European Convention on the Recognition of the Legal Personality of INGOs, which came into force in 1991.[48]

Information on IO Secretariats in the Yearbook *and the UIA Journal*

The UIA has not been a major player within the UN: its action on the legal status of INGOs remained without success. However, its role in regularly publishing information on both IGOs and INGOs deserves credit. In contrast to patchy pre-1945 numbers, its *Yearbooks* provide a clear picture of IO numbers.[49] As the remainder of this chapter will show, UIA publications also hold significant information on international secretariats, including numbers of headquarters, officers and staff, which are rarely used in IO literature and merits further consideration.

In January 1949, the UIA launched its *UIA Monthly Review*, which was renamed *NGO Bulletin* in 1951, *International Associations* in 1954 and *Transnational Associations* in 1977 (until 2005). This digitally available journal, with articles in both English and French, complements the *Yearbook* significantly. Its editors and authors used UIA data and information in the journal to present overviews of numbers of IOs, officers, staff, budgets and languages,[50] and figures and trends of people attending international conferences.[51] Other articles discussed state participation in IGOs[52] and some early inter-organizational relations.[53] The journal also matters because, over the years, it covered topics that are relevant for secretariats, for instance the training of European civil servants, simultaneous interpretation at international conferences and within IGOs, the observer status within IGOs as well as IOs and public opinion. Several aspects of international congresses were discussed, such as nomenclature, proceedings, new trends, rise and growth of international meetings, designing and printing, use of 'multi-meetings' of INGOs and IGOs in the same place as well as the facilitation of network processes.

Yearbook information on IO secretariats is limited and refers to a permanent secretariat or rotation of secretariats among national members. It also mentions 'primary' points of contact (headquarters addresses) and 'secondary' contacts, such as the office of the president, regional or continental offices, journal editor and (for INGOs) the representative at the UN. Addresses have been published since the beginning, statistics since 1966. With regard to numbers of IO headquarters (see Table 10.4), UIA data shows that Europe has remained dominant, despite its share falling from 82 to 58.9 per cent between 1951 and 2011.[54] North America's share grew to 12.8 per cent in 2011, Asia's to 11.3, South America's to 7.7 and Africa's to 6.2. Figure 10.1 distinguishes between IGO and INGO headquarters in 2011.

In 1958, the UIA provided numbers regarding IO officers and staff for the first time. Table 10.4 depicts the number of officers between 1954 and 1958, based on the *Yearbook* and journal. It also shows gender representation in a smaller number of IOs in 1958. Other UIA publications provide insights into the numbers of paid and voluntary staff. In 1958, the UN and specialized agencies employed 10,972 staff members (plus in 1955 2,200 technical assistance experts), the European Community

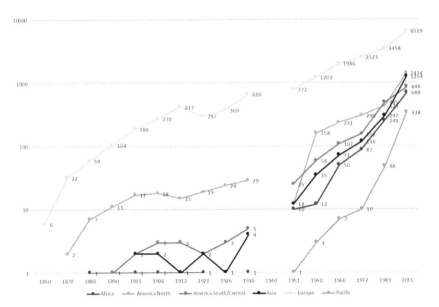

Figure 10.1 Location of IO headquarters by continent, 1951–2011. *Source:* Table 5 in *Yearbook of International Organizations, 1970–1971* (Brussels: UIA, 1970), 880; *Yearbook of International Organizations 1983–1984*, vol. 7 (Munich: K.G. Saur, 1983); Figure 3.10 in *Yearbook of International Organizations, 2011–2012*, vol. 5 (Leiden: Brill, 2011), 80–105. The total number of recorded international organizations is greater than the sum of those listed here because of unknown addresses.

1,012 and other IGOs 5,884. By 1962, the total of paid IGO staff had risen from 17,828 to 23,881.[55] Whereas voluntary work at IGOs was negligible, it provided 23 per cent of INGO staff. Yet INGOs too had seen a growth in the number of employees – from 5,998 in 1958 to 7,742 by 1962. The average number of staff of IGOs was 137, of INGOs roughly seven, of whom five were paid.[56] Since staff development has long been ignored in IO research, these numbers are a useful starting point for further research into the internal affairs of IOs. The UIA also published practical overviews of officers and departments of IGO secretariats in charge of official relations with INGOs in its journal.[57] When the UIA published its International Associations Statutes Series in 1988, it included UN staff rules and regulations.[58]

Section 8 of recent *Yearbooks* is called 'Who represents international organizations?', with the 2011–12 *Yearbook* providing data (collected in 2009) on birth dates, gender and citizenship of IO officers, languages spoken by them and areas of interest.[59] Such material can also provide valuable information for research into gender distribution within IO secretariats, which is receiving growing scholarly attention.[60] Of the 24,116 persons who represent organizations in the *Yearbook's* Figure 8.8, 21.9 per cent are female, 53.2 per cent male and 25 per cent unknown. Table 10.5 provides information on the citizenship of male and female IO officers per continent in 2009.

Table 10.5 Citizenship of male and female IO officers per continent in 2009

	Africa	Americas	Asia	Australasia/ Oceania	Europe
Men (number of IOs)	193 (352)	483 (822)	253 (450)	78 (139)	1564 (2,587)
Women (number of IOs)	31 (69)	106 (185)	41 (75)	22 (34)	274 (438)

Source: Figure 8.3 in *Yearbook of International Organizations, 2011–2012* (Leiden: Brill, 2011), 272–5. Data collected in 2009, based on 3,080 persons from 157 countries whose citizenship or nationality is known; numbers are also provided per country.

In 1955, Eyvind Tew was the first author to raise the question of 'Who is who in international organizations?' within the UIA journal, referring to the 6,892 office holders mentioned in the most recent *Yearbook*.[61] In both 1963 and 1964, the UIA issued a *Who's Who in International Organizations*, listing members of governing bodies, regional representatives and chairpersons. The *Yearbook*'s eleventh edition, published in 1966, had the term 'officers' in its subtitle: 'the encyclopaedic dictionary of international organizations, their officers, their abbreviations'. In 1992, the first edition of a three-volume *Who's Who in International Organizations: A Biographical Encyclopaedia of More than 12,000 Leading Personalities* was published, with new editions in 1996 (13,000 personalities), 2000 (14,000), 2003 (19,000) and 2006 (21,000). Since 2007, the *Who's Who in International Organizations* appears as an additional Volume 6 to the *Yearbook*, covering 16,000 personalities in 2015–16.

The *Who's Who* series aims to provide 'information on the principal personalities involved in the development, operation and coordination of international organizations, associations, institutes, programmes and other bodies described in the Yearbook', 'an easy means of checking biographical details of significant individuals on the multinational and global levels' and 'a resource for the development of inter-organizational relationships' as well as to improve access to information on IOs. The *Yearbook*'s online introduction argues that this *Who's Who* is unique in that it 'concentrates on the human role in the international organizational network' and answers to questions such as 'who are the people making and carrying out decisions in international organizations?', 'what other responsibilities do they have?', 'what is their background?' and 'what do they have in common?'.[62] Having gone through the *Who's Who* as an editor of a biographical dictionary myself, I noticed that information provided per person is not very extensive, not equally structured like in many other 'Who's Whos' and differs widely in terms of the information provided per individual.[63] These limitations exist because the UIA does not use structured questionnaires, but relies on information provided by IOs.

UIA Information on INGO Secretariats

The UIA uses the abbreviation 'NGO' rather than 'INGO', but its focus has been on internationally active NGOs. Over the decades, articles in its journal explored a variety of aspects relating to their work, examining questions of definitions, classification and taxonomy as well as covering the work of individual organizations. Early on, the periodical featured pieces on NGOs.[64] The discussion of INGOs and their role within the international system remained a recurring topic in the UIA's journal. For instance, in 1972, it presented extensive material on a Milan-based UIA seminar that had explored the 'philosophy of non-governmental organization.'[65] One of the seminar's contributors, the pioneering peace studies scholar Johan Galtung, authored a range of articles for the UIA, for instance analysing the role of INGOs in 'world decision-making' in a 1986 piece.[66] By the 1990s, discussions on the role of INGOs in the context of globalization began to figure prominently in the periodical's pages.[67] Trade union activist Peter Waterman contributed several pieces in which he considered the role of social movements in the promotion of global solidarity.[68]

In light of its wider interest in INGOs, it is hardly surprising that the UIA's periodicals also examined the staff and structure of such organizations.[69] This included descriptions of the responsibilities of INGO secretaries-general as well as an inventory on the 'duties of officers'.[70] Other articles focused on careers in INGOs and techniques to improve training as well as efficiency and effectiveness.[71] Lawrence Young assumed that the behaviour and characteristics of INGO secretaries-general both reflected and shaped the characteristics of the organization itself. Using sixteen indicators, he discerned six types of secretaries-general – 'patriarchs', 'outsiders', 'followers', 'national leaders', 'careerists' and 'internationalists'. 'Patriarchs' were found to be least peace-oriented in the goals they identified for their organizations, while 'followers' and 'national leaders' were more peace-oriented. Great differences between the six types were found in the length of membership in the INGO, previous organizational histories, salary figures and age for secretary-general.[72]

In 1974 Kjell Skjelsbaek – who had previously written about the growth of INGOs – published the results of an INGO survey in the UIA's journals.[73] He was somewhat surprised that staff contacts with members were so infrequent and that there was less contact with IGOs than with other INGOs and even less with national governments. Fifty per cent of INGOs had no contacts with IGOs. Skjeelsbaek regarded this number as plausible, as roughly one-third of all INGOs had consultative status with one or more IGOs and as some interaction was likely to take place outside that status. Almost 70 per cent had never had any contact with national governments. Quite a few secretaries-general were personal friends and did business with each other. The majority of them were middle-aged, with two-thirds knowing at least three languages. Most of the respondents were 'organizational' persons with extensive administrative experience, often in addition to specific professional competence. They had experience in other organizations and had held other positions in their INGO before becoming secretary-general. Ninety-two per cent were men. In spite of frequent complaints about IGOs from INGO officers, quite a few of them were prepared to advise friends to work in IGOs.

The UIA often encountered the practical question of how to run an INGO secretariat. In the 1970s, one contribution to its journal argued that a secretariat should have the qualities of both a manager and an ambassador and be assisted by a qualified assistant, a secretary-typist, a sales assistant and a bookkeeper, all paid in the currency of the secretary's host country. The secretariat should arrange its files by subject, have a reference library and conduct sound financial management for current operations and initiating new projects.[74] Faced with the growth in new NGOs and the expansion of existing ones during the early 1990s, Bonnie Koenig commented on their preference for decentralized structures in order to increase involvement of members or constituent groups, regardless of their geographical location. She argued that INGO leaders had to believe in the organization's internationalism and translate this belief into their everyday actions and decisions. Given the special challenge of working with people and organizations from different cultures, ethnicities, nationalities and religions, helpful qualities included an international outlook and knowledge, multicultural sensitivity, the 'civil service' philosophy to remain neutral as well as communication, facilitation and language skills. While expanding, existing NGOs needed to look at ways to share decision-making abilities; meanwhile, newly created INGOs had to seek diverse representation on their committees, boards and staff.[75]

From the start, the UIA journal provided legal and comparative information on the consultative status of INGOs with ECOSOC and the UN's specialized agencies. It reported on meetings of the ECOSOC Committee on NGOs and published related texts and addresses by UN secretaries-general.[76] In 1955, a special issue on the UN's tenth anniversary focused on the background of Article 71 and the first ten years of practice.[77] The 1962–1963 *Yearbook* provided some numbers of consultative relations (see Table 10.6).

The UIA journal frequently featured articles on relations between NGOs and the UN. It traced the development of the consultative status, for instance the passing of a new ECOSOC resolution in 1968, as well as covering the general review of arrangements for UN consultations with INGOs in 1995 and the Panel of Eminent Persons on UN–Civil Society Relations.[78]

Table 10.6 Consultative relations of INGOs with the UN and its specialized agencies in 1962

UN ECOSOC A	UN ECOSOC B	UN ECOSOC Register	ILO	FAO	UNESCO A	UNESCO B/C
10	124	198	6 + 52	36 + 17	22	112 + 66

WHO	ICAO	ITU	WMO	IMCO	IAEA	UNICEF
57	27	28	11	10	19	70

Source: Yearbook of International Organizations, 1962–3 (UIA: Brussels, 1962), 95–105; details on categories and additional numbers with ILO, FAO and UNESCO B/C: 104–5.

Conclusion

The *Yearbook of International Organizations* is best known among scholars for its quantitative data on IOs. However, it may be questioned whether researchers have always paid full attention to potential inconsistencies in its data, or have been aware of the potential to harvest additional information from sources such as the UIA's journal.

In seeking specific information – in this case on international secretariats of IOs – this chapter has stressed the value of combining material from the *Yearbook* and the UIA's periodical. The journal complements the *Yearbook* because its authors discussed a variety of topics relating to the internal life of IGOs and INGOs, also using UIA data in specific ways. Some articles considered quantitative data, for instance on international conferences, headquarters, staff and gender, or presented more precise calculations. On one occasion, it did so in comparison with data from the Correlates of War project, whose database on IGOs has become a competitor to the *Yearbook*. Such articles as well as some counting of my own have helped to make up for the *Yearbook*'s missing numbers of IOs between 1909 and 1951 and to correct its low 1909 number of INGOs.

Information on the nature, development and mechanisms of international secretariats is crucial to understanding how IOs work. UIA information on the structure of international secretariats as such is limited, particularly before the late 1940s, but numbers about international conferences and the geographical distribution of IO headquarters reveal trends and show inequalities between continents. By the late 1950s, a few *Yearbooks* provided numbers of IO officers and staff, as well as data about birth dates, gender and citizenship. The availability of such information might encourage the examination of staff development within IGOs and INGOs, which remain under-researched fields. Moreover, as has been shown, articles in the UIA journal can add to the understanding of internal developments within secretariats. Unfortunately, the *Yearbook*'s 'Who's Who' publication – relevant for material on executive heads and other senior officers – shows serious weaknesses, because it relies on incomplete information provided by the IOs and not on structured questionnaires as used by other 'Who's Whos'.

In line with the UIA's background as an NGO, information on INGO secretariats is more extensive than on IGO secretariats. Articles in the UIA journal cover a variety of topics on both the functioning of NGOs in international society and the internal mechanisms of INGOs, such as the qualities of secretaries-general and the running of a secretariat. The journal is also informative about consultative relations that INGOs have developed with ECOSOC and UN specialized agencies. Digging deeper into the UIA's *Yearbook* and journal can thus provide manifold insights.

Notes

I am grateful to Marti Huetink of Brill Publishers and the Brussels UIA staff for giving me access to older *Yearbooks*, as several libraries only keep the latest edition(s).

1 Craig Murphy, *International Organization and Industrial Change: Global Governance since 1850* (Cambridge: Polity, 1994), 111–12.

2 Digital copies are freely available on the UIA's website: http://www.uia.org/journals (accessed 9 October 2017).

3 Michael Davies, *The Administration of International Organizations: Top Down and Bottom Up* (Aldershot: Ashgate, 2002).

4 Ernst Haas, *Beyond the Nation-State: Functionalism and International Organization* (Stanford, CA: Stanford University Press, 1964), 100–3.

5 Robert Cox and Harold Jacobson, eds, *The Anatomy of Influence: Decision Making in International Organization* (New Haven, CT: Yale University Press, 1973), 397–400.

6 Frank Biermann and Bernd Siebenhüner, eds, *Managers of Global Change: The Influence of International Environmental Bureaucracies* (Cambridge, MA: MIT Press, 2009), 7.

7 Jörn Ege and Michael Bauer, 'International Bureaucracies from a Public Administration and International Relations Perspective', in *Routledge Handbook of International Organization*, ed. Bob Reinalda (London: Routledge, 2013), 143–5.

8 Liesbet Heyse, 'From Agenda Setting to Decision Making: Opening the Black Box of Non-Governmental Organizations', in *The Ashgate Research Companion to Non-State Actors*, ed. Bob Reinalda (Farnham: Ashgate, 2011), 277–90.

9 Jutta Joachim, 'Non-Governmental Organizations and Decision Making in the United Nations', in *Ashgate Research Companion*, ed. Reinalda, 301.

10 Elizabeth Bloodgood, 'The *Yearbook of International Organizations* and Quantitative Non-State Actor Research', in *Ashgate Research Companion*, ed. Reinalda, 19–33.

11 Francis S. L. Lyons, *Internationalism in Europe 1815–1914* (Leiden: Sijthoff, 1963), 62.

12 Madeleine Herren, *Internationale Organisationen seit 1865: Eine Globalgeschichte der internationale Ordnung* (Darmstadt: WBG, 2009).

13 Paul Reinsch, *Public International Unions: Their Work and Organization* (Boston: Ginn, 1911), 155–6; Daniel Laqua, *The Age of Internationalism and Belgium, 1880–1930* (Manchester: Manchester University Press, 2013).

14 Gustave Moynier, *Les Bureaux internationaux des unions universelles* (Geneva: Cherbuliez and Fischbacher, 1892), 21–3.

15 Asher Hobson, *The International Institute of Agriculture: An Historical and Critical Analysis of Its Organization, Activities and Policies of Administration* (Berkeley, CA: University of California Press, 1931), 77–9; Bob Reinalda, *Routledge History of International Organizations: From 1815 to the Present Day* (London: Routledge, 2009), 129.

16 Murphy, *International Organization*, 112.

17 Reinalda, *Routledge History*, 179.

18 Ibid., 190–2.

19 See entries in *IO BIO: Biographical Dictionary of Secretaries-General of International Organizations*, ed. Bob Reinalda, Kent Kille and Jaci Eisenberg. Available online: https://www.rul.nl/fm/iobio (accessed 9 October 2017).

20 Alfred Hermann Fried, 'Le Bureau paneuropéen', *La Vie Internationale*, fascicule 38 (1910): 1–9; Dennis Myers, 'La Concentration des organismes internationaux publics', *La Vie internationale* 10 (1913): 97–122.

21 Paul Otlet, *La Fin de la guerre* (Brussels: Oscar Lamberty, 1914), 20 Art. IXa, b; idem, *Constitution mondiale de la Société des nations* (Geneva: Atar and Crès, 1917), 170–1; W. Boyd Rayward, *The Universe of Information: The Work of Paul Otlet for*

Documentation and International Organization (Moscow: VINITI, 1975), 203–5. For Otlet's focus on nations: Laqua, *Age of Internationalism*, 26–30.

22 Alex Wright, *Cataloging the World: Paul Otlet and the Birth of the Information Age* (Oxford: Oxford University Press, 2014), 164.

23 *Répertoire des organisations internationales* (Geneva: Société des Nations, 1921), 9–10.

24 In French in 1921, 1923, 1925 and 1936; in English in 1922, 1924, 1929 and 1937.

25 Council Document A43(B)1421, 5 September 1921; Georges Patrick Speeckaert, 'The Union of International Associations: Its Origines, Aims and First Activities (1907– 1944)', *Transnational Associations* 31, no. 3 (1979): 81.

26 Figure 5.2 in *Yearbook of International Organisations*, 2015–16, vol. 5 (Leiden: Brill, 2015), 174.

27 See the comments in Lyman C. White, *The Structure of Private International Organizations* (Philadelphia, PA: Ferguson, 1933), 238–9.

28 Egon Ranshofen-Wertheimer, *The International Secretariat: A Great Experiment in International Administration* (Washington, DC: Carnegie Endowment, 1945).

29 Felix Morley, *The Society of Nations: Its Organization and Constitutional Development* (Washington, DC: Brookings Institution, 1933), ch. VIII and IX.

30 Helen Moats, 'The Secretariat of the League of Nations: International Civil Service or Diplomatic Conference?' (PhD diss., University of Chicago, 1936).

31 Karen Gram-Skjoldager, 'Drummond, Eric James', in *IO BIO*. Available online: https://www.ru.nl/fm/iobio (accessed 9 October 2017). See also Karen Gram-Skjoldager and Haakon O. Ikonomou, 'The Construction of the League of Nations Secretariat: Formative Practices of Autonomy and Legitimacy in International Organizations', *The International History Review*, published on 21 December 2017. Advance access online via https://doi.org/10.1080/07075332.2017.1409792 (accessed 19 September 2018). Gram-Skjoldager is currently leading a project on 'The Invention of International Bureaucracy: The League of Nations and the Creation of International Public Administration *c.* 1920–1960', funded by the Danish Research Council.

32 David Mitrany, 'The Functional Approach to World Organization', *International Affairs* 24, no. 3 (1948): 350–63.

33 James Arthur Salter, *Allied Shipping Control: An Experiment in International Administration* (Oxford: Clarendon Press, 1921); Leonie Holthaus and Jens Steffek, 'Experiments in International Administration: The Forgotten Functionalism of James Arthur Salter', *Review of International Studies* 42, no. 1 (2015): 114–35. On the way in which the experiences with the League Secretariat affected debates about the future shape of international bureaucracy, see Benjamin Auberer, 'Digesting the League of Nations: Planning the International Secretariat of the Future, 1941–1944', *New Global Studies* 10, no. 3 (2016): 393–426.

34 Lyons, *Internationalism*, 13–14; Georges Patrick Speeckaert, *Les 1,978 organisations internationales fondées depuis le congrès de Vienne* (Brussels: UIA, 1957).

35 *Répertoire des organisations*, 1921, 9–10.

36 Jon Pevehouse, Timothy Nordstrom and Kevin Warnke, 'The Correlates of War 2 International Governmental Organizations Data Version 2.0', *Conflict Management and Peace Science* 21, no. 2 (2004): 101–19; Jonas Tallberg, Thomas Sommerer, Theresa Squatrito and Christer Jönsson, *The Opening Up of International Organizations: Transnational Access in Global Governance* (Cambridge: Cambridge University Press, 2013), 9.

37 Michael Wallace and J. David Singer, 'Intergovernmental Organization in the Global System, 1815–1964: A Quantitative Description', *International Organization* 24, no. 2 (1970): 272; Table 14 in *Yearbook of International Organizations, 1970–1971* (Brussels: UIA, 1970): 885.

38 'A Hundred Years of International Meetings', *UIA Monthly Review* 1, no. 1 (1949): 6, where numbers are also given per year.

39 Geneviève Devillé, 'The Rise and Growth of International Meetings', *International Associations* 13, no. 5 (1961): 342.

40 'Handbook of International Organizations', *Nature* 142, no. 3594 (1938): 508.

41 James O. C. Jonah, 'Secretariat: Independence and Reform', in *The Oxford Handbook on the United Nations*, ed. Thomas G. Weiss and Sam Daws (Oxford: Oxford University Press, 2007), 166.

42 'Resolution adopted by the Economic and Social Council concerning the Handbook of Inter-National Organizations', *UIA Monthly Review* 2, nos. 8–9 (1950): 183.

43 UN Document E/2489.

44 UN Document E/2088.

45 Bloodgood, 'The *Yearbook*', 22.

46 Anthony Judge, 'International Organizations: An Overview', *Yearbook of International Organizations 1985–6*, vol. 6 (Munich: K.G. Saur, 1985), 1591–1606.

47 *Yearbook of International Organizations, 2015–16*, vol. 1 (Leiden: Brill, 2015), 15–21.

48 Documents available online: http://www.uia.org/archive/statutes-series/app3 and http://www.uia.org/archive/statutes-series/app4 (accessed 9 October 2018).

49 'Historical Overview of Numbers of International Organizations by Type 1909–2015' in *Yearbook of International Organizations, 2015–2016*, vol. 5 (Leiden: Brill, 2015), 33–5.COW data: 237 IGOs in 1964 (*Yearbook*: 179) and 496 in 2010 (*Yearbook*: 241). The COW data is available online: http://www.correlatesofwar.org/data-sets/IGOs (accessed 21 December 2017).

50 Georges Patrick Speeckaert, 'The Evolution of International Structure', *International Associations* 10, no. 9 (1958): 612–19; Eyvind Tew, 'The Organizational World', *International Associations* 12, no. 12 (1960): 732–7.

51 Geneviève Devillé, 'Congress Phenomena', *International Associations* 9, no. 6 (1957): 345–51.

52 Geneviève Devillé, 'La Participation des États aux Organisations Internationales', *International Associations* 9, no. 10 (1957), 707–12; 'Participation of Sovereign States in the United Nations and the Specialized Agencies', *International Associations* 13, no. 8 (1961): 534–8; Eyvind Tew, 'Représentation nationale dans les organisations internationales', *International Associations* 15, no. 11 (1963), 688–93; 'National Participation in International Organizations', *International Associations* 20, no. 6 (1968): 394–404.

53 Lawrence Whetten, 'Formal versus Informal Relationships among Inter-Governmental Organizations', *International Associations* 18, no. 2 (1966): 74–82, idem 'Administrative Relationship among International Organizations' 19, no. 7 (1967): 466–8; David Horton Smith with Anthony Judge, 'Inter-Organizational Networking', *Transnational Associations* 30, no. 10 (1978): 429–34.

54 My calculations, based on Figure 10.1.

55 Schedule 1 in *Yearbook of International Organizations, 1962–1963* (Brussels: UIA, 1962), 16.

56 'An Insoluble Puzzle?', *International Associations* 10, no. 9 (1958): 651–2.

57 For example 'Intergovernmental Officers and Departments in Charge of Official Relations with International Non-Governmental Organizations', *International Associations* 16, no. 1 (1964): 31–2; 'Directory of Departments and Offices of the UN Secretariat, UN Programmes, Specialized Agencies and Other Intergovernmental Organizations Dealing with Non-Governmental Organizations', *Transnational Associations* 39, no. 4 (1987): 229–34; 'Directory of Departments and Offices of the United Nation Secretariat, United Nations Programmes, Specialized Agencies and Other Intergovernmental Organizations Dealing with Non-Governmental Organizations', *Transnational Associations* 42, no. 5 (1990): 292–302.

58 Appendix 1 of the *International Associations Statutes Series* (1988). Available online: http://www.uia.org/archive/legal-status-5-7 (accessed 9 October 2017).

59 Section 8, 'Who Represents International Organizations?' in *Yearbook of International Organizations 2011–2012*, vol. 5 (Leiden: Brill, 2011), 267–99.

60 Kirsten Haack, 'Breaking Barriers? Women's Representation and Leadership at the United Nations', *Global Governance* 20, no. 1 (2014): 37–54.

61 Eyvind Tew, 'Who's Who in International Organizations', *International Associations* 7, no. 2 (1955): 87–91.

62 'Introduction to *Who's Who*'. Available online: http://ybio.brillonline.com/ybguide/bio-intro (accessed 30 March 2018).

63 Looking for specific officers should include searching section C in the bibliographic volume 4 (added to the *Yearbook* in 1996) on 'Publications Concerning Transnational Nongovernmental and Intergovernmental Organizations', with section G2 covering 'INGO/IGO Case Studies of Personalities'; also G1 ('INGO/IGO Case Studies on Organizations') and K ('Intergovernmental Organizations').

64 Lyman White, '"Peace by Pieces": The Role of Non-Governmental Organizations', *UIA Monthly Review* 1, no. 7 (1949): 103–7; idem, 'Non-Governmental Organizations and Democracy', *NGO Bulletin* 5, no. 11 (November 1953): 437–48; David Mitrany, 'An Advance in Democratic Representation', *International Associations* 6, no. 6 (1954): 136–8.

65 Geneviève Devillé, 'Milan 1972: la philosophie de l'organisation non-gouvernementale', followed by a series of speeches, *International Associations* 25, no. 3 (1972): 147–62.

66 Johan Galtung, 'International Organizations and World Decision-Making', *Transnational Associations* 38, no. 4 (1986): 220–4.

67 Jan Aart Scholte, 'Globalisation and Social Change (Part I)', *Transnational Associations* 50, no. 1 (1998): 2–11; idem, 'Globalisation and Social Change (Part II)', *Transnational Associations* 50, no. 2 (1998): 62–79.

68 Peter Waterman, 'Globalisation, Civil Society, Solidarity', *Transnational Associations* 46, no. 2 (1994): 66–85.

69 Geneviève Bockstael, 'La Structure des Organisations Internationales Non Gouvernementales', *International Associations* 10, nos. 4 and 5 (1958): 251–4 and 308–12; Veenou Lall, 'Non-Governmental Organizations: Some Data on Their Structure', *International Associations* 16, no. 12 (1964): 742–5. Georges Patrick Speeckaert, 'On the Structure and Functioning of International Non-Governmental Organizations', *International Associations* 18, no. 3 (1966): 140–50.

70 'Duties of Officers', *International Associations* 17, no. 12 (1965): 718–22.

71 See, for example, 'A Simple Decision Game as Training Aid for NGO Officers', *International Associations* 19, no. 10 (1967): 759–72.

72 Lawrence Young, 'Secretaries-General in International Non Governmental Organizations (INGOs)', *International Associations* 23, no. 7 (1971): 396–403.

73 Kjell Skjelsbaek, 'A Survey of International Nongovernmental Organizations', *International Associations* 26, nos. 5 and 6–7 (1974): 267–70 and 352–4. For an example of Skjelsbaek's earlier work, see 'The Growth of International Non-Governmental Organization in the Twentieth Century', *International Organization* 25, no. 3 (1971): 420–42.

74 W. van der Brugghen, 'The Management of an NGO Secretariat', *Transnational Associations* 29, no. 5 (1977): 204–6.

75 Bonnie Koenig, 'The Management of International Non-Governmental Organizations in the 1990s', *Transnational Associations* 48, no. 2 (1996): 66–72.

76 See, for example, U Thant, 'Message of the UN Secretary General to the Non Governmental Organizations', *International Associations* 17, no. 2 (1965): 68; 'Keynote Address by Secretary-General Boutros-Ghali to the 47th DPI/NGO Conference', *Transnational Associations* 47, no. 6 (1995): 345–9.

77 Themed issue 'Tenth Anniversary of the United Nations', *International Associations* 7, no. 9 (1955).

78 Themed issue 'Review of the Consultative Status of Non-Governmental Organizations at United Nations', *International Associations* 20, no. 9 (1968); Marcel Merle, 'A Legal Tangle: The "Status" of Non-Governmental International Organizations between International Law and National Laws', *Transnational Associations* 47, no. 6 (1995): 324–30; 'The Cardoso Report. We the Peoples: Civil Society, the United Nations and Global Governance', *Transnational Associations* 56, no. 3 (2004): 209–13.

Chapter 11

MAPPING INTERNATIONALISM: CONGRESSES AND ORGANIZATIONS IN THE NINETEENTH AND TWENTIETH CENTURIES

Martin Grandjean and Marco H. D. van Leeuwen

The Union of International Associations' documentation on international non-governmental organizations (INGOs) is a treasure trove for historians and social scientists alike. INGOs are part and parcel of the modern world. They both reflect and influence social, political, cultural and economic conditions around the globe. They occupy a space of human activity in between, but connected to, the market and the state, and this space seems to be growing.[1] The present chapter seeks to show how a historical investigation into this space might benefit from the use of UIA data.

As other contributions to this volume have noted, the UIA aims to register the key activities of all INGOs that exist or have ever existed. As anyone familiar with historical databases would immediately admit, a database with such a large geographical (the globe) and temporal span (in principle that of human history, though in practice mostly the past two centuries) cannot, and never will be, complete in its coverage. This is also acknowledged by the UIA and is partly caused by the fact that most of the data is provided by the organizations themselves.[2] For the present purpose – namely the visualization of various long-term developments – we will, however, assume that it can nonetheless offer a representative picture. For practical reasons, we focus on the period between 1800 and 1970, concentrating on two UIA datasets: the annual congress calendar and the *Yearbook* series, featuring all organizations that meet the UIA's definition of an INGO.

Mapping International Congresses

The UIA's material is a testimony to the internationalization of science and technology over more than a century. But it is, first and foremost, a means for understanding the internationalist movement itself and, in particular, its Brussels epicentre. The establishment of an institution responsible for federating international associations, congress bureaus and other technical organizations is in itself of significance, especially if it collects information on its own activities. UIA data can help to shed light on specific kinds of international congresses, but also support enquiries into the broader phenomenon of 'the international congress'.[3] Such material can complement existing studies that mostly focus on the nineteenth and early twentieth centuries, owing to the early availability of data for this period.[4]

Before conducting a global analysis of the data on international congresses, we need to consider the UIA's role when it started gathering information in the early twentieth century. Without challenging the intrinsic value of cataloguing projects for congresses, international organizations or centralized summaries of their decisions and publications, it appears that these initiatives were based on two pragmatic strategies that sought to place the UIA at the centre of the 'network' of internationalism. First of all, the UIA did not as such create links within a well-defined subject community like other organizations that bring together experts in a specific field. However, by providing a central service, it could boast of participating fully in internationalist work. In the logic of communication, the one that offers visibility to all the others is soon considered an important player, since, if its publications are echoed sufficiently, it is through them that the public become aware of the activity of these organizations. By becoming a servant of this community, the UIA sought to establish itself as an unavoidable factor.

To this internal perspective, which sought to ensure the UIA's credibility among international bureaux – some of which had already existed for several decades and did not necessarily have any reason to rely on such a 'union' – we can add a second, external perspective related to the relationship between the UIA and society. Assessing the visible manifestation of internationalism was also a way to prove to the world that this internationalism existed. Accordingly, UIA lobbying activities sought to convince decision makers and the wider public that internationalism was not a temporary phenomenon but rather a long-term trend that was progressing rapidly. And what better way than statistics on congresses and organizations to objectify this reality?

The UIA and its founders were, of course, not the only ones to make this observation. In the early twentieth century, several individuals sought to describe internationalism and provide figures to demonstrate its extent. Pierre-Yves Saunier's chapter in this volume has noted Alfred Fried's work, which subsequently resulted in a collaborative venture with the UIA. Other examples included the legal scholar – and later Governor of Connecticut – Simeon Eben Baldwin, who in 1907 discussed international congresses 'as forces working towards the solidarity of the world'.[5] Moreover, John Culbert Farie devoted his 1913 doctoral thesis to documenting *The Rise of Internationalism*. The preface to its published version in 1915 inevitably referenced the outbreak of the First World War, while noting that his work sought to provide 'evidence of the extent of the growth of internationalism and the magnitude of a crime which retards its growth'.[6] His own listing of international congresses had slightly fewer elements than the UIA's, but he adopted a similar quantitative approach. He found that 'there are several reasons for thinking that ... private congresses afford a truer index of the real growth of internationalism than official conferences',[7] because they were more spontaneous, because the discussion there was less conditioned by official rigidity and because they were more varied, moving beyond the traditional questions of diplomatic conferences (health, standardization, measures, conservation, communications, trade, security and international legislation).[8]

It is important to note that collection logic has evolved over time. As far as the pre-1945 years are concerned, it was only between 1907 and 1914 that the UIA possessed the resources to register congresses as they were being held. Staff directly entered information into a large card directory when these events were announced by the associations organizing them. It was also during these early years that the UIA's founders gathered information on earlier international congresses. When it eventually published two volumes of past international congresses much later, in 1960 and 1964, the data for the pre-1919 period was based on the work of La Fontaine and Otlet before the First World War.[9] Yet even in the UIA's formative years, greater emphasis was placed on the listing of organizations than of congresses. After the First World War, the production of congress lists was not a priority either: in addition to the *Répertoire des Organisations Internationales*, which partly replaced the *Annuaire de la Vie Internationale*, the UIA published the *Code des Voeux des Associations Internationales*, which grouped together their resolutions.

The collection of information on congresses was only really initiated after the resumption of the UIA's activities around 1950. It no longer undertook a large and sometimes heterogeneous census of all congresses; instead, it was limited to a core group of the main international organizations, whose congresses were then listed on a self-declaration basis.[10] When viewing Figure 11.1, this needs to be borne in mind: at first sight, it seems to suggest that from 1920 until the mid-1950s, the number of international congresses was much smaller than in the pre-war years. However, this apparent drop was not simply a consequence of the First World War, but reflected the fact that information was gathered on a more limited basis. The nature of the corpus changed, and all interpretations of the data must take this into account. In more recent decades, the activities of the UIA have seen further changes and its selection of organizations varied according to the needs of the UN, especially after 1978.[11] Moreover, the acceleration in the number of congresses from the 1960s led to an unparalleled expansion of the corpus, which makes it more difficult to compare it to the early years. For this reason, our analysis – which, after all, is a preliminary exploration – confines itself to the period before the 1960s.

With regard to the dataset and its limits, it should also be noted that the two world wars clearly interrupted the continuity of the congresses. In the case of the Second World War, the UIA database lists a few dozen meetings outside Europe, but the lists published by the UIA indicate no congresses being held during the First World War. While it is evident that only a very limited number of events could have taken place during these years, this complete void was due to a conscious decision made by the publishers of the second volume not to integrate the 275 congresses contained in their original files and covering the period August 1914 to December 1918. They regarded the vast majority of them as mere announcements of conferences that were then cancelled.[12] This kind of decision is obviously problematic, but the intervention was probably necessary and reminds us that a historical dataset is always the product of such a construction. It is therefore certain that other events appearing in Otlet and La Fontaine's files were also congresses announced but that did not materialize, whatever the year.

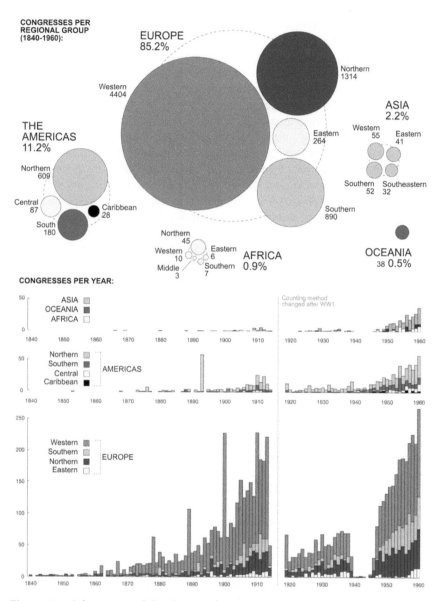

Figure 11.1 Sub-continental distribution of international congresses, 1840–1960. Above: Distribution of the total number of congresses between 1840 and 1960 in the main sub-continental divisions (United Nations geoscheme). The colours do not indicate a concentration but help to identify the regions in the histograms. Below: Annual breakdown by continent/sub-continent. *Source:* UIA database / Martin Grandjean.

If we look at the global geographical distribution of international congresses between 1840 and 1960 (Figure 11.1), we notice that this internationalism remained an essentially European phenomenon for a long time. Hosting more than 85 per cent of congresses during the whole period, Europe accounted for almost 92 per cent of such events prior to the First World War. Apart from this, only the Americas hosted a significant proportion of congresses – at just over 11 per cent (7 per cent before 1914). A sub-continental division offers another image of this distribution. Indeed, even if a more detailed classification is far from perfect,[13] it makes it possible to highlight the unbalanced situation in these two continents, with in both cases one region hosting two-thirds of the congresses. In Europe, most congresses were organized in the West (Germany, France and their Belgian, Dutch, Swiss and Austrian neighbours), although we see a gradual diversification from the 1950s onwards with the development of Northern Europe (Great Britain and Scandinavia) and Southern Europe (the Iberian and Italian peninsulas, the Balkans and Greece) as destinations for international meetings. In America, the North (the United States and Canada) hosted more congresses than the rest, but as the rest was less affected by the Second World War, diversification reached it earlier. From 1940, Latin America hosted half of the international congresses. On the other hand, it is only since the 1950s that international organizations gradually turned to Asia for their meetings.

But beyond these descriptive statistics, which make it possible to set the framework, to characterize the dataset and to contextualize 'the congress', the most obvious lesson from this brief quantitative survey is the confirmation that universal expositions played a central role in structuring the activity of international organizations in the late nineteenth century. The world's fairs in Paris were particularly important since, as Figure 11.1 shows, there were indeed clear peaks in 1867, 1878, 1889 and 1900.[14] As for Europe, we also note the early influence of the London international exhibition of 1862, as well as the peak recorded for Brussels in 1910, the richest year for congresses before the First World War (n=259) and the year that saw the final step towards the creation of the UIA. Even this did not equal the popularity of Paris a decade earlier, since only eighty-three congresses were held in Brussels in 1900 compared with a little over 200 in the French capital. On the subject of world's fairs, we refer in particular to the work of Claude Tapia and Jacques Taieb, who carried out a similar study of congress data, focusing on Paris's particular position as well as some thematic issues.[15] Outside Europe, the Chicago World's Fair of 1893 is also perfectly visible on the American histogram, since in that year fifty-eight congresses were held in the United States, including fifty-five in Chicago itself (the world total was ninety-five).

However, the logic that prevailed during the organization of a congress did not rest solely on the choice of country but rather on the choice of city with conference facilities, with means of transportation for maximum international access and, above all, with an international reputation for hosting institutions directly related to the congress theme. Consequently, among the states in question, only a handful of cities hosted the majority of congresses. Between 1840 and 1960, the twelve states most frequently hosting an international congress represented 85 per cent of the total number of events, a proportion that was actually as high as 90 to 95 per cent before 1914. And inside these few countries, one city, usually the capital, accounted on average for two-thirds of the congresses held in that country.

In Europe, as shown in Figure 11.2, the vast majority of congresses took place in the highly urbanized and industrialized region running from Manchester to Milan.[16] In addition to being the most densely populated part of Western Europe, it is

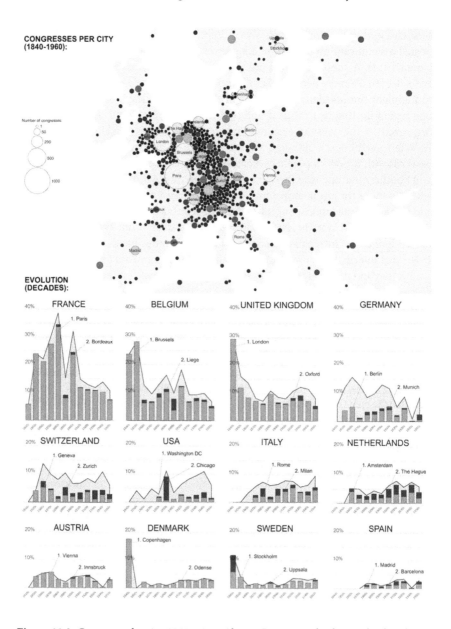

Figure 11.2 Congresses by city, 1840–1960. Above: Cartogram displaying the distribution of congresses by city between 1840 and 1960. The map is lightly anamorphic to expand areas where dots might overlap, especially in the European Megalopolis between Milan and Manchester. Only the two principal cities of the twelve principal countries are named. Below: Evolution in the twelve first countries, by decade, as a percentage of the world total. The surface is the percentage for the country, the light bar is the principal city and the dark bar is the second city (stacked). *Source:* UIA database / Martin Grandjean.

also its geographical centre. But of the more than 700 congress cities, only 102 hosted ten or more meetings between 1840 and 1960, and only fourteen of them hosted hundred or more.[17] This very inequitable distribution, which cannot be fully explained by the universal expositions, shows that certain cities were rapidly becoming true poles of internationalism. France hosted the largest number of international congresses by far – more than 20 per cent of the total up to 1914, with peaks of over 30 per cent in some decades, followed by stabilization at around 13 per cent during the interwar years and after the Second World War. Not surprisingly, the most popular French congress city was its capital, hosting more than three quarters of the international events organized in France. The difference with the province is striking.

The histograms that accompany Figure 11.2 compare these values by decade for the top twelve congress host countries between 1840 and 1960 (as a proportion of the global total). By comparing the total proportion for a country (area marked by a line) with the score for its first two cities (light grey bars for the first and dark grey bars for the second), it becomes very clear that the dominance of the French capital was characteristic of states whose political, cultural and social activity was very strongly centralized. In contrast, in federal states and those that history and geography have organized around several urban centres (Germany, Switzerland, the United States and, to a lesser extent, Belgium, Italy and the Netherlands), the proportion of events hosted by the two principal cities compared with the national total was much smaller. As a sign of the diversification of congress venues at the end of the nineteenth century, the three great classical destinations of Paris, Brussels and London gradually lost ground in relative terms, stabilizing at around 10 per cent for the French capital and 8 per cent for the Belgian and British from the beginning of the twentieth century. Note that the very high proportions recorded during the first three decades, especially in France, Belgium, the UK, Denmark and Sweden, reflected the very low frequency of congresses and should not be interpreted as a trend but as an edge effect. It is also observed that among the twelve countries hosting the most international congresses, Switzerland was the only one whose first city was not its capital (Geneva and Zurich were more popular than Bern). In the United States and in the Netherlands, the capital narrowly took first place, ahead of Chicago and The Hague (the seat of government and parliament).

As already observed in the histograms for the main congress cities, temporality is an aspect difficult to combine with the spatial approach that interests us here. As the global displacement is fairly invisible on a short temporal scale, we may summarize the annual 'centre of gravity' per decade. This type of representation (Figure 11.3), which is generally used in studies dealing with the planet's economic or demographic centre of gravity,[18] makes it possible to globalize an analysis that would otherwise have been complicated. It shows a clear evolution in annual averages, from black (1840) to white (1960), from north-east to south-west. This trend is even more evident when looking at the averages by decade.

Logically, the annual centre of gravity of international congresses is generally located in a region close to the London-Brussels-Paris triangle. The extreme years

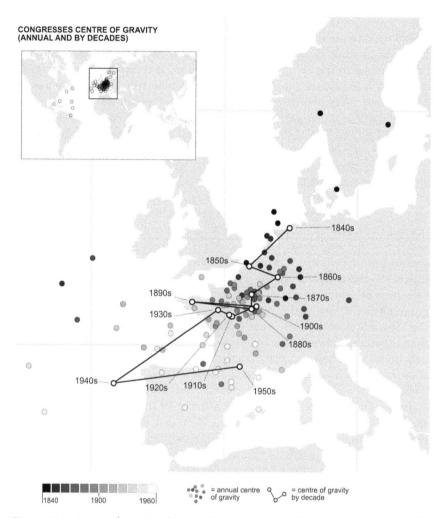

Figure 11.3 Centre of gravity of international congresses, 1840–1960. Evolution of the annual centre of gravity (dots), and its average, by decade (linked dots). *Source:* UIA database / Martin Grandjean.

are not inconsistent with this trend, but they might be coincidental variations. Indeed, during the earliest the very small number of congresses means these averages were very easily influenced by one or more events in Copenhagen or Stockholm, for example. It should also be noted that seven annual averages are not displayed on the European map but appear on the Atlantic coast of the American continent: these are the years 1893 (Chicago World's Fair) and 1940 to 1945, during which almost no congresses took place in Europe. These exceptional years also explain why the centres of gravity in the 1890s and 1940s break the relatively linear evolution of the other averages by decade.

If the centre of gravity changed little between 1870 and the Second World War, the period since 1950 saw a shift towards the South. This was the result of new destinations in the Americas as well as in Asia, Africa and Oceania. In conjunction with this development, the slight shift from East to West is explained by the number of international congresses increasing more rapidly in the Americas than in Asia (Figure 11.1). However, during the 1950s, Europe still hosted 78 per cent of all international congresses (61 per cent for Western and Northern Europe only).

Two Centuries of Data on International Non-Governmental Organizations

The UIA's *Yearbook* defines an INGO as an organized body, having a permanent headquarters and governing body, being non-governmental and international in orientation, that has its aims and projects in, and funding and members from, at least three countries. In practice, it also excludes multinational criminal and multinational commercial organizations.[19] Grassroots movements without an organized body and permanent headquarters are excluded by definition, even if such a movement covers large parts of the globe.[20] Depending on the interests of the researcher, this might be an advantage or a disadvantage, but one can see why they are excluded: such movements are more fluid and therefore less likely to answer the questionnaire the UIA sends them.[21] The definition of what constitutes an INGO thus has its limits, especially with regard to permanency and formality, and it was not entirely static over time.

What can historians learn from analysing the data on organizations? Figure 11.4 shows the number of new INGOs by decade and continent of their headquarters (1800–1979), excluding those organizations for which the continent is unknown.

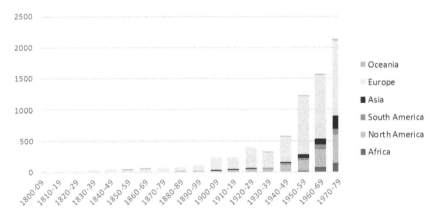

Figure 11.4 Number of new INGOs, by the decade of foundation and known continent of headquarters, 1800–1979. *Source:* UIA database, November 2016 / Marco H. D. van Leeuwen.

There are indeed many organizations for which relevant information is missing, presumably because for many of the older short-lived organizations it has not been possible to gather such information retrospectively.[22] The figure shows an overall growth in numbers in all periods except for those prior to the First World War and the Second World War. By far the most organizations had their headquarters in Europe, followed by North America. The aims of many INGOs lay at least partly outside Europe. The British and Foreign Anti-Slavery Society – currently named Anti-Slavery International – founded in London in 1839 is sometimes even regarded as the first INGO. And many organizations developed a global reach: the YMCA (founded in 1855), the International Vegetarian Union (1907), the International Chamber of Commerce (1919), the Comintern (1919), the World Council of Churches (1948), the International Planned Parenthood Federation (1948), Amnesty International (1961) and the International Lesbian, Gay, Bisexual, Trans and Intersex Association (1981).

Even in the nineteenth century, however, some organizations were *founded* outside Europe, and by its last decade INGOs had become a truly global phenomenon. Some organizations actively sought to combat European influences, as was the case with the Indian National Congress (1885) or the Muslim Brotherhood (1928). During the twentieth century, the globalization of INGO work led John Boli and George Thomas to speak of a 'world culture'. Obviously, most of the organizations founded during the two world wars were set up outside Europe, notably in Latin America. One example was the South American Football Federation CONMEBOL (1916).[23] Although Figure 11.4 ends with 1970–79, this process of globalization has increased since then, with a growing proportion of organizations based in Asia, South America or Africa.[24]

The UIA data covers INGOs of various types. In the following sections, we zoom in on a subset that is often seen as constituting the core – the 'genuinely international non-governmental organizations'.[25] The UIA data covers only a fraction of the organizations in the *Yearbook* – the genuinely international NGOs existing in 1988 or having existed before that year but now being defunct. Table 11.1 makes clear which types of organization are in the dataset (active organizations types B, C and D, and similar organizations that have ceased to exist and are part of type H). It includes a clear minority (though arguably the most international) of all organizations covered by the UIA. The table uses data from 1988 to facilitate comparison with other records that we will use, as explained below.

We have at our disposal two datasets – both of which were kindly provided by its creators: one from the UIA and one used by Boli and Thomas in their seminal publications on the history of INGOs. The UIA file and the Boli/Thomas (BT) file relate to the same of organizations, but they differ in some other respects. The BT file contains a small number of numerical variables keyed in from the 1988 *Yearbook* for most organizations, and the 1984 *Yearbook* for defunct organizations. The UIA file has more variables, including text strings. The UIA file, for example, gives us the name of an organization, their predecessor/successor and the countries in which it was active, whereas the BT file gives us the ID but not the name, and the number of countries but not their names.

Table 11.1 Organizations covered by the UIA, by section, in 1988

		IGO	NGO	Total
Conventional international bodies				
A	Federations of international organizations	1	41	42
B	Universal membership organizations	33	422	455
C	Intercontinental membership organizations	45	796	841
D	Regionally oriented membership organizations	230	3259	3489
	Total conventional	309	4518	4827
Other international bodies				
E	Organizations emanating from places, persons, bodies	751	1996	2747
F	Organizations of special form	590	1538	2128
G	Internationally oriented national organizations	52	8273	8325
	Total other	1393	11807	13200
Special sections				
H	Dissolved or apparently inactive organizations	240	2109	2349
R	Religious orders and secular institutes	0	690	690
S	Autonomous conference series	63	406	469
T	Multinational treaties and intergovernmental agreements	1634	0	1634
	Total special	1937	3205	5142
Total of all of the above		**3639**	**19530**	**23169**
Unconfirmed bodies				
J	Recently reported bodies, not yet confirmed	137	1341	1478
U	Untraceable (or currently inactive nonconventional) bodies	262	4033	4295
	Total unconfirmed	399	5374	5773
Grand total all sections		4038	24904	28942
%		14.0	86.0	100

Source: UIA, *Yearbook of International Organizations 1988–1989*, vol. 2 (Munich: K. G. Saur, 1988), Appendix 7.

Given that the UIA file contains more detailed information than the BT file, it would seem the better dataset to work with, certainly if one is willing to make the effort to transform texts into the numerical values that make the BT file so neat to work with. However, the BT file does have extra information of two types: a categorization designed by Boli and Thomas of the work fields of an organization, and a variable indicating whether an organization was still active in 1988 or defunct by then, and, if so, whether this was due to its dissolution or a merger, for example. To preserve this extra information, we merged the UIA file with the BT file, although we lose cases in the process.[26] This merger does, however, make it possible to compare the categorization of work fields by the UIA with that of Boli and Thomas.[27] We start in 1800 and end in 1973. In our data, there are only four organizations predating 1800.[28] Although the UIA-BT file includes INGOs founded up to and including 1988, we stop in 1973 as that is the first year for which coverage by the UIA is thought to have become as complete as it was ever to become. It took some time before all new INGOs were included in the UIA files. As the UIA website says: 'In preparing and updating the organization profiles, the UIA gives priority to information received from the organizations themselves, then checks this information against other sources (periodicals, official documents,

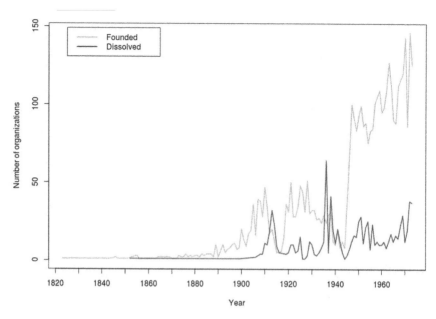

Figure 11.5 INGOs, by year of foundation and year of dissolution, 1800–1973. *Source:* Boli-Thomas and UIA datasets / Marco H. D. van Leeuwen.

media, etc.) to present a reliable picture of a dynamic situation.' This timeframe is about fifteen years, meaning that by 1988, one can assume that the UIA had a comprehensive picture of all INGOs that existed in 1973.[29]

What does the UIA-BT file tell us about the history of 'genuine' INGOs? Figure 11.5 shows the year of foundation for the INGOs in the UIA-BT file in the period 1800–1973. Figure 11.4 did something similar, but by decade for all organizations for which the UIA gathered data, whereas Figure 11.5 shows the year of foundation for our subset of genuine INGOs in our merged UIA-BT file. The graph also depicts the number of INGOs terminated per year. Though not entirely surprising, it is still useful to document the fact that more organizations disbanded and fewer were established during and before the two world wars.[30] In both periods, there were even more dissolutions than foundations.[31]

Boli and Thomas created a categorization of the work fields of the organizations in the dataset. They labelled these fields 'primary aims' and also created another variable for those organizations that covered further areas, which they labelled 'secondary aims'. Here we look at the primary aims only, of which there are forty.[32] The UIA currently also has its own categorization of work fields for organizations, termed 'subject headings' in the dataset. We present these aims and categories as word clouds in Figure 11.6. The word cloud based on the BT file shows clearly that, in order of prominence, the main work fields for INGOs were medicine, commerce, agriculture, sports, natural sciences, religion, education, social sciences, labour and services. As the UIA's dataset has many more categories than the BT categorization, the word cloud

Boli Thomas   UIA

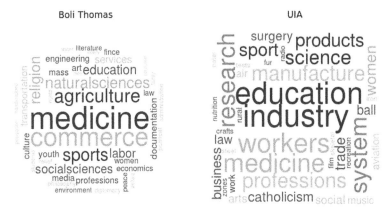

Figure 11.6 Word clouds for INGO work fields, according to the Boli-Thomas classification and the UIA-classification, 1800–1973. *Source:* Boli-Thomas and UIA datasets / Marco. H. D. van Leeuwen.

Period 1: 1800–72 (N = 27)   Period 2: 1873–1913 (N = 483)   Period 3: 1914–45 (N = 812)   Period 4: 1946–73 (N = 2830)

Figure 11.7 Word clouds for INGO work fields, by sub-period, 1800–1973 (Boli-Thomas categories). *Source:* Boli-Thomas dataset / Marco H. D. van Leeuwen.

based on its material is not strictly comparable, but the figure shows many similarities in terms of the prominence of particular work fields. There appears to be no easy way to make a crossover between the current UIA and BT categorizations of work fields.[33]

Figures 11.7 and 11.8 show the same word clouds for INGO work fields as before, albeit in miniature form, by sub-period. It is interesting to see how, according to both the UIA and BT categorizations, the organizations founded in the first period were focused mostly on Christianity/religion, in the second period on workers/ labour issues, and in the fourth on industry/commerce. The word clouds for the third period appear not to be especially similar, but this might in large measure be due to differences in coding – for example, educational work fields are coded into separate disciplines by Boli and Thomas, but as one category by the UIA. Overall, the comparison between the two independently made classifications suggests that both do a good job in capturing the work fields of INGOs, despite the difficulty in narrowing this down to one or two categories. Both categorizations

Figure 11.8 Word clouds for INGO work fields, by sub-period, 1800–1973 (UIA categories). *Source:* UIA dataset / Marco H. D. van Leeuwen.

are static in nature, though, and subtle changes in work field over time therefore remain invisible.

Conclusion

Datasets this rich in temporal, geographical and thematic coverage are a feast for historians. While we have no reason to assume major flaws in terms of these records, it is inevitable that some organizations will have been missed, especially as the datasets essentially rely on self-reporting. At present, there is no yardstick to measure the degree of completeness. This problem is likely to be greater, the further one goes back in time and the more ephemeral, marginal or informal the organization in question was. Related to that is the fact that, for some older, more short-lived, marginal and informal organizations, there are many gaps in the data. It would be strange if this were not the case, but it is fair to acknowledge this and also to note that it would probably require much collaborative work by historians to fill in these gaps.

The UIA *Yearbook* is primarily meant to serve the world of international NGOs. This implies that, although the UIA has been gathering data for a long time and does consider the history of the organizations, these records do not provide everything that a historian of INGOs might wish for, as a historical review is not the UIA's stated aim. It seeks to document the world of INGOs in a certain year, rather than tracing it over time. The UIA stores the information on name changes or mergers in the 'history field', but in our data for 1988, there is only one organization and not the precursors. As the *Yearbook* documents only the situation with regard to, for example, aims and regional coverage in that particular year, the historian faces the problem not only of counting, but also, to some extent, of characterizing the aims and coverage as they evolved over time.

In other words, any given *Yearbook* will only give us a snapshot in any given year. This might not be a concern for the UIA as a service provider, or to those who use its information to study the world of INGOs in 2017. But for historians, or social scientists with an interest in historical processes, it might. Potentially, this problem can be contained in several ways, notably by incorporating from the 'history' field of the UIA data; by going back to older yearbooks and incorporating information from previous decades;[34] or by undertaking detailed studies of one or more organizations.[35]

Notwithstanding these limitations, we have been able to sketch some possibilities of using UIA data to trace the historical development of international non-governmental organizations. We have seen that the material can be used to provide an overview of the geographical distribution of international congresses since the second half of the nineteenth century. Our investigation has shown that this phenomenon was essentially centralized in a handful of cities, quickly identified as capitals of internationalism, and that it was only after the Second World War that diversification gathered momentum. By using UIA data, we have been able to visualize the number of INGO foundations and dissolutions over time as well as the shift from Europe and the West to a more global distribution. Moreover, we have traced patterns and processes of relations among INGOs and their work fields over time. The word clouds in the final section show that regardless of whether one uses the UIA's own classifications or those by Boli and Thomas, one will gain a similar picture of the changing work fields.

In a review of the UIA material, Elizabeth Bloodgood has drawn attention to the fact that despite the inherent attraction of the topic to historians, and despite the quality of the UIA data, there is not much quantitative transnational research on NGOs. She believes this paradox to be the result of several factors, including heuristic requirements requiring collaborative scholarship and the dominant social science research paradigms focusing on exceptionality rather than 'commonalities across cases, places and time'.[36] While we have stressed the potential pitfalls of using UIA information historical purposes, its use for research on non-governmental organizations is evident. Alongside other recent endeavours, the chapters in the present volume suggest that the era of what one might term the 'social-science history of international non-governmental organizations' has truly started.[37]

Notes

The authors are grateful for the UIA's kind assistance, for valuable comments by Pierre-Yves Saunier and the editors of this volume and for Chris Gordon's work in editing the text. Martin Grandjean wrote the part on the conferences, while Marco van Leeuwen wrote the section on INGOs. Marco van Leeuwen also wishes to thank John Boli and George Thomas for providing their database on the INGOs. He is grateful, too, to the EUI Research Council for providing a grant allowing him to visit the UIA headquarters in Brussels under the programme 'European Trajectories in the Quest for Welfare and Democracy: Voluntary Associations, Families and the State, 1870s–1990s', convened by Laura Downs. Last but not least, he is indebted to Agata Troost for her highly valuable help throughout.

1   See, for example, John Boli and George M. Thomas, eds, *Constructing World Culture: International Non-Governmental Organizations since 1875* (Stanford, CA: Stanford University Press, 1999); Thomas Davies, *NGOs: A New History of Transnational Civil Society* (London: Hurst, 2013); Davide Rodogno, Bernhard Struck and Jakob Vogel, eds, *Shaping the Transnational Sphere: Experts, Networks and Issues from the 1840s to the 1930s* (New York: Berghahn, 2015); Christian Topalov, ed., *Laboratoires du nouveau siècle: les nébuleuse réformatrice et ses réseaux en France, 1880–1914* (Paris: EHESS, 1999); Pamala Wiepking and Femida Handy, eds, *The Palgrave Handbook of Global Philanthropy* (New York: Palgrave, 2015).

2   'Editorial Problems and Policies' (Appendix 10.3), in UIA, *Yearbook of International Organizations, 2015–16*, vol. 1 (Leiden: Brill, 2015), 15–21.

3   Eric Brian, 'Y a-t-il un objet *Congrès*? Le cas du Congrès international de statistique (1853–1876)', *Mil Neuf Cent. Revue d'histoire Intellectuelle* 7, no. 1 (1989): 9–22; Christophe Prochasson, 'Les Congrès: lieux de l'échange intellectuel. Introduction', *Mil Neuf Cent. Revue d'histoire Intellectuelle* 7, no. 1 (1989): 5–8.

4   See Anne Rasmussen, 'Jalons pour une histoire des congrès internationaux au XIXe siècle: régulation scientifique et propagande intellectuelle', *Relations Internationales* 62 (1990): 115–33., Claudia Tapia and Jacques Taieb, 'Conférences et congrès internationaux de 1815 à 1913', *Relations Internationales* 5 (1976): 11–35; Nico Randeraad, 'Triggers of Mobility: International Congresses (1840–1914) and their Visitors', in *Mobility and Biography* [*European History Yearbook*, vol. 16], ed. Sarah Panter (Boston: De Gruyter, 2015), 63–82.

5   Simeon E. Baldwin, 'The International Congresses and Conferences of the Last Century as Forces Working Toward the Solidarity of the World', *The American Journal of International Law* 1, no. 3 (1907): 565–78.

6   John Culbert Faries, *The Rise of Internationalism* (New York: W.D. Gray, 1915), 6.

7   Faries, *The Rise of Internationalism*, 73.

8   Faries himself established this classification. Ibid., 47 et seq.

9   *Les Congrès Internationaux de 1681 à 1899, Liste Complète* (Brussels: UIA, 1960) and *Les Congrès Internationaux de 1900 à 1919, Liste Complète* (Brussels: UIA, 1964).

10 Data for the years after 1919 are taken from the UIA database: 'The International Congress Calendar'. Available online: https://uia.org/calendar (accessed 9 October 2017). On this subject, see Elizabeth Bloodgood, 'The Yearbook of International Organizations and Quantitative Non-State Actor Research', in Reinalda, *The Ashgate Research Companion to Non-State Actors*, 19–34.

11 Evelyn L. Bush, 'Measuring Religion in Global Civil Society', *Social Forces* 85, no. 4 (2007): 1645–65.

12 *Les Congrès Internationaux de 1900 à 1919*, 3.

13 This classification is based on the United Nations geoscheme of the UN Statistics Division, M.49 standard.

14 On Paris congresses and universal expositions, see Anne Rasmussen, 'Les Congrès internationaux liés aux Expositions universelles de Paris (1867–1900)', *Mil Neuf Cent. Revue d'histoire Intellectuelle* 7, no. 1 (1989): 23–44.

15 Tapia and Taieb, 'Conférences et congrès internationaux de 1815 à 1913'. See, for example, p. 15.

16 The famous 'blue banana' introduced by Brunet. See Roger Brunet, *Les Villes 'européennes'* (Paris: DATAR / La Documentation française, 1989).

17 Paris (1,074), Brussels (532), London (512), Rome (260), Vienna (236), Berlin (187), Copenhagen (182), Amsterdam (170), Stockholm (163), The Hague (161), Geneva

(149), Zurich (133), Berne (106) and Washington DC (100). Followed by Liège (99), Milan (97), Madrid (97), Chicago (90), Munich (89), Antwerp (88), Budapest (86), New York (73), Oslo (70), Ghent (62) and Hamburg (55).

18 Danny Quah, 'The Global Economy's Shifting Centre of Gravity', *Global Policy* 2, no. 1 (2011): 3–9.

19 See 1.3 'Types of Organization' (Appendix 10.3: 'Editorial Problems and Policies'). Available online: https://uia.org/system/files/pdf/v5/2017/10_3.pdf (accessed 26 January 2018).

20 Nitza Berkovitch, 'The Emergence and Transformation of the International Women's Movement', in Boli and Thomas, *Constructing World Culture*, 100–27, identified 195 such organizations in the UIA Yearbooks from 1950 to 1993. She cites evidence of a larger number of organizations, especially of the network type not included in the Yearbook.

21 The UIA can also be seen as a service provider for INGOs that pay a membership fee, and many grassroots movements cannot do that.

22 For around half the organizations in the period between 1800 and 1979, the location of their headquarters is unknown.

23 John Boli and George Thomas, 'INGOs and the Organization of World Culture', in *Constructing World Culture*, ed. idem, 32–3.

24 Membership outside Europe has also grown. See Anheier, Glasius and Kaldor, 'Introducing Global Civil Society', 5. This was especially so in low- and middle-income countries.

25 John Boli and George M. Thomas, 'World Culture in the World Polity: A Century of International Non-Governmental Organization', *American Sociological Review* 62, no. 2 (1997): 171–90, and Boli and Thomas, *Constructing World Culture*; Bloodgood, 'The Yearbook of International Organizations and Quantitative Non-State Actor Research', 19–33. See the *Yearbook*'s 'Types of Organization' section (as cited in note 19).

26 We merged the UIA file with the BT file using an ID that was identical after deleting the second letter in the BT file (which used the ID style with double first letters in use by the UIA in 1988). In some cases, we could not find a match as the ID number had changed after 1988. We continued to work only with the organizations we could match, as this enabled us to use the additional variables in the BT file and make comparisons between the BT classification and that of the UIA. Although we lost a considerable number of cases as a result, the new file had 4,152 INGOs founded between 1800 and 1973.

27 Boli and Thomas, drew up their own classification. See idem, 'INGOs and the Organization of World Culture', 49.

28 The 2016 Yearbook lists 202 organizations founded before 1800 because it covers many other types of organization than are in our dataset. See Table 1.

29 As noted in Boli and Thomas, 'INGOs and the Organization of World Culture', 21 and Jackie Smith and Dawn Wiest, 'The Uneven Geography of Global Civil Society: National and Global Influences on Transnational Association', *Social Forces* 84, no. 2 (2005): 621–52.

30 See for example, by Michael Barnett, *Empire of Humanity: A History of Humanitarianism* (Ithaca, NY: Cornell University Press, 2011); Davies, *NGOs*; Boli and Thomas, 'INGOs and the Organization of World Culture', 23. See also two seminal studies: Kjell Skjelsbaek, 'The Growth of International Nongovernmental Organization in the Twentieth Century', *International Organization* 25, no. 3 (1971): 420–42; Michael Wallace and J. David Singer, 'Intergovernmental Organization in the Global System, 1815–1964: A Quantitative Description', *International Organization* 24, no. 2 (1970): 239–87.

31 The foundation years are derived from the UIA file and have no missing values. The failure years are derived by combining categories of the variable Failure Type created by Boli and Thomas: 1 – inactive or dissolved; 2 – merged or absorbed; 3 – replaced; 4 – no longer international. In the case of 232 organizations, we do not know in what year they failed. The true level of failure is thus somewhat higher than the line in the graph suggests. If the 232 missing cases were disproportionally from around the First and Second World Wars, the failure line would surpass the foundation line even more than the graph suggests.

32 These fall under a smaller number of larger categories. This variable has sixty-seven missing cases. Boli and Thomas also created a variable to capture which organizations had another, secondary, aim; this occurred only in a minority of cases (there are 3,026 organizations without a secondary aim).

33 The UIA has 2,284 more detailed work fields, some of them repeated in various broader categories, and 134 broader ones, including the regional categories (for example 'Africa'). Boli and Thomas have forty more detailed work fields and thirteen more general ones. While the many detailed UIA subject headings could be matched to broader categories also created by the UIA, using a matrix file kindly provided by the UIA, the smaller subject headings (for example 'political') match with multiple broader categories (such as 'government' and 'metapolitics'). In addition, there are multiple subject headings per organization, corresponding to multiple broader categories, and choosing the first one could be misleading, since they are ordered alphabetically. Therefore, the first subject heading is not necessarily the one that best describes the organization. For these reasons, we postponed automatically mapping UIA work fields onto BT work fields.

34 As Smith and Wiest, 'The Uneven Geography of Global Civil Society', did for a group of organizations.

35 As has been done in several chapters in the seminal study commissioned by Boli and Thomas, *Constructing World Culture*.

36 Bloodgood, 'The Yearbook of International Organizations', 19.

37 Amanda Murdie and David R. Davis, 'Looking in the Mirror: Comparing INGO Networks Across Issue Areas', *Review of International Organizations* 7, no. 2 (2012): 177–202; Patricia Bromley, 'The Rationalization of Educational Development: Scientific Activity among International Nongovernmental Organizations', *Comparative Education Review* 54, no. 4 (2010): 577–601; Jackie Smith and Dawn Wiest, *Social Movements in the World-System: The Politics of Crisis and Transformation* (New York: Russel Sage Foundation, 2012).

EPILOGUE: THE UIA IN THE TWENTY-FIRST CENTURY

Nancy Carfrae

The UIA is noteworthy for its long-lasting efforts in documenting the development and activity of global civil society. While adapting to changing needs, technologies and financial models over the decades, it has remained largely consistent in its purpose and methodology: collecting and organizing data on international associations was one of the original purposes that founders Henri La Fontaine and Paul Otlet set for the organization, and the UIA's activities still embody these principles. Especially since its re-establishment in the late 1940s, the curation of its database is a raison d'être for the organization.

The UIA's data was intended to be objective, neutral and apolitical in nature, but once mobilized, it became a powerful tool carving out a space for the development and affirmation of global civil society. The UIA gave shape to its database of international organizations and was in turn shaped by that database until the distinction between the organization itself and its database has become, essentially, non-existent. The UIA's purpose continues to be primarily to *document* the existence and activities of international organizations, and, by disseminating its documentation, to *promote* the contribution international organizations make to society.

This epilogue complements the scholarly chapters that form the main part of this book. Our contribution outlines the activities of the organization today as they are viewed by the UIA staff members who have collaborated in authoring this piece. We provide an overview of the data the UIA makes available through the *Yearbook of International Organizations* and other publications, and the events and structures it has set up to promote the work of international organizations.

The Yearbook

The *Yearbook of International Organizations* lies at the heart of the UIA's activities. As Pierre-Yves Saunier's chapter has shown, the documentation of international activities, bodies and associations has been intrinsic to the UIA's work from its very beginnings as the Office Central des Institutions Internationales in 1907. Following the organization's relaunch in the late 1940s, the *Yearbook* soon became part of its attempts to establish links with the nascent UN system. In 1949, representatives of the UIA, the UN and the UN Interim Committee of Non-Governmental Organizations agreed that the best way to rebuild the UIA would be to conceive it as a centre for documentation, study, service and the promotion of closer relations between international associations – a development that Philip Post and Nico Randeraad have traced in their contribution to this volume.[1] In 1950, a special ECOSOC resolution established cooperation between the UN and the UIA for the purposes of preparing the *Yearbook*.[2] UNESCO and ECOSOC granted consultative status to the UIA in 1952 and 1953 respectively; today the UIA enjoys associate status with UNESCO. With the UN's moral support, the UIA carried on compiling the *Yearbook of International Organizations*. In 1970, on the occasion of the UIA's sixtieth anniversary, the then director-general of UNESCO wrote:

> UNESCO has several special reasons for gratitude towards the Union. I would like to mention the fruitful collaboration which has arisen between both institutions, in the matter of scientific terminology, the circulation of scientific documentation, and the research which has been carried out on the subject of peace.[3]

The current reality is that most UN institutions and departments maintain their own directories of the non-governmental bodies they cooperate with, using the *Yearbook* only as a supplementary source.

Over the years, the *Yearbook* has grown in many ways. After a change in publisher in 1983, it expanded to three volumes, allowing for a commensurate expansion in printed information. Since then, Volume 1 contains the organization profiles. Volume 2 is dedicated to the geographical index and Volume 3 to the subject index. The expansion was in part due to a broadening of the criteria in response to the changing nature of international organizations and more fluid or specialized structures: more bodies became eligible for inclusion. In March 2018, at the end of the annual editorial cycle for the *Yearbook*'s 55th edition, the database contained descriptions of over 76,000 organizations past and present. About 1,000 newly detected organizations are added to the database every year.

The methodology to obtain, sustain and update the various interlinked UIA databases has changed little over the decades. The organizations themselves have always been the editors' first port of call, and every year up to 30,000 organizations are sent a letter or an email inviting them to update their profiles, both of their organization itself and of their organization's events. Typically, an invitation includes either a copy of the organization's profile and its meetings profiles, or – more commonly nowadays – a link to where the profiles can be viewed online.

In the past, it all happened on paper: the profiles were printed and inserted in an envelope, along with explanatory documents and lists and questions, and mailed to the principal office of the organization. The early 2000s still saw the UIA offices and corridors lined with shelves holding thousands of paper files: documents, brochures and newsletters; paper proofs with corrections, annotations, and additions. With the increasingly widespread general use of electronic communication new opportunities arose: proofs could be sent by email and corrected proofs could be returned the same way; now organizations can also opt to log in to the UIA website to view and comment on the profile. Experience shows, however, that a paper letter still yields the best results, though the paper-filled shelves have become a faint memory.

Along with the dozens of replies that still arrive every day, the UIA also receives a steady flow of newsletters, journals, magazines, annual reports and similar documents. Here, too, paper has largely been replaced by electronic versions. In whatever format, they were and still are used to double-check the information in the databases. Often such sources provide useful information on several organizations at once. With the growth of the internet, organization websites are mined as well.

The corrections, modifications and amplifications received from organizations in response to the proofs remain the UIA's primary source of information when maintaining and updating its databases, but they are not the only one. Editors review every reply and double-check against other documents or websites in an attempt to ensure that the final profile meets UIA standards of uniform presentation and objective style.

For those conducting research in the domain of international organizations, the *Yearbook* and its sister publications can be useful instruments. The chapters by Bob Reinalda, Marco van Leeuwen and Martin Grandjean have shown how such data can be used, while Pierre-Yves Saunier has commented on the ways in which other scholars have drawn on data published by the UIA. Notwithstanding the limitations that have been noted elsewhere in this book, UIA data sheds light on the history of a single international organization and on the history and evolution of global civil society more widely. Major divisions can be made on geographical, thematic or chronological criteria.

Today, in these early years of the UIA's second century, its audiences continue to be diverse: international associations seeking contact and partnerships with like-minded bodies; governmental ministries and departments dealing with foreign development policies or with internal economic strategies; academics in the social and political sciences (such as international relations or economics) and those interested in collective actions in any domain (such as environmental studies or community health); university and state libraries; and businesses with an interest in Corporate Social Responsibility. An important audience since the 1950s has been the meetings industry – including national, regional and civic tourist authorities, service providers as well as convention centres and other meetings venues – which increasingly recognizes the value of international associations as partners. The diversity of the UIA's audience has always been a challenge. Even with new online measuring tools, it has been difficult to design and implement the functionalities of the online databases to meet the needs of such a diverse audience. A sustained dialogue between the UIA and users of its databases aims to improve and diversify those functionalities.

In the mid-1990s, the UIA began the compilation of two new databases. The first was biographical, with profiles of the principal personalities involved in the development, operation and coordination of the international bodies described in Volume 1 of the *Yearbook*. In 1992, this resulted in a new series, *Who's Who in International Organizations*, which carried on until 2006 and five editions. The second was a bibliographic database, built on the UIA's bibliographic work in earlier decades, of published works about global civil society; in 1996, this resulted in a fourth volume becoming part of the *Yearbook* set. In 2001, a fifth volume, dedicated to statistical summaries, was added in order to meet the growing demand for more detailed statistical tables. Finally, from 2007 until 2017, the *Who's Who* series was incorporated into the *Yearbook* series as Volume 6; in 2018 a new Volume 6 focusing on the United Nations' Sustainable Development Goals was launched. In 1999 the growing number of organization profiles necessitated publishing Volume 1 in two bound volumes, thus making the printed *Yearbook* series today an annual collection of seven books of up to 1,500 pages each.

Notwithstanding these additional volumes in the *Yearbook* series, the growth of the database made it impractical to publish in printed form all the information it holds. A CD-ROM version, *Yearbook / Annuaire Plus*, was first produced in 1995 and continued until a fifteenth edition in 2008. Meanwhile, the world changed and the internet proved it could offer a much larger scope: the *Yearbook Online* was launched in 2000.

The numbers are, however, only one aspect of UIA's wealth. Any one edition of the *Yearbook of International Organizations* has encyclopaedic features, providing a unique snapshot of the international association world of that year. Moreover, as the editorial treatment, structure and methodology have remained largely constant over the decades, the set of editions over the years is a resource of over a hundred years of comparable data. It is possible to research, compare, evaluate and contrast the scope of organizations in any given year, to detect trends in global civil society as a whole over time, and to track the evolution of any individual organization from its beginnings until the present day. Some organizations listed in the *Yearbook* – such as the Theosophical Society, the International Law Association, the International Olympic Committee and the UIA itself – have been active for over a century, and their history has been captured year after year in the *Yearbook*. The continuity and extent of the UIA's database allow us to explore a multitude of questions: how did a given event in world history affect civil society? When and where did disciplines or concerns, such as human rights or environmental questions, emerge and become reflected in international association life? What did the UN look like fifty years ago? With every new edition and update of the *Yearbook Online*, the UIA makes a larger picture of civil society available.

Gathering and Publishing Data beyond the Yearbook

From the beginning the *Yearbook of International Organizations* (and its predecessors) included information on events held by the profiled organizations. In 1959, the UIA started publishing the *International Congress Calendar,* with a separate profile for each event, with additional information where possible. In 2004 the *Calendar Online* joined the *Yearbook Online*. The *Calendar* database currently contains almost half a million past and future meetings and grows by about 12,000 meetings a year. Like the *Yearbook*, the *Calendar* is a barometer of civil society, a window onto its scope of activity, its breadth of subjects, its regional tendencies, and its interaction with and attraction to the public.

To meet the needs of a wider audience, and in line with UIA's Statutes 'to encourage and undertake all activity aimed at promoting the development and efficiency of non-governmental networks',[4] the UIA launched the *Open Yearbook* and *Open Calendar* in 2013. These are free and public online versions of the databases, with more limited functionalities and content than those available by subscription. They are a first step towards finding new ways to make the UIA databases more widely accessible and available so as to support the activities of organizations worldwide.

Since the 1951 edition of the *Yearbook*, the UIA has extracted and published statistical information from the organization profiles. The method of extraction has always been simple: certain elements of data are counted and totalled. The UIA has seldom attempted more sophisticated analyses; its merit lies in its consistency, with the same tables produced on an annual basis. When new demands and new tools have allowed the extraction of other information, the earlier tables have been continued in order to avoid losing the value of comparability. The reliability of the extractions has increased as data has become digitized, though deviations in even the oldest tables are negligible given the simplicity of the methodology.

The two most regular and most significant compilations of UIA statistics are the *International Meetings Statistics Report*, published annually since 1960, and the *Yearbook of International Organizations, Volume 5*, published annually since 2001. The former features statistics on the international meetings that have taken place worldwide in the preceding year, drawn from the database of the *Calendar*. The report's format has changed over the years – significantly in 1984 with major advances in digitalization of the databases – but the method of data collection and selection has remained consistent. Since 2003, all data for the report is extracted anew each year so that summaries of earlier years are also updated annually on the basis of newly received information.

Each volume of the *Yearbook* has always contained some statistical summaries of its contents. With the addition of Volume 5, space became available to add to these summaries both in breadth and in depth. The summaries published in Volume 5 are standard; once again, their merit is their comparability with earlier summaries because the same sources and the same methods and criteria have been used over several decades. In addition, customized statistical tables are produced on demand, usually at the request of scholars who thus exercise significant influence on the development and improvement of statistical summaries.

The *Survey on International Meeting Issues* is a periodic, large-scale survey covering multiple aspects of meetings held by international organizations. The survey is designed to help those involved in the process of organizing international association meetings – whether the associations themselves or the professionals assisting them – to get a sense of changes over the years and the challenges of the current environment. The first survey was undertaken in 1985; a seventh edition was completed in 2018. The participants in the survey are the international associations listed in the *Yearbook*. While the questions have been adjusted with each edition, and some new ones have been added, the results are comparable over time due to the consistent methodology.

The UIA's *Encyclopedia of World Problems and Human Potential* is a logical extension to the *Yearbook* and *Calendar*. The *Encylopedia* starts from the premise that an international organization tends to be formed to solve what its founders conceive to be a problem, and to solve that problem using strategies chosen by those founders, with both the perception of the problem and the choice of the strategy springing from the founders' value systems. By focusing on both problems and strategies, and on both constructive and destructive values, the *Encyclopedia* endeavours to encompass the issues, the responses to them, and the complexity of both. The *Encyclopedia* was first published in printed form in 1976 and has been online since 2000.[5] In 2017 the online *Encyclopedia* was relaunched in a new format intended to enable greater community sourcing and interactivity.

Events and Education

From its earliest days, the UIA has not only documented international organizations, it has also brought representatives of international bodies together, starting with the two World Congresses of International Associations in 1907 and in 1910 and with the 'Quinzaines Internationales' during the 1920s. Similar events followed, such as the 'Meeting of International Congress Organizers and Technicians' (a series that started in 1959) and the 'World Forum of Transnational Associations' (1980). The UIA's various journals contributed to its educational project, from the *Bulletin des Associations Internationales* in 1943 to the last edition of *Transnational Associations* in 2005.[6] While the UIA has had no journal since 2005, initiatives such as the present volume provide fresh opportunities for developing its dialogue with the academic world.

The UIA still brings together representatives of the international community through its Associations Round Table project. In keeping with the UIA's overall goals, the purpose of the Round Tables is for participants to acquire ideas, skills and contacts. The first event was an academic session in 2007; by 2012 the Round Table had grown to 200 participants for a full-day programme by and about international associations and the common challenges they face. Recognizing that many associations have limited resources, making travel to events problematic, the UIA expanded its Round Table project geographically as well as numerically: the first Associations Round Table Asia-Pacific was held in 2013, and in 2014 the Associations Round Table Europe began rotating across the continent.

It is noteworthy that, in education as in documentation, continuity is a prominent characteristic of the UIA's activities. The topics discussed at the UIA Round Tables resemble those discussed at the World Congresses of the early twentieth century: organization and governance; democracy and social engagement; membership and partnership; communication and public awareness. To reach an even broader audience, the UIA offers its educational expertise at events attracting diverse associations, such as trade fairs within the congress industry, and academic sessions. The UIA also contributes to the educational programmes of other organizations by sitting on programme committees and providing speakers.

From its earliest years, the UIA has recognized the importance of international meetings and congresses to international association life. This recognition has led to a decades-long engagement with what is now known as the meetings industry: convention bureaux, congress centres, congress organizers and travel agencies, hotels and other similar businesses. The UIA also initiated the first international meetings of this industry, which led to the creation of trade groups such as the International Association of Conference Interpreters (AIIC), founded in 1953, the International Association of Convention Centres (AIPC), founded in 1958, the Association Internationale des Traducteurs de Conférence (International Association of Conference Translators; AITC), founded in 1962, and the International Association of Professional Congress Organisers (IAPCO), founded in 1968.

As these examples illustrate, the UIA has retained a diverse range of activities beyond the *Yearbook*, the centrepiece of its work. It cooperates closely with two sister organizations, the European Society of Association Executives (ESAE) and the Federation of International and European Associations Established in Belgium (FAIB), especially regarding the educational programme of each organization. As a result of this cooperation, it was involved in establishing an Executive Masters in International Association Management in partnership with the Solvay School of Economics and Management at the Université Libre de Bruxelles in 2015, with twenty to twenty-five students successfully completing the six-month programme each year since.

The UIA's two online fraud monitors are another initiative: the *Fraud Monitor* for events and the *Directory Scams Fraud Alert* for publications. Both provide information about possible fraudulent activity affecting associations in whatever way, but particularly in the field of conferences and publications. Scams can masquerade as either real or fraudulent international organizations, whether governmental or non-governmental, or as development agencies, organizers of international conferences, or publishers of directories or journals. While not having the resources or the mandate to provide specific advice to, or take action on behalf of, victims of such scams, the UIA maintains the monitors as one step in countering the ways in which scams undermine legitimate communications or events.

Looking to the Future

The UIA's viability depends on moral and financial support from an increasing diversity of bodies. The UIA receives no government funding (though the Belgian government subsidized it until the late 1970s). While some of its data is freely and publicly accessible online, a major part of the UIA's income is derived from selling its publications. Clients include the libraries of academic institutions, multinational corporations, intergovernmental organizations, professional groupings, and of the meetings and service industries. Further income is generated by customized reports and by advertising in the UIA newsletter or on its website. Financial support also comes from sponsorships, partnership agreements and donations. An important form of support is the voluntary sharing of knowledge and time: membership on the UIA governing bodies; assisting in the secretariat; speaking at UIA educational events. The current annual budget is approximately 550,000 Euros.

The future of the UIA depends very much on its personnel and on its governance structure, which has remained stable since its re-establishment in 1949–50. Its governing body is the General Assembly, comprised of the 'Active Members'. From its ranks, the General Assembly elects fifteen to twenty-one members who form the UIA's council. The latter body appoints some of its members to a bureau (headed by the president), which in turn oversees the work of the secretariat. The secretariat carries out the daily work of the UIA and is led by the secretary-general, who also sits on the bureau. The staff in the secretariat embody the UIA's continuity. Many of the current seventeen staff members have served for over twenty years. While such stability may be questioned elsewhere, as possibly tending to stagnation, it greatly benefits the UIA's documentation work to have experienced and dedicated staff.

On the premise that historical information is useful to global civil society development and activity, the relevance of the UIA's contribution – its comparable and methodologically consistent historical data – increases with each passing year. Continuing this work is therefore the cornerstone of the UIA's plans for the future. However, it recognizes that collecting information is only half the job: disseminating it to the widest possible audience is an essential corollary. Improving access to its data, providing deeper and more diverse search functionalities and broadening the audience base therefore form the second layer of UIA's future plans. To this end, the UIA welcomes, and listens carefully to, suggestions for improvements from its current users.

The UIA aims to promote the contribution international organizations make to society. One way of doing this is by providing education, hence the UIA's commitment to furthering and increasing its educational offerings. This takes most concrete form in the Round Table project, seizing every opportunity to bring practical and accessible education to an ever-increasing number of international organization workers.

A more ambitious goal is to be a voice for global civil society, to promote its interests, to lobby for recognition of its contributions and for measures to facilitate those contributions. In this, the UIA would be carrying out the promise of earlier initiatives, such as its role in the creation of the *European Convention on the Recognition of the Legal Personality of International Non-Governmental Organisations* in 1986.

That the UIA has lasted for so long can be credited to its single-mindedness in pursuing its goals, to its consistency in its methodology, and to the dedication and imagination of its founders as well as its current leadership, staff and supporters. It welcomes those wishing to contribute to its future.

Notes

This epilogue was written with the assistance of Cyril Ritchie, Rachele Dahle, Clara Fernández López, Liesbeth van Hulle, Joel Fischer and Judy Wickens.

1 Georges Patrick Speeckaert, 'A Glance at Sixty Years of Activity (1910–1970) of the Union of International Associations', in UIA, *Union of International Associations, 1910–1970: Past, Present, Future* (Brussels: UIA, 1970).
2 See ECOSOC Resolution 334 B (XI): 'The Committee unanimously expressed its appreciation of the value and usefulness of the Yearbook of International Organizations published by the Union of International Associations. Members voiced the hope that the work of the Union would become even better known both to the public and to Member States and that its continuation would be secured.'
3 René Maheu, 'Tributes on the Occasion of the 60th Anniversary of the Union of International Associations', in *Union of International Associations, 1910–1970*, 4–7.
4 UIA Statutes, 2005. Available online: https://uia.org/statutes (accessed 23 July 2018).
5 The 1976 edition appeared under the title Yearbook of World Problems and Human Potential. In 1994, a CD-ROM edition 'Encyclopedia Plus' was also published.
6 *La Vie Internationale* (1912–21); *Bulletin des Associations Internationales* (1943–4); *UIA Bulletin Mensuel* (1949–50); *NGO Bulletin* (1951–3); *International Associations* (1954–76); *Transnational Associations* (1977–2005).

INDEX